The Theatre Experience

The Theatre Experience

FIFTEENTH EDITION

EDWIN WILSON
Professor Emeritus
Graduate School and University Center
The City University of New York

ALVIN GOLDFARB
President and Professor Emeritus
Western Illinois University

Mc Graw Hill

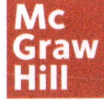

THE THEATRE EXPERIENCE

Published by McGraw Hill LLC, 1325 Avenue of the Americas, New York, NY 10019. Copyright ©2023 by Edwin Wilson. All rights reserved. Printed in the United States of America. No part of this publication may be reproduced or distributed in any form or by any means, or stored in a database or retrieval system, without the prior written consent of McGraw Hill LLC, including, but not limited to, in any network or other electronic storage or transmission, or broadcast for distance learning.

Some ancillaries, including electronic and print components, may not be available to customers outside the United States.

This book is printed on acid-free paper.

1 2 3 4 5 6 7 8 9 LWI 27 26 25 24 23 22

ISBN 978-1-265-22551-3
MHID 1-265-22551-6

Cover Image: *Used by permission of Michael Courier, photographer; Porchlight Music Theatre; William Morey, costume designer; and actors: Stephen Allen, Shantel Cribbs, Ariel Dorsey, Jared David Michael Grant, Nicole Lambert, Bernell Lassai, Ivory M. Leonard IV, Aalon Smith, and Aeriel Williams*

All credits appearing on page or at the end of the book are considered to be an extension of the copyright page.

The Internet addresses listed in the text were accurate at the time of publication. The inclusion of a website does not indicate an endorsement by the authors or McGraw Hill LLC, and McGraw Hill LLC does not guarantee the accuracy of the information presented at these sites.

mheducation.com/highered

About the Authors

Edwin Wilson attended Vanderbilt University, the University of Edinburgh, and Yale University, where he received an MFA and the first Doctor of Fine Arts degree awarded by Yale. He has taught theatre at Vanderbilt, Yale, and, for over 30 years, at Hunter College and the Graduate Center of the City University. Wilson has produced plays on and off Broadway and served one season as the resident director of the Barter Theatre in Abingdon, Virginia. He was the assistant to the producer on the Broadway play *Big Fish, Little Fish* directed by John Gielgud and starring Jason Robards and of the film *Lord of the Flies* directed by Peter Brook. On Broadway, he co-produced *Agatha Sue, I Love You* directed by George Abbott. He also produced a feature film, *The Nashville Sound*. He was the moderator of *Spotlight*, a television interview series on CUNY-TV and PBS (1989–1993), 91 half-hour interviews with outstanding actors, actresses, playwrights, directors, and producers, broadcast on 200 PBS stations in the U.S. Selected interviews can be seen on YouTube.

For 22 years he was the theatre critic of the *Wall Street Journal*. A long-time member of the New York Drama Critics Circle, he was president of the Circle for several years. He was on the board of the John Golden Fund for 45 years and served a term as president of the Theatre Development Fund **(TDF)**, whose board he was on for 23 years. He has served a number of times on the Tony Nominating Committee and the Pulitzer Prize Drama Jury. He is also the author or co-author of two other widely used college theatre textbooks in the United States. The fourteenth edition of his pioneer book, *The Theater Experience*, was published by McGraw Hill. The seventh edition of the theatre history textbook, *Living Theatre* (co-authored with Alvin Goldfarb), published previously by McGraw Hill, has been published by W. W. Norton. He is also the editor of the volume *Shaw on Shakespeare* and his well-received memoir, *Magic Time,* a chronicle of his years in and around theatre, was published by Smith and Kraus in 2020.

Alvin Goldfarb is president emeritus and professor emeritus of Western Illinois University. Dr. Goldfarb has also served as provost, dean of fine arts, and chair of the Department of Theatre at Illinois State University. Throughout his administrative career, he continued to teach theatre courses. Dr. Goldfarb is most recently an adjunct professor at the Chicago Conservatory for the Performing Arts at Roosevelt University. He holds a PhD in theatre history from the City University of New York, a master's degree from Hunter College of CUNY, and a bachelor's degree from Queens College of CUNY, graduating Phi Beta Kappa.

Dr. Goldfarb is the co-author of *Living Theatre* as well as co-editor of *The Anthology of Living Theatre* with Edwin Wilson. Dr. Goldfarb is also the co-editor, with Rebecca Rovit, of *Theatrical Performance During the Holocaust: Texts, Documents, Memoirs,* which was a finalist for the National Jewish Book Award. He has published numerous articles, reviews, and annotated bibliographies in scholarly journals and anthologies, many of which focus on theatre during the Holocaust and its representation in post–World War II drama and theatre. Currently, Dr. Goldfarb serves as the lead scholar for the online *Holocaust Theatre Catalog*, which is hosted at the University of Miami's Sue and Leonard Miller Center for Contemporary Judaic Studies. His interest in this area was inspired by his parents, who were survivors of the Holocaust.

Dr. Goldfarb has served as a member of the Illinois Arts Council and president of the Illinois Alliance for Arts Education. He also served for six years as a member and treasurer of Chicago's Joseph Jefferson Theatre Awards Committee, which recognizes excellence in the Chicago theatre, as well as a board member of the Arts Alliance of Illinois. He currently is a member of the board of Congo Square Theatre in Chicago.

Dr. Goldfarb has received service awards from the Illinois Theatre Association and the American College Theatre Festival. He also received alumni awards from the CUNY Graduate Center's Alumni Association and Hunter College, CUNY.

To the memory of my wife, Catherine.

To my children Deborah Goldfarb and Jason Goldfarb

Contents in Brief

PART 1	**The Audience**	**1**
1	The Audience: Its Role and Imagination	5
2	Background and Expectations of the Audience	27
3	Theatre Spaces	47

PART 2	**The Performers and the Director**	**71**
4	Acting for the Stage	75
5	The Director and the Producer	101

PART 3	**The Designers**	**129**
6	Scenery	133
7	Stage Costumes	157
8	Lighting and Sound	179

PART 4	**The Playwright and the Play**	**203**
9	Creating the World of the Play	207
10	Dramatic Structure and Dramatic Characters	225
11	Theatrical Genres	253
12	Alternative and Experimental Dramatic and Theatrical Forms	287
13	Diverse and Inclusive Plays, Playwrights, and Theatrical Forms	301

Plays That May Be Read Online	331
Glossary	334
Notes	338
Index	339

Contents

PART 1
The Audience 1

Chapter 1   **The Audience: Its Role and Imagination**   5

The Mediated Arts: Film and Television   6

The Contrast Between Theatre, Film, Television, and Streamed Media   7

Theatre Is Transitory and Immediate   8

Human Beings—The Focus of Theatre   9

The Chemistry of the Performer-Audience Contact   9

Theatre as a Group Experience   10
    Psychology of Groups   10
    How Audience Composition Affects the Theatre Experience   12

The Separate Roles of Performers and Spectators   14
    How Should the Audience Be Involved?   14
    Audience Participation through Direct Action   14

The Imagination of the Audience   16
    Tools of the Imagination: Symbol and Metaphor   18
    The "Reality" of the Imagination   19

The Imaginary Worlds of Theatre   21
    Realistic Elements of Theatre   21
    Departures from Realism: Nonrealistic Elements of Theatre   22
    Combining the Realistic and the Nonrealistic   22
    Distinguishing Stage Reality from Fact   23

Summary   25

(Arctic-Images/Corbis Documentary/Getty Images)

Chapter 2   **Background and Expectations of the Audience**   27

Background of Individual Spectators   28

Background Information on the Play or Playwright   28

Background of the Period   29
    Theatre and Society   29
    Modern Theatre and Culture   31

(Sara Krulwich/The New York Times/Redux)

xi

Expectations: The Variety of Experiences in Modern Theatre 33
 Broadway and Touring Theatre 34
 Resident Professional Theatre 34
 Alternative Theatre: Off-Broadway and Elsewhere 35
 Young People's and Children's Theatre 35
 College and University Theatre 36
 Community and Amateur Theatre 37
 Diverse and Global Theatres 37

The Audience, Critic, Reviewer, and Blogger 38
 The Critic, Reviewer, and Blogger 38
 Online Theatre Critics and Reviewers: New Approaches 39
 Preparation for Criticism 40
 Fact and Opinion in Criticism 40
 Critical Criteria 41

The Dramaturg or Literary Manager 42

The Audience's Relation to Criticism 43
 The Audience's Independent Judgment 43

Summary 44

Chapter 3 Theatre Spaces 47

Creating the Environment 47

Theatre Spaces 48
 Proscenium or Picture-Frame Stage: History and Characteristics 49
 Arena Stage: History and Characteristics 53
 Thrust Stage: History and Characteristics 55
 Alley or Traverse Theatre Space 60
 Created and Found Spaces 61
 All-Purpose Theatre Spaces: The Black Box 66

Special Requirements of Theatre Environments 67
 Evaluating the Theatre Space 68

Summary 69

(Oli Scarff/Getty Images)

PART 2
The Performers and the Director 71

Chapter 4 Acting for the Stage 75

Acting in Everyday Life 75
 Social Roles 75
 Personal Roles 76

Acting in Life versus Acting on Stage 76

Three Challenges of Acting 77
 Making Characters Believable 78
 Physical Acting: Voice and Body 87
 Synthesis and Integration 94

Evaluating Performances 97

Summary 99

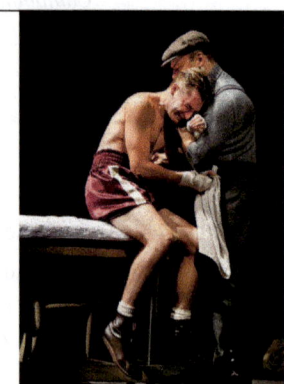
(Sara Krulwich/The New York Times/Redux)

xii   Contents

Chapter 5 **The Director and the Producer** 101

    The Theatre Director   101

    The Traditional Director   102
        The Director and the Script   102

    The Auteur Director and the Postmodern Director   109
        The Auteur Director   109
        The Postmodern Director   111

    The Director and the Production: The Physical Production   111

    The Director's Work with the Performers   112
        Casting   112
        Diversity and Inclusion in Directing: Inclusive Casting   113
        Rehearsals   114
        The Director as the Audience's Eye   114
        Movement, Pace, and Rhythm   116
        Technical Rehearsal   116
        Dress Rehearsal   117
        Previews   117
        The Director's Collaborator: The Stage Manager   118
        The Director's Collaborator: The Choreographer   119
        The Director's Collaborators: The Fight Director and the Intimacy Director   120
        The Director's Collaborator: The Dramaturg   120

    The Director's Power and Responsibility   121

    The Producer or Managing Director   123
        The Commercial Producer   123
        Noncommercial Theatres   124
        The Producer and Director's Collaborator: The Production Manager   125

    Completing The Picture: Playwright, Director, and Producer   127
        Evaluating Directing   127

    Summary   128

(Liz Lauren/Richard Hein)

PART 3
The Designers 129

Chapter 6 **Scenery** 133

    The Audience's View   133

    The Scene Designer   134

    A Brief History of Stage Design   134

    Scenic Design Today   135
        The Scene Designer's Objectives   135
        Elements of Scene Design   141
        The Process of Scene Design   148

    The Scene Designer's Collaborators and the Production Process   150
        Designing a Total Environment   153
        Evaluating Scene Design   154

    Summary   155

(T. Charles Erickson)

Chapter 7 **Stage Costumes** 157

Costumes for the Stage 157
   Objectives of Costume Design 157
   The Process of Costume Design 158
   The Costume Designer at Work 164
   The Costume Designer's Resources 164
   The Costume Designer's Collaborators 167

Related Elements of Costume Design 168
   Makeup 168
   Hairstyles and Wigs 171
   Masks 171
   Millinery, Accessories, and Crafts 175

Coordination of the Whole 176
   Evaluating Costume Design 177

Summary 177

(Sara Krulwich/The New York Times/Redux)

Chapter 8 **Lighting and Sound** 179

Stage Lighting 179
   A Brief History of Stage Lighting 179
   Objectives and Functions of Lighting Design 181
   The Lighting Designer 186

Sound in the Theatre 193
   Sound Reproduction: Advantages and Disadvantages 193
   The Sound Designer 195
   Understanding Sound Reproduction and Sound Reinforcement 195
   Sound Creates the Environment 197
   Sound Technology 197

Special Effects in Lighting and Sound 199
   Evaluating Lighting and Sound Design 200

Summary 201

(Sara Krulwich/The New York Times/Redux)

PART 4
The Playwright and the Play 203

Chapter 9 **Creating the World of the Play** 207

The Subject and Verb of Drama: People and Action 209
Structural Conventions: The Rules of the Game 209
   Limited Space 210
   Limited Time 210
   Strongly Opposed Forces 211
   A Balance of Forces 212
   Incentive and Motivation 212

Creating Structure 213
   Plot versus Story 213

(Anne Cusack/Contributor/Getty Images)

xiv   Contents

  The Opening Scene   213
  Obstacles and Complications   215
  Crisis and Climax   215
 Point of View   216
  The Dramatist's Point of View   217
  Society's Point of View   219
 Summary   221

Chapter 10   Dramatic Structure and Dramatic Characters   225

 Dramatic Structure   225
  Characteristics of Climactic Structure   225
  Characteristics of Episodic Structure   227
  Combinations of Climactic and Episodic Form   232
  Rituals as Dramatic Structure   233
  Patterns as Dramatic Structure   234
  Serial Structure   234
  Structure in Experimental and Avant-Garde Theatre   234
  Structure in Musical Theatre   236
  Diversity and Inclusion in Dramatic Structure: Feminist Structure   237
 Dramatic Characters   238
  Extraordinary Characters   238
  Representative or Quintessential Characters   239
  Stock Characters   243
  Minor Characters   244
  A Narrator or Chorus   245
  Nonhuman Characters   246
  The Audience and Character Types   247
  Juxtaposition of Characters   247
  Orchestration of Characters   248
 Summary   250

(Robbie Jack/Corbis/Getty Images)

Chapter 11   Theatrical Genres   253

 Types of Drama   253
 Tragedy   254
  Traditional Tragedy   255
  Modern Tragedy   256
 Heroic Drama   257
 Bourgeois or Domestic Drama   260
 Melodrama   262
 Comedy   263
  Characteristics of Comedy   263
  Techniques of Comedy   265
  Forms of Comedy   266
 Tragicomedy   269
  What Is Tragicomedy?   269
  Modern Tragicomedy   270

(Geraint Lewis/Alamy Stock Photo)

Contents   xv

Theatre of the Absurd   272
   Absurdist Plots: Illogicality   272
   Absurdist Language: Nonsense and Non Sequitur   275
   Absurdist Characters: Existential Beings   275

Musical Theatre   276
   Antecedents   276
   The Book Musical Is Born   277
   A High Point of Musicals   278
   Musicals after 1975   280

Summary   284

Chapter 12   Alternative and Experimental Dramatic and Theatrical Forms   287

Expressionism, Surrealism, Epic Theatre, and Theatre of Cruelty   288

Other Nontraditional and Experimental Forms   289

Two Forms that Bridge the Traditonal and Nontraditional   294

Traditional Genres and Forms Continue and Transform   297

Summary   298

(Sara Krulwich/The New York Times/Redux)

Chapter 13   Diverse and Inclusive Plays, Playwrights, and Theatrical Forms   301

Diverse Multicultural Theatre and Playwrights   301
   African American Theatre and Playwrights: Introduction   302
   African Theatres and Drama   302
   African American Theatres and Playwrights   305
   Asian American Playwrights and Theatres   308
   Latinx Theatre   310
   Indigenous Theatres and Playwrights   312

Feminist Theatre and Women Playwrights   316

LGBTQ Theatre and Playwrights   321

Global Theatre   325

Summary   330

(Emon Hassan/The New York Times/Redux)

Plays That May Be Read Online   331

Glossary   334
Notes   338
Index   339

xvi   Contents

Preface

ACTIVE AUDIENCE PARTICIPANTS, ACTIVE CLASS PARTICIPANTS

The Theatre Experience prepares students to be well-informed, well-prepared theatre audience members. With an audience-centered narrative that engages today's students, a vivid photo program that brings concepts to life, and features that teach and encourage a variety of skill sets, students master core concepts and learn to think critically about theatre and the world around them. As a result, students are better prepared for class, and better prepared for theatregoing.

Engage with Your Role

- True to its original vision—to focus on the audience's experience of attending a live theatre performance—the 15th edition of *The Theatre Experience* **opens with three chapters that focus on the student as an audience member**. Topics include the difference between being at a live performance and watching a dramatic performance on film, TV, or an electronic device; the enhancement of the experience aided by the proper preparation and background; and the awareness of the role of the audience in live theatre.

(VisitBritain/Eric Nathan/Getty Images)

xvii

- **Play Links** allow you to read many of the plays mentioned in the text online. Any play referenced in the text that can be found online is highlighted in blue typeface when first mentioned in a chapter. Should you want to read one of these plays, you can refer to the list that precedes the Glossary at the end of the book and find its URL. Titles are listed alphabetically.

  The plays can be used to highlight key concepts and to complement the discussions found in *The Theatre Experience,* 15th edition. In addition, many of the new "Thinking about Theatre" and "Experiencing Theatre" exercises can also be supplemented and enhanced with examples from these plays.

Master the Basics

Parts Two, Three, and Four cover the important elements of theatre: acting, directing, design, and playwriting. The authors' efficient structure and succinct style set up students for a clear understanding of the basic concepts, freeing up valuable class time for deeper discussions and more personal engagement with course concepts.

Photo Essays and a dynamic art program allow students to visualize the core theatrical concepts introduced in each chapter. Topics include modern domestic drama (Chapter 11), forms of comedy (Chapter 11), costumes and masks (Chapter 7), uses of stage lighting (Chapter 8), and others.

Think Critically and Engage Actively

Based on feedback from instructors and students, the 15th edition of *The Theatre Experience* offers both time-tested and newly revised text features that help students deepen their understanding and appreciation of the theatrical experience.

- **"Playing Your Part"** is a feature in each chapter that includes two distinct sets of questions and activities that emphasize thinking and engaging critically.
  - **"Experiencing Theatre"** activities help students actively engage with the concepts of the text. These exercises ask students to undertake activities within the classroom or to understand how aspects of their everyday lives connect to core concepts discussed in the text.

PLAYING YOUR PART: EXPERIENCING THEATRE

1. If you were to write a play about your life, what would you choose as your opening scene? What would some of your complications be? Would there be a climactic moment?
2. If you were to write a play about a family you know (your own or another), what point of view would you take? Why? Are there strongly opposed forces or balanced forces in this family?
3. If you were told you were going to have to attend a play that lasted over four hours, what would your reaction be? Why? What are your traditional expectations about the space and time of a play?
4. After watching a popular film, describe how the opening scene aids in setting the action. Describe one or two of the complications in the film. Can you discuss the film's point of view?

- "**Thinking about Theatre**" questions challenge students to analyze and examine elements of a theatre experience.

> **PLAYING YOUR PART: THINKING ABOUT THEATRE**
>
> 1. Think of a play you have read or seen where the main character encounters one impediment or roadblock after another. Describe the various obstacles that must be overcome before the end of the play.
> 2. Think of a play or musical you have seen or read where two major characters are in conflict with one another. Describe the two characters and explain the source of their conflict. How does it play out?
> 3. Think of a situation some people saw as very serious, but another person viewed as humorous. Explain what you believe led different people to see it so differently. What was your own feeling—was the incident funny or sad?

- "**In Focus**" boxes, also appearing in every chapter, help students understand and compare different aspects of theatre. They address historical perspectives on theatre, contemporary applications of technology, issues of theatrical structure, and global and other current issues in theatre, such as color-blind and nontraditional casting. Theatre artists such as Peter Brook and Josef Svoboda are also featured.

WHAT'S NEW IN THE 15TH EDITION OF *THE THEATRE EXPERIENCE*

The 15th edition of *The Theatre Experience* has been updated, taking note of new talent that has appeared on the scene as well as new approaches to writing, directing, acting, and design presented in previous editions. New plays, new productions, new approaches, and new subject matter have all been recognized and explained. At the same time, well-established forerunners in the theatre universe, whether Greek, Roman, Elizabethan, or later, have been looked at anew. All of this has been reviewed in light of the COVID-19 pandemic and, following the murder of George Floyd, the recognition of the need for diversity, inclusion, and equity in the contemporary theatre and the need to confront systemic racism.

The most significant changes in the 15th edition is moving all of the design chapters to Part Three of the book so that all of the production elements are discussed before turning to plays and playwriting. Part Four, now focuses on the playwright and the play with discussion of musical theatre being added to the chapter on genres. In addition, two new chapters use previous historic material in the context of playwriting and plays. Chapter 12 focuses on experimental and alternative forms of drama and theatre. Chapter 13 reviews diverse and inclusive playwrights, plays, and theatre artists.

Selected Chapter-by-Chapter Changes

For greater inclusivity, all gender-specific terminology and references have been removed as appropriate throughout the eleventh edition of *The Theatre Experience*.

Part One: The Audience
- Added new paragraph on COVID-19 and Theatre.
- New discussion on how COVID-19 impacted other audience events, including sports and the Biden inauguration.

Chapter 1: The Audience: Its Roles and Imagination
- New section header "The Contrast between Theatre, Film, Television, and Streamed Media."
- Added coverage on streamed and Zoomed[WU3] performances during COVID-19.
- Updated examples of shows filmed for TV or film, including *Hamilton* and *The Prom*.
- Added research on how audiences' hearts beat in rhythm during parts of shows.
- New material on the 2020 production of *Boys in the Band* done by Chicago's Windy City Playhouse in an immersive fashion.
- Added new box "In Focus: The COVID-19 Pandemic and Theatre."
- Added a new coverage on "Distinguishing Stage Reality from Fact" using *Fairview* by African American playwright Jackie Sibblies Drury.

Chapter 2: Background and Expectations of the Audience
- Added new coverage of August Wilson and his ten-play cycle.
- Added material on how marginalized peoples are underrepresented or stereotyped in certain theatres.
- Added coverage of *Slave Play* as an example of a contemporary play and the marginalization of underrepresented peoples in the theatre.
- Added a new section "Diverse and Global Theatres."
- Updated and revised "The Audience, Critic, Reviewer, and Blogger" to include new online forms.

Chapter 3: Theatre Spaces
- Added new coverage of alley or traverse theatre spaces.
- Added new section on site-specific and immersive spaces.

Chapter 4: Acting for the Stage
- Updated the "In Focus: The Profession of Acting and Technology" box to include coverage on new apps that allow actors to work on auditions and scheduling.
- Provided new example in "In Focus: Puppetry Around the World box."
- Added a new section "Diversity and Inclusion in Acting Training."

Chapter 5: The Director and the Producer
- Reorganized and revised "The Director's Collaborator: The Dramaturg" and provided a longer section on other collaborators.

- Revised the "In Focus: Color Conscious, Color Blind, and Nontraditional Casting box.
- Revised coverage of "The Director's Collaborator: The Stage Manager."
- Revised coverage of "The Director's Collaborator: The Choreographer."
- Updated material on "The Director's Collaborator: The Fight Director and the Intimacy Director."
- Added new box "In Focus: Technology for Directors and Their Collaborators."
- Moved boxed material on color conscious casting into the main text as part of a new section "Diversity and Inclusion in Directing: Inclusive Casting."

Chapter 6: Scenery
- Replaced as far as possible the term "nonrealistic" to "departures from realism."
- Replaced older example of a design concept with the 2019 Broadway production of *Oklahoma*.
- Revised coverage of the central image and metaphor.
- Added coverage of hand held technology in scene design.
- Updated the box "In Focus: New Design Materials: Video and Projection Design."
- Added a new box "In Focus: App Technology for Scene Design."
- Added a new box "In Focus: Scene Design in Film and Television."

Chapter 7: Stage Costumes
- Added new example (*Frozen*) of on-stage costume change.
- Revised examples of prosthetics.
- Revised coverage of wigs. Provided new example.
- Provided new example of the use of masks.
- Added new box "In Focus: Costume Design in Film and Television."
- Added new box "In Focus: Touch Tours and Audio Description."
- Revised box "In Focus: Technology and Costume Design" to include the use of apps and hand held devices.

Chapter 8: Lighting and Sound
- Updated text when referring to technology to include "tablets" or "hand held devices" when referring to computer-controlled light and sound.
- Added text with examples in "Sound Creates the Environment."
- Added new box "In Focus: Lighting and Sound Design in Film and Television."
- Added new box "In Focus: Inclusivity and Sound Technology" that addresses the needs of the hearing impaired.
- Added new box "In Focus: App Technology for Lighting and Sound Design."

Chapter 9: Creating the World of the Play
- Added coverage of Luis Alfaro's adaptations of *Electra, Oedipus Rex, and Medea* that focus on contemporary immigrant community issues.
- Included reference to Matthew Lopez's *The Inheritance* and Marsha Norman's *'Night Mother*, as contemporary examples of creative usage of theatrical time.

- Added new example of Troy Maxson, in *Fences*, to the coverage of incentive and motivation.
- Added August Wilson's work to the discussion of family dramas.
- Updated the section "Point of View" with coverage of Jeremy O' Harris's *Slave Play*.
- Revised coverage of the enlightenment and age of progress with a critique of white privilege, colonialism, and the enslavement of Africans.

Chapter 10: Dramatic Structure and Dramatic Characters
- Added new section "Diversity and Inclusion in Dramatic Structure: Feminist Structure."
- Updated the section "People, Places, and Events Proliferate" with a new example: Tony Kushner's *Angels in America*.
- Updated the section "Combinations of Climactic and Episodic Form" with coverage of August Wilson's ten-play cycle about Black life in the United States.
- Expanded coverage of "Structure in Musical Theatre" with a new example: *Hamilton*.
- Updated the section "A Narrator or Chorus" with reference to *Fairview* by African American playwright Jackie Sibblie Drury.
- Expanded and revised the section "Orchestration of Characters" by adding August Wilson to the exiting discussion of Chekhov.

Chapter 11: Theatrical Genres
- Added new section on musical theatre.
- Updated examples used to explain genres.

Chapter 12: Alternative and Experimental Dramatic and Theatrical Forms
- New chapter that focuses on all of the alternative and experimental forms of the twentieth and twenty-first centuries, including surrealism, expressionism, theatre of cruelty, epic theatre, happenings environmental theatre, postmodernism, performance art, political theatre, and documentary drama.

Chapter 13: Diverse and Inclusive Plays, Playwrights, and the Theatrical Forms
- New chapter that focuses on diverse playwrights, theaters, and theatre artists, including African American theatre, Latinx theatre, Asian American theatre, indigenous theatre, Feminist theatre, and LGBTQ theatre. In addition the chapter concludes with a brief discussion of global theatre.

CONNECT: ENHANCING THE THEATRE EXPERIENCE

Connect combines the content of *The Theatre Experience* with award-winning adaptive tools that help students prepare for their time in class with you. The tools in Connect help students understand and retain basic concepts: parts of the theatre, the creative artists and technicians who make it happen, and the tradition and historical background from which theatre springs. When students successfully master concepts using McGraw Hill's Connect, you can spend more class time discussing theatre and theatrical performances, fostering a greater appreciation for the course and inspiring students to become lifelong audience members. Connect is reliable, easy to use, and can be implemented on its own or paired with your school's learning management system. Contact your McGraw Hill Higher Education representative to learn more or to speak with an instructor who already uses Connect for his or her theatre courses.

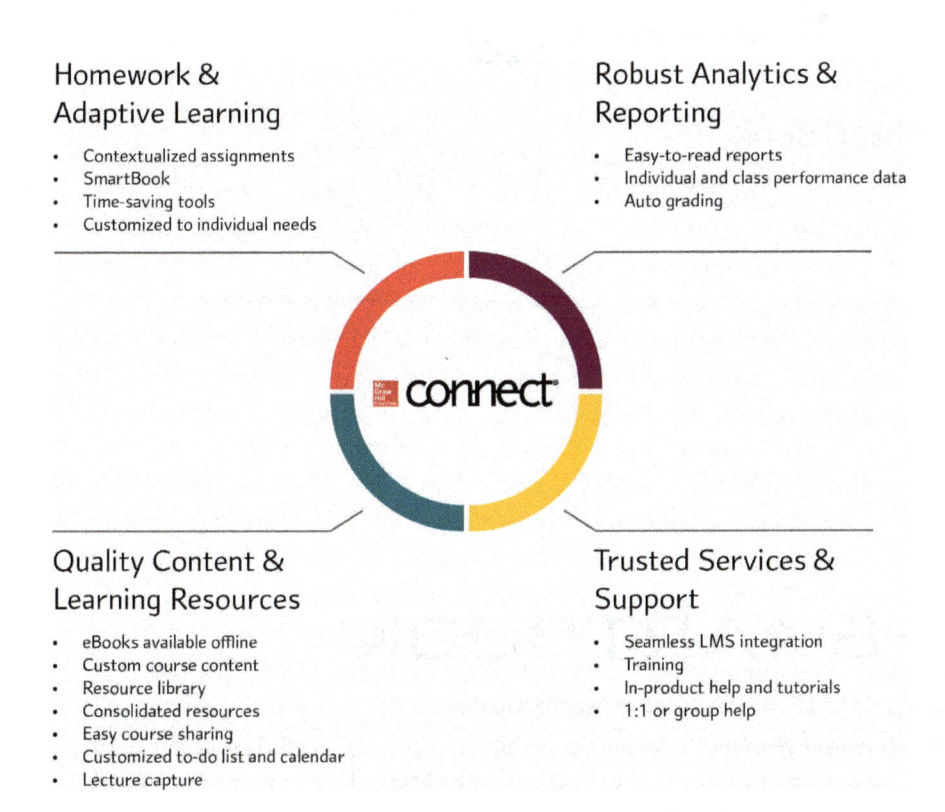

Homework & Adaptive Learning
- Contextualized assignments
- SmartBook
- Time-saving tools
- Customized to individual needs

Robust Analytics & Reporting
- Easy-to-read reports
- Individual and class performance data
- Auto grading

Quality Content & Learning Resources
- eBooks available offline
- Custom course content
- Resource library
- Consolidated resources
- Easy course sharing
- Customized to-do list and calendar
- Lecture capture

Trusted Services & Support
- Seamless LMS integration
- Training
- In-product help and tutorials
- 1:1 or group help

Connect for *The Theatre Experience* now includes two ways to read: an eBook and SmartBook. The eBook provides a simple, elegant reading experience, available for offline reading on a tablet. SmartBook creates a personalized online reading experience by highlighting the most impactful concepts that a student needs to learn. Students periodically test their knowledge as they read, and SmartBook adapts accordingly, highlighting content based on what the student knows and doesn't know. Real-time reports quickly identify the concepts that require more attention from individual students—or the entire class.

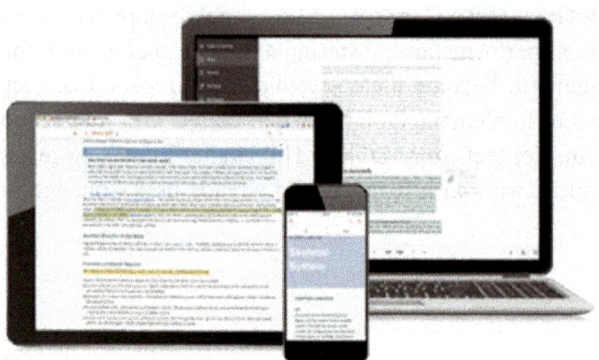

SmartBook

DESIGNED FOR
- Preparing for class
- Practice and study
- Focusing on key topics
- Reports and analytics

SUPPORTS
- Adaptive, personalized learning
- Assignable contents
- Tablet iOS and Android apps

eBook

DESIGNED FOR
- Reading in class
- Reference
- Offline reading
- Accessibility

SUPPORTS
- Simple, elegant reading
- Basic annotations
- Smartphone and tablet via iOS and Android apps

Support for Instructors and Students

The Theatre Experience offers a wealth of supplemental materials to aid both students and instructors, including the Instructor's Manual and both computerized and print versions of the Test Bank.

For students, resources keyed directly to this edition include:

- The Theatre Goer's Guide, which is an excellent introduction to the art of attending and critiquing a play. This guide will assist students in everything from making theatre reservations and knowing when to applaud to evaluating a performance and doing web research.
- Detailed explanations and examples of major theatrical forms and movements.
- Synopses of plays.

Craft your teaching resources to match the way you teach! With McGraw Hill Create, you can easily rearrange chapters, combine material from other content sources, and quickly upload content you have written, like your course syllabus or teaching notes. Search through thousands of leading McGraw Hill textbooks, and arrange your book to fit your teaching style. Create even allows you to personalize your book's appearance by selecting the cover and adding your name, school, and course information. Order a Create book and you'll receive a complimentary print review copy in 3-5 business days or a complimentary electronic review copy (eComp) via e-mail in about one hour. Go to www.mcgrawhillcreate.com today and register. Experience how McGraw Hill Create empowers you to teach your students your way.

ACKNOWLEDGMENTS

The original author, Edwin Wilson, would like to thank Professor Alvin Goldfarb for his invaluable and indispensable contribution to this and the previous edition of *The Theatre Experience*. As coauthor on *Living Theatre* and *Theatre: The Lively Art,* Al's ideas, his research and writing skills, his originality and imagination, and his persistence have been indispensable in completing this, the first volume on which he serves as co-author. Both authors believe this is the most audience-oriented and concise version of *The Theatre Experience* of the entire series.

Professor Wilson first developed many of the ideas in this book while teaching a course in Introduction to Theatre at Hunter College of the City University of New York. To his former students and colleagues at Hunter, he expresses his continuing appreciation. Also, to those professors and other experts who have contributed importantly to prior versions, he expresses his continuing appreciation. They include Alexis Greene, Naomi Stubbs, Susan Tenneriello, Donny Levit, and Frank Episale.

In addition, Professors Wilson and Goldfarb express our gratitude to Professor Jeff Entwistle for his prodigious contribution to the chapters on design, and we also thank Professor Laura Pulio for her helpful suggestions on acting. We extend our appreciation to Shanesia Davis who provided input to our acting chapter and suggested the additions on alley theatre spaces and touch tours. A special thanks also to Professor Oliver W. Gerland and his fellow teachers at the University of Colorado. We would also like to thank Professor Scott Walters, University of North Carolina–Asheville, for developing the first teacher and student study guide materials for *The Theatre Experience,* and Professor John Poole, Illinois State University, for his revisions that are now found in the instructor resources.

We'd also like to thank the following reviewers who have contributed to this edition:

James Bell, Grand Valley State University
Scott Boyd, Middle Tennessee State University
Chris Gray, Illinois Central College
Richard Hansen, Middle Tennessee State University
Ethan Krupp, Bloomsburg University of Pennsylvania
Jeannine Russell, Wichita State University

Through twenty-six editions of our three textbooks published by McGraw Hill, including the previous edition of this text, our colleague Inge King, the incredible photography expert, discovered every photograph that appeared in every edition of every text. Inge is amazing as well as being an irreplaceable colleague and there is no way adequately to acknowledge her taste and abiding loyalty, as well as her creativity.

At the same time, a new photography editor, Emily Tietz, has taken over the duties of researching and obtaining permission for illustrations in this and the previous edition of *The Theatre Experience*. Emily has proved to be resourceful, energetic, and persistent in these endeavors as well as a person with excellent taste. We are most grateful to her.

At McGraw Hill we express our gratitude to the following:

Katie Stevens
Sarah Remington
Elisa Odoardi
Lisa Bruflodt
Brianna Kirschbaum

Design Elements: Audience Sitting in Theatre (theatre): Ron Chapple/Photodisc/Getty Images; Studio Light (spotlights): Exactostock/SuperStock

Part One

The Audience

1 The Audience: Its Role and Imagination

2 Background and Expectations of the Audience

3 Theatre Spaces

THE AUDIENCE
The basic encounter in the theatre is the exchange, the chemistry, the electricity between the audience and the actors performing onstage. The presence of the audience sets live theatre apart from all other forms of dramatic entertainment. Here the audience is gathered for a production of *A Midsummer Night's Dream* in Shakespeare's Globe Theatre on the South Bank of the River Thames on July 16, 2013, in London, England. (Oli Scarff/Getty Images)

Part One | The Audience

We may not realize it, but when we attend the theatre, we, as spectators, are essential to the experience. To be complete, each one of the performing arts—opera, ballet, symphony concerts as well as theatre—requires an audience. Whether watching a classic, like *Romeo and Juliet,* or a modern family play, like *Fences,* for most of us, it is likely that our first encounter with the dramatic work was on film, television, computer, or a handheld digital device. No matter how impressed we were with seeing a play or a musical in this format, however, it must be remembered that the experience of watching television or a movie is quite different from attending the theatre. With electronic or digital media, we are looking at a screen on which there are no live people but only images of people. And the experience of being in the presence of a living, breathing person makes all the difference. Another way of putting this is to say that the audience is not an incidental factor in a theatrical performance; if we are audience members, we become an indispensable element in what is occurring.

At a theatrical performance, we become keenly aware of the actors onstage. What we may not realize is that the actors are just as aware of our presence. Laughter at a comedy or a deep silence at a tense moment in a serious drama is communicated directly to the actors and has a very real effect on their performance.

In a number of events other than the performing arts, spectators often play a key role. For example, most sports contests—football, baseball, basketball, soccer, tennis, NASCAR races—elicit huge interest from fans. This is true whether the sports event is at the high school, college, or professional level. In other spheres as well, the participation of viewers is crucial. Political conventions and political rallies depend on large, supportive crowds to be considered successful. A good example is a national nominating convention. The hall where the event takes place becomes a giant stage set, with a stagelike platform, backdrops, and carefully arranged positions for entrances and exits. The programs are carefully scripted to build to a climax, with a finale consisting of stirring music and

Fans cheering at the NASCAR Sprint Cup Series auto race in Martinsville, Virginia. (Don Petersen/AP Images)

Seen here is a group of people gathered to watch the August 21, 2017, eclipse of the sun. (Volkan Furuncu/Anadolu Agency/Getty Images)

literally thousands of balloons dropping from the ceiling.

During the COVID-19 pandemic in 2020 and 2021, we clearly saw how the absence of fans and supportive crowds impacted sporting events, political conventions, and the 2021 inauguration of President Joe Biden. In many instances, there were attempts to simulate the presence of spectators. For example, televised football games were accompanied by digitally created background spectators sounds. However, we were always aware that there was a missing element: live fans.

Despite the similarity between theatre events and sports events, there is one unmistakable difference. Theoretically, a sports contest could take place in an empty stadium (as many did during the COVID-19 pandemic) and still be considered complete: though the thrill and the excitement would be missing, the results would be entered in the record book, and the won–lost statistics would be just as valid as if the game had taken place before a large crowd.

This is not true for the performing arts. Each theatre, ballet, or opera performance, each musical concert is intended specifically to be presented in the presence of an audience, which is an absolutely essential part of the event. Of course, any of these can be recorded digitally or otherwise (again as was done with Zoom readings and recordings during the pandemic), but listening to or viewing one of these is not the same as attending a live event. In a very real sense, a theatre performance at which no audience is actually present is *not* a performance. It may be a rehearsal of some kind, but the performance occurs only when the actors perform in the presence of a live audience.

In Part One we will explore who makes up the audience, how audiences are created, how they differ from one another, how they respond to what is happening onstage, and how they interact with performers.

The audience at a performance of *The Two Gentlemen of Verona* at Shakespeare's Globe in London. (Gideon Mendel/Getty Images)

The audience watching a 3D movie. (Image Source/Getty Images)

3

The Audience:
Its Role and Imagination

Live theatre: The performance of a dramatic event by a group of actors in the presence of their counterparts, the audience members.

The title of this book tells us that attending the theatre is an experience. It is an experience, but more than that, it is a *unique* experience. Along with the other performing arts—music, dance, and opera—it occurs only in the presence of an audience. Music can consist of a concert by a symphony orchestra, a pop concert before thousands, or an intimate cabaret performance: the key factor is that there is a live audience in attendance. The same would be true of dance: it could be a formal ballet in a concert hall or a modern dance group in a small, intimate setting. However, it occurs only when there is a live audience present. A presentation by any performing arts group involves a different dynamic from the appreciation of other artworks such as painting, sculpture, literature, or a filmed or digitally captured and distributed performance. A live theatre production, for instance, changes from moment to moment and night to night, as the audiences encounter a series of shifting impressions and stimuli. It is a kaleidoscopic adventure through which the audience passes, with each instant a direct, immediate experience.

The transitory nature of the performing arts sets them apart in other ways from literature and the visual arts. A painting, a piece of sculpture, a novel, or a collection of poems is a fixed object. When it leaves the artist's hands (or, in the case of a book, when it leaves the printer's shop), it is complete. In a world of change and uncertainty, these objects remain the same. Today, the statue of the *Winged Victory* at the Louvre Museum in Paris is the same majestic figure that was fashioned 2,200 years

◀ **THE ROLE OF THE AUDIENCE**

The audience and the performers are the two essential elements of theatre: both are required for theatre to occur. The presence of the audience sets theatre apart from the experience of watching a theatrical presentation on film, on television, or in any other electronic medium. A comparison can be made to the theatricality of a rock performance and the impact on the audience by the performers. Here the audience watches and reacts to the performance of Pall Oskar, an Icelandic pop singer, songwriter, and disc jockey, performing in Harpa Concert Hall, Reykjavik, Iceland. (Arctic-Images/Corbis Documentary/Getty Images)

ago on the island of Samothrace in Greece. When we see this statue, we are looking at a soaring figure, facing into the wind, which is essentially what the Greeks saw at the time it was created. A theatre production changes from performance to performance because of differences in audience responses or in slight changes in the interactions among the cast members. And once a specific production is over, that production no longer exists.

Beyond the transitory nature of theatre, a second point to be made is that theatre alone among the performing arts centers entirely on human beings and their behavior, a point that we will discuss in more detail later in this chapter. A case could be made that opera focuses on people as well, but it should be remembered that though opera deals with human beings and their actions, it does so primarily through the medium of music. Confirmation of this fact is that operas are invariably identified by the name of the composer, never the playwright or librettist. It is always Mozart's or Verdi's opera, never the writer's opera. Music, of course, is sound: the notes produced by a singer or instrumentalist bringing alive a musical score. And dance is motion, the graceful, sometimes incredible movements made by performers in ballet, modern and popular dance, or tap.

THE MEDIATED ARTS: FILM AND TELEVISION

mediated arts The mediated arts, which include radio, film, television, digital streaming, and the like, are performances captured or recorded through the use of other types of media.

Standing between the performing arts and the fixed arts (painting, sculpture, literature) is a third art form: the ***mediated arts*** (radio, film, television, digital streaming, and the like), that is, performances captured or recorded through the use of other types of media. Whereas the other art forms have been with us for thousands of years, this third art form is relatively new. Ever since the inception of these various media, there have been dire warnings that each one would make the performing arts—especially live theatre—obsolete. Beginning in the early years of the twentieth century, mechanical and electronic inventions came fast and furiously. First there was radio, then black-and-white cinema, followed by movies in color; after that, television, again first in black and white and then in color and later, in quick succession, an electronic smorgasbord of digital devices (such as microcomputers, smartphones, and tablets) that now allow for the streaming of performances (recorded and even live), and so forth.

At every step of the way it was argued that live theatre could not possibly withstand this onslaught of rivals that were so readily accessible and so much less expensive. Why go to the theatre when we could see the same thing so much more easily in our neighborhood or at home and at such a sharply reduced cost? Surely this overwhelming electronic competition would lead to a sharp diminution of theatre attendance. Oddly enough, however, the falling off of live theatre has not happened; in fact, theatre attendance has noticeably increased. Live theatre today takes place at varying levels of professionalism in more locations across the United States (and the globe, for that matter) than at any time in its history. In the chapter "Background and Expectations of the Audience," we will discuss in detail the breadth and depth of live theatre across the United States and our global theatre. In the meantime, we should examine why live theatre can thrive in the midst of what appears to be unbeatable competition. The answer lies in the nature of a dramatic performance by actors in the presence of a live audience.

The essence of live theatre is that it is immediate and spontaneous; it happens at a given moment before our very eyes. We are there watching it; more important, we are actually participants in the event. The twentieth-century critic Walter Kerr (1913-1996), for whom a Broadway theatre is named, explained what it means for audience and actors to be together:

> It doesn't just mean that we are in the personal presence of performers. It means that they are in *our* presence, conscious of us, speaking to us, working for and with us until a circuit that is not mechanical becomes established between us, a circuit that is fluid, unpredictable, ever-changing in its impulses, crackling, intimate. *Our* presence, the way we respond, flows back to the performer and alters what he does, to some degree and sometimes astonishingly so, every single night. We are contenders, making the play and the evening and the emotion together. We are playmates, building a structure. This never happens at a film because the film is already built, finished, sealed, incapable of responding to us in any way. The actors can't hear us or feel our presence; nothing we do, in our liveness, counts. We could be dead and the film would purr out its appointed course, flawlessly, indifferently.[1]

THE CONTRAST BETWEEN THEATRE, FILM, TELEVISION, AND STREAMED MEDIA

As Walter Kerr suggests, one way to explain the special nature of live theatre is to contrast a drama seen in a theatre with one shown on film, television, or streaming. Both present a story told in dramatic form—an enactment of scenes by performers who speak and act as if they were the people they represent. The same actor can play Juliet in *Romeo and Juliet* by William Shakespeare (1564-1616) on both stage and screen. Not only the dramatization and the acting but also other elements, such as scenery and costumes, are often similar on stage and screen. In fact, many films and television specials have been based on stage productions: *A Chorus Line, The Phantom of the Opera, The Importance of Being Earnest, Les Misérables, The Prom, Hamilton*, and numerous plays by Shakespeare. Also, one can learn a great deal about theatre from watching a play on film, television, or streamed, which can also give us many of the same feelings and experiences that we have when watching a theatre performance.

Moreover, the accessibility of film, television, and streaming means that they play a crucial role in our overall exposure to the depiction of dramatic events and dramatic characters. During the pandemic shutdown of the theatres in 2020 to 2021, audiences turned to these media as the only means to have theatrical experiences.

As important as the similarities are, however, there is a crucial difference between experiencing live theatre or watching it on television, film, or streamed. We are not speaking here of the technical capabilities of these media, the ability to show outdoor shots taken from helicopters, cut instantaneously from one scene to another, or create special effects such as those in science fiction films like the popular Marvel superhero films.

No, the most significant—in fact, the overriding—difference between films and theatre is the *performer-audience relationship.* The experience of being in the presence of the performer is more important to theatre than anything else. With a film or with television, we are always in the presence of an *image,* never a person.

The American playwright Jean-Claude van Itallie (b. 1936) has explained the importance of the performer-audience relationship in theatre, and how theatre differs from films and television:

> Theater is not electronic. Unlike movies and unlike television, it does require the live presence of both audience and actors in a single space. This is the theater's uniquely important advantage and function, its original religious function of bringing people together in a community ceremony where the actors are in some sense priests or celebrants, and the audience is drawn to participate with the actors in a kind of eucharist.[2]

The Irish playwright Conor McPherson (b. 1971), who has had great success in theatre and film, also points out how the two art forms are distinct by comparing the difference between a rock band playing a live performance and its recorded music:

> Ultimately the difference between making films and putting plays on is analogous to the band of musicians who go into the studio to record an album and the completely different world of performing the music live to an audience. If you want to play live, you'd better be able to play well. . . . It's a great feeling to see a talented person perform live in front of you. Curiously, the live experience both demystifies the performer and at the same time creates a whole other set of mysteries: "How do they do that?"[3]

THEATRE IS TRANSITORY AND IMMEDIATE

As noted earlier, live theatre performance changes from moment to moment as the audience encounters and impacts a series of shifting impressions and stimuli. Each instant is a direct, immediate experience.

The essence of literature and the visual arts is to catch something at a moment in time and freeze it. With the performing arts, however, that is impossible because the performing arts are not objects but events. Specific objects—costumes, props, scenery, a script—are a part of theatre, but none of these constitute the art. Bernard Beckerman (1921–1985), Shakespeare scholar and director, explained the difference:

> Theater is nothing if not spontaneous. It occurs. It happens. The novel can be put away, taken up, reread. Not theater. It keeps slipping between one's fingers. Stopping, it stops being theater. Its permanent features, facets of activity, such as scenery, script, stage, people, are no more theater than the two poles of a generator are electricity. Theater is what goes on between the parts.[4]

Plays are often printed in book form, like literature, and many novels and short stories contain extensive passages of dialogue that could easily be scenes in a play. But there is an important difference between the two forms. Unlike a novel, a play is written to be performed. In some respects a script is to a stage production as a musical score is to a concert, or an architectural blueprint is to a building: it is an outline for a performance.

Drama can be studied in a classroom in terms of imagery, character, and theme, but with drama, study of this sort takes place *before* or *after* the event. It is a form of preparation for or follow-up to the experience; the experience is the performance itself. Obviously, we have more opportunities to read plays in book form than to see them produced; but when we read a play, we should always attempt to visualize the other aspects of a production in our mind's eye.

HUMAN BEINGS—THE FOCUS OF THEATRE

Books often focus on people, but they can also focus on science or nature; music focuses on sound; abstract painting and sculpture focus on shapes, colors, and forms. Uniquely among the arts, theatre focuses on one thing and one thing only—human beings. This is true even though different plays emphasize different human concerns, from profound problems in tragedy to pure entertainment in light comedy. And even when the performers play animals, inanimate objects, or abstract ideas, theatre concentrates on the human concerns involved.

In the modern world, human beings have lost the central place they were once believed to occupy in the universe. In the Ptolemaic view of the universe, which prevailed until the sixteenth century—when Copernicus theorized that Earth revolved around the sun—it was assumed that Earth was the center of everything. In science, we have long since given up that notion, particularly in light of explorations in outer space and other transformative discoveries regarding our universe. The human being has become seemingly less and less significant, and less and less at the center of things. But not in theatre, where the preoccupations of human beings are still the core, the center around which other elements orbit.

THE CHEMISTRY OF THE PERFORMER–AUDIENCE CONTACT

The fascination of being in the presence of a famous person or observing firsthand a special occasion is difficult to explain but not difficult to verify. No matter how often we have seen a favorite star in the movies or have seen a singer on television or listened to his or her songs on a handheld device, we will often go to any lengths to see the performer in person. Probably, at one time or another, each of us has braved bad weather and shoving crowds to see celebrities at a parade, a political rally, or a concert. Even a severe rainstorm will not deter many of us from seeing our favorite star at an outdoor concert. The same pull of personal contact draws us to the theatre. At the heart of the theatre experience, therefore, is the performer-audience relationship: the immediate, personal encounter whose chemistry and magic give theatre its special quality.

As suggested earlier, during a stage performance the performers can hear our laughter, can sense our silence, and can feel our tension as audience members. In short, we, as audience, can affect, and in subtle ways change, the performance. At the same time, as members of the audience, we watch the performers closely, consciously or unconsciously asking ourselves questions: Are the performers convincing in their roles? Will they do something surprising? Will they make a mistake? At each moment, in every stage performance, we, as fully participating audience members, should be looking for answers to questions like these. Actually two experiences are occurring almost simultaneously: our individual experience, which is highly personal; and the group experience, which we will discuss below.

THEATRE AS A GROUP EXPERIENCE

Certain arts—such as painting, sculpture, and literature—provide solitary experiences. The viewer or reader contemplates the work alone, at their own pace. This is true even in a museum: although many people may flock to look at a single painting and are with each other, they respond as individuals, one by one. In the performing arts, however, including theatre, the group experience is indispensable.

The performing arts share this trait with other communal events such as religious services, spectator sports, and celebrations. Before the event can take place, a group must assemble, at one time and in one place. When people are gathered together in this way, something mysterious happens to them. Though still individuals, with their own personalities and backgrounds, they take on other qualities as well, qualities that often overshadow their independent responses.

Psychology of Groups

Not all crowds are alike. Some are aggressive, such as an angry mob that decides to riot or a gang that terrorizes a neighborhood. Others are docile—a group of spectators on a sidewalk observing a juggler, for example. A crowd at a football game is different from a congregation at a religious observance; and a theatre crowd is distinct from any of these. In spite of being different, however, the theatre audience shares with all such groups the special characteristics of the *collective mind*. Becoming part of a group is a crucial element of the theatre experience. For a time, we share a common undertaking, focused on one activity—the performance of a play. Not only do we laugh or cry in a way we might not otherwise; we also sense an intangible communion with those around us. When a collection of individuals respond more or less in unison to what is occurring onstage, their relationship to one another is reaffirmed. If there is a display of cruelty at which we shudder, or sorrow by which we are moved, or pomposity at which we laugh, it is reassuring to have others respond as we do. For a moment we are part of a group sharing an experience; and our sorrow or joy, which we thought might be ours alone, is found to be part of a broad human response. There have even been physiological studies that prove audience members' hearts beat in similar ways during specific moments in productions.

IN FOCUS: THE COVID-19 PANDEMIC AND LIVE THEATRE

The worldwide COVID-19 pandemic caused economic hardships globally in 2020 and 2021. People were forced to shelter in place in many countries, including China, Italy, and the United States. Social distancing became the norm as governments asked its citizens to help stop the spread of the virus, which was particularly deadly for elderly populations and those with preexisting health conditions.

The pandemic took a toll on theatres and theatre artists, since productions and playhouses had to be closed across the world, in the same way that theatres were forced to close during Shakespeare's time in England due to the plague. In 1593, the plague caused the London theatres to shut down for 14 months. From 1603 to 1613, the theatres were closed for a total of 78 months due to the raging disease.

In 2020 and 2021, some theatres streamed productions at the same time they would have been presented live and sold "tickets" for online access codes. Still, these performances were digitally recorded so never changed from night to night. In addition, audience members watched on computers or tablets, or streamed to TV sets by themselves and could pause the events to leave and return.

Even when watching live streamed events on Zoom or other social media, audiences were limited to those family members at home or to individuals. While a noble attempt to keep theatre alive during a worldwide crisis, streaming could not replace being in the presence of live performers and in the presence of other audience members.

But we could see the ongoing appeal of theatre, ironically, during the shutdown of theatres across the globe due to the COVID-19 pandemic. The shutdown illustrated the resilience of live theatre and how much audiences missed live performances. As noted earlier, theatres streamed previously recorded productions and even staged some new ones via Zoom and other online media. A recorded version of the hit musical *Hamilton* was presented on Disney+ streaming channel earlier than expected due to audience demand. The National Theatre in London streamed several of its past productions.

Some theatres opened as soon as they could for actual performances, using very limited casts, social distancing for actors and backstage personnel, and reduced audience seating. Australia was able to reopen a production of the musical *Come From Away* in January 2021 after theatres there were closed for over 300 days. In April 2021, 378 days after Broadway shut down, a Broadway theatre reopened for a 36-minute show with two stars and only 150 audience members, all wearing masks and socially distanced. Broadway theatres, as well as theatres around the United States, reopened for full productions by the fall of 2021.

The closing of theatres during the pandemic reminded audiences everywhere how unique the live theatre experience is and how much theatre is and always will be part of our lives and our history. As one audience member said after the reopening of the first Broadway theatre: "I think I was smiling every second, just feeling being in a room with people again and having a shared human experience was incredible."[1]

During the COVID-19 pandemic theatres were initially forced to shutdown to prevent spread of the virus. In 2021, some theatres attempted to open again using masking and social distancing for performers and audience members. Shown here is a COVID-safe production of the musical *Kiss Me Kate* staged at Western Illinois University. *https://www.facebook.com/wiutheatredance/photos/a.195941867112610/5428105970562814/?type=3*
(Photo provided courtesy of Western Illinois University Visual Production Center. Costume Design by Jeannie Galioto. Scenic Design by Gerald "Andy" Trusley. Lighting Design by Joshua Wroblewski.)

1. "First Broadway Theatre Opens Its Doors Since the Covid-19 Pandemic Began." https://www.cnn.com/2021/04/03/us/broadway-st-james-theatre-ny-popsup-first-performance-trnd/index.html

Chapter 1 *The Audience: Its Role and Imagination*

THEATRE AS A GROUP EXPERIENCE

In theatre, the size, attitude, and makeup of the audience affect the overall experience. The theatre can be large or small, indoors or outdoors, and the audience can be people of similar tastes and background or a collection of quite varied individuals. Shown here is a production of *Pride and Prejudice*, a play being performed to a large audience at the Regents Park Open Air Theatre in London. (VisitBritain/Eric Nathan/Getty Images)

How Audience Composition Affects the Theatre Experience

Although being part of a group is an essential element of theatre, groups vary, and the makeup of a group will alter a theatrical event. Some audiences are general—for instance, the thousands who attend outdoor productions such as the Shakespeare festival in Ashland, Oregon, and *Unto These Hills,* which is a play about the Cherokee Indians presented each summer on a Cherokee reservation in western North Carolina. General audiences include people of all ages, from all parts of the country, and from all socioeconomic levels. Other audiences are more homogeneous, such as spectators at a high school play, a children's theatre production, a Broadway opening night, a political play, or a performance in a prison.

Another factor affecting our experience in the theatre is our relationship to the other members of the audience. If we are among friends or people of like mind, we feel comfortable and relaxed, and we readily become part of the group experience. On the other hand, if we feel alien—for example, a young person with an older group or a liberal with conservatives—we may feel estranged from the group as a whole. The people with whom we attend theatre may strongly influence our response to the total event. But theatre might also have the capacity to bring us together as an audience and performers to explore, respect, and discover our differences and similarities.

IN FOCUS: GLOBAL CONNECTIONS

Augusto Boal: The Theatre of the Oppressed

If ever there were an international theatre figure in recent times, it was Augusto Boal (1931–2009). Born in Brazil, Boal (pronounced "Bo-AHL") attended Columbia University in the United States. Returning to Brazil, he began working in the Arena Theatre in São Paulo. At first he directed conventional dramatic works, but Boal was a man with a powerful social conscience. During his early years he began to develop his philosophy of theatre. He concluded, for example, that mainstream theatre was used by the ruling class as a soporific, a means of sedating the audience and inoculating it against any impulse to act or revolt. In other words, conventional theatre oppressed ordinary citizens, especially the underprivileged.

Boal also became fascinated with the relationship of actors to audience members. He established a partnership between them, and he felt strongly that spectators should participate in any theatre event, that a way must be found for them to become performers, and a part of the action. In putting these theories into practice, he began to present *agitprop* plays, that is, plays with a strong political and social message. He experimented with several versions of such plays. One was the Invisible Theatre, in which actors, seemingly spontaneously, presented a prepared scene in a public space such as a town square or a restaurant. Another was his Forum Theatre, in which a play about a social problem became the basis of a discussion with audience members about solutions to the problem.

Considered an enemy of the authoritarian government in Brazil for his work in the 1960s, he was jailed in 1971 and tortured. Released after a few months, he was exiled from his native land. Following that he lived in various countries: Argentina, Portugal, and France. He decided along the way that his approach should be less didactic than it had been, that he would be more effective if he engaged audiences in the theatrical process rather than confronting them. This was the basis of his Theatre of the Oppressed, which became the cornerstone of his lifework from then on. He wrote a book by that title, which appeared in 1974.

Augusto Boal (Sucheta Das/AP Images)

In 1985 Boal returned to Brazil. From that point until his death, for the next quarter century, he traveled all over the world directing, lecturing, and establishing centers furthering the Theatre of the Oppressed. He also wrote other books, which were widely read. His approach to theatre found adherents in more than forty countries. Wherever the Theatre of the Oppressed was established, its productions challenged injustice, especially in poor and disenfranchised communities where citizens are often without a voice or an advocate. In his later years he was looked upon by many as the most inspirational person of his time in propagating socially oriented theatre.

THE SEPARATE ROLES OF PERFORMERS AND SPECTATORS

It is important to note the difference between *observed* theatre and *participatory* theatre. In observed theatre, as audience members we participate vicariously or empathetically with what is happening onstage. Empathy is the experience of mentally or emotionally entering into the feelings or spirit of another person—in this case, a character onstage. Sometimes we will not be in tune with the characters onstage but will react vehemently against them. In either situation, though, we are participating empathetically. We might shed tears, laugh, pass judgment, sit frozen, or tremble with fear. But we participate through our imagination while separated from the action.

There are also times when observers and audience members participate in a theatre event. In rituals and ceremonies in parts of Africa and among certain tribes of Native Americans, those attending have become, in effect, participants, joining in the singing and dancing, for instance. At a number of contemporary theatre events spectators have also been urged to take part. For example, one of the chief aims of the Theatre of the Oppressed created by Augusto Boal was to eliminate the distinction between audience members and performers. In Boal's philosophy, every spectator could be and should be an actor, and he developed a number of strategies to bring this about.

How Should the Audience Be Involved?

The attempt to involve audience members directly springs from a desire to make theatre more immediate and intense, and such work can be innovative and exciting. It remains, however, an exception to the kinds of theatre most of us are likely to encounter. The theatre most of us will experience requires a degree of distancing, in the same way that all art requires a certain perspective. Imagine trying to get the full effect of a large landscape painting when standing a few inches from the canvas: one would see only the brushstrokes of a single tree or a small patch of blue sky. To perceive and appreciate a work of art, we need distance. This separation, which is called *aesthetic distance,* is as necessary in theatre as in any other art.

aesthetic distance Physical or psychological separation or detachment of audience from dramatic action, usually considered necessary for artistic illusion.

In the same way that we must stand back from a painting to get its full effect, so too, as theatre spectators we must be separated from the performance in order to see and hear what is happening onstage and absorb the experience. If an audience member becomes involved in the proceedings or goes onstage and takes part in the action, as often occurred in a Boal production, he or she reverses roles and becomes a performer, not a spectator. The separation between performers and spectators remains.

Audience Participation through Direct Action

Today a range of educational or therapeutic activities employ theatrical techniques. The aim is not a performance viewed by an audience, as such. Those who take part in such activities are not performers in the usual sense, and there is no attempt to follow a written script. Rather, the emphasis is on education, personal development, or therapy—fields in which theatre techniques have opened up new possibilities. In schools, for example, creative dramatics, theatre games, and group improvisations have proved invaluable for self-discovery and the development of healthy group attitudes. By acting out hypothetical situations or giving free rein to their imagination, children can build self-confidence, discover their creative potential, and overcome their inhibitions.

In some situations, creative dramatics can teach lessons that are difficult to teach by conventional means. Playwriting, too, has often proved to be an invaluable educational tool. Students who write scenes, whether autobiographical or fictional, find the experience not only fulfilling but also enlightening. In addition to creative dramatics, a wide range of other activities—*sociodrama, psychodrama,* and *drama therapy*—incorporate theatrical techniques. For adults as well as children, these activities have come to the forefront as educational and therapeutic methods. In sociodrama, the members of participating groups—such as parents and children, students and teachers, or legal authorities and ordinary citizens—explore their own attitudes and prejudices. One successful approach is *role reversal.* A group of young people, for instance, may take the part of their parents while the adults assume the roles of the children; or members of a street gang will take the roles of the police, and the police

DRAMA THERAPY
Theatre techniques can be used for educational and therapeutic purposes. Shown here is a moment from the play *Circle Mirror Transformation*, by Annie Baker and directed by Sam Gold, at Playwrights Horizons in New York in 2009 that depicts the use of theatre for therapeutic purposes. The actors in this scene (from left to right) are: Tracee Chimo, Deirdre O'Connell, Heidi Schreck, Reed Birney, and Peter Friedman. (Sara Krulwich/The New York Times/Redux)

will take the roles of the street gang. In such role playing, both groups become aware of deep-seated feelings and arrive at a better understanding of one another.

Psychodrama uses some of the same techniques as sociodrama but is more private and interpersonal; in fact, it can become so intense that it should be carried out only under the supervision of a trained therapist. In psychodrama, individual fears, anxieties, and frustrations are explored. A person might reenact a particularly traumatic scene from childhood, for example. In participatory drama, theatre is a means to another end: education, therapy, group development, or the like. Its aim is not public performance, and there is little emphasis on a carefully prepared, expertly performed presentation before an audience; in fact, just the opposite is true. In observed drama, on the other hand, the aim is a professional performance for spectators, and this requires a separation between the performers and the audience—the "aesthetic distance" described earlier.

Participatory and Immersive Theatre There are some times, however, when observers and audience members are invited, even urged, to participate actively together in a theatre event. In the 1960s, for example, many politically and socially engaged theatre groups created productions in which spectators were encouraged to ignore the traditional boundaries between audience members and performers. In other words, instead of viewing the stage action as taking place in a separate space, audience members were asked to see the stage and the viewing area as a single entity.

In recent years a new phenomenon, ***immersive theatre,*** has become popular internationally. In immersive theatre, the audience plays an active role in some way, often moving through a performance space, sometimes even choosing where they go

immersive theatre In immersive theatre, audience members play an active role in some way, often moving through a performance space, sometimes even choosing where they should go within that space and what they should see and do. Many such productions use transformed, redesigned spaces as well as requiring audience members to engage in a complete sensory experience (touch, smell, even taste of foods and drink).

Chapter 1 *The Audience: Its Role and Imagination*

within that space and what they see and do. Many immersive productions use transformed, redesigned spaces as well as require the audience member to engage in a complete sensory experience (touch, smell, even taste of foods and drink). The goal is an attempt to personalize the experience for each audience member while still emphasizing the social interaction between small groups in the audience, as well as with the performers.

An example of such a work is *Sleep No More* (2003), an adaptation of Shakespeare's *Macbeth,* which the British company Punchdrunk has staged successfully in New York and London. Another group, the Australian theatre company One Step at a Time Like This, also focuses on immersive theatrical experiences. Their production *En Route,* for example, takes individual audience members through city spaces connecting those spaces to theatrical interactions with individual performers along the way. In Chicago, Windy City Playhouse stages immersive works, including *Southern Gothic* (2018), in which 30 audience members move from room to room, eavesdropping on the hosts and guests of a unique birthday celebration that is more and more out of control. In 2020, this theatre revived *Boys in the Band,* a significant 1968 drama about gay life in New York, in an immersive environment.

Although there has been a long history of participatory theatre where audience members are asked to take an active role, the most traditional role of audience members in the contemporary theatre is as observers.

THE IMAGINATION OF THE AUDIENCE

For those who create it, theatre is a direct experience: a performer walks onstage and embodies a character; a carpenter builds scenery; a scene designer paints it. For these people the experience is like cutting a finger or being held in an embrace: the pain or the warmth is felt directly and physically. Members of a theatre audience experience a different kind of pain or warmth. As spectators in a theatre, we sense the presence of other audience members; we observe the movements and gestures of performers and hear the words they speak; and we see costumes, scenery, and lighting. From these we form mental images or make imaginative connections that provoke joy, laughter, anger, sorrow, or pain. All this occurs, however, usually without moving from our seats.

We naturally assume that those who create theatre are highly imaginative people and that their minds are full of vivid, exciting ideas that might not occur to the rest of us. If we conclude, however, that we in the audience have only a limited theatrical imagination, we do ourselves a great injustice. As we saw earlier, theatre is a two-way street—an exchange between performers and audience—and this is nowhere more evident than in the creation of *illusion.* Illusion may be initiated by the creators of theatre, but it is completed by the audience.

In the eerie world of William Shakespeare's *Macbeth,* when three witches appear out of the mist or when Banquo's ghost interrupts the banquet, we know it is fantasy; witches and ghosts like those in *Macbeth* do not appear in everyday life. In the theatre, however, we take such fantasy at face value. In Shakespeare's own day, for instance, a convention readily accepted by audiences was that women's parts were played by boy actors. Shakespeare's women characters—Juliet, Desdemona, Lady

Macbeth—were not acted by women, as they are today, but played by boys. Everyone in the audience at an Elizabethan theatre knew that the boys were not actually women but accepted without question the notion that a boy actor was presenting an impression or an imitation of a woman. The film *Shakespeare in Love* (1998) afforded a fascinating glimpse of this: the actress Gwyneth Paltrow plays a young woman portraying a boy actor (in secret), while her acting partner is a young man playing a young woman portrayed by a boy (in the open).

Along with fantasy, we, as audience members, accept drastic shifts in time and space. Someone onstage dressed in a Revolutionary uniform says, "It is the winter of 1778, at Valley Forge," and we do not question it. What is more, we accept rapid movements back and forth in time. *Flashbacks*—abrupt movements from the present to the past and back again—are a familiar technique in films and television shows, but they are also commonplace in modern drama. A similar device often used in drama is *anachronism*. An anachronism involves placing some character or event outside its proper time sequence: for example, having people from the past speak and act as if they were living today. Medieval mystery and morality plays frequently contained anachronisms.

The medieval play *Abraham and Isaac,* for instance, is set in the time of the Old Testament, but it makes several references to the Christian trinity—a religious concept that was not developed until centuries later. The medieval audience accepted this shift in time as a matter of course, just as we do in theatre today.

In his frequently revived play *Angels in America* (1993), Tony Kushner includes a number of bizarre and fantastic characters or events. For example, a

THE IMAGINATION OF THE AUDIENCE
The audience and the performers are the two essential elements of theatre: both are required for theatre to occur. One aspect of the audience's participation is the use of its imagination. For the Broadway musical *Avenue Q*, audience members were expected to focus on the puppets as well as the clearly visible performers/operators. Shown here is a scene presented at the 2004 Tony Awards. Left to right are: Jennifer Barnhart, Rick Lyon, and John Tartaglia. (Sara Krulwich/The New York Times/Redux)

flashback In a narrative or story, movement back to a time in the past to show a scene or an event before the narrative resumes at the point at which it was interrupted.

PLAYING YOUR PART: EXPERIENCING THEATRE

1. Watch a scene from the film *Les Misérables*. Now try to imagine why it would be different as a live theatrical experience.
2. Read aloud the balcony scene from Shakespeare's *Romeo and Juliet*. What is realistic about the scene? What are some nonrealistic elements?
3. Discuss your favorite current nonrealistic film or television show. What fantastic elements are most appealing? Why?
4. Discuss a recent film or television show that you felt was realistic. What was real about it? What wasn't real?
5. Read a speech from a play (or a paragraph from a novel) aloud in class. How did your classmates affect your reading? How would you describe your class as an audience? Homogeneous? Heterogeneous? Explain.

character in the play called Mr. Lies is an imaginary person created in the mind of Harper, a housewife who is addicted to pills. Near the end of part 1, Mr. Lies takes Harper on a fantasy trip to the Antarctic. At the very end of part 1, an angel crashes through the ceiling and speaks to Prior, a man ill with AIDS. In the theatre, then, our imagination allows us to conceive of people and events we have never seen or experienced and to transcend our physical circumstances to the point where we forget who we are, where we are, or what time it is. How is this possible? It happens because in the theatre our imagination works for us just as it does in everyday life.

The musical *Hamilton* uses anachronisms in many ways to draw parallels between our country's past and its present.

Tools of the Imagination: Symbol and Metaphor

We can understand this process better if we look closely at two tools of our imagination: symbol and metaphor.

symbol A sign, a visual image, an object, or an action that signifies something else; a visual embodiment of something invisible. A single image or sign stands for an entire idea or larger concept—a flag is a symbol for a nation; a logo is a symbol for a corporation.

Functions of Symbols In general terms, a *symbol* is a sign, token, or emblem that signifies something else. A simple form of symbol is a sign. Some signs stand for a single, uncomplicated idea or action. In everyday life we are surrounded by them: road signs, such as an S-shaped curve; audible signals, like sirens and foghorns; and a host of mathematical and typographical symbols: $, 1/4, @, &. We sometimes forget that language itself is symbolic; the letters of the alphabet are only lines and curves on a page. Words are arrangements of letters that by common agreement represent something else. The same four letters mean different things depending on the order in which they are placed: *pear, reap, rape*. These three words set different imaginative wheels in motion and signal responses that vary greatly from word to word.

At times, symbols exert incredible emotional power; a good example is a flag, embodying a nation's passions, fears, and ambitions. Flags are symbols: lines, shapes, and colors that in certain combinations become immediately recognizable. Like flags, some symbols signify ideas or emotions that are far more complex and profound than the symbol itself. The cross, for example, is a symbol of Christ and, beyond that, of Christianity as a whole. Whatever form a symbol takes—language, a flag, or a religious emblem—it can embody the total meaning of a religion, a nation, or an idea.

Functions of Metaphors A similar transformation takes place with metaphor, another form of imaginative substitution. With metaphor we announce that one thing is another, in order to describe it or point up its meaning more clearly. (In poetry, you will remember, a simile says that one thing is *like* another; metaphor simply states directly that one thing *is* another.) The Bible is filled with metaphors. The psalmist who says, "The Lord is my shepherd," or who says of God, "Thou art my rock and my fortress," is speaking metaphorically. He does not mean literally that God is a shepherd, a rock, or a fortress; he is saying that God is similar to and has qualities like these things. Just as with symbols, metaphors are part of the fabric of life, as the following common expressions suggest:

"How gross."

"They are off the wall."

"It's a slam dunk."

"Give me the bottom line."

"That's cool."

We are saying one thing but describing another. When someone describes a person or event as "cool," the reference is not to a low temperature but to an admirable quality. The term *slam dunk* comes from basketball, but in everyday parlance is applied to a wide range of activities that have nothing to do with sports. We can see from these examples that metaphors, like symbols, are part of daily life.

The "Reality" of the Imagination

Our use of symbol and metaphor shows how large a part imagination plays in our lives. Millions of automobiles in the United States can be brought to a halt, not by a concrete wall, but by a small light changing from green to red. Imagine attempting to control traffic, or virtually any type of human activity, without symbols. Beyond being a matter of convenience, symbols are necessary to our survival.

The same holds true for metaphor. Frequently we find that we cannot express fear, anxiety, hope, or joy—any of the deep human feelings—in descriptive language. That is why we sometimes scream. It is also why we have poetry and use metaphors. Even scientists, the men and women we are most likely to consider realists, turn to metaphor at crucial times. They discuss the "big bang" theory of the origin of the universe and talk of "black holes" in outer space. Neither term is "scientific," but both terms communicate what scientists have in mind in a way that an equation or a more logical phrase could not.

Dreams provide another example of the power of the imagination. We dream that we are falling off a cliff; then, suddenly, we wake up and find that we are not flying through the air but lying in bed. Significantly, however, the dream of falling means more to us than the objective fact of lying in bed. Theatre functions in somewhat the same way. Though not real in a literal sense, it can be completely—even painfully—real in an emotional or intellectual sense. The critic and director Harold Clurman (1901-1980) gave one of his books on theatre the title *Lies Like Truth*. Theatre—like dreams or fantasies—can sometimes be more truthful about life than a mundane, objective description. This is a paradox of dreams, fantasies, and art, including theatre: by probing deep into the psyche to reveal inner truths, they can be more real than outward reality.

THE POWER OF SYMBOLS
Symbols and metaphors, though not real in a literal sense, have enormous power to influence our lives; in that respect, they become "realer than real." A forceful symbol of the bravery, tragedy, and losses of the Vietnam War is the wall designed by Maya Lin in Washington, D.C., where the names of those who died are etched into the side of the memorial. (Win McNamee/Getty Images)

IN FOCUS: THE CONTRAST BETWEEN REALISM AND DEPARTURES FROM REALISM

The distinction between realistic techniques in theatre and those forms that depart from realistic techniques becomes clearer when the two approaches are examined side by side. This distinction is present in all aspects of theatre.

Realistic Techniques	"Departures from Realism" Techniques
STORY	
Events that the audience knows have happened or might happen in everyday life: Blanche DuBois in Tennessee Williams's *A Streetcar Named Desire* goes to New Orleans to visit her sister and brother-in-law.	Events that do not take place in real life but occur only in the imagination: in Kushner's *Angels in America*, a character in a housewife's mind takes her on an imaginary trip to the Antarctic.
STRUCTURE	
Action is confined to real places; time passes normally, as it does in everyday life: the hospital room setting in Margaret Edson's *Wit* is an example.	Arbitrary use of time and place: in August Strindberg's *The Dream Play*, walls dissolve and characters are transformed, as in a dream.
CHARACTERS	
Recognizable human beings, such as the priest and the nun in John Patrick Shanley's *Doubt*.	Unreal figures like the ghost of Hamlet's father in William Shakespeare's *Hamlet* or the three witches in *Macbeth*.
ACTING	
Performers portray people as they behave in daily life: the men on a summer holiday in the country house in Terrence McNally's *Love! Valor! Compassion!*	Performers portray animals in the musical *The Lion King*; they also engage in singing, dancing, and acrobatics in musical comedy or performance art.
LANGUAGE	
Ordinary dialogue or conversation: the two brothers trying to get ahead in Suzan-Lori Parks's *Topdog/Underdog*.	Poetry such as Romeo speaks to Juliet in Shakespeare's play; or the song "Tonight" in the musical *West Side Story*.
SCENERY	
Rooms of a real house, as in Edward Albee's *Who's Afraid of Virginia Woolf?*	Abstract forms and shapes on a bare stage—for example, for a Greek play such as Sophocles's *Electra*.
LIGHTING	
Light onstage appears to come from natural sources—a lamp in a room, or sunlight, as in Ibsen's *Ghosts*, where the sunrise comes through a window in the final scene.	Shafts of light fall at odd angles; also, colors in light are used arbitrarily. Example: a single blue spotlight on a singer in a musical comedy.
COSTUMES	
Ordinary street clothes, like those worn by the characters in August Wilson's *The Piano Lesson*.	The bright costumes of a chorus in a musical comedy; the strange outfit worn by Caliban, the half-man, half-beast in Shakespeare's *The Tempest*.
MAKEUP	
The natural look of characters in a domestic play such as Lorraine Hansberry's *A Raisin in the Sun*.	Masks worn by characters in a Greek tragedy or in a modern play like the musical *Beauty and the Beast*.

THE IMAGINARY WORLDS OF THEATRE

As theatre audience members, we are asked to accept many kinds of imaginary worlds. One way to classify these imaginary realms is as *realism* and **departures from realism (or nonrealism).** At the outset, it is essential to know that in theatre the term *realistic* denotes a special application of what we consider "genuine" or "real." A realistic element is not necessarily more truthful than a nonrealistic element. Rather, in theatre, realistic and nonrealistic denote different ways of presenting reality.

Realistic Elements of Theatre

In theatre, a realistic element is one that resembles *observable* reality. It is a kind of photographic truth. We apply the term *realistic* to those elements of theatre that conform to our own observations of people, places, and events. Realistic theatre follows the predictable logic of everyday life: the law of gravity, the time it takes a person to travel from one place to another, the way a room in a house looks, the way a person dresses. With a realistic approach, these conform to our normal expectations. In realistic theatre, we are called upon in our imaginations to accept the notion that what we see onstage is not fantastic but real, even though we always know we are in the theatre and not watching an actual event.

We are quite familiar with realism in films and television. Part of the reason is mechanical. The camera records what the lens "sees." Whether it is a bedroom in a house, a crowded city street, or the Grand Canyon, film captures the scene as the eye sees it. Theatre too has always had realistic elements. Every type of theatre that is not pure fantasy has realistic aspects. For example, characters who are supposed to represent real people must be rooted in a human truth that audiences can recognize. When we are so readily able to verify what we see before us from our own experience, it is

realism Broadly, an attempt to present onstage people, places, and events corresponding to those in everyday life.

nonrealism (or departures from realism) All types of theatre that depart from observable reality.

REALISTIC AND NONREALISTIC THEATRE CONTRASTED
These scenes illustrate some of the differences between two approaches to the make-believe of theatre. At the left we see Gabriel Brown as George Murchison, Edena Hines as Beneatha Younger, and Susan Kelechi Watson as Ruth Younger in the Westport Country Playhouse production of Lorraine Hansberry's *A Raisin in the Sun*. In contrast, the scene at the right is from a revival of an avant-garde production presented at the Brooklyn Academy of Music of *Einstein on the Beach*, directed and designed by Robert Wilson. Note the abstract setting, the eerie lighting, the symbolic characters. This kind of theatre contrasts sharply with realism. (*left*: T Charles Erickson *right*: Sara Krulwich/The New York Times/Redux)

easy to identify with it and to accept its authenticity. For this reason, realistic theatre has become firmly established in modern times, and it seems likely to remain so.

Departures from Realism: Nonrealistic Elements of Theatre

Departures from realism includes every technique that does not conform to our observations of surface reality: poetry instead of prose, ghosts rather than flesh-and-blood people, abstract forms for scenery, and so forth. Again, we find a counterpart in films and television. The extremely popular vampire and zombie films and television shows present us with fantastic characters and situations. All of the *Star Wars* films have intriguing digitally generated characters and effects, which is one of the reasons audiences look forward to each of the new additions to the series.

In theatre, the argument for *departures from realism* (or *nonrealism*) is that the surface of life—a real conversation, for instance, or a real room in a house—can never convey the whole truth, because so much of life occurs in our minds and imagination. If we are depressed and tell a friend that we feel "lousy" or "awful," we do not even begin to communicate the depth of our feelings. It is because of the inadequacy of ordinary words that people turn to poetry, and because of the inadequacy of other forms of daily communication that they turn to music, dance, art, sculpture, and the entire range of symbols and metaphors discussed earlier.

A wide range of theatrical techniques and devices fall into the category of departures from realism or nonrealism. One example is the ***soliloquy,*** in which a solitary character speaks to the audience, expressing in words a hidden thought. Another example is ***pantomime,*** in which performers pretend to be using objects that are not actually present, such as drinking from a cup or opening an umbrella. Many aspects of musical comedy are nonrealistic. People in various human circumstances do not break into song or dance as they do in musicals like *Guys and Dolls, West Side Story, Wicked, The Book of Mormon, Hamilton* or *The Prom.* One could say that any activity or scenic device that transcends or symbolizes reality tends to be nonrealistic.

soliloquy Speech in which a character who is alone onstage speaks inner thoughts aloud.

pantomime A form of theatrical presentation that relies on dance, gesture, and physical movement without speech.

NONREALISTIC ELEMENTS
Realism has been a major approach to theatre since the late nineteenth century, but for hundreds of years before that, theatre incorporated many unrealistic elements. One example is Shakespeare's use of ghosts, spirits, and various otherworldly creatures. Shown here in a Royal Shakespeare Company production of *The Tempest,* directed by Gregory Dora, with Simon Russell Beale as Prospero (front center) and Mark Quartley as Ariel, a spirit. This production was staged at Stratford Upon Avon in 2016. (Geraint Lewis/Alamy Stock Photo)

Combining the Realistic and the Nonrealistic

In discussing realistic and nonrealistic elements of theatre, we must not assume that these two approaches are mutually exclusive. The terms *realistic* and *nonrealistic* are simply a convenient way of separating those parts of theatre that correspond to our observations and experiences of everyday life from those that do not. Most performances and theatre events contain a mixture of realistic and nonrealistic elements. In acting, for example, a Shakespearean play calls for a number of nonrealistic qualities or techniques. At the

Part One   The Audience

same time, any performer playing a Shakespearean character must convince the audience that he or she represents a real human being.

To take more modern examples, in *The Glass Menagerie* by Tennessee Williams (1911–1983), and in *Our Town* by Thornton Wilder (1897–1975), one of the performers serves as a narrator and also participates in the action. When the performer playing this part is speaking directly to the audience, his actions are nonrealistic; when he is taking part in a scene with other characters, they are realistic.

Distinguishing Stage Reality from Fact

Whether theatre is realistic or nonrealistic, it is different from the physical reality of everyday life. In recent years there have been attempts to make theatre less remote from our daily lives. For example, plays have been presented that were largely transcripts of court trials or congressional hearings. This was part of a movement called *theatre of fact,* which involved reenactments of material gathered from actual events. Partly as a result of this trend, theatre and life have become intertwined. Television has added to this with *docudramas,* dramatizing the lives, for example, of ordinary, often actual people who become heroic. There has also been a vogue for what is called "reality television," in which real people are put in stressful situations with a presumably unplanned outcome.

FACT-BASED THEATRE
A popular form that has emerged in the past half century is theatre based on facts. This includes documentary theatre taken from court trials, congressional hearings, and interviews. Shown here is Lynn Japjit Kaur, center, as Jyoti Singh Pandey, a woman who died in 2012 after she was gang-raped and tortured in New Delhi, in the play *Nirbhaya*. The testimony of five Indian women describing their experiences of sexual abuse is used by South African playwright and director Yael Farber to create a harrowing documentary drama that was performed internationally, including at the Lynn Redgrave Theater in New York in 2015. (Sara Krulwich/The New York Times/Redux)

This kind of interaction—and sometimes confusion—between life and art has been heightened, of course, by the emergence of television and film documentaries that cover real events but are also edited. In addition, today we have "staged" political demonstrations and hear of "staged news." In politics staged events have become commonplace: a presidential or senatorial candidate visits a flag factory, an aircraft carrier, or an elementary school for what is called a "photo opportunity." When news becomes "staged" and theatre becomes "fact," it is difficult to separate the two.

These developments point up the close relationship between theatre and life; nevertheless, when we see a performance, even a re-creation of events that have actually occurred, on some level we are always aware of being in a theatre. Most of us have seen plays with a stage setting so real we marvel at its authenticity: a kitchen, for instance, in which the appliances actually work, with running water in the faucets, ice in the refrigerator, and a stove on which an actor or actress can cook. What we stand in awe of, though, is that the room *appears* so real when we know, in truth, that it is not. We admire the fact that, not being a real kitchen, it looks as if it were. We are abruptly reminded of the distinction between stage reality and physical reality when the two lines cross. If an actor unintentionally trips and falls onstage, we suddenly shift our attention from the character to the person playing the part. Has he hurt himself? Will he be able to continue? A similar reaction occurs when a performer forgets lines, or a sword falls accidentally during a duel, or a dancer slips during a musical number.

We remember the distinction, also, at the moment when someone else *fails* to remember it. Children frequently mistake actions onstage for the real thing, warning the heroine of the villain's plan or assuming that blows on the head of a puppet actually hurt. There is a famous story about a production of *Othello* in which a spectator ran onstage to prevent the actor playing Othello from strangling Desdemona. Most people, however, are always aware of the difference; our minds manage two seemingly contradictory feats simultaneously: on the one hand, we know that an imagined event is not objectively real, but at the same time we accept it completely as fantasy. This is possible because of what the poet and critic Samuel Taylor Coleridge (1772–1834) called the "willing suspension of disbelief." Having separated the reality of art from the reality of everyday life, the mind is prepared to go along unreservedly with the reality of art.

PLAYING YOUR PART: THINKING ABOUT THEATRE

1. Think of an event you have recently attended in person: a rock concert, a circus, a dance or musical presentation, a religious or memorial service. Explain what it meant to you to be present, in the same space at the same time as those performing or officiating. What was the feeling, the emotion, the stimulation you experienced that would not have been the same if you had watched the event on television?

2. During a performance you may observe a puppet or group of puppets who appear as real as people we deal with every day. Or you may see on a bare stage two or three props (a tree, for example, or a throne) and you assume you are in a forest or a royal palace. Why do you think during a performance we are able to let our imaginations take over? Is this something we also do in everyday life?

3. While watching a performance you may dissolve into laughter or cry real tears. The whole time, on some level, you know what you are observing is not "real." But does this matter? In some sense is the experience real? What is the relationship between a theatre experience such as this and an experience in daily life?

The Pulitzer Prize winning play *Fairview* (2018) by Jackie Sibblies Drury, begins as a theatrically realistic work, with the audience observing a birthday party being given by a Black family for a grandmother. But eventually, the audience is shatteringly reminded that they are in the theatre and in turn of the racist world off stage. The play makes us realize that nothing in the theatre is ever real and that true reality only exists off the stage.

SUMMARY

1. During the past 100 years, theatre has been challenged by a succession of technological developments: silent movies, radio, talking movies, television, and electronic handheld devices. It has survived these challenges partly because of the special nature of the performer–audience relationship.
2. In 2020 and 2021, live theatre was challenged by the worldwide shutdowns caused by the COVID-19 pandemic. The desire for live performance resulted in streamed and Zoom hosted performances. Still, there was a clamor for a return to live performances.
3. The relationship between performer and audience is "live": each is in the other's presence, in the same place at the same time. It is the exchange between the two that gives theatre its unique quality.
4. Theatre—like the other performing arts—is a group experience. The composition of the audience has a direct bearing on the effect of the experience.
5. Participants and spectators play different roles in the theatre experience; the role of spectators is to observe and respond.
6. There is a difference between participating in theatre by direct action and by observation. In the former situation, nonactors take part, usually for the purpose of personal growth and self-development. In the latter, a presentation is made by one group to another, and the spectators do not participate physically in the experience.
7. For the observer, theatre is an experience of the imagination and the mind. The mind seems capable of accepting almost any illusion as to what is taking place, who the characters are, and when and where the action occurs.
8. Our minds are capable of leaps of imagination, not just in the theatre but in our everyday lives, where we use symbol and metaphor to communicate with one another and to explain the world around us.
9. The world of the imagination—symbols, metaphors, dreams, fantasies, and various expressions of art—is "real," even though it is intangible and has no objective reality. Frequently it tells us more than any form of logical discourse about our true feelings.
10. Theatre makes frequent use of symbols and metaphors—in writing, acting, and design—and theatre itself can be looked upon as a metaphor.
11. Theatre calls upon audiences to imagine two kinds of worlds: realistic and nonrealistic. Realistic theatre depicts things onstage that conform to observable reality; nonrealistic theatre includes the realm of dreams, fantasy, symbol, and metaphor. In theatre, realism and nonrealism are frequently mixed.
12. In order to take part in theatre as an observer, it is important to keep the "reality" of fantasies and dreams separate from the real world. By making this separation, we open our imagination to the full range of possibilities in theatre.

Design Elements: Audience Sitting in Theatre (theatre): Ron Chapple/Photodisc/Getty Images; Studio Light (spotlights): Exactostock/SuperStock

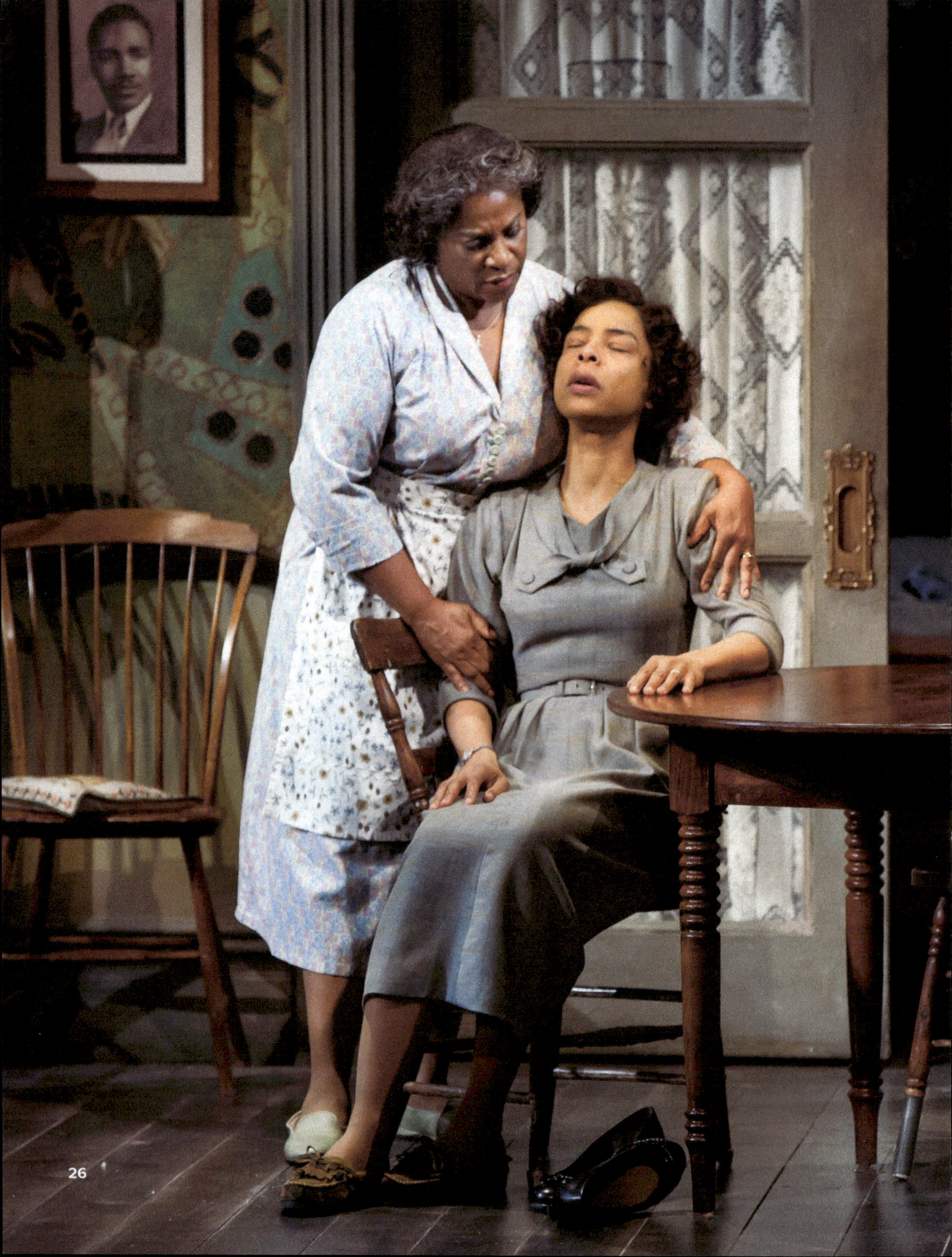

2

Background and Expectations of the Audience

We are soon going to attend a theatre performance, either for personal enjoyment or as a class assignment. As a soon-to-be audience member is there a way we can prepare so that the production will be more entertaining or more meaningful? Are there steps we can take beforehand that will enhance the experience, make it more rewarding, and make us a more engaged audience member? The answer to these questions is "yes."

In a sense, this entire book is a preparation for going to the theatre. Chapter by chapter it explains the various elements of a production—the acting and directing, the script, the scenic and costume design—and how all these fit together in the final stage presentation. But initially, before getting to these specifics, there is information and preparation that will make attending a specific production more exciting and pleasurable, as well as make us a more informed, engaged, and knowledgeable audience member.

For one thing, when we attend a theatre event, we bring more than our mere presence; we bring a background of personal knowledge and a set of expectations that shape the experience. Several important factors are involved:

1. Our family and personal history, knowledge, and memories.
2. Our awareness of the social, political, and philosophical world in which the play was written or produced—the link between theatre and society.
3. Our knowledge about the play and playwright.
4. Our personal expectations concerning the event: what we anticipate will happen at a performance. As we will see, misconceptions about what the theatre experience is or should be can lead to confusion and disappointment.

◀ **THE AFRICAN AMERICAN EXPERIENCE**

Members of a theatre audience come to a performance with individual, personal backgrounds, which can make the experience more meaningful. An example would be an African American audience member seeing A Raisin in the Sun, *which depicts an African American family trying to move into a home in an all-white neighborhood in mid-twentieth century, originally opening on Broadway in 1959. Shown here is a 2014 revival at the Barrymore Theatre in New York, directed by Kenny Leon. From left to right are: LaTanya Richardson Jackson and Sophie Okonedo. (Sara Krulwich/The New York Times/Redux)*

BACKGROUND OF INDIVIDUAL SPECTATORS

A background element that each of us brings to a theatre performance as an audience member is our own individual memories and experiences. Each of us has a personal catalog of childhood memories, emotional scars, and private fantasies. Anything we see onstage that reminds us of this personal world will have a strong impact on us. When we see a play that has been written in our own day, we bring with us also a deep awareness of the world from which the play comes, because we come from the same world. Through the books we have read, through newspapers and television, through our discussions with friends, we have a background of common information, values, and beliefs. Our shared knowledge and experience are much larger than most of us realize, and they form a crucial ingredient in our theatre experience.

The play *A Raisin in the Sun* by Lorraine Hansberry (1930–1965) tells the story of an African American family in Chicago in the late 1950s whose members want to improve their lives by finding better jobs and moving to a new neighborhood. But they face a number of obstacles put in their way by racism. Many African Americans—and other persons from underrepresented groups who have experienced racism—can readily identify with this situation. They may know from personal experience what the characters are going through or recognize the ongoing systemic racism confronted by the Younger family.

BACKGROUND INFORMATION ON THE PLAY OR PLAYWRIGHT

Often to enhance our experience of attending a theatre production we need additional information about a play or a playwright. For instance, a play may contain difficult passages or obscure references, which it is helpful to know about before we see a performance. As an example, we can take a segment from Shakespeare's *King Lear:* the scene in the third act when Lear appears on the heath in the midst of a terrible storm. Earlier in the play, Lear divided his kingdom between two of his daughters, Goneril and Regan, who he thought loved him but who, he discovers, have actually deceived him. Gradually, they have stripped him of everything: his possessions, his soldiers, his dignity. Finally, they send him out from their homes to face the wind and rain in open country. As the storm begins, Lear speaks the following lines:

> Blow, winds, and crack your cheeks! Rage! Blow!
> You cataracts and hurricanoes, spout
> Till you have drenched our steeples, drowned the cocks!

In the first line, the expression "crack your cheeks" refers to pictures in the corners of old maps showing a face puffed out at the cheeks, blowing the wind. Shakespeare is saying that the face of the wind should blow so hard that its cheeks will crack. In the second line, "cataracts and hurricanoes" refers to water from both the heavens and the seas. In the third line, "cocks" refers to weathercocks on the tops of church steeples; Lear wants so much rain to fall that even the weathercocks on the steepletops will be submerged. If we are aware of these meanings, we can join them with the sounds of the words—and with the rage the actor expresses in his voice and gestures—to get the full impact of the scene.

In contemporary theatre, playwrights frequently use special techniques that will confuse us if we do not understand them. The German playwright Bertolt Brecht (1898-1956), who lived and wrote in the United States during the 1940s, wanted to provoke his audiences into thinking about what they were seeing. To do this, he would interrupt a story with a song or a speech by a narrator. His theory was that when a story is stopped in this manner, audience members have an opportunity to consider more carefully what they are seeing and to relate the drama onstage to other aspects of life.

If we are not aware that this is Brecht's purpose in interrupting the action, we might conclude that he was simply a careless or inferior playwright. Here, as in similar cases, knowledge of the play or playwright is indispensable to a complete theatre experience.

The African American playwright August Wilson (1945-2005) wrote a ten-play cycle that dramatized Black life in the United States, each play set in a separate decade of the twentieth century. Wilson wanted to chronicle the ongoing systemic racism in the United States as well as Black strength, community, and resiliency in the face of that oppression. Wilson's works are influenced by Black history, music, culture, and religious beliefs. Audience members attending his works can have a greater appreciation if they understand his intentions and have an awareness of his dramatic techniques.

BACKGROUND OF THE PERIOD

Even when we identify closely with the characters or situation in a play and we have knowledge about the play and the playwright, often in drama from the past there are elements we cannot understand unless we are familiar with the history, culture, and philosophy of the period when it was created. This is because there is a close connection between any art form and the society in which it is produced.

Theatre and Society

Art does not occur in a vacuum. All art, including theatre, is related to the society in which it is produced. Artists are sometimes charged with being "antisocial," "subversive," or "enemies of the state," and such accusations carry the strong suggestion that artists are outsiders or invaders rather than true members of a culture. To be sure, art frequently challenges society and is sometimes on the leading edge of history, appearing to forecast the future. More often than not, however, such art simply recognizes what is already present in society but has not yet surfaced. A good example is the abstract painting that developed in Europe in the early twentieth century. At first it was considered a freakish aberration, an unattractive jumble of jagged lines and patches of color with no relation to nature, truth, or anything human. In time, however, abstract art came to be recognized as a genuine movement, and the disjointed and fragmentary lines of abstract art seemed to reflect the quality of much of modern life.

Art grows in the soil of a specific society. With very few exceptions—and those are soon forgotten—art is a mirror of its age, revealing the prevailing attitudes, underlying assumptions, and deep-seated beliefs of a particular group of people. Art may question society's views or reaffirm them, but it cannot escape

AUDIENCE MEMBER'S PERSONAL BACKGROUND
The personal background of individual audience members will affect their experience in attending a theatre production. Young people from diverse ethnic and cultural backgrounds who have worked together on a project or other undertaking will have a better understanding than others of a theatre piece such as *Emotional Creature* by Eve Ensler, shown here, with the actor Ashley Bryant in the foreground. In the play, six young actors from different countries around the globe develop an involvement in their mutual social problems that inspires them to express their feelings in monologues, songs, and dance.
(Sara Krulwich/The New York Times/Redux)

them; the two are as indissolubly linked as a person and his or her shadow. When some speak of art as "universal," they mean that the art of one age has so defined the characteristics of human beings that it might speak to another age; but we should never forget that every work of art first emerges at a given time and place and can never be adequately understood unless the conditions surrounding its birth are also understood.

We should also remember that too often "universal" has meant representing the majority population to the exclusion of those being marginalized or representing those peoples in negative ways. For example, the theatre of the United States has either marginalized or represented negatively people of color throughout most of its history. Women and those in the LGBTQ communities have been dealt with in the same way.

Two societies that produced an astonishing output of dramatic works were Athens, Greece, in the fifth century BCE and the Elizabethan period (named for Queen

Elizabeth I) in England. The former gave us the tragedies of Aeschylus, Sophocles, and Euripides as well as the comedies of Aristophanes. It was during the Elizabethan era that William Shakespeare, Christopher Marlowe, and Ben Jonson emerged. In each instance the advances in politics, science, philosophy, and the arts in general provided the environment in which these theatrical works could emerge.

In understanding the dramatic works of each period, it is helpful to understand what was occurring in society generally. We should also recognize the negative representations of marginalized populations in some of these works, such as women in the Greek comedies, Jews in Elizabethan dramas, and Africans in Shakespeare's plays, by understanding the gender, racial, and religious biases of the eras. The same is true of any period or culture known for its theatrical works, whether in the past or present, or the place where it occurs—in Asia, Western Europe, or around the globe.

THEATRE REFLECTS SOCIAL ISSUES
Theatre can be a powerful tool in calling attention to social and political injustices. A good example is Lynn Nottage's Pulitzer Prize-winning play *Sweat*, directed by Kate Whoriskey. The play is set in Reading, Pennsylvania, and dramatizes the impact of global economic changes on blue-collar steelworkers as they lose their livelihoods and their humanity and camaraderie are eroded. (Sara Krulwich/The New York Times/Redux)

Modern Theatre and Culture

Moving to the contemporary period, we find once again a link between theatre and society. Modern society, especially in the United States, is heterogeneous. We have people of different races, religions, sexual orientations, and national backgrounds living side by side. Moreover, the twentieth century was marked by increasingly swift global communication. By means of television, computers, and the Internet, an event occurring in one place can be flashed instantaneously to the rest of the world. Text messaging and social media, such as Facebook and Twitter, now make us aware of events instantaneously. By these means, too, people are continually made aware of cultures other than their own.

When cultures and societies are brought together, we are reminded not only of the many things people may have in common but also of the differences among us. At the same time that we are brought together by immediate global communications, other aspects of life have become increasingly fragmented. A number of institutions that had held fairly constant through many centuries—organized religion, the family, marriage—have been seriously challenged in the century and a half preceding our own day. Discoveries by Charles Darwin (1809–1882) about evolution, by Karl Marx (1818–1883) on economics, by Sigmund Freud (1856–1939) about the importance of the unconscious, and by Albert Einstein (1879–1955) on relativity questioned and threatened long-established views of the universe, of religion, economics, psychology, and science.

Similar changes in viewpoint and discoveries about nature have continued to the present, the cumulative effect of which has been to make human beings much less certain of their place in the cosmos and of their mastery of events. Today, in the early twenty-first century, life appears much less unified and less ordered than it once did.

IN FOCUS: HISTORICAL PERSPECTIVES

Women in Greek and Elizabethan Theatres

Did women attend theatre in ancient Greece? In Elizabethan England, why were women forbidden to appear onstage? These are only two of many significant and intriguing questions that arise when one examines the role of women at various times in theatre history. And, of course, they are inextricably linked to larger questions about the treatment of women in society in every age.

In Athenian society of ancient Greece, only male citizens had the right to participate in politics. Although women counted as citizens, they were generally excluded from the institutions of government. They were thus also excluded from appearing onstage in the annual spring theatre festival called the City Dionysia. The plays were written and acted by men, even though many feature important women characters. A broader social question is whether women were allowed to attend the dramatic festivals as spectators. There appears to be no conclusive answer, and the question continues to perplex classical scholars. Even if a select number of women were at performances—after all, men brought their male slaves to the theatre—the plays primarily address a large male audience. Contemporary sources supporting the view that women attended theatre are fragmentary and inconclusive; for instance, a character in *The Frogs* by Aristophanes (c. 447–388 BCE) remarks ironically that all decent women committed suicide after seeing one of Euripides's plays. Later commentaries, such as an often-repeated story that a few women who saw the chorus of Furies in *The Eumenides* by Aeschylus (525–456 BCE) had miscarriages, are discounted because women did attend theatre after the classical period.

One argument for the attendance of women is the important role women often played in other aspects of the cultural life of the city-state. They contributed to civic life, for example, by playing leading roles in religious ceremonies, celebrations, and other ritual activities. In fact, they were creatively involved in theatre at other festivals. Because the public activities of women were regulated in order to protect their reputation, women entertainers came to be associated with indecent behavior. Even so, popular entertainments included women performers as singers, dancers, acrobats, and musicians.

In the sixteenth century, actresses appeared onstage in continental Europe. Also, women had appeared in medieval theatre productions in England, but in the English public theatres in the time of Elizabeth I (r. 1558–1603), women were forbidden by law to appear onstage. Although some actors rose to become celebrities, actresses were often associated with "public women" or prostitutes—particularly by Puritans who viewed theatre as an immoral profession. Women roles therefore were played by boys, notable for their ability to imitate feminine beauty and grace. An exception to the prohibition of actresses was the appearance of Italian singers and French actresses who performed in England for both the nobility and commoners. Outside the public theatres, historians identify a vast, hidden tradition of woman performance gleaned from private documents, such as letters and diaries. At court and in manor houses aristocratic women took part in extravagant spectacles called masques; parish dramas and pageants included women members of the community; other women worked as traveling entertainers. The disapproval of women performing in public changed with the restoration of the monarchy in 1660, when actresses were finally permitted to appear in licensed theatres.

Prepared by Susan Tenneriello, Baruch College, CUNY.

We must add to these developments the effect of the horrific events that have occurred over the past 125 years: the two World Wars, the second of which saw the Holocaust, the extermination of millions of Jews and others by the Nazi regime; the highly controversial Vietnam War; terrorism and the effects on our society of the events of 9/11; more recently, the Iraq and ongoing Afghanistan wars; and the continuing systemic racism and rise of violent white supremacy in the United States and in European nations.

All of these developments are reflected in our theatre today, which is fragmented and *eclectic*, and embraces different styles and traditions. The theatre productions we attend today may come from around the world and from artists from marginalized and underrepresented peoples (though as was apparent during the 2020 and 2021 protests against systemic racism, the U.S. and European theatres reflect the white privilege and ongoing exclusion of artists of color in those societies), and range from the darkest of tragedies to the lightest of comedies to the highly experimental works, created by dramatists who write on many subjects and in many diverse styles.

A typical theatre company today performs a wide range of plays. In a single season, the same company may present a tragedy by Shakespeare, a farce by the French dramatist Molière (1622-1673), a twentieth-century drama by the Spanish writer Federico García Lorca (1898-1936), a play like *Eurydice,* by Sarah Ruhl (b. 1974), a contemporary drama like *Slave Play* by Black playwright Jeremy O. Harris (b. 1989), as well as a one-person show by a performance artist.

The three periods we have discussed—the Greek, the Elizabethan, and the modern—are examples of the close relationship between a society and the art and theatre it produces. One could find comparable links in every culture and period. It is important to remember, therefore, that whatever the period or culture in which it was first produced, drama is woven into the fabric of its place and time.

To sum up, for our purposes it is important to realize that when we go to the theatre, it is extremely helpful to be aware of the period and circumstances in which a play of whatever sort was created. These are things our professors and instructors can help us with, but things we should also research ourselves as future audience members.

EXPECTATIONS: THE VARIETY OF EXPERIENCES IN MODERN THEATRE

If we have not often been to the theatre, we might expect that all theatre experiences will be much alike. In fact, most of us go to the theatre for entirely different reasons. Some of us enjoy the escape offered by movies and television and are interested primarily in light entertainment. If we attend a dinner theatre or a Broadway musical, we do not want to be faced with troublesome problems or serious moral issues. Instead, we are looking for something that will be amusing and perhaps include music, dancing, and beautiful scenery and costumes.

On the other hand, some of us want to be stimulated and challenged intellectually, politically, and emotionally. It must be remembered, too, that many of us like both of these kinds of theatre. At times we may seek light entertainment and at other times, meaningful drama. Not only do performances vary in the type of theatre they offer, but they also take place in a variety of settings, and this too has an effect on the nature of the experience. In the mid-twentieth century, in the United States "the theatre" was largely synonymous with one kind of experience: Broadway. In the last several decades this has changed radically—further evidence of how diversity in theatre reflects the overall diversity in contemporary life. In the opening chapter we mentioned different places where the great variety of theatre events might be experienced today. In the pages that follow we examine these opportunities in more detail.

Broadway and Touring Theatre

Broadway is the name of the oldest professional theatre in New York City: it refers specifically to plays performed in the large theatres in the district near Times Square in New York City. From 1920 until the early 1950s, most new plays written in the United States originated there, and productions in other areas were usually copies of Broadway productions. Productions sent on tour from Broadway to the rest of the country are exact replicas of the original. Scenery is duplicated down to the last detail, and performers from New York often play roles they had played on Broadway.

Because our society is diverse and complex, however, and because theatre reflects society, no one form of theatre today can speak equally to all of us. As if in response to the complexity of the modern world, in the second half of the twentieth century people began searching for new forms in theatre and for alternative locations in which to present theatre.

BROADWAY THEATRE
Productions in the major theatres in New York City—collectively known as Broadway—are usually characterized by elaborate scenic elements, first-rate acting, and scripts with wide appeal: either new works or revivals. Shown here is a scene from the award-winning *Hamilton,* which has become a theatrical phenomenon. It depicts the founding fathers of the United States in a postmodernist fashion, employing nontraditional casting and rap music. *Hamilton* is written and composed by Lin-Manuel Miranda. The hip-hop retelling of the nation's founding was one of several shows in a strikingly diverse Broadway season where race and American history were front-and-center topics. The actors from left to right are: Lin-Manuel Miranda, Renee Elise Goldsberry, Phillipa Soo and Jasmine Cephas Jones, in the production directed by Thomas Kall. (Sara Krulwich/The New York Times/Redux)

Resident Professional Theatre

One significant development, which began in a few cities in the 1950s and has since spread across the country, is resident professional theatre, sometimes known as *regional theatre.* Theatre companies have been formed, and theatre facilities built, for the continuing presentation of high-quality professional productions to local residents. The performers, directors, and designers are generally high-caliber artists who make theatre their full-time profession.

Most cities have developed theatres that present a series of plays over a given span of time, with each play being performed for about four to twelve weeks. Among the best-known of these theatres are the Arena Stage in Washington, D.C., the Long Wharf in New Haven, the American Repertory Theater in Boston, the Actors Theatre of Louisville, the Alley Theatre in Houston, the Goodman Theatre in Chicago, the Milwaukee Repertory Theater, the Guthrie Theater in Minneapolis, the Seattle Repertory Theatre, and the Mark Taper Forum in Los Angeles.

Among African American theatres, which developed to give greater opportunities to Black theatre artists, examples are Towne Street Theatre of Los Angeles, the North Carolina Black Repertory, Congo Square Theatre in Chicago, Penumbra Theatre in Minneapolis, Karamu House in Cleveland, and the Black Repertory Company of St. Louis. A season of plays in these theatres will usually include both new plays and classics, and theatregoers are encouraged to buy a season subscription.

Along with resident companies, there are now a number of permanent summer theatre festivals and Shakespeare festivals throughout the United States and Canada. Among the best known are the Shakespeare festivals at Stratford, Ontario; San Diego, California; Cedar City, Utah; and Ashland, Oregon.

Alternative Theatre: Off-Broadway and Elsewhere

In New York City *off-Broadway theatre* began in the 1950s as an alternative to Broadway, which was becoming increasingly costly. Off-Broadway theatres were smaller than Broadway theatres—most of them had fewer than 200 seats—and were located outside the Times Square area. Because off-Broadway was less expensive than Broadway, it offered more opportunity for producing serious classics and experimental works. Off-Broadway itself, however, became institutionalized in the 1960s and 1970s, and small independent groups developed *off-off-Broadway,* which produced a wide variety of offerings wherever inexpensive space was available—churches, lofts, warehouses, large basements.

THEATRE AWAY FROM THE MAINSTREAM
In addition to traditional mainstream theatre, there are important active alternatives, such as off-Broadway, off-off-Broadway, and avant-garde theatre artists, not only in major cities but also in many other places around the world. One example is the work of playwright-director Richard Maxwell, whom the *New York Times'* theatre critic Ben Brantley refers to as the most significant experimental playwright in current U.S. theatre. Maxwell's works are presented at small off-off-Broadway spaces and internationally. Shown here are Janet Coleman and Alex Delinois in a scene from Maxwell's *Neutral Hero,* staged in 2012 at the Kitchen, an avant-garde performance space in New York. (Sara Krulwich/The New York Times/Redux)

An important development in American theatre is that counterparts to off-off-Broadway have been established in other major cities across the United States—Washington, Atlanta, Chicago, Minneapolis, Los Angeles, San Francisco, Seattle—where small theatre groups perform as alternatives to large organizations. It is in these smaller theatres, in New York and across the country, that most experimental and new works are performed.

In addition, all across the country there are cabaret and dinner theatres in which the atmosphere of a nightclub or restaurant is combined with that of a theatre. In these informal settings, guests eat and drink before watching a performance.

Young People's and Children's Theatre

A branch of theatre that has earned an important place in the overall picture is children's theatre, sometimes called *theatre for youth.* These theatres include a wide spectrum from the most sophisticated professional organizations to semiprofessionals to improvisational groups to undertakings that are predominately amateur or educational. The aim in all cases, however, is to provide a theatrical experience for young people. In some cases it is to offer school-age children an opportunity to see first-class productions of plays dealing with people and subjects in which they might be personally interested. In other cases, the emphasis is on dramatizing the lives of significant figures in history—Abraham Lincoln, Martin Luther King Jr., Eleanor Roosevelt—or giving dramatic life to literary classics such as *Tom Sawyer* or *Huckleberry Finn*.

A number of young people's or children's theatre organizations across North America have a long history and feature first-class theatre spaces and production facilities. Moreover, the caliber of those responsible for their productions—performers, designers, directors, and so on—is excellent and the equal of any professional regional or not-for-profit theatre. Among those in this category are the Children's Theatre Company of Minneapolis, the Children's Theatre of Charlotte, the Orange County Children's Theater, the Nashville Children's Theatre, and TheatreworksUSA in New York City.

College and University Theatre

In the last few decades, *college* and *university theatre* departments have also become increasingly important, not only in teaching theatre arts but also in presenting plays. In some localities, college productions are virtually the only form of theatre offered. In other areas, they are a significant supplement to professional theatre.

The theatre facilities in many colleges are excellent. Most large colleges and universities have two or three theatre spaces—a full-size theatre, a medium-size theatre, and a smaller space for experimental drama—as well as extensive scene shops, costume rooms, dressing rooms, and rehearsal halls. Productions are usually scheduled throughout the school year.

The quality and complexity of these productions vary. In some places, productions are extremely elaborate, with full-scale scenery, costumes, lighting, and sound. Colleges vary, too, in the level of professionalism in acting. Many colleges use only

COLLEGE AND UNIVERSITY THEATRE
A vital segment of theatre in the United States is the many productions mounted by theatre departments in colleges and universities, which often achieve a high degree of professionalism. They also provide excellent training for theatre practitioners, as well as affording audiences first-rate productions. Seen here are (left to right) Danny Pancratz, Nathan Grant, and T. J. Nichols in a production of Molière's *The Miser* at Western Illinois University, directed by Professor Jeannie M. Woods. (Courtesy of Western Illinois University Visual Production Center/Larry Dean, photographer)

PLAYING YOUR PART: EXPERIENCING THEATRE

1. Imagine that you are required to attend a production of a play by Shakespeare. What knowledge do you have about the playwright and the period? What other information would help you better prepare for the presentation?
2. Search the Internet for a website of a regional theatre closest to your community. What types of plays is the theatre doing? Would you be interested in attending the whole season or just one or two productions? Why? What does that say about the types of plays you like?
3. Tour the theatre(s) and backstage areas of your university theatre. What surprised you about these spaces?
4. Read a review online by a *New York Times* or *Chicago Tribune* theatre critic. Which of the criteria discussed in this chapter does he or she address? How did the critic help you decide whether you might want to see the production?

performers from the undergraduate theatre program. If a college has a master's degree program, it will use both graduate and undergraduate performers. Colleges or universities may also bring in outside professionals to perform along with students. Most college and university theatres offer a variety of plays, including classics and experimental plays rarely done by professional theatres.

Community and Amateur Theatre

In addition to the many forms of professional theatre, and to college and university theatre, another area in which theatre activity thrives is community and amateur theatre. In hundreds of locations throughout the United States and Canada, and in many parts of the world, one finds semiprofessional or nonprofessional theatres serving local communities. In some cases, those involved—actors, directors, designers, crew members—have had professional training and experience but have chosen not to pursue a full-time career, for a number of reasons. Along with the part-time professionals, community theatres often include amateurs who also love the theatre. Many of these theatres approach their productions—the selection of plays, rehearsals, the building of scenery, advertising, and ticket sales—in much the same way as their professional counterparts, and in many cases, the level of work is surprisingly good. In many parts of the country, community and amateur theatres afford the only live theatre available to audiences.

Diverse and Global Theatres

People throughout the world are becoming aware of the diverse, multiracial, and multicultural aspects of contemporary society, as is true in the United States. In the late nineteenth and early twentieth centuries, the United States wanted to be known as the "melting pot," the goal of people who came here was to become assimilated and integrated into the prevailing, privileged white, European culture (and we might add, male, as women during this era still had to fight for basic rights, such as the right to vote). People of color were excluded from this supposed "melting pot."

In recent decades, however, we have become aware that such a homogeneous culture has many biases and privileges certain members of society; as a result, we find a trend to recognize, maintain, and celebrate our differences and, at the same time, to recognize the systemic racism, sexism, and homophobia that continues in our society and the theatre world. Many organizations have emerged that present productions by and for specific marginalized groups, including Black, Latinx, Asian American, Native American, feminist, and LGBTQ theatre companies. We will discuss diversity, equity, and inclusion and these theatres more fully in the next chapter.

Global theatre means theatre not just in the Western tradition but theatre from around the world. There is a rich tradition of theatre in Asia. In India, theatre began more than 2,000 years ago, and Chinese theatre a few centuries after that, while Japanese theatre was established by 800 CE. In Africa, in pre-Columbian Latin America, and in the Native American cultures of North America, there are rich traditions of rituals and ceremonies that have recognizable elements of theatre: costumes; song and dance; and impersonation of people, animals, and divinities.

The various ways in which we see theatrical traditions from different nations and cultures influence one another today were relatively rare prior to 1900. Today we live in a world where such cross-cultural relationships are extremely easy due to modern transportation and communication. *New York Times* columnist Thomas Friedman, in *The World Is Flat,* analyzes how globalization has affected business and industry in contemporary society. One can no longer tell whether a product is made by a company in a specific country, since most major corporations are multinational. The automobile industry clearly reflects the trend toward industrial globalization, as does the technology industry. A car created today by a Japanese, Korean, or German manufacturer may be fully or partially assembled in the United States. A PC, cell phone, or tablet may be manufactured in China and sold in the United States, but the twenty-four-hour help desk may be located in India.

The same is true in today's theatre. Theatre artists cross national boundaries to stage their works with artists of other countries. Popular works tour the world and cross-pollinate other theatrical ventures. International theatre festivals bring artists of various nationalities to interact with those in the host community. In addition, traditional theatrical techniques from differing countries may be fused together to create a unique contemporary work.

THE AUDIENCE, CRITIC, REVIEWER, AND BLOGGER

Most of us who go to the theatre or the movies, or who watch a television show, are amateur critics. When we say about a performance, "It started off great, but it fizzled," or "The star was terrific, just like someone in real life," or "The woman was OK, but the man overacted," or "The acting was good, but the story was too downbeat for me," we are making a critical judgment. The difference between a critic/reviewer and those of us in the audience is that the former presumably is better informed about the event and has developed a set of critical standards by which to judge it.

The Critic, Reviewer, and Blogger

A *critic,* loosely defined, is someone who observes theatre and then analyzes and comments on it and ideally serves as a knowledgeable and highly sensitive audience member. Audiences can learn from critics not only because critics impart information and judgments but also because a critic shares with an audience the point of view of the spectator. Unlike those who create theatre, critics sit out front and watch a performance just as other members of the audience do. Critics generally write serious articles that appear in newspapers, magazines, and books.

A familiar type of critic is the reviewer. A *reviewer,* who usually works for a newspaper, a magazine, a television station or a professional blog, reports on what has occurred at the theatre. He or she will tell briefly what a theatre event is about, explaining that it is a musical, a comedy, or a serious play, and perhaps describing its plot. The reviewer might also offer an opinion about whether or not the event is worth seeing. The reviewer is usually restricted by time, space, or both.

In recent years, the power and significance of theatre critics and reviewers in newspapers and magazines has greatly diminished, even with those publications having online versions. Some estimate that about 20 years ago, there were around 100 full-time theatre critics working for traditional publications; now there are probably fewer than 20. For example, the *New York Daily News* now shares a Broadway theatre critic with the *Chicago Tribune*. The other major newspaper in Chicago, the *Sun-Times,* employs a series of freelance critics rather than one full-time critic.

In addition, many point out that the majority of theatre critics and reviewers do not represent our multicultural society and that there are inherent biases in the work of most critics and reviewers.

Today, therefore, audiences are seeking information and opinions about productions in new online media.

Online Theatre Critics and Reviewers: New Approaches

In addition to critics and reviewers whose opinions appear in the traditional print media (which is also now available online) or on television, we have a new source of theatre criticism: popular websites and blogs. Many of these sites, such as *Theatremania.com,* have their own theatre reviewers; other sites may have critics who send in their opinions. Some individuals have set up their own websites and blogs for expressing their views about theatre productions.

There have also been some new models for theatre journalism and criticism on the Web. In Miami, *Artburst Miami* is an online site funded by local government and foundations that carries reviews and news stories about local theatre and arts events, employing paid freelance journalists. Atlanta has a similar website. *Rescripted* is a Chicago online collective of ten young Chicago theatre artists, most of them artists of color, who critically engage with the city's theatre scene. The goal is to bring underrepresented voices into criticism. *Show Score* is a website supported by private funds that pulls together a database of about 320,000 online users, aggregating their opinions about shows in New York, making it the theatre version of *Rotten Tomatoes* (which captures audiences' opinions of movies) or *TripAdvisor*.

Individual opinions posted on the Web about theatre productions, therefore, have become another tool audience members use and can also be found on social media sites such as Facebook, Twitter, Snapchat, Instagram, YouTube, and even Yelp. Social media allows all of us to function as reviewers and to respond to productions we see. Some theatres request that audience members "like" their Facebook pages in response to productions. Some theatres have set aside specific seats in their theatres, known as "tweet seats." Audience members sitting in these sections can tweet to their Twitter followers their instantaneous reactions to a production, while not distracting other spectators. Some theatres also have personnel backstage who tweet about the show while it is going on.

Another recent development that allows audience members to become part of the critical process is known as *dial testing*, wherein audiences electronically respond to shows that are still being developed. Their responses might then be used to affect the final product. Some theatres use *focus groups* (that is, selected audience members) to provide feedback about a show that is still in development. Often, these methods are used to test reactions to theatre productions that are meant to reach a wide audience and have commercial, box office success. Some theatres e-mail questionnaires to audience members who have attended their productions. Smaller theatres that produce new, cutting-edge works would probably not ask potential audience members to respond in these ways.

At times these assessments of a production can be helpful and informative, but a word of caution is in order. A number of self-appointed reviewers may have little or no background in theatre criticism or, in fact, in theatre itself. They enjoy being part of the wider world of theatre criticism, but may not have the credentials to do so. In other words, these amateur critics may not have the necessary preparation for criticism. In the same way we do not take any or every online review of a product as an expert evaluation, we should do the same when we read responses to theatrical presentations in the various social media.

Preparation for Criticism

The critic and reviewer, whether in traditional print media or on the Web, should have a thorough background in theatre to make criticism more meaningful to audiences. These commentators should have a full knowledge of theatre history, acting, directing, and design. The critic/reviewer/blogger must be familiar with plays written in various styles and modes and should know the body of work of individual writers. Also, the critic ought to be able to relate what is happening in theatre to what is happening in the other arts and, beyond that, to events in society generally and be open to those artists who are underrepresented in the theatre. In addition, the person commenting on theatre should understand the production elements discussed in this book—directing, acting, dramaturgy, and design.

Fact and Opinion in Criticism

In reading the commentary of the reviewer, in print or online, it is important to distinguish between *fact* and *opinion*. Facts may provide helpful information in understanding a play; for example, to know that in Shakespeare's time, men played all the women parts would help explain why a director might make that choice today in assigning actors to their roles. Opinions can also be helpful, but audience members should carefully weigh them against their own knowledge and experience. In addition to our professors and instructors, a critic, reviewer, or blogger can often make us aware of information we might not otherwise have known; for example, by explaining a point that was confusing to the audience or noting how a particular scene in a play relates to an earlier scene. They might also offer background material about the playwright, the subject matter of the play, or the style of the production. Such information can broaden our understanding and appreciation of a production we are about to see. The more we know about what a playwright is attempting to do and why a playwright arranges scenes in a certain way, the better we will be able to judge the value of a theatre event we attend.

A good example would be an explanation by a critic of the intentions and techniques of the playwright Maria Irene Fornés (1930-2018) in her play *Fefu and Her Friends*. The first act takes place in the living room of Fefu's New England home. The audience sits in one location watching the action in the living room. The second act, however, is presented in four different locations, spaces in the theatre such as backstage, offstage, in the lobby, or in a rehearsal hall. One represents a lawn outside the house, a second a bedroom, a third the study, and the fourth the kitchen. The characters in the play split up and perform separate scenes in each of the four locations. The scenes are supposed to be occurring all at the same time. The audience is

CRITICS PROVIDE BACKGROUND

Certain plays, both past and present, can prove difficult for an audience to understand fully, especially when first seen. Included in this group are avant-garde or experimental plays. A good example of the latter is *Fefu and Her Friends* by Maria Irene Fornés, which focuses on eight women. During the course of the action, the audience is divided into four groups and taken to four separate locations to see different scenes. Without the proper orientation, this unusual arrangement might at first prove confusing. Shown here are Julianna Margulies as Emma and Joyce Lynn O'Connor as Fefu in a production at the Yale Repertory Theatre. (Gerry Goodstein/Yale Repertory Theatre)

divided into four groups as well and members move from one location to the next; the scenes in the separate locations are repeated four times so that each group of audience members can see them. For the third act of the play, the audience reassembles in the main auditorium to watch a scene again in the living room, onstage.

Among other things, Fornés uses the second act to break out of the usual theatre setting. She also wants to show the fragmentation of life as well as its simultaneity. She wants the audience to get a sense of life overlapping and continuing in different places in addition to those on which we usually focus. If the construction of the play, as well as Fornés's purpose and techniques, have been explained to us prior to our seeing the play, then we, as audience members, will be better prepared to understand the experience when we attend a performance.

Critical Criteria

In commenting on a theatre production, a critic, reviewer, or those of us who present our opinions through social media traditionally ask three questions as a guide to arriving at judgments, criteria that will also aid the rest of us to be better informed about a production we have seen and to better explain our reactions to it.

What Is Being Attempted?

One of the first questions is: *What is the play, and the production, attempting to do?* This question must be raised both about the script and about the production. Is the play a tragedy meant to raise significant questions and stir deep emotions? Is it a light comedy intended to entertain and provide escape? Is it a political drama arguing for a point of view?

Have the Intentions Been Achieved?

A second question is: *How well have the intentions of the playwright been carried out?* If a theatre piece originates with an acting ensemble or with a director, the question is: *How well have the intentions of the original creators been realized?* A theatre company may be producing an acknowledged masterpiece such as *Hamlet* or *Macbeth,* in which case the question becomes how well the play has been acted, directed, and designed. Have the performers brought Shakespeare's characters to life convincingly and excitingly? Or has the director—perhaps by striving to be too original in approach and staging, without helping us as audience members understand why she or he has done so—distorted Shakespeare's intentions beyond recognition?

In the case of a new script, one must also ask how well the playwright has realized his or her own intentions. If the play is intended to probe deeply into family relationships—parents and children or husbands and wives—how convincingly and how insightfully has the dramatist accomplished this? If the intention is to entertain, to make the audience laugh, the question to be asked is: Just how funny is the play? Did it succeed in providing entertainment? Was it clever, witty, and full of amusing situations, or did it fall flat?

Do You Believe the Attempt Was Worthwhile; A Subjective Point of View?

A third question to ask when judging a production falls more into the realm of personal taste and evaluation and should be approached carefully: *Is the play or production worth doing?* Many critics think that anything that succeeds at giving pleasure and providing entertainment is as worthwhile in its own way as a more serious undertaking. Others, however, do not. In cases like this, readers of criticism and viewers of a performance must make up their own minds.

If audience members are aware of these criteria, they not only can note whether critics—in print, on television, or online—address these questions but also can ask the questions for themselves.

Readers should, however, always be aware of the biases of those who judge artistic works because those biases may inappropriately affect how they respond to these questions. As noted, many theatre artists have pointed out that the majority of critics, reviewers, and initially bloggers were white males who may not have been receptive to or even understood the works of artists of color. Their positions of privilege may not make them open to differing points of view about race, gender, or sexual orientation.

As theatregoers, we should also be aware that we bring our own background and biases to the theatre experience and that we should always think about how those might impact us as we discuss theatrical productions we have attended and to always be open to other points of view.

THE DRAMATURG OR LITERARY MANAGER

Sometimes when we enter a theatre, we see in the theatre program an article or note written by the theatre's dramaturg. The term ***dramaturg (or literary manager)*** comes from a German word for "dramatic adviser." In Europe, the practice of having a

dramaturg (or literary manager) On the staff of a theatre, a person who consults with and advises authors and directors, writes program notes, and edits scripts.

dramaturg attached to a theatre goes back well over a century. In the United States, the role of the dramaturg is relatively new; in recent years, however, many regional professional groups and other not-for-profit theatres have engaged full-time dramaturges. Among the duties frequently undertaken by dramaturges are discovering and reading promising new plays, working with playwrights on the development of new scripts, identifying significant plays from the past that may have been overlooked, conducting research on previous productions of classic plays, preparing reports on the history of plays, researching criticism and interpretations of plays from the past, and writing articles for the programs that are distributed when plays are produced.

Just as a good critic/reviewer can be helpful to audience members, so, too, can a perceptive dramaturg. He or she is usually the person who prepares educational material for students and teachers who attend performances. And if there is a discussion with audiences and members of the artistic team before or after a performance, the dramaturg often leads such a discussion.

THE AUDIENCE'S RELATION TO CRITICISM

As suggested earlier, when we, as audience members, combine awareness of criticism with the theatre event itself, the experience can be greatly enhanced: background information and critical appraisals are added to our own firsthand reactions. There are cautionary notes, however, of which we should be aware.

The Audience's Independent Judgment

Quite often critic/reviewers state unequivocally that a certain play is extremely well written or badly written, beautifully performed or atrociously performed, and so on. Because these so-called authorities often speak so confidently and because their opinions appear in print or on the Internet, their words have the ring of authority. But as theatregoers, we should reserve our own judgment and should certainly not be intimidated by this.

In certain large cities—New York, Chicago, Los Angeles, London, Paris—where a number of critics and reviewers in various media comment on each production,

THE AUDIENCE'S JUDGMENT
Critics and reviewers can be enormously helpful to theatre audiences in providing background material, critical criteria, and other information. In the end, though, audience members should make up their own minds. A good example is the Broadway musical *Spider-Man: Turn Off the Dark*, which opened to negative reviews from critics, but was somewhat of a commercial success with audiences. (Sara Krulwich/The New York Times/Redux)

PLAYING YOUR PART: THINKING ABOUT THEATRE

1. Think of a contemporary play or musical you have seen in which the characters and the story remind you of something you are familiar with in your own life. How did the knowledge of the real event help you appreciate and understand what you saw onstage?
2. Imagine two friends viewing the same theatre production. One friend is captivated, feeling that what he or she saw was genuine and moving, a deeply affecting experience. The other friend was not moved and felt that the performance was artificial and inauthentic. Why do you think the same performance can elicit two such different reactions?
3. Make a list of all the places near your hometown or near your college where live theatre is presented. Have you ever attended a performance at one of these theatres? Describe the kind of physical theatre it is. Describe the experience; what was it like?

there is a wide range of opinion. It is not unusual for some critic/reviewers to find a certain play admirable, while others find the same play quite inferior, and still others find a mixture of good and bad. This implies that there is no absolute authority among such people, and that we should make up our own minds. If a critic/reviewer, for example, dislikes a certain play because he or she finds it too sentimental and you happen to like that kind of sentiment, you should not be dissuaded from your own preferences. Attending the theatre is a unique, individual experience—it is *your* experience—and you must trust and be guided by your own judgment. And always remember all judgments, whether by professionals or by us, have inherent biases and we should be aware of that when reading about or commenting on productions.

SUMMARY

1. Each individual attending a theatre event brings to it a personal background of experience that becomes a vital ingredient in his or her response.
2. Theatre—like other arts—is closely linked to the society in which it is produced; it mirrors and reflects the attitudes, philosophy, and basic assumptions of its time.
3. Spectators attending a play written in their own day bring to it an awareness of their society's values and beliefs, and this background information forms an important part of the overall experience.
4. A play from the past can be better understood if the spectator is aware of the culture from which it came.
5. For any play that presents difficulties in language, style, or meaning, familiarity with the work itself can add immeasurably to a spectator's understanding and appreciation of a performance.
6. With an unfamiliar work, it is also helpful to learn about the playwright and his or her approach to theatre.
7. Expectations about the nature of the theatre experience affect our reaction to it. The various experiences in theatre today in the United States include Broadway and touring theatre; resident professional theatre; alternative theatre; young people's and children's theatre; college and university theatre; community and amateur theatre; and multiethnic, multicultural, global, and gender theatre.

8. Most people who attend theatre events are amateur critics, making judgments and drawing conclusions about what they see.

9. The professional critic has several tasks: to understand exactly what is being presented, including the intentions of the playwright and the director; to analyze the play, the acting, and the direction, as well as other elements such as scenery and lighting; to evaluate the presentation—was this worth doing? Does it serve a purpose?

10. People commenting on theatre can be divided into *reviewers,* who report briefly on a theatre event in newspapers, in magazines, or on television, and *critics,* who write longer articles analyzing in depth a performance or the work of a playwright.

11. The dramaturg or literary manager is a position that originated in Europe and is now found in many theatres in the United States, particularly not-for-profit theatres. The dramaturg analyzes scripts, advises directors, and works with playwrights on new dramas.

12. Audience members must realize that critics, too, have their limitations and prejudices and that ultimately each individual spectator must arrive at his or her own judgment regarding a theatre event.

Design Elements: Audience Sitting in Theatre (theatre): Ron Chapple/Photodisc/Getty Images; Studio Light (spotlights): Exactostock/SuperStock

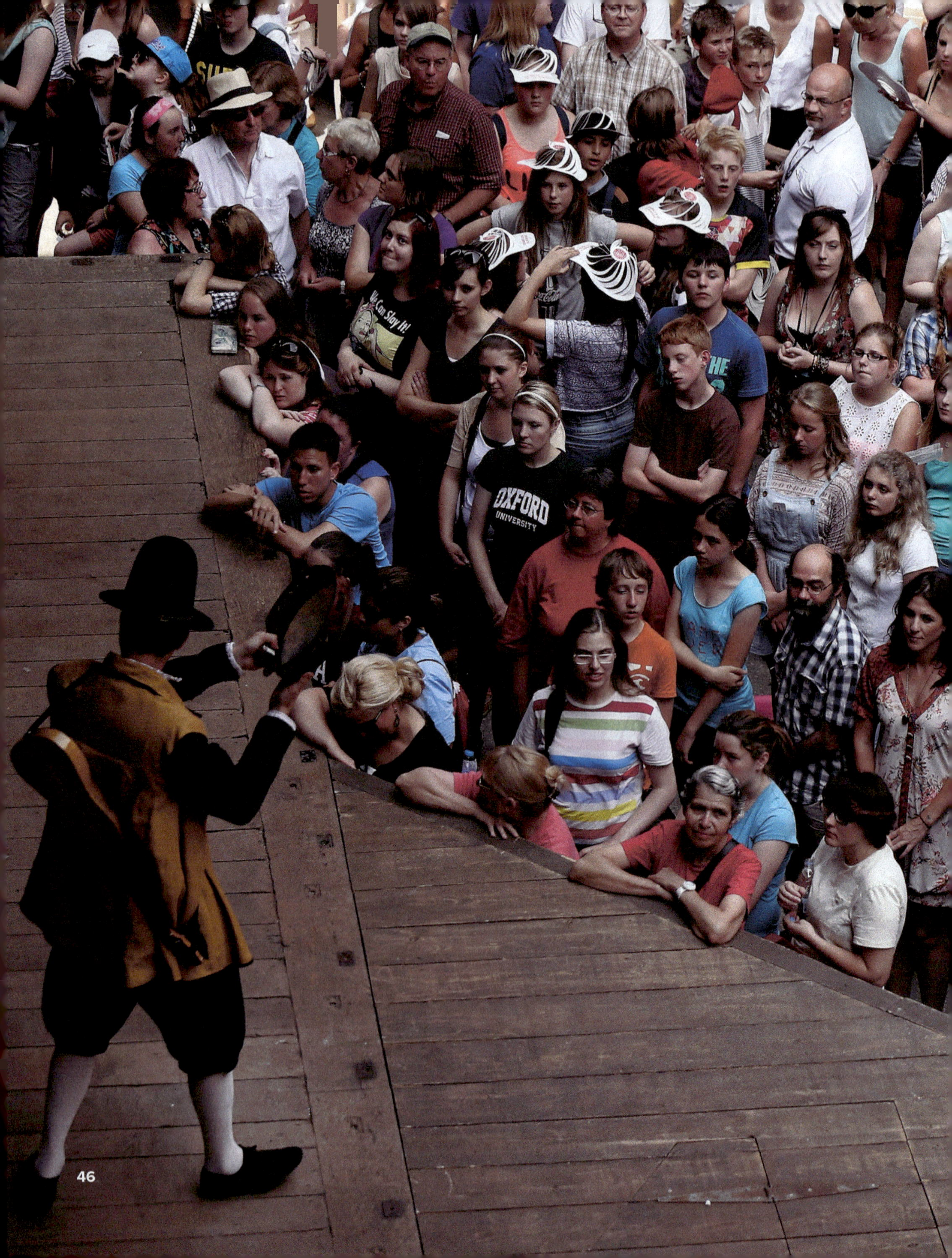
OXFORD
UNIVERSITY

Theatre Spaces

When we attend the theatre, our experience begins in advance. Sometimes we read or hear reports of the play online or in print; we anticipate seeing a particular actress or actor or a specific type of production; we buy tickets and make plans with friends to attend; and before the performance, we gather outside the theatre space with other members of the audience.

CREATING THE ENVIRONMENT

When we arrive inside a theatre building or other space for a performance, we immediately take in the environment in which the event will occur. The atmosphere inside the space for a production has a great deal to do with our mood in approaching a performance, not only creating expectations about the event but also conditioning the experience once it gets under way. As spectators, we have one feeling if we come into a formal setting, such as a picture-frame stage surrounded by carved gilt figures, with crystal chandeliers and red plush seats in the auditorium. We have quite a different feeling if we come into an old warehouse converted for a performance, with bare brick walls, and a stage in the middle of the floor surrounded by folding chairs. We may have a different feeling if we enter into an outdoor performance space.

For many years people took the physical arrangement of theatres for granted. This was particularly true in the period when all houses were facsimiles of the Broadway theatre, with its proscenium, or picture-frame, stage. Since the 1950s, however, not only have people been exposed to other types of theatres, they have also become more aware of the importance of environment. Many experimental groups have deliberately made awareness of the environment a part of the experience. And even in the commercial Broadway theatre there have been experiments with transforming the environment.

An example of such a production is *Natasha, Pierre & the Great Comet of 1812*. This musical, based on a section of Leo Tolstoy's novel *War and Peace*, was first produced in a 99-seat off-Broadway house and then to accommodate even larger audiences in a tent in Manhattan's Meatpacking District. (The use of a tent reflects how theatre spaces can be created anywhere.) In 2016, the play opened at the Imperial Theatre, a Broadway playhouse that can seat over 1,400 audience members.

◀ **STAGE SPACES: AN OUTDOOR THRUST STAGE**
The Globe Theatre in London is a recreation of the Elizabethan thrust stage on which many of Shakespeare's plays were staged with the audience on three sides, this is one of the oldest and most popular configurations for a theatre performance space. Shown here are audience members, standing in the pit near the stage, preparing to watch a production of Shakespeare's A Midsummer Night's Dream *at the Globe in 2013. (Oli Scarff/Getty Images)*

In order to transform this traditional proscenium arch theatre into an immersive space that feels like a nineteenth-century Russian supper club, set designer Mimi Lien added red velvet curtains surrounding the entire audience area. In addition, portraits line all the walls of the theatre; a wooden curving road goes through the middle of the orchestra, bringing actors into the midst of audience members, and brilliant chandeliers come down from the ceiling, engulfing the audience. Staircases lead from the traditional orchestra level to the upper seating area for audience members; tables and chairs replace five rows of seats usually used for spectators (the only physical change in the theatre), with ramps and the curving road being built on existing seats. In the center of the Imperial Theatre there is a constructed oval that again thrusts the performance into the audience.

What was the goal of transforming this traditional Broadway theatre for *Natasha, Pierre & the Great Comet of 1812?* Director Rachel Chavkin, when she describes the reaction of an audience member, indicates that the goal is to immerse the audience, to integrate them into the world of the production to become part of the action, blurring the distinction between performance and spectator space. The director explained: "A woman walked in the theatre one day... and she was like, 'Where's the stage?' The answer is: There isn't one. Or it's everywhere, which is the joy of it."[1]

Designer Lien says the Imperial was transformed so that the experience begins from the moment the audience enters: "Then you come inside, and I really wanted that moment of stepping inside to be impactful," she says. "This feeling of a warm, lush, opulent cocoon-like space was really important to us, and so we have hung onto that every step of the way."[2]

The feeling we have about the atmosphere of a theatre building as we enter the space has always been an important element in the experience. In the past, spectators may not have been conscious of it, but they were affected by it nevertheless. Today, with the many varieties of theatre experience available to us, the first thing we should become aware of is the environment in which an event takes place: whether it is large or small, indoors or outdoors, formal or informal, familiar or unfamiliar.

At times scenic designers are able to alter the architecture of a theatre space to create a new arrangement or configuration, as we explained was done for *Natasha, Pierre & the Great Comet of 1812*. If the auditorium space is too large for a specific production, balconies might be blocked off, or the rear of the orchestra might be closed in some manner. Also, the decor can be altered: bright colors, banners, and bright lighting could create a festive atmosphere in a space that is ordinarily formal and subdued. The first thing for us, as audience members, is to note the general characteristics of the space: Is it formal or informal? Is it large or small? Next, the question of the configuration of stage and audience seating is discussed.

THEATRE SPACES

A consideration of environment leads directly to an examination of the various forms and styles of theatre buildings, including the arrangements of audience seating. Throughout theatre history, there have been five basic stage arrangements, each with its own advantages and disadvantages, each suited to certain types of plays and certain types of productions, and each providing the audience with a somewhat different experience. They are (1) the ***proscenium,*** or picture-frame, stage; (2) the

---

proscenium ("pro-SEEN-ee-um") Arch or frame surrounding the stage opening in a box or picture stage.

arena Stage entirely surrounded by the audience; also known as *circle theatre or theatre-in-the-round.*

thrust stage Stage space that thrusts into the audience space; a stage surrounded on three sides by audience seating.

black box A theatre space that is open, flexible, and adaptable, usually without fixed seating. The stage–audience configuration can be rearranged to suit the individual requirements of a given production, making it both economical and particularly well suited to experimental work.

fourth wall Convention, in a proscenium-arch theatre, that the audience is looking into a room through an invisible fourth wall.

arena, or circle, stage; (3) the ***thrust*** stage with three-quarters seating;[3] (4) *created* and *found* stage spaces; and (5) all-purpose, multipurpose, or ***"black box"*** theatre spaces, out of which a version of any one of the other four can be created.

Proscenium or Picture-Frame Stage: History and Characteristics

Perhaps the most familiar type of stage is the proscenium (pro-SEEN-ee-um), or picture-frame, stage. Broadway-style theatres, which for many years were models for theatres throughout the country, have proscenium stages.

The term *proscenium* comes from *proscenium arch,* the frame that separates the stage from the auditorium and that was first introduced in Italy during the Renaissance in the seventeenth century. Today this frame is not an arch but a rectangle. As the term *picture-frame stage* suggests, it resembles a large frame through which the audience looks at the stage. Another term for this type of stage is ***fourth wall,*** from the idea of the proscenium opening as a transparent glass wall through which the audience looks at the other three walls of a room.

Because the action takes place largely behind the proscenium opening, or frame, the seats in the auditorium all face in the same direction, toward the stage, just as seats in a movie theatre face the screen. The auditorium itself—the ***house,*** or ***front of the house,*** as it is called—is slanted downward from the back to the stage. (In theatre usage, the slant of an auditorium or stage floor is called a ***rake***.) The stage is raised several feet above the auditorium floor to aid visibility. There is usually a balcony (sometimes two balconies) protruding about halfway over the main floor. The main floor, incidentally, is called in American usage the *orchestra.* (In ancient Greek theatre, the orchestra was the circular acting area at the base of the hillside amphitheatre, but in modern usage, it is the main floor of the theatre, where the audience sits.) In certain theatres, as well as concert halls and opera houses that have the proscenium arrangement, there are horseshoe-shaped tiers, or ***boxes,*** which ring the auditorium for several floors above the orchestra.

The popularity of the proscenium stage on Broadway and throughout the United States in the nineteenth century and the early twentieth century was partly due to its wide acceptance throughout Europe. Beginning in the late seventeenth century, the proscenium theatre was adopted in every European country. For the next two centuries in Europe, both the mechanics of stage machinery and the artistry of scene painting improved steadily, allowing designers to create extraordinary stage pictures.

An Italian, Giacomo Torelli (1608–1678), developed methods of moving scenery on and off stage felicitously, and throughout the eighteenth century, members of one family, the Bibiena family, dominated the art of scene painting. The Bibiena sets usually consisted of vast halls, palaces, or gardens with towering columns and arches that framed spacious corridors or hallways, which disappeared into an endless series

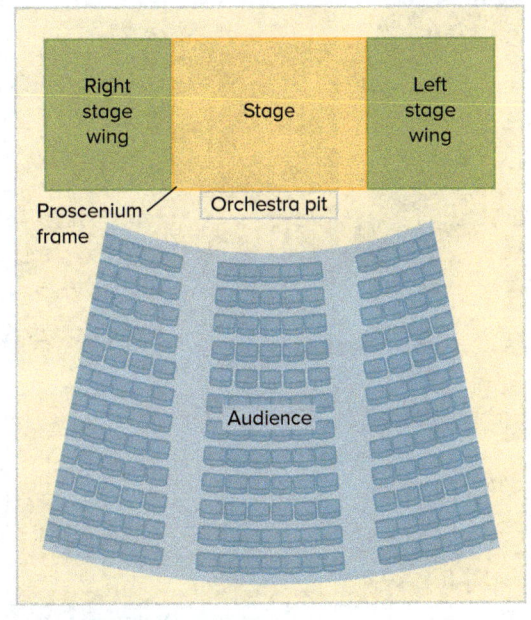

PROSCENIUM THEATRE
The audience faces in one direction, toward an enclosed stage encased by a picture-frame opening. Scene changes and performers' entrances and exits are made behind the proscenium opening, out of sight of the audience.

front of the house Portion of a theatre reserved for the audience; sometimes called simply the *house.*

rake (1) To position scenery on a slant or at an angle other than parallel or perpendicular to the curtain line. (2) An upward slope of the stage floor away from the audience.

orchestra A circular playing space in ancient Greek theatres; in modern times, the ground-floor seating in a theatre auditorium.

box Small private compartment for a group of spectators built into the walls of traditional proscenium-arch and other theatres.

THE PROSCENIUM THEATRE
The traditional proscenium theatre resembles a movie theatre in terms of audience seating: All the seats face in one direction, toward the stage. The frame of the stage is like a picture frame, and behind the frame are all the elements of the visual production such as scenery, painted drops, pieces that move across the stage, platforms, steps, and perhaps the interior of a room or several rooms. The theatre shown here, the Bolton Theatre at the Cleveland Play House, is an excellent example of a proscenium theatre. It was redesigned by the architect Philip Johnson and renovated in 1983. (Paul Tepley/Courtesy of Cleveland Play House)

A MODERN PROSCENIUM-STAGE THEATRE
In this cutaway drawing we see the audience seating at the left, all facing in the one direction, toward the stage. Behind the orchestra pit in the center is the apron on the stage and then the proscenium frame, behind which are the flats and other scenic elements. Overhead, scenery can be raised into the fly loft above the stage area.

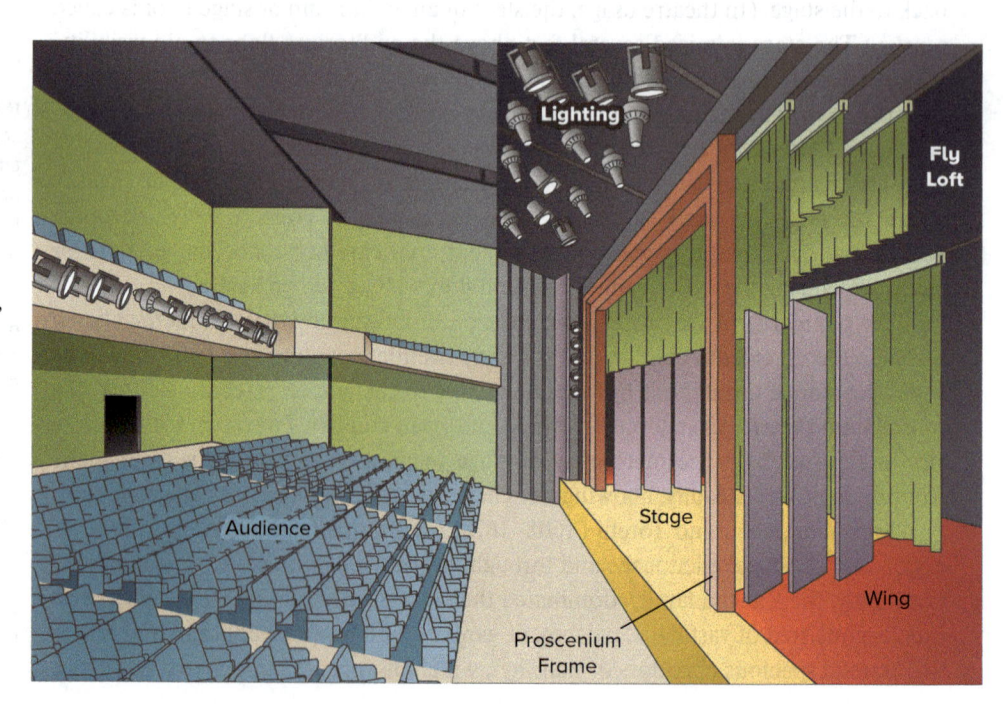

50   Part One   The Audience

A BIBIENA SET FOR A FORMAL PROSCENIUM THEATRE

The standard theatre throughout Europe and the United States from the eighteenth century to the early twentieth century was a formal proscenium space. The audience sat in a downstairs orchestra, in balconies, and in side boxes facing an ornate picture-frame stage. Impressive scenery and other visual effects were created and changed behind the curtain that covers the proscenium opening. In the eighteenth century, the Bibiena family from Italy created scene designs on a grand scale for such theatres throughout Europe. They painted backdrops with vistas that seemed to disappear into the far distance. This scene is by Giuseppe di Bibiena (1696–1757). (akg-images/Newscom)

of vistas as far as the eye could see. At times during this period, audiences, as well as scene designers and technicians, became so carried away with spectacle that the visual aspects were emphasized to the exclusion of everything else, including the script and the acting.

Although there have been many changes in theatre production, and today we have a wide variety of production approaches, we are still attracted to ingenious displays of visual effects in proscenium theatres. This is especially true of large musicals such as *The Phantom of the Opera*, *The Lion King*, *Wicked*, *Aladdin*, and *Charlie and the Chocolate Factory*. Because the machinery and the workings of scene changes can be concealed behind a proscenium opening, this type of stage offers a perfect arrangement for spectacle. It can also be true of plays that require spectacular scenery, such as *Harry Potter and the Cursed Child, Parts One and Two*.

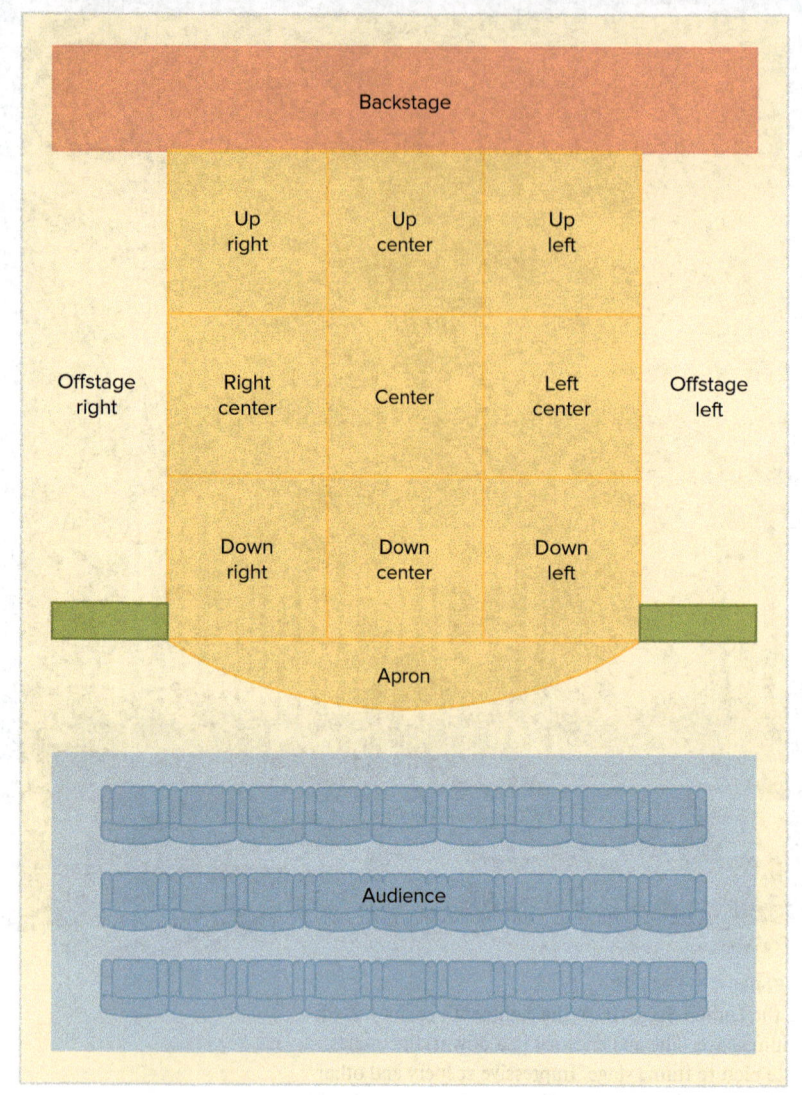

STAGE AREAS

Various parts of the stage are given specific designations. Near the audience is *downstage*; away from the audience is *upstage*. *Right* and *left* are from the performers' point of view, not the audience's. Everything out of sight of the audience is *offstage*. Using this scheme, everyone working in the theatre can carefully pinpoint stage areas.

stage right Right side of the stage from the point of view of a performer facing the audience.

stage left Left side of the stage from the point of view of a performer facing the audience.

downstage Front of the stage, toward the audience.

upstage At or toward the back of the stage, away from the front edge of the stage.

There are other advantages to the proscenium stage. Realistic scenery—a living room, an office, a kitchen—looks good behind a proscenium frame; the scene designer can create the illusion of a genuine, complete room more easily with a proscenium stage than with any other. Also, the strong central focus provided by the frame rivets the attention of the audience. There are times, too, when we want the detachment, the distancing, that a proscenium provides.

There are disadvantages as well, however. As we have seen, the proscenium stage creates a temptation to get carried away with visual pyrotechnics. In addition, a proscenium stage tends to be remote and formal. Some of us, as spectators, prefer the intimacy and informality—the experience of being close to the action—found in the arena and thrust theatres.

Physical Layout: The Proscenium Arch To designate areas of the stage, usually in a proscenium theatre, scene designers, directors, performers, and technicians use terminology peculiar to theatre. *Stage right* and *stage left* mean the right side and the left side of the stage, respectively, as seen from the position of a performer facing the audience. (In other words, when we, as spectators, in the auditorium look at the stage, the area to their left is known as right stage and the area to their right as left stage.)

The area nearest to us, the audience, is known as *downstage*; farthest away from us is *upstage*. The designations downstage and upstage come from the eighteenth and nineteenth centuries, when the stage was *raked*, that is, sloped downward from front to back. As a result of this downward slope, the performer farthest away from the audience was higher, or "up," and could be seen better. Also, performers downstage from, or below, an upstage performer would be forced to turn their backs on the audience when addressing them. This is the origin of the expression "to upstage" someone. Today, the term is used whenever one performer grabs the spotlight from everyone else or calls attention to themself by any means whatever. At first, however, it meant simply that one performer was in a better position than the others because

For large-scale productions the proscenium theatre is ideal. The scenery and other elements can be hidden above, behind, and around the stage and then moved into the main stage area, as if by magic. Costumes can be displayed at their finest. In addition, the scale of the scenic effects can be extensive and sometimes electrifying. Shown here is a spectacular scene from Disney's *Aladdin,* performed during the 68th annual Tony Awards at Radio City Music Hall in New York on June 8, 2014. (Sara Krulwich/The New York Times/Redux)

that performer was standing farther back on the raked stage and therefore was higher.

Arena Stage: History and Characteristics

To some of us, proscenium theatres, decorated in gold and red plush, look more like temples of art than theatres. We prefer a more informal, intimate theatre environment. A movement in this direction began in the United States just after World War II, when a number of theatre practitioners decided to break away from the formality of proscenium theatres. This was part of an overall desire to bring many aspects of theatre closer to everyday life: acting styles, the subject matter of plays, the manner of presentation, and the shape of the theatre space. One form this reaction took was the *arena stage*—a return to one of the most ancient stage arrangements.

From as far back as we have records, we know that tribal ceremonies and rituals, in all parts of the world, have been held in some form of circle space. For example, many scholars believe that the ancient Greek theatre evolved from an arena form. In an arena theatre (also called *circle theatre* or *theatre-in-the-round*) there is a playing space in the center of a square or circle, with seats for spectators all around it. The arrangement is

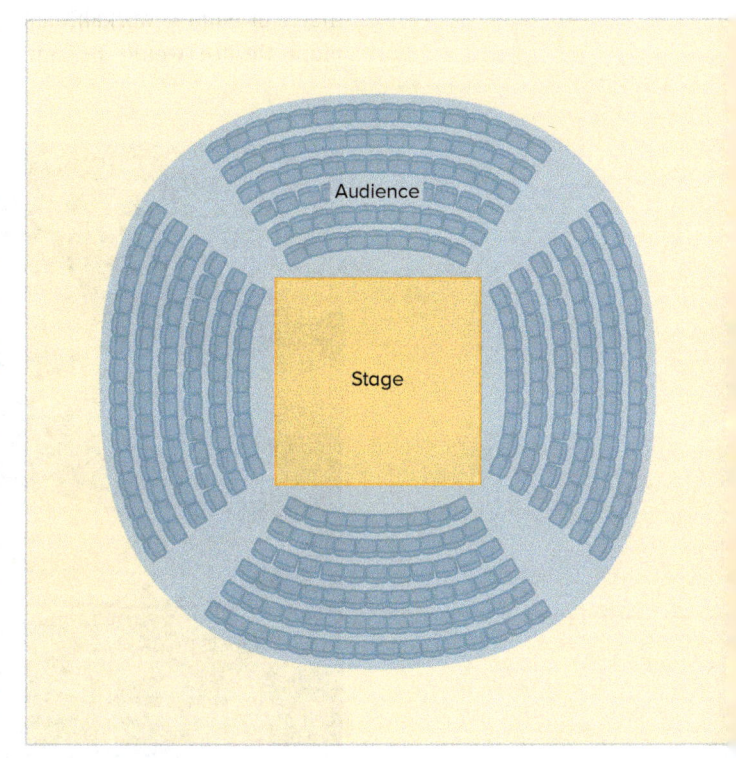

PLAN OF AN ARENA STAGE
The audience sits on four sides or in a circle surrounding the stage. Entrances and exits are made through the aisles or through tunnels underneath the aisles. A feeling of intimacy is achieved because the audience is close to the action and encloses it.

Chapter 3 *Theatre Spaces*

similar to that in sports arenas featuring boxing or basketball. The stage may be a raised area a few feet off the main floor, with seats rising from the floor level; or it may be on the floor itself, with seats raised on levels around it. When seating is close to the stage, there is usually some kind of demarcation indicating the boundaries of the playing area.

One advantage of the arena theatre is that it offers more intimacy than the ordinary proscenium. With the performers in the center, even in a larger theatre, we can be closer to them. If the same number of people attend an arena event and a proscenium event, at least half of those at the arena will be nearer the action: Someone who would have been in the twelfth row in a proscenium theatre will be in the sixth row in an arena theatre. Besides, with this proximity to the stage, the arena theatre has another advantage: There is no frame or barrier to separate the performers from us.

Beyond these considerations, in the arena arrangement there is an unconscious communion, basic to human behavior, which comes when people form a circle—from the embrace of two of us, to a circle for children's games, to a larger gathering where we form an enclosure around a fire or an altar. It is no coincidence that virtually all of the earliest forms of theatre were "in the round."

A practical advantage of the arena theatre is economy. All you need for this kind of theatre is a large room: You designate a playing space, arrange rows of seats around the sides, hang lights on pipes above, and you have a theatre. Elaborate scenery is impossible because it would block the view of large parts of the audience. A few pieces of furniture, with perhaps a lamp or sign hung from the ceiling, are all you need to indicate where a scene takes place. Many low-budget groups have found that they can build a workable and even attractive theatre-in-the-round when a proscenium theatre would be out of the question. These two factors—intimacy and

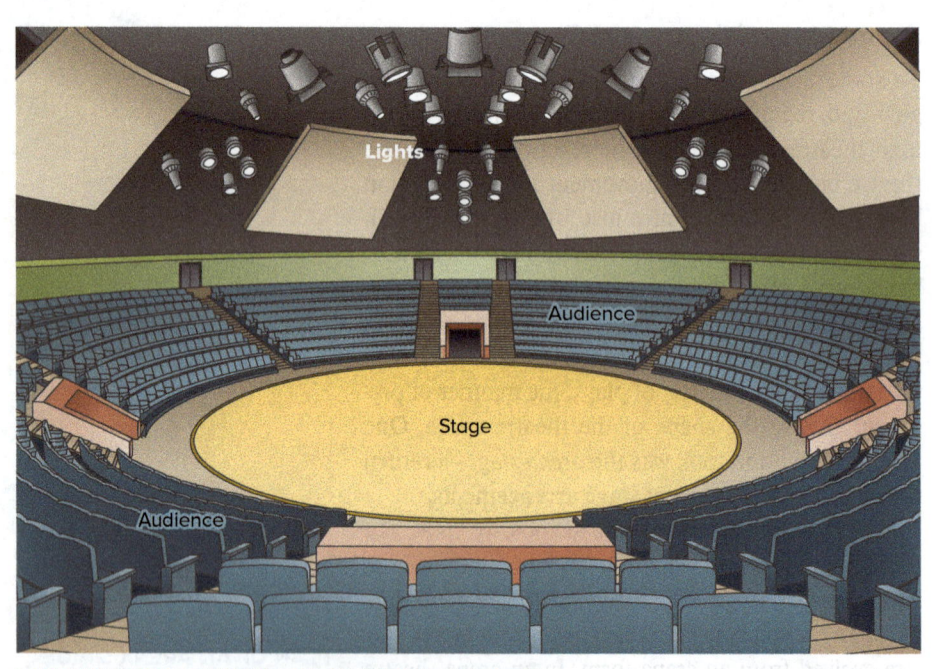

THE STAGE AND SEATING IN AN ARENA THEATRE
The arena theatre attempts to capture the immediacy of primitive theatre. It uses the barest essentials of stage scenery but the full resources of contemporary stage lighting.

ARENA STAGE
With an arena stage, also referred to as a circle stage or theatre-in-the-round, the audience surrounds the stage area on all sides. In addition to aisles for audience members to enter, there are passages that the performers use to enter and leave the stage. One effect of the arena stage is to create a close rapport between actors and audience. Seen here is the Arena Stage in Washington, D.C., designed by Bing Thom Architects. (View Pictures/Universal Images Group/Getty Images)

economy—no doubt explain why arena theatre is one of the oldest stage forms, as well as one still very much in use today.

In spite of its long history, however, and its resurgence in recent years, the arena stage has often been eclipsed by other forms. One reason is that its design, while allowing for intimacy, also dictates a certain austerity. As we noted before, it is impossible to have elaborate scenery because that would block the view of many spectators. Also, the performers must make all their entrances and exits along aisles that run through the audience, and they can sometimes be seen before and after they are supposed to appear onstage. The arena's lack of adaptability in this respect may explain why some of the circle theatres that opened twenty or thirty years ago have since closed. A number survive, however, and continue to do well. Among the best-known are the Arena Stage in Washington, D.C., and Circle in the Square in New York City. In addition, throughout this country there are a number of *tent theatres* in arena form where musical revivals and concerts are given.

Thrust Stage: History and Characteristics

Falling between the proscenium and the arena is a third type of theatre: the *thrust stage* with three-quarters seating. In one form or another, this U-shape arrangement has been the most widely used of all stage spaces. In the basic arrangement for this type of theatre, we sit on three sides, or in a semicircle, enclosing a stage, which protrudes into the center. At the back of the playing area is some form of ***stage house*** providing for the entrances and exits of the performers as well as for scene changes.

stage house Stage floor and the space around it to the side walls, as well as the space above it up to the grid.

Chapter 3 *Theatre Spaces*   55

THRUST STAGE WITH THREE-QUARTERS SEATING

The stage is surrounded on three sides by the audience. Sometimes seating is a semicircle. Entrances and exits are made from the sides and backstage. Spectators surround the action, but scene changes and other stage effects are still possible.

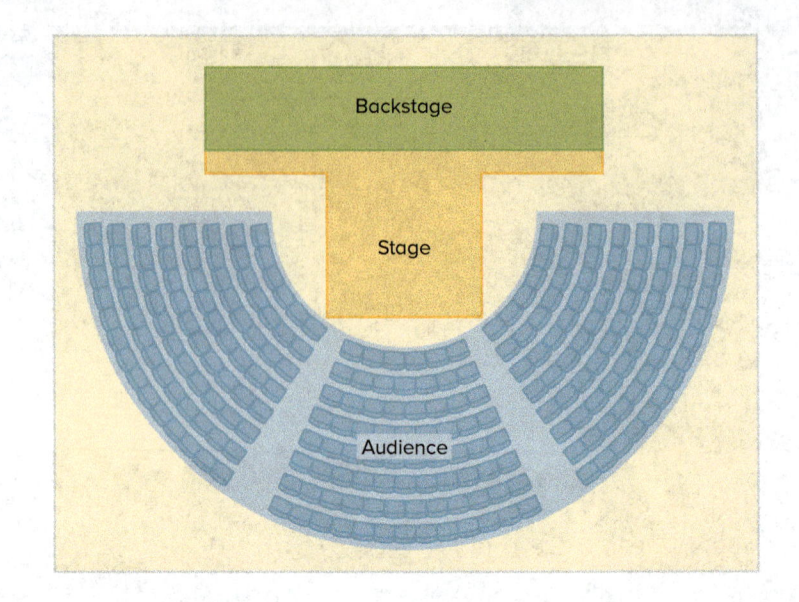

The thrust stage combines some of the best features of the other two stage types: the sense of intimacy and the "wraparound" feeling of the arena and the focused stage placed against a single background found in the proscenium.

The thrust stage was developed by the classical Greeks for their tragedies and comedies. They adapted the circle used for tribal rituals and other ceremonies—the circle called the *orchestra*—by locating it at the base of a curving hillside. The slope of the hill formed a natural amphitheatre for the spectators. At the rear of the orchestra circle, opposite the hillside, was placed a stage house, which had formal doors through which characters made their entrances and exits and served as a background for the action. The stage house also provided a place for the actors to change their costumes. The largest Greek theatres seated 15,000 or more spectators. While they were originally wooden structures in the classical Greek era, their design was duplicated in stone structures all over Greece in the following two centuries. Remnants of these stone theatres remain today throughout that part of the world in such places as Epidaurus, Priene, Ephesus, Delphi, and Corinth, to name a few.

The Romans, who took the Greek form and built it as a complete freestanding structure, had a theatre that was not strictly a thrust stage but a forerunner of the proscenium. Instead of using the natural amphitheatre of a hillside, they constructed a stone building, joining the stage house to the seating area and making the orchestra a semicircle. In front of the stage house, decorated with arches and statues, they erected a long platform stage where most of the action occurred.

Another example of the thrust stage is found in the medieval period, when short religious plays began to be presented in churches and cathedrals in England and parts of continental Europe. Around 1200 CE, performances of these religious plays were moved outdoors. One popular arrangement for these outdoor performances was the ***platform stage***. A simple platform was set on trestles (it was sometimes called a *trestle stage*), with a curtain at the back, which the performers used for entrances and costume changes. The area underneath the stage was closed off and provided, among other things, a space from which devils and other characters could appear, sometimes in

platform stage Elevated stage with no proscenium.

THE ORIGINAL THRUST STAGE: THE GREEK AMPHITHEATRE
An original prototype of the thrust stage was the amphitheatre in ancient Greece. Shown here is the theatre at Epidaurus, Greece. The seating surrounds the playing area on three sides. Acting took place on the raised platform at the back, but also in the circular area that is thrust into the audience. Among many other remarkable traits of these theatres are the incredible view of the mountains in the distance and the amazing acoustics of the theatre. A person in the back, top row can hear an actor speaking without any artificial amplification. (Jose Fuste Raga/Getty Images)

a cloud of smoke. In some places the platform was on wheels (a *wagon stage*) and was moved from place to place through a town. The audience stood on three sides of the platform, making it an improvised thrust stage. This type of stage was widely used from the thirteenth to the fifteenth centuries in England and various parts of Europe.

The next step following the wagon stage was a thrust stage that appeared in England in the sixteenth century, just before Shakespeare began writing for the theatre. A platform stage would be set up at one end of the open courtyard of an inn. The inns of this period were three or four stories high, and the rooms facing the inner courtyard served as boxes from which spectators could watch the performance. On the ground level, spectators stood on three sides of the stage. The fourth side of the courtyard, behind the platform, served as the stage house. An interesting coincidence is that an almost identical theatre took shape in Spain at the same time. The inns in Spain were called *corrales,* and this name was given to the theatres that developed there.

The formal English theatres of Shakespeare's day, such as the Globe and the Fortune, were similar to the inn theatres: The audience stood in an open area around a platform stage, and three levels of spectators sat in closed galleries at the back and sides. A roof covered part of the stage; at the back of the stage, some form of raised area served for balcony scenes (as in *Romeo and Juliet*). At the rear of the stage, also, scenes could be concealed and then "discovered." On each side at the rear was a door used for entrances and exits.

wagon stage (or, Wagon) Low platform mounted on wheels or casters by means of which scenery is moved on- and offstage.

corral Theatre building of the Spanish golden age, usually located in the courtyard of a series of adjoining buildings.

Chapter 3 *Theatre Spaces* 57

THE CLASSIC SPANISH STAGE

A variation on the thrust stage used in Elizabethan England is the Spanish *corral*. A version of this stage, uncovered by accident in 1953, is shown here in Almagro, Spain, where a theatre festival is held each year. Not strictly speaking a thrust stage, it has all the other components of a Renaissance outdoor theatre, with the platform stage and audience seating in boxes or a balcony around three sides. (Calle Montes/Photononstop Images/Media Bakery)

These theatres were fascinating combinations of diverse elements: They were both indoors and outdoors, some spectators stood while others sat, and the audience was composed of almost all levels of society. The physical environment must have been stimulating: Performers standing at the front of the thrust stage were in the center of a hemisphere of spectators on three sides around them, as well as above and below. These theatres held 2,000 to 3,000 spectators, but no one in the

A MODERN THRUST STAGE

The thrust stage, with a stage area extending into audience seating that surrounds it on three sides, is one of the oldest arrangements, having been used by the Greeks and by the Elizabethans in the time of Shakespeare. It has been revived successfully in the modern period and is widely used in Europe and the United States. A good example is the recently renovated Mark Taper Forum in Los Angeles. (Craig Schwartz)

58   Part One   The Audience

audience was more than sixty feet or so from the stage, and most people were much closer. Being in the midst of so many people, enclosed on all sides but with the open sky above, must have instilled a feeling of great communion among audiences and performers. Something of the same feeling can be recaptured when one visits today the Globe Theatre in London, modelled after the original Elizabethan playhouse.

Shortly after Shakespeare's day, in the latter part of the seventeenth century, there were two significant theatrical developments in England, in Spain, and throughout Europe: (1) the theatre moved almost completely indoors and (2) the stage began a slow but steady retreat behind the proscenium opening, partly because performances were indoors, but more because the style of theatres changed. For more than two centuries the thrust stage was in eclipse, not to reappear until about 1900, when a few theatres in England began using a version of the thrust stage to produce Shakespeare. The return of the thrust stage resulted from a growing realization that Elizabethan plays could be done best on a stage similar to the one for which they had been written.

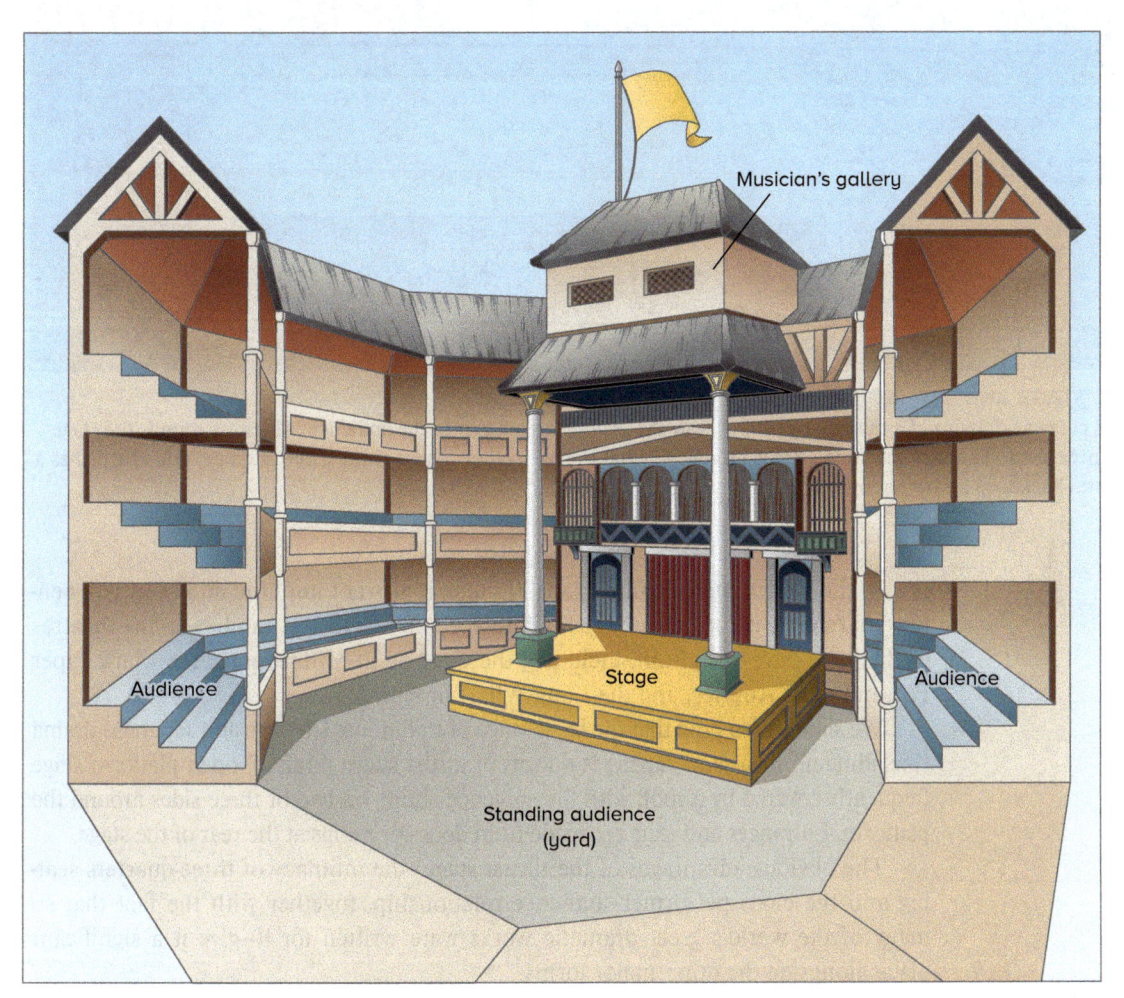

AN ELIZABETHAN PLAYHOUSE
This drawing shows the kind of stage on which the plays of Shakespeare and his contemporaries were first presented. A platform stage juts into an open courtyard, with spectators standing on three sides. Three levels of enclosed seats rise above the courtyard. There are doors at the rear of the stage for entrances and exits and an upper level for balcony scenes.

Chapter 3 *Theatre Spaces*   59

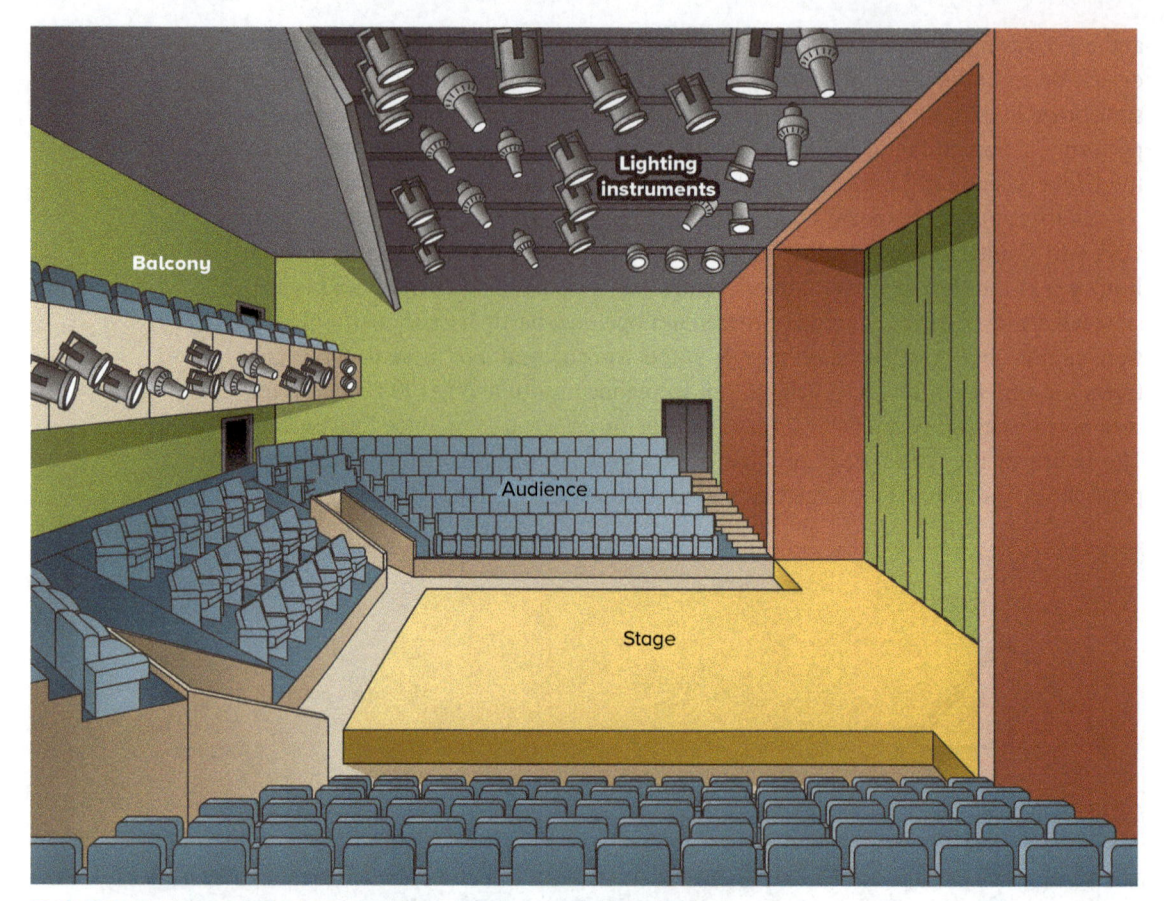

THE STAGE AND SEATING AREA OF A THRUST-STAGE THEATRE
This cutaway drawing of a thrust stage shows how the playing area juts into the audience, which surrounds the stage on three sides. This configuration affords intimacy, but at the back (shown here at the right) is an area that furnishes a natural backdrop for the action.

In the United States and Canada, though, it was not until the mid-twentieth century that the thrust stage came to the fore again. Since then a number of fine theatres of this type have been built, including the Guthrie in Minneapolis, the Mark Taper Forum in Los Angeles, and the Long Wharf in New Haven.

We should also note that the basic stage of traditional Chinese and Japanese drama (including nō theatre in Japan) is a form of thrust stage: a raised, open platform stage frequently covered by a roof, with the audience sitting on two or three sides around the platform. Entrances and exits are made from doors or ramps at the rear of the stage.

The obvious advantages of the thrust stage—the intimacy of three-quarters seating and the close performer-audience relationship, together with the fact that so many of the world's great dramatic works were written for it—give it a significant place alongside the other major forms.

Alley or traverse space
In this type of space the audiences its on opposite sides of the stage facing each other.

Alley or Traverse Theatre Space

Another unique form of theatre arrangement is the *alley or traverse* theatre space. (This arrangement is also sometimes referred to as a corridor stage.) In this type of

Part One The Audience

ALLEY STAGE
The alley stage has audience members sitting on opposite sides of the stage almost like a runway. Shown here is the alley stage being used for the 2020 production of *I'm Not Your Perfect Mexican Daughter* staged at Chicago's Steppenwolf Theatre.(Michael Brosilow)

space, the audience sits on opposite sides of the stage facing each other. The type of space is very much like the catwalk used by models in fashion shows.

Like the arena and thrust stages, actors must be blocked so that both sides of the audience can see the action and not feel that they are missing important moments. There can also only be limited amounts of scenery.

The alley stage arrangement also allows for greater audience–actor intimacy and is frequently used for productions that require direct address to or interaction with the audience.

Created and Found Spaces

After World War II a number of avant-garde theatre artists, such as the Polish director Jerzy Grotowski (1933–1999), undertook to reform theatre at every level. Since the various elements of theatre are inextricably bound together, their search for a more basic kind of theatre included a close look at the physical arrangement of the playing area and its relationship to the audience.

The Performance Group, which, for example, led spectators one at a time into its adaptation of the Greek tragedy *The Bacchae, Dionysus in 69*, is typical in this regard. It presented its productions in a large garage converted into an open theatre space. At various places in the garage, scaffolding and ledges were built for audience seating. The Performance Group, like other modern avant-garde companies, owed a great debt to a Frenchman, Antonin Artaud (1896–1948), one of the first theatre people to examine in depth the questions raised by the avant-garde. An actor and director who wrote a series of articles and essays about theatre, Artaud was brilliant but inconsistent (he spent several periods of

> # PLAYING YOUR PART: EXPERIENCING THEATRE
>
> 1. Rearrange your classroom seating into proscenium, arena, and thrust configurations, if possible. Read a speech aloud from a play or a paragraph from a novel to the class in each of these configurations. How is your presentation affected by the arrangement of the space?
> 2. Visit a gym or sports arena on your campus. What is the configuration of the space? How does it relate to a theatre environment? What type of popular entertainment might be staged there?
> 3. Find an outdoor space on your campus that might be used for theatre. What type of presentation would you stage there? Why?

his life in mental institutions). Many of Artaud's ideas, however, were to prove prophetic: Notions he put forward in the 1920s and 1930s, considered impossible or impractical at the time, have since become common practice among experimental theatre groups. Among his proposals was one on the physical theatre:

> We abolish the stage and auditorium and replace them by a single site, without partition or barrier of any kind, which will become the theater of the action. A direct communication will be reestablished between the spectator and the spectacle, between the actor and the spectator, from the fact that the spectator, placed in the middle of the action, is engulfed and physically affected by it. This envelopment results, in part, from the very configuration of the room itself. Thus, abandoning the architecture of present-day theaters, we shall take some hangar or barn which we shall have reconstructed according to processes which have culminated in the architecture of certain churches or holy places, and of certain temples in Tibet.[4]

Some of Artaud's ideas were put into practice when the movement to explore new concepts became widespread. In the generation after Artaud, Jerzy Grotowski included the physical arrangements of stage space in his experiments. Not only Grotowski but others in the avant-garde movement developed theatre space in a variety of ways.

Nontheatre Buildings   Artaud mentioned a barn or hangar for performances. In recent years virtually all kinds of structures have been used: lofts, warehouses, fire stations, basements, churches, breweries, and gymnasiums. This practice should not be confused with the conversion of unusual spaces to full-scale theatres, which has numerous precedents in the past; historically, indoor tennis courts, palace ballrooms, and monastery dining halls have been converted into theatres. We are, instead, describing here the use of nontheatre structures as they are, with their original architectural elements intact, and carving out special areas for acting and viewing—as with the garage used by the Performance Group.

site-specific companies
Theatre groups that create productions for specific nontheatre locations.

Site-Specific and Immersive Theatre Spaces   In our contemporary theatre, *site-specific theatre* refers to a production created for a unique, found location that was not intended to be used as a theatre. In site-specific theatre, the chosen space is made to fit the needs of the specific production and will probably not be used again

SITE-SPECIFIC THEATRE: CREATED AND FOUND SPACE

Shown here are two examples of site-specific theatre. In the first, a formal garden in the Aberglasney Gardens in Wales is the site of a performance by young actors dressed in black and white using the garden space as their stage. The second example shows the Polish theatre company Biuro Podrozy in a production of *Macbeth,* using its trademark stilts on a street, at the Edinburgh Fringe Festival in Edinburgh, Scotland. (top: Keith Morris/Alamy Stock Photo bottom: Jeff J Mitchell/Getty Images)

Chapter 3 *Theatre Spaces*

Immersive theatre In immersive theatre, audience members play an active role in some way, often moving through a performance space, sometimes even choosing where they should go within that space and what they should see and do. Many such productions use transformed, redesigned spaces as well as requiring audience members to engage in a complete sensory experience (touch, smell, even taste of foods and drink).

for theatre after that production. *Site-specific companies* are theatre groups that create productions for specific nontheatre locations.

Another popular current movement that has also led us to reconsider traditional theatre spaces is **immersive theatre.** In an immersive production, audience members are asked to become part of the production, often having to move through spaces (often not in theatre spaces but found or site-specific spaces) and to interact with the performers.

The English company Punchdrunk, for example, staged the immensely popular *Sleep No More,* an adaptation of Shakespeare's *Macbeth*, in three abandoned warehouses in Manhattan with the audiences moving through various spaces, supposedly in a 1930s hotel. A recent article about the increasing popularity of this type of theatre highlighted twenty-five New York theatre companies and artists who create immersive theatre work. There are many other examples of immersive theatre companies and productions throughout the United States and worldwide, using traditional theatre spaces, found spaces, and site-specific spaces.

Adapted Spaces One frequent practice was using or creating a space to fit a play, rather than (as is normally the case) making the play fit the space. Grotowski, in particular, pursued the notion of finding a different, appropriate configuration for each production. In Grotowski's production of the *Doctor Faustus* story, for example, the theatre was filled with two long tables at which spectators sat as if they were guests at a banquet hosted by Faustus. The action took place at the heads of the tables and even on the tabletops. For his production of *The Constant Prince,* a fence was built around the playing area, and the audience sat behind the fence, looking over it like spectators at a bullfight. In recent decades there have been similar attempts to deal with theatre spaces in many parts of Europe and the United States.

Street Theatre One development—which was actually a return to practices in medieval Europe—is theatre held outdoors in nontraditional settings. A good example is *street theatre.* Generally, street theatre is of three types: (1) plays from the standard repertoire presented in the streets; (2) *neighborhood theatre,* in which an original play deals with problems and aspirations of a specific population of a city, such as Puerto Ricans, African Americans, or Italians; and (3) *guerrilla theatre,* aggressive, politically oriented theatre produced by an activist group in the streets in an attempt to persuade us to become more politically involved, such as street presentations during the Occupy Wall Street movement in 2012.

Whatever the form, the important point for our purposes is that these productions take place not in theatre buildings but in places like streets, parks, hospitals, jails, and bus stations.

In these productions, theatre is brought to those of us who might not otherwise see it. Also, audiences in such unusual settings are challenged to rethink what theatre is all about. On the other hand, there are inherent disadvantages to impromptu productions in the streets or other "found spaces": The audience must be caught on the run, and there is rarely time for more than a sketch or vignette. Nor are there facilities

WAITING FOR GODOT IN A SITE-SPECIFIC PRODUCTION
Wendell Pierce (left) and J. Kyle Manzay rehearsing *Waiting for Godot*, directed by Paul Chan, and staged in the badly damaged Gentilly neighborhood of New Orleans in November 2007, following Hurricane Katrina. Chen, an artist, wanted his site specific production to reflect the interminable waiting for help from the federal government. He also created cardboard signs posted around the city to advertise his unique staging. (Lee Celano/The New York Times/Redux)

for presenting a fully developed work—but often that is not the purpose of these undertakings in the first place.

Multifocus Environments

An approach that sometimes accompanies these unusual arrangements is ***multifocus theatre.*** In simple terms, this means not only that there is more than one playing area, such as the four corners of the room (as Artaud suggested in one article), but also that something is going on in several of them simultaneously. This is somewhat like a three-ring circus, where we see an activity in each ring and must either concentrate on one or divide our attention among two or three.

There are several theories behind the idea of multifocus theatre. One is that a multifocus event is more like everyday life; if you stand on a street corner, there is activity all around you—in the four directions of the streets, in the buildings above—not just in one spot. You select which area you will observe, or perhaps you watch several areas at one time. The argument is that in theatre, you should have the same choice. In multifocus productions no single space or activity is supposed to be more important than any other. We either take in several impressions at once and synthesize them in our own mind or select one item as most arresting and concentrate on that. There is no such thing as the "best seat in the house"; all seats are equally good, because the activity in all parts of the theatre is equally important. Sometimes multifocus theatre is joined with *multimedia theatre*—presentations that offer some combination of acting, films, video, dance, music, slides, and light show.

multifocus theatre An environment in which there is more than one playing area.

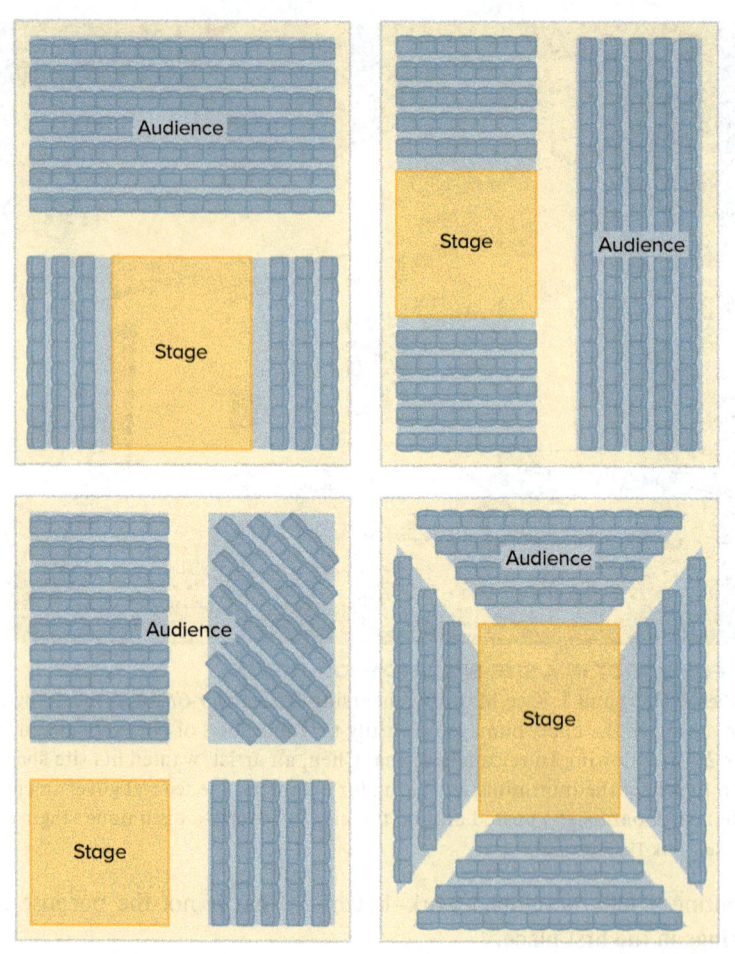

THE MULTIPURPOSE OR "BLACK BOX" THEATRE

A popular type of modern theatre is the multipurpose space, sometimes called a "black box." It consists of an open space with perhaps a pipe grid on the ceiling from which lighting and sound instruments can be suspended. A stage platform can be positioned at any place in the space, and movable chairs for spectators can be placed around the playing area. The diagrams suggest some of the possibilities of stage arrangements in a multipurpose theatre.

All-Purpose Theatre Spaces: The Black Box

Because of the interest in a variety of spaces in modern theatre production and the requirements of many different kinds of productions, a number of theatre complexes, including many college theatre departments and regional theatres, have built spaces that can be adapted to an almost infinite variety of configurations. Seats, lights, platforms, levels—every aspect of such a theatre is flexible and movable.

In this kind of space the designers can create a proscenium, a thrust, an arena, or some combination of these, but the designers can also create corner stages, island stages, and multifocus arrangements with playing areas in several parts of the studio. This space is sometimes referred to as a *black box* because it is often an empty rectangular space into which various audience seating and stage arrangements can be introduced.

IN FOCUS: POPULAR PERFORMANCE SPACES

Many spaces used for live popular entertainments are reminiscent of theatre environments. Arenas used for sports, circuses, and rock concerts are configured much like theatrical spaces discussed in this chapter. Madison Square Garden in New York; Soldier Field in Chicago; the Rose Bowl in Pasadena, California; and university sports arenas are all large spaces that primarily house sporting events but are also used for rock concerts and other popular spectacles. Madison Square Garden, for example, has housed circuses, elaborate rock concerts, and music award ceremonies. This means that an arena like the Garden is often equipped with the most innovative technology for lighting, stage, and sound effects.

Spectacular performance spaces for magicians, circuses, concerts, and stage extravaganzas are found in all of the major hotels in Las Vegas. Live entertainment is also presented in fairgrounds and amusement parks across our country.

These spaces for popular performances are most often configured in the round, with spectators surrounding the events. Some are configured three-quarters round. The reason is to maximize the number of audience members, as well as to create an electrifying interactive entertainment. With these configurations, we, as spectators, are also able to watch and possibly influence each other's reactions.

Such popular performance spaces are usually extremely large, much larger than environments created exclusively for theatre. For example, the Rose Bowl accommodates over 90,000 fans for football games. Even a comparatively small collegiate athletic facility, Western Hall on the Western Illinois University campus, can accommodate approximately 5,000 spectators.

The relationship between spaces for popular entertainments and theatrical environments is complex. Throughout theatre history, the same spaces were used for popular arts and for theatrical performances. Modern theatre artists have experimented with staging dramatic performances within spaces created for concerts and circuses.

For that matter, the performance qualities of sports, the circus, and rock concerts underscore their shared heritage with the theatrical arts. It is not surprising, then, that their spaces are also similar and often multipurpose.

PLAYING YOUR PART: THINKING ABOUT THEATRE

1. As discussed in this chapter, there are five major types of stage spaces: proscenium, arena, thrust, found space, and black box. What do you think are the advantages and disadvantages of each? On which type of stage space would you prefer to watch a performance?
2. Using information from this chapter, explain which type of stage space you would feel is best suited for the following productions: a large-scale musical, an intimate personal drama, a Shakespearean drama, and a play of political protest.
3. The size of theatre spaces can range from fewer than 100 spectators to more than 3,000. What do you consider an ideal-sized theatre for the following types of productions: a musical, a Shakespearean play, a modern family drama? Suggest the ideal number of audience seats and the shape and size of the ideal stage space for each.

SPECIAL REQUIREMENTS OF THEATRE ENVIRONMENTS

Simply assigning a theatre to a category does not adequately describe the environment; we must also take into account a number of other variables. Two theatres may be of the same type and still be quite different in size, atmosphere, and setting. The experience in a small off-off-Broadway-type thrust theatre will be far different from that in a thrust theatre several times larger, such as the Guthrie in Minneapolis. The experience in a 99-seat arena theatre at a university would be quite different than in the 886-seat arena playhouse used for musicals at the suburban Chicago Marriott Lincolnshire. Also, one theatre may be indoors and another of the same type outdoors.

There are other factors that architects, producers, and designers must take into account, one of which is the human scale. No matter what the configuration, the performer is the basic scale by which everything is measured in theatre. Theatre architects, as well as scenic and lighting designers, must always keep this in mind, and we should be aware of it as well. When the theatre environment and the stage space violate this human scale in some way, problems are created for performers and us.

There is also the question of appropriateness. By *appropriateness* we mean the relationship of a stage space to a play or production. A large-scale musical requires a full stage—usually a proscenium stage—and a large auditorium from which we can get the full effect of the spectacle. However, an intimate, small-cast family drama with its intense personal confrontations might require a small playing area so that we are close enough to the action to make a connection with the characters onstage.

Rather than being limited to one type of building and one type of stage, we are fortunate today in having a full range of environments in which to experience theatre. Taken all in all, whether single-focus or multifocus, indoors or outdoors, the recent innovations in theatre milieus have added new alternatives, rich in possibilities, to the traditional settings for theatrical productions. They have also called attention to the importance of environment in our total theatre experience.

Evaluating the Theatre Space

While we do not often think about evaluating the use of theatre space for a production, it is an element that can affect audience engagement and the work of the theatre artists. When we attend a theatre production, there are key questions we should ask ourselves as we interact with the environment used for staging:

1. What type of theatre was it? How large or small? How opulent or elaborate? How simple or modern? What type of stage did it have: proscenium, thrust, arena, or some other type? Was it a found space? How did the area for the actors relate to the audience seating?
2. What were the size and shape of the playing space? Were any modifications made to a preexisting space?
3. What sort of atmosphere did the space suggest? How was that atmosphere created?
4. Did the space seem to meet the needs of the play (such as special performance requirements or technical requirements)? Did it affect the production and, if so, how?
5. Did the space seem appropriate for the type of play you were seeing (an intimate family drama, a spectacular musical, a classical tragedy, a work by Shakespeare, etc.)?

SUMMARY

1. The atmosphere and environment of the theatre space play a large part in setting the tone of an event.
2. Experimental theatre groups in recent years have deliberately made spectators aware of the environment.
3. Throughout theatre history there have been five basic stage and auditorium arrangements: proscenium, arena, thrust, traverse or alley, created or found space, and all-purpose or "black box" spaces.
4. The proscenium theatre features a picture-frame stage, in which the audience faces directly toward the stage and looks through the proscenium opening at the "picture." The proscenium stage aids illusion: Placing a room of a house behind the proscenium, for example, allows the scene designer to create an extremely realistic set. This type of stage also allows elaborate scene shifts and visual displays because it generally has a large backstage area and a fly loft. It also creates a distancing effect, which works to the advantage of certain types of drama. At the same time, however, the proscenium frame sets up a barrier between the performers and the audience.
5. The arena or circle stage places the playing area in the center with the audience seated in a circle or square around it. This offers an economical way to produce theatre and an opportunity for great intimacy between performers and spectators, but it cannot offer full visual displays in terms of scenery and scene changes.
6. The thrust stage with three-quarters seating is a platform stage with seating on three sides. Entrances and exits are made at the rear, and there is an opportunity for a certain amount of scenery. This form combines some of the scenic features of the proscenium theatre with the intimacy of the arena stage.
7. Created or found space takes several forms: use of nontheatre buildings, site-specific adaptation of a given space to fit individual productions, immersive spaces, use of outdoor settings, street theatre, multifocus environments, and all-purpose spaces.
8. The theatre space referred to as a *black box* is an open, adaptable space that can be configured into a variety of stage–audience arrangements, providing for maximum flexibility and economy.
9. Size and location (indoors or outdoors, etc.), along with the shape and character of a theatre building, affect the environment.

Design Elements: Audience Sitting in Theatre (theatre): Ron Chapple/Photodisc/Getty Images; Studio Light (spotlights): Exactostock/SuperStock

Part Two

The Performers and the Director

4 Acting for the Stage

5 The Director and the Producer

THE PERFORMERS TAKE THE STAGE

Actors are at the heart of theatre. They embody the characters as well as project the story, language, and emotional qualities of the play. Seen here is Gabriel Brown (front) dancing in August Wilson's *Joe Turner's Come and Gone* at the Mark Taper Forum in Los Angeles in 2013. At left are January LaVoy and Glynn Turman, and at right are Vivian Nixon and Keith David. (Gary Friedman/Los Angeles Times/Getty Images)

Part Two | The Performers and the Director

Performers, by their presence, set theatre apart from films, television, and the visual arts; they serve as the direct, immediate contact that we, as members of the audience, have with theatre. More than that, performers embody the heart and soul of theatre. The words of a script, the characters created by a dramatist, and the scenery and costumes come to life only when an actor or actress steps onto a stage.

Acting, however, is not confined to theatre. Of course, there is acting on film and television. But there are also many forms of "acting" in our daily lives. Most of us might be surprised to learn that acting is almost as old as the human race. From the earliest days of civilization, people have mimicked other people and have told stories, imitating the voices and gestures of the characters in those stories. There have also been rituals and ceremonies in which the celebrants wore costumes and performed assigned roles—one example is the person officiating in a religious service.

Another familiar type of "acting" in daily life is imitation. A good example is the attempt by individuals to copy the lifestyle of a hero—a singer, a film actor, or some other well-known personality. The imitator adopts the same wardrobe, the same stance, the same physical movements, and the same hairstyle as the hero or heroine. Another form of imitation is mimicry. Someone who tells a story or recounts an event copies the voices and gestures of the persons being described. A second type of "acting" prevalent in our daily lives is role playing. Much has been written about role playing in recent years, and a currently popular term is *role*

Religious celebrations, such as the Jewish bar mitzvah—shown here at the Western Wall in Jerusalem—have many things in common with theatre. (Richard T. Nowitz/Corbis Documentary/Getty Images)

Virtually all types of ceremonies and performances worldwide—ancient and modern, religious and secular—have theatrical elements. Here, in Mali, West Africa, teetering on stilts high above village audience members, masked Dogon dancers imitate a long-legged waterbird. (alantobey/Getty Images)

model, referring to people whose lives, or "roles," serve as models or guides for others.

On the less admirable side, how often have we had a behind-the-scenes revelation of the behavior of a politician, a movie star, or a corporate executive just before the person is to appear at a press conference? Sometimes the person is scowling, peppering his or her language with profanity and invective, speaking sharply to assistants. Then, suddenly, when the person moves before the television cameras, he or she breaks into a smile and takes on the persona of someone who is affable, pleasant, and charming. In a public appearance, the person is playing a "role." Looked at from a different perspective, in the age of the Internet, of Facebook, Twitter, and YouTube, a certain kind of acting in everyday life has become commonplace. As George Vecsey, a columnist for the *New York Times,* has written, "In the YouTube era, everybody under a certain age is a performer."

We have been speaking of "acting" in everyday life. When we turn to acting for the stage, we will observe that for all the similarities, there are significant, even crucial, differences between imitation or role playing in daily life and the acting that takes place onstage. For one thing, everyone concerned—audiences as well as those onstage—will recognize that it is a performance. It is a conscious act that requires not only talent but a tremendous amount of training and discipline. In Part Two, we will look at the art and craft of theatrical performance. We will also look at the role of a person who works most closely with actors: the director.

PERFORMING IN EVERYDAY LIFE

Many activities not usually thought of as theatre are theatrical in nature. Here are individuals, dressed in costumes, performing in the St. Patrick's Day Parade along 5th Avenue in New York City on March 17, 2016.
(Stuart Monk/Shutterstock)

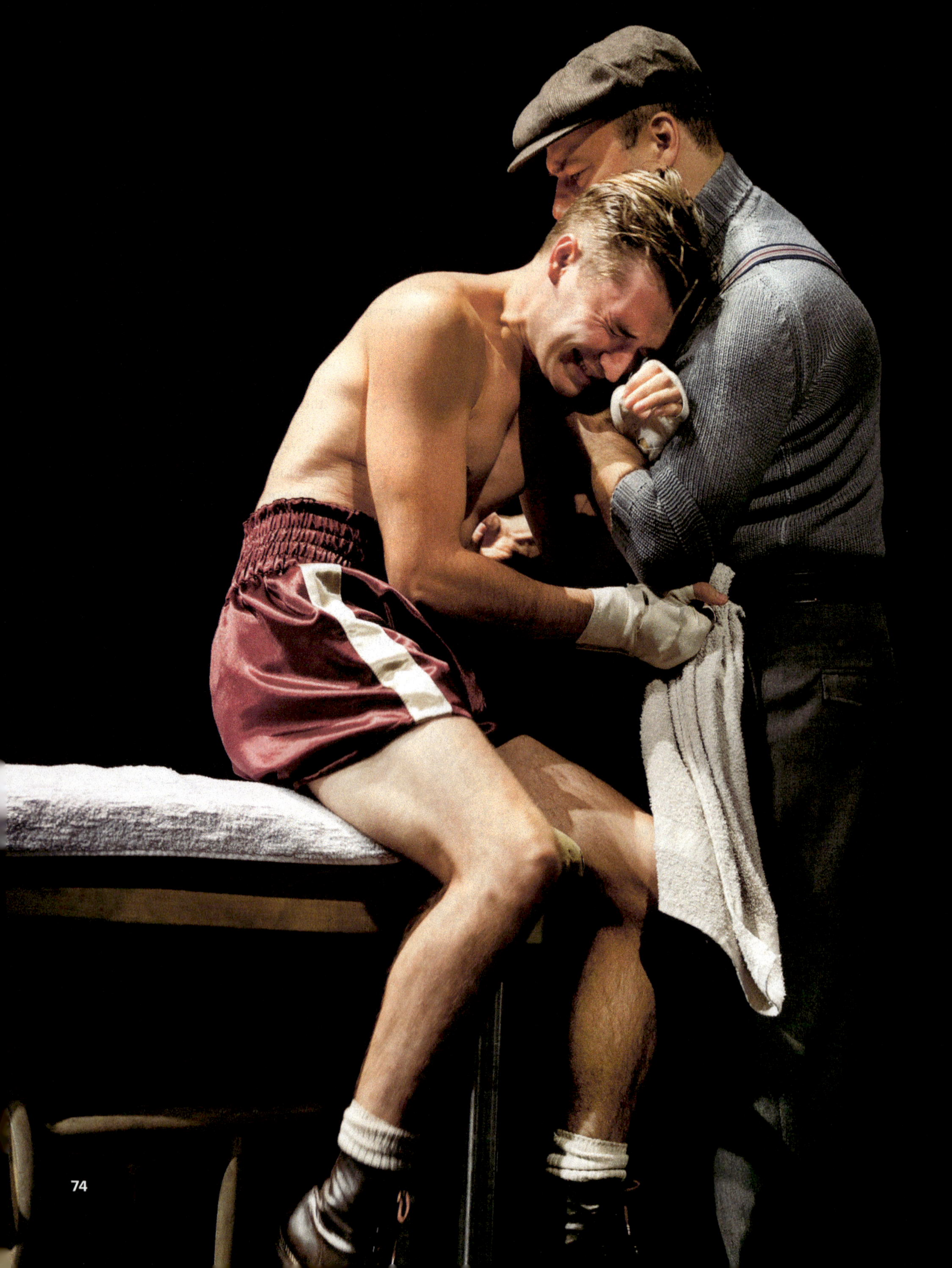

4

Acting for the Stage

At the heart of the theatre experience is the exchange between actors and the audience. We in the audience observe the performers on stage: their gestures and their movements. And we listen to their words. Actors, in turn, are acutely aware of us in the audience: our presence and our reactions and responses. Previously we have focused on the role of the audience at a performance; in this chapter we examine the art and craft of acting for the stage. Before we turn to the stage actor, however, we should take note of another type of performance in which we are all participants: acting in everyday life, that is, the various roles in our daily lives.

ACTING IN EVERYDAY LIFE

Two examples of acting in daily life are imitation and role playing. The first of these, *imitation,* is found on all levels of society and at all ages. Children, for example, are among the best imitators in the world, and we are often amused by a child who imitates a parent or some other grown-up. As we grow older, imitation continues to be a part of our experience: in every class in school, from elementary school through college, there is usually one person—a clever mimic—who imitates the teacher or the principal with great humor, and sometimes with cruelty.

The second type of acting in everyday life we mentioned is *role playing,* which can generally be divided into two categories: social and personal.

imitation To simulate or copy behavior observed in real life.

role playing In everyday life, the acting out of a particular role by copying the expected social behavior of that position.

Social Roles

Social roles are general roles recognized by society: parent, child, police officer, store clerk, teacher, student, business executive, physician, and so on. Every culture expects certain types of behavior from people who are assigned specific social roles, sometimes resulting in stereotyping or oppressing those individuals. For many years in Western culture, for example, the roles of women as secretaries, teachers, or housewives were considered subordinate to the roles of men and the only ones deemed appropriate for them. Even today when women hold positions similar to those of men in business and the professions, they frequently receive a lower salary

◀ **STAGE ACTING**

To play a character convincingly, an actor must develop both outer techniques and inner emotional resources. This is true whether performing in a classical play or a modern, realistic play. Shown here from a scene in a Broadway revival of Golden Boy *by Clifford Odets is Seth Nurmich as the boxer and Danny Burstein as his trainer. (Sara Krulwich/The New York Times/Redux)*

for the same job. The women's movement challenged the notion of subservient roles for women. So entrenched was the idea, however, that it took an entire movement to call it into question. (One aspect of this movement was *consciousness raising:* making people aware of sexist social attitudes toward women.) Before changes could begin to be made in the subordinate roles women were forced to play, everyone had to understand that these *were* social roles imposed upon them by a male-dominated, patriarchal society and were clearly unacceptable.

As noted, there continues to be active women's movements across the globe. Recently, the #MeToo movement has focused on the issues of sexual harassment and sexual assault in the workplace. Equal pay for equal work is an ongoing political battle in the United States, and there have been large-scale women's protest marches in 2017 and 2018.

Personal Roles

Aside from social roles, we develop personal roles with our family and friends. For example, some people become braggarts, boasting of their (sometimes imaginary) feats and accomplishments and embellishing the truth to appear more impressive than they are. Others become martyrs, constantly sacrificing for others and letting the world know about it. Still others are conspirators, people who pull their friends aside to establish an air of secrecy whenever they talk. Frequently, two people fall into complementary roles: one dominant and the other submissive, one active and the other passive.

ACTING IN LIFE VERSUS ACTING ON STAGE

Some of the differences between stage acting and acting in daily life are obvious. For one thing, actors onstage are always being observed. In real life there may be observers, but their presence is not essential to an event. Bystanders on a street corner where an accident has occurred form a kind of audience, but their presence is incidental and unrelated to the accident itself. Onstage, however, the performer is always on display and often in the spotlight.

Acting onstage, too, requires a performer to play roles they do not play in life. A scene between a parent and child arguing about money, or between spouses or partners discussing whether or not to have children, is one thing when it is actually occurring in our lives but something quite different onstage. Generally, the roles we play in life are genuine. A parent who accepts responsibilities toward children does not just play a parent; that person *is* a parent. Someone who writes novels does not just play a novelist; that person *is* one.

In real life, a lawyer knows the law; but onstage, an actor playing the role of a lawyer may not know the difference between jurisprudence and habeas corpus and probably has never been inside a law school. Playing widely divergent parts or parts outside their personal experience requires performers to stretch their imagination and ability. For example, a young actor at one time or another might be called on to play parts as dissimilar as the fiery, independent Antigone in the play by Sophocles; the vulnerable, love-struck Juliet in Shakespeare's *Romeo and Juliet*; and the neurotic, obsessed leading character in Strindberg's *Miss Julie.* Beyond playing different

REAL-LIFE ROLES SEEN ONSTAGE
Roles onstage are often similar to roles people are called on to play in real life. Cheerleaders at athletic events are a good example. Here we see a scene from *Bring It On: The Musical,* about rival high school cheerleading squads. (Sara Krulwich/The New York Times/Redux)

roles at different times, performers are even called on at times to *double,* that is, perform several parts in one play.

Another significant difference between acting for the stage and "acting" in life is that dramatic characters are not real people. Any stage character—Joan of Arc, Antigone, Oedipus, Hamlet, Willy Loman—is a symbol or an image of a person. Stage characters are fictions created by dramatists and performers to represent people. They remind us of people—in many cases they seem to *be* these people, but they are not. The task of the performer in attempting to make the characters onstage *appear* to be real requires not only talent but training and discipline as well.

THREE CHALLENGES OF ACTING

Theatre actors and actresses face three major challenges:

1. To make characters believable—inner truth.
2. Physical acting—the use of the voice and body.
3. Synthesis and integration—combining inner and outer skills.

Chapter 4 *Acting for the Stage* 77

To understand the first two challenges of acting, we will examine them separately. We begin with making characters believable and then turn to the craft of acting—specific physical and vocal techniques required in performances.

Making Characters Believable

One major aspect of the craft of acting is credibility: the ability to make those of us in the audience believe in the characters that appear onstage, to make the characters convincing.

The Development of Realistic Acting

From the mid-seventeenth century on, serious attempts were made to define the craft or technique of credible, natural acting. Such an approach became more important than ever at the end of the nineteenth century, when drama began to depict characters and situations close to everyday life. Three playwrights—Henrik Ibsen of Norway, August Strindberg of Sweden, and Anton Chekhov of Russia—perfected a type of drama that came to be known as *realism*. This drama was called realistic because it closely resembled what people could identify with and verify from their own experience. In performing plays by these dramatists, not only the spirit of the individual dramatic characters but also the details of their behavior had to conform to what people saw of life around them.

The Stanislavski System: A Technique for Realistic Acting

Before the realistic drama of the late 1800s, individual performers, through their own talent and genius, had achieved believability onstage, but no one had developed a system whereby it could be taught to others and passed on to future generations. The person who eventually did this most successfully was the Russian actor and director Konstantin Stanislavski. A cofounder of the Moscow Art Theater in Russia and the director of Anton Chekhov's most important plays, Stanislavski was also an actor. By closely observing the work of great performers of his day and by drawing on his own acting experience, Stanislavski identified and described what these gifted performers did naturally and intuitively. From his observations he compiled and then codified a series of principles and techniques.

We might assume that believable acting is simply a matter of being natural, but Stanislavski discovered first of all that acting realistically onstage is extremely artificial and difficult. He wrote:

> All of our acts, even the simplest, which are so familiar to us in everyday life, become strained when we appear behind the footlights before a public of a thousand people. That is why it is necessary to correct ourselves and learn again how to walk, sit, or lie down. It is essential to reeducate ourselves to look and see, on the stage, to listen and to hear.[1]

To achieve this "reeducation," Stanislavski said, "the actor must first of all believe in everything that takes place onstage, and most of all, he must believe what he himself is doing. And one can only believe in the truth." To give substance to his ideas, Stanislavski developed a series of exercises and techniques for the performer, among them the following.[2]

TECHNIQUES OF ACTING: THE IMPORTANCE OF SPECIFICS
Konstantin Stanislavski believed that performers should concentrate on specifics. In *The Glass Menagerie*, the playwright Tennessee Williams has provided the character Laura with a collection of glass animals with which she is preoccupied. Shown here are Rachel Caywood as Laura Wingfield and Michael Mitchell as Jim O'Connor, the gentleman caller, staged at the Davis Performing Arts Center in Washington, D.C. (The Washington Post/Getty Images)

Relaxation. When he observed the great actors of his day, Stanislavski noticed how fluid and lifelike their movements were. They seemed to be in a state of complete freedom and relaxation, letting the behavior of the character come through effortlessly. He concluded that unwanted tension has to be eliminated and that the performer must at all times attain a state of physical and vocal relaxation.

Concentration and observation. Stanislavski also discovered that gifted performers always appeared fully concentrated on some object, person, or event while onstage. Stanislavski referred to the extent or range of concentration as a *circle of attention.* This circle of attention can be compared to a circle of light on a darkened stage. The performer should begin with the idea that it is a small, tight circle including only that performer and perhaps one other person or one piece of furniture. When a strong circle of attention has been established, the performer can enlarge the circle outward to include the entire stage area. In this way performers will stop worrying about the audience and lose their self-consciousness.

Importance of specifics. One of Stanislavski's techniques was an emphasis on concrete details. Performers should never try to act in general, he said, and should never try to convey a feeling such as fear or love in some vague, amorphous way. In life, Stanislavski said, we express emotions in terms of specifics: someone who is anxious might twist a handkerchief, an angry child throws a rock at a trash can, a nervous business person jangles keys. Performers must find similar concrete activities. Stanislavski points out how Shakespeare has Lady Macbeth in her sleepwalking scene—at the height of her guilt and emotional upheaval—try to rub blood off her hands.

The performer must also conceive of the situation in which a character exists—what Stanislavski referred to as the *given circumstances*—in terms of specifics. In what kind of space does an event take place: formal, informal, public, domestic? How does it feel? What is the temperature? The lighting? What has gone on just before? What is expected in the moments ahead? Again, these questions must be answered in concrete terms.

Chapter 4   *Acting for the Stage*

IN FOCUS: DEMANDS OF CLASSICAL ACTING

Before the twentieth century, the challenges facing performers were dictated by the very specific demands of the type of theatre in which performers appeared. Both classic Greek theatre and traditional Asian theatre stressed formal movement and stylized gestures similar to classical ballet. The chorus in Greek drama both sang and danced its odes, and Asian theatre has always had a significant component of singing and dancing. In addition, Greek performers wore masks, and Asian performers often wore richly textured makeup.

In Western theatre, from the time of the Renaissance through the nineteenth century, actions onstage were not intended to replicate the movements or gestures of everyday life. For example, performers would often speak not to the character they were addressing but directly to the audience. In England during the eighteenth and nineteenth centuries, acting alternated between exaggerated and more natural styles. Throughout this period, every generation or so someone would emerge who was praised for performing in a less grandiose, more down-to-earth way. But exaggerated or not, performance before the twentieth century was more formal and stylized than the acting we are accustomed to today, especially in films and on television.

In Western theatre, from the fifth century BCE in Greece to the middle of the nineteenth century, vocal demands were greater than they are today. The language of plays was most often poetry, and poetry—with its demanding rhythms, sustained phrases, and exacting meters—required intensive training in order for the performer to speak the lines intelligently and distinctly. There were problems of projection, too. A Greek amphitheatre was an acoustical marvel, but it seated as many as 15,000 spectators in the open air, and throwing the voice to every part of the theatre was no small task.

In Elizabethan England, Christopher Marlowe, a contemporary of Shakespeare, wrote superb blank verse that made severe demands on performers' vocal abilities. One example is found in Marlowe's *The Tragical History of D. Faustus*. Here is a speech by Faustus to Helen of Troy, who has been called back from the dead to be with him:

> O' thou art fairer than the evening's air
> Clad in the beauty of a thousand stars;
> Brighter art thou than flaming Jupiter
> When he appear'd to hapless Semele;
> More lovely than the monarch of the sky
> In wanton Arethusa's azured arms;
> And none but thou shalt be my paramour![3]

These seven lines of verse are a single sentence and, spoken properly, will be delivered as one overall unit, with the meaning carried from one line to the next. How many of us could manage that? A fine classical actor can speak the entire passage as a whole, giving it the necessary resonance and inflection as well. Beyond that, the actor can stand onstage for two or three hours delivering such lines.

No one would expect a performer today to act in a classical play in the manner in which it was originally presented; such a performance would no doubt seem ludicrous. Besides, we do not know exactly how classical acting looked or sounded. At the same time, it should be clear that any performer today who is appearing in a play from the past must develop a special set of skills and be able to respond successfully to a number of challenges. Not only should an actor have the necessary psychological and emotional tools—a Hamlet, for instance, who must express a wide range of emotions as well as contradictory impulses, or an Ophelia who must play a "mad scene" in which she has lost her mind—but the same actor must also master the necessary physical and vocal techniques. Physically, an actor playing Hamlet would have to move with confidence as well as with the precision of a dancer. The actor would also be required to climb steps and levels with ease, and since Hamlet must engage in sword fighting, the performer must have mastered fencing techniques.

The Social Status of the Performer

On the subject of historical acting styles, we should also note that through the centuries there has been a wide fluctuation in the social and political positions of performers. First, it is important to be aware that in several key periods of theatre history, women were prohibited from performing at all. Two prime examples are the theatre of ancient Greece—the era of the playwrights Aeschylus, Sophocles, and Euripides—and the Elizabethan age, during which Shakespeare and his contemporaries wrote. In both periods women could not even appear onstage. In Roman theatre, women were allowed to perform, but only in a lower form of theatre known as *mime*. In Europe, during the Renaissance, acting became more professional, but the social position of actors was still problematic. Women began to appear with acting troupes in Italy and Spain, but in Spain it was required that any woman in a company be a relative (wife, mother, sister) of one of the leaders of the troupe.

The next point to be noted is that frequently in the history of acting, performers were regarded as quite low on the social scale. An early exception was the classical period in Greece. Because theatre presentations were part of a religious festival, actors were treated with dignity. Still, there was distrust of the actor. Through most of theatre history, however, this was not the case. An example of the problems faced by actors is the fate of the French playwright and actor Molière. Though he was one of the most renowned theatre artists of his day, France at that time had laws preventing actors from receiving a Christian burial, and thus Molière was buried secretly at night. When women began to appear on the English stage in the Restoration period, after 1660, they were regarded by some as on a par with courtesans or prostitutes. Other people, however, accepted them into high society, and one performer Nell Gwynn, was a mistress of the king. During the eighteenth and nineteenth centuries there were a number of famous and celebrated stars on the European continent, in England, and in the United States. In England, when the actor Henry Irving was knighted in 1895, it was felt that actors had finally arrived socially.

In Asian theatre, performers for many centuries were primarily men, though a unique phenomenon occurred at the beginning of kabuki in Japan. Kabuki began in the early seventeenth century with all-women troupes. Social disruptions arose, however, because of feuds over the sexual services of the women, and in 1629 the shogun forbade performances of women's kabuki. From that point on, kabuki was all-male, as were nō theatre and puppet theatre, bunraku.

ACTING IN THE PAST
Acting requirements in the past were often different from those of today. Forceful, sometimes exaggerated movements and a powerful voice were two essentials for successful performers. Actors were expected to declaim their lines and strike impressive poses while wearing elaborate costumes. An example from the late eighteenth century is an actress in the costume for a character in *Athalie* by Jean Racine. (Historical Picture Archive/Getty Images)

Inner truth. An innovative aspect of Stanislavski's work has to do with inner truth, which deals with the internal or subjective world of characters—that is, their thoughts and emotions. The early phases of Stanislavski's research took place while he was also directing the major dramas of Anton Chekhov. Plays like *The Sea Gull* and *The Cherry Orchard* have less to do with external action or what the characters say than with what the characters are feeling and thinking but often do not verbalize. It becomes apparent that Stanislavski's approach would be very beneficial in realizing the inner life of such characters. Stanislavski had several ideas about how to achieve a sense of inner truth, one being the ***magic if.*** *If* is a word that can transform our thoughts; through it we can imagine ourselves in virtually any situation. "*If* I suddenly became wealthy . . ." "*If* I were vacationing on a Caribbean island . . ." "*If* I had great talent . . ." "*If* that person who insulted me comes near me again . . ." The word *if* becomes a powerful lever for the mind; it can lift us out of ourselves and give us a sense of absolute certainty about imaginary circumstances.

magic if Stanislavski's acting exercise that requires the performer to ask, "How would I react *if* I were in this character's position?"

Action onstage: What? Why? How? Another important principle of Stanislavski's system is that all action onstage must have a purpose. This means that the performer's attention must always be focused on a series of physical actions (also called *psychophysical actions*), linked together by the circumstances of the play. Stanislavski determined these actions by asking three essential questions: What? Why? How? An action is performed, such as opening a letter (the *what*). The letter is opened because someone has said that it contains extremely damaging information about the character (the *why*). The letter is opened anxiously, fearfully (the *how*), because of the calamitous effect it might have on the character.

Through line of a role. According to Stanislavski, in order to develop continuity in a part, the actor should find the ***superobjective*** of a character. What is it, above all else, that the character wants during the course of the play? What is the character's driving force? If a goal can be established toward which the character strives, it will give the performer an overall objective. From this objective can be developed a *through line* that can be grasped, as a skier on a ski lift grabs a towline and is carried to the top. Another term for through line is *spine*. To help develop the through line, Stanislavski urged performers to divide scenes into units (sometimes called *beats*). In each unit there is an objective, and the intermediate objectives running through a play lead ultimately to the overall objective.

superobjective What the character wants above all else during the course of the play.

Ensemble playing. Except in one-person shows, performers do not act alone; they interact with other people. Stanislavski was aware that many performers tend to "stop acting," or lose their concentration, when they are not the main characters in a scene or when someone else is talking. This tendency destroys the through line and causes the performer to move into and out of a role. That, in turn, weakens *ensemble playing*—the playing together of all the performers.

ensemble playing Acting that stresses the total artistic unity of a group performance rather than individual performances.

Stanislavski and Psychophysical Action

Stanislavski began to develop his technique in the early twentieth century, and at first he emphasized the inner aspects of training; for example, various ways of getting in touch with the performer's unconscious. Beginning around 1917, however, he began to look more and more at purposeful action, or what he called *psychophysical action*. A student at one of his lectures that year took note of the change: "Whereas action previously had been taught as the expression of a previously established 'emotional state,' it is now action itself which predominates and is

CHALLENGES OF ACTING
Actors must understand the circumstances of a play, the motivations of their characters, and they must listen carefully, sensing each other's actions and moods, and responding alertly. Seen here are Adina Verson (left), and Katrina Lenk in *Indecent* by Paula Vogel directed by Rebecca Teichman at off-Broadway's Vineyard Theatre in 2016. The play chronicles the controversial original production of the Yiddish play *God of Vengeance*, a work by Sholem Asch that caused a scandal when produced on Broadway in 1923. The actors in the show must understand the circumstances of the time, the reasons for the controversy, create a sense of ensemble (since they are supposed to be a theatre troupe presenting the story), and be able to learn dialects and speak some Yiddish. (Sara Krulwich/The New York Times/Redux)

the key to the psychological."[4] Rather than seeing emotions as leading to action, Stanislavski came to believe that it was the other way around: purposeful action undertaken to fulfill a character's goals was the most direct route to the emotions.

Modern Approaches to Realistic Acting in the United States
In the second half of the twentieth century, there were three broad approaches to actors' training in the United States. Two of these derived from the methods of Stanislavski. In the 1930s and 1940s a number of performers and directors in the United States became greatly interested in the ideas of Stanislavski. One of these, Lee Strasberg, a founder of the Actors Studio in New York City, focused on the inner aspects of Stanislavskian theory. Strasberg emphasized a technique called *emotional recall,* a tool intended to help performers achieve a sense of emotional truth onstage. By recalling sensory impressions of an experience in the past (such as what a room looked like and the temperature and any prevalent odors in the room), emotions associated with that experience are aroused and can be used as the basis of feelings called for in a role in a play.

Though the teachings of Strasberg and his followers were successful with certain performers, other acting teachers, such as Stella Adler (1902–1992) and Sanford Meisner (1905–1997), felt that Strasberg emphasized the inner aspects of acting to the exclusion of everything else. Following the lead of Stanislavski in his later approach with psychophysical action, they balanced the emphasis on inner resources with the inclusion of given circumstances and purposeful action.

emotional recall
Stanislavski's exercise that helps the performer present realistic emotions. The performer feels a character's emotion by thinking of the conditions surrounding an event in his or her own life that led to a similar emotion.

photo essay

The Actor's Range

In theatre, performers are often called on to play a wide range of diverse parts. Frequently, too, actors portray people unlike themselves. Many performers welcome this challenge. An American actor who has demonstrated tremendous versatility is John Douglas Thompson, shown here in five contrasting roles.

(Sara Krulwich/The New York Times/Redux

John Douglas Thompson as the lead in Eugene O'Neill's *The Emperor Jones,* Irish Repertory Theatre, 2009.

John Douglas Thompson as Richard III in a production of that play at Shakespeare & Company, Lenox, MA.

(Kevin Sprague/Studio Two)

84

Kate Arrington, John Douglas Thompson, and Salvatore Inzerillo in Eugene O'Neill's *The Iceman Cometh* at the Goodman Theatre.

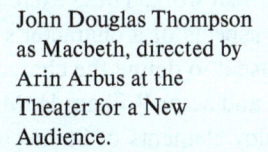

(Liz Lauren/Richard Hein)

John Douglas Thompson as Macbeth, directed by Arin Arbus at the Theater for a New Audience.

(Sara Krulwich/The New York Times/Redux)

John Douglas Thompson as Othello, Merritt Janson as Desdemona, directed by Tony Simotes, Shakespeare & Company, 2008.

(Kevin Sprague/Studio Two)

85

Other well-known acting teachers who emphasize approaches to creating realistic performances are Uta Hagen (1919-2004), the director Lloyd Richards (1919-2006), Robert Cohen (b. 1938), Robert Benedetti (b. 1939), and playwright David Mamet (b. 1947) working with actor William H. Macy (b. 1950).

Hagen, in her book *Respect for Acting,* places a large emphasis on emotional recall and sense memory in general. She provides a number of exercises that enable students to pull from past experiences in their own lives as a means of reaching the emotions required within the context of any given role. Hagen's idea is not to allow the student to become overwhelmed by past emotion, but to use it as a springboard into the action of the play.

In *Acting One,* Robert Cohen encourages students to use text as an instrument of action. In an exercise that he calls the "Contentless Scene," he has students memorize the same text. He then asks them to perform the scene but changes the given circumstances of the scene each time. The outcome is the obvious realization that the words are not nearly as important as the meaning behind them. And, clearly, without solid given circumstances, actors are simply saying lines instead of using those lines to further the action of the play.

Robert Benedetti in *The Actor at Work* focuses on the actor's body and how performers can use it to help shape character. Using a variety of movement exercises, Benedetti encourages students to explore elements of rhythm, time, weight, intensity, and space through improvisational work. These exercises allow the students to start with the "outside" (physical) aspects of a character's definition. Once the physical form is found, they can then use it to define the character's inner life (emotion).

Playwright David Mamet and actor William H. Macy, in their approach, known as "practical aesthetics," employ elements of Stanislavski and Meisner. Actors analyze a scene to discover what is literally happening, as well as what his or her character wants from the others in that scene.

THE CRAFT OF ACTING: PHYSICAL DEMANDS
Among the many skills involved in becoming a performer are various vocal and physical skills—speaking clearly and distinctly, "projecting" the voice into the auditorium, moving gracefully, and meeting a variety of physical challenges, including sword fights, such as the one shown here. The scene is from a production of Tony Kushner's adaptation of Pierre Corneille's *The Illusion,* at A Noise Within Theatre in Pasadena, CA. (Craig Schwartz)

There are, of course, many other teachers and professional schools of acting. For example, Chicago's Steppenwolf Theatre offers acting training, emphasizing their "Chicago style" of realistic performance. The important thing for students of acting is to explore different methods of and approaches to acting, such as those outlined earlier, and decide which techniques and types of training—or which combination of these—work best for them. Ultimately each individual actor must develop his or her own methodology.

Diversity and Inclusion in Acting Training   As can be seen from our previous review of actor training, most of the methods discussed are based on European and American models with the marginalization of diverse voices and approaches in preparing actors. While some Asian techniques have been incorporated in Western actor training, performers of color have pointed out that most acting training does not recognize their unique backgrounds and cultural experiences.

Inspired by the Black Lives Matter movement, a group of BIPOC (Black, indigenous, and People of Color) theatre artists authored a document entitled "We See You, White America" in which they called for changes in the methods and materials of actor training that recognize the diverse background of those studying.

The best-selling *Black Acting Methods: Critical Approaches* (2016) by Sharrell D. Luckett and Tia M. Shaffer outsold works by Stanislavski and Uta Hagen in its first year of publication. *Black Acting Methods* includes essays by actors, directors, and teachers of color who focus on Afrocentric, rather than Eurocentric, approaches to performance training.

In 2017, Sherrill Lockett founded the Black Acting Methods Studio which centers on the backgrounds of its students of color as the key issue in their training. The Studio refers to this as the Lockett Paradigm. The Black Acting Methods Studio offers master classes, talks, and residencies for higher education institutions, one-on-one coaching, and an online virtual university, which was particularly significant during the COVID-19 pandemic shutdown.

There are also other African American theatre artists with well-known training programs, including Susan Batson, an actor, director, and playwright, who established the Black Nexus studio in Los Angeles and New York and which is now The Susan Batson Studio. In addition, many of the long-standing acting schools recognized their need to further diversify their faculties for greater inclusion. For example, the H-B Studios, founded in 1945 by Uta Hagen and director Herbert Berghof, added African American actor Keith David and the Cuban born playwright Eduardo Machado to its faculty in recent years.

Physical Acting: Voice and Body

We have been looking at training that helps actors make stage characters truthful and believable. We turn now to a second aspect of actor training: the instruments of the performer, specifically the voice and the body.

Physical elements have always been important in the art of acting. Traditional theatre makes strong demands on the performer's body. In Shakespeare, for instance, performers must frequently run up and down steps or ramps, confront other characters in sword fights, and enact prolonged death scenes. Anyone who has seen an impressive sword fight onstage senses how difficult it must be. A duel, in which the

IN FOCUS: THE PROFESSION OF ACTING AND TECHNOLOGY

The profession of the actor has been affected in very unique ways by the development of technology. *Backstage*, an online and print magazine that provides information for those working in theatre, film, and other media, published an article entitled "How Has Technology Changed Your Acting Career?"[5] The actors' responses were intriguing and suggest ongoing changes to the profession of the actor.

Many pointed to the ability to access casting sites online from wherever they are living or performing, on any mobile device, in order to request auditions for theatre productions, films, and television series. The opportunity to audition via Skype or FaceTime without having to change geographical location allows the actor to be engaged with the global theatre and media industries. One multilingual performer noted that she was able to act in a production in France while searching for casting opportunities in Los Angeles.

Resumes and headshots can be photoshopped and digitally manipulated so that an actor can, for example, be seen in different costumes or against various backgrounds. These can now be e-mailed or accessed through a performer's website. (Many theatre artists maintain websites that contain links to resumes, photos, and videos.)

Actors may create YouTube presentations of auditions and past performances that can be accessed electronically. Casting directors sometimes check an actor's Instagram account for examples of their work. Also, some casting directors might be influenced by the number of followers a performer has on social media, particularly when trying to cast a show that will appeal to a specific audience demographic. The musical *Mean Girls* cast a replacement actor in 2019 based on that performer's large Instagram following.

Actors can also communicate with their fans through Facebook and Instagram accounts as well as Twitter accounts. (Stars, of course, have staff who sometimes oversee those accounts.)

Even preparing for an audition has changed. There are apps that help actors find auditions and keep track of their upcoming auditions. Actors can "run their lines" for a monologue with online audio programs and apps. There is an app that can connect you online to a last-minute rehearsal partner. Actors can "run their lines" for a monologue with online audio programs and apps. Accents and dialects can be Googled and found on the Web. There are digital musical rehearsal apps that allow musical theatre performers to hear and learn their parts via their smartphone, tablet, or computer. And actors can self-tape an audition using an app without having to deal with any technical issues.

A few theorists and theatre artists have even suggested that actors could be replaced by technology, using 3D images or other digitally created representations. An extreme example is the music-theatre production by German composer Heiner Goebbels, *Stifter's Things* (2008), in which five upside-down, remotely controlled grand pianos that performed and even moved threateningly toward the audience on runners were the only "actors." The production combined light, sound, and recorded text. The question, of course, remains: Is this a unique concert, is it an art installation, or is it theatre without actors?

Still, as one of the actors in the *Backstage* article emphasized, once rehearsals and performances begin, the work of the actor, in most instances, is still "old fashioned" or traditional. Even with all the technology surrounding the actor in the rehearsal room and on stage, the human dynamic between the live actor and the audience is indispensable in any kind of traditional theatre and that is why theatre has survived.

---

combatants strike quickly at one another—clashing swords continually without hitting each other—resembles a ballet in its precision and grace, and it entails a great deal of physical exertion. Adept physical movement is also required in modern realistic acting. For example, an activity in a modern play analogous to a sword fight would be a headlong fall down a flight of stairs or two people engaged in a knife fight, like the one in Arthur Miller's *A View from the Bridge*.

PERFORMING IN CLASSICS TODAY
Contemporary performers in classic plays must have vocal training to be able to speak and project poetry properly; they must have the physical training necessary to engage in sword fights and other activities; and they must be familiar with the historical eras of the playwrights and of the texts they are to perform. Here we see Stephen Fry as Malvolio and Mark Rylance as Olivia in Shakespeare's *Twelfth Night*, in a Shakespeare's Globe production with an all-male cast directed by Tim Carroll. (Geraint Lewis/Alamy Stock Photo)

As to the importance of voice training, because of microphones and sound amplifications, today we have increasingly lost our appreciation of the power of the human voice. But in the past, public speakers from Cicero to Abraham Lincoln stirred people with their oratory; and throughout its history, the stage has provided a natural platform for stirring speeches. Beginning with the Greeks and continuing through the Elizabethans, the French and Spanish theatres of the seventeenth century, and other European theatres at the close of the nineteenth century, playwrights wrote magnificent lines that performers, having honed their vocal skills to a fine point, delivered with zest. Any performer today who intends to act in a revival of a traditional play must learn to speak and project stage verse, which requires much the same kind of vocal power and breathe control as opera.

In order to develop projection and balance it with credibility, a performer must train and rehearse extensively. For example, that performer might use breathing exercises, controlling the breath from the diaphragm rather than the throat so that vocal reproduction will have power and can be sustained. Many of these exercises are similar to those used by singers. Also, head, neck, and shoulder exercises can be used to relax the muscles in those areas, thus freeing the throat for ease of projection. In the nearby chart we see a group of elementary vocal and body exercises. It must be stressed that these are basic exercises that represent only the earliest beginnings of a true regimen of exercises for the voice and body.

The Actor's Instrument: Voice and Body Throughout the twentieth century, at the same time that many acting teachers were focusing on the inner life of the actor, another group of teachers and theoreticians were turning to a different aspect, the physical side of performing. This includes the freeing and development of the voice and body and combining these with improvisation to create maximum flexibility, relaxation, and imagination in the actor's instrument—his or her voice and body.

Chapter 4 *Acting for the Stage*

IN FOCUS: WARM-UP EXERCISES FOR BODY AND VOICE

To give an indication of the types of exercises performers must undertake during their years of training—and during their careers as professionals—it is interesting to look at some samples of warm-up exercises. The exercises here are designed to relax the body and the voice. The following are typical warm-up exercises for *body* movement:

1. Lie on your back; beginning with the feet, tense and relax each part of the body—knees, thighs, abdomen, chest, neck—moving up to the face. Note the difference in the relaxation of various muscles and of the body generally after the exercise is completed.
2. Stand with feet parallel, approximately as far apart as the width of the shoulders. Lift one foot off the ground and loosen all the joints in the foot, ankle, and knee. Repeat with the other foot off the ground. Put the feet down and move to the hip, spine, arms, neck, etc., loosening all joints.
3. Stand with feet parallel. Allow all tension to drain out of the body through the feet. In the process, bend the knees, straighten the pelvis, and release the lower back.
4. Begin walking in a circle; walk on the outside of the feet, then on the inside, then on the toes, and then on the heels. Notice what this does to the rest of the body. Try changing other parts of the body in a similar fashion and observe the effect on feelings and reactions.
5. Imagine the body filled with either helium or lead. Notice the effect of each of these sensations, both while standing in place and while walking. Do the same with one body part at a time—each arm, each leg, the head, etc.

The following *vocal* exercises free the throat and vocal cords:

1. Standing, begin a lazy, unhurried stretch. Reach with your arms to the ceiling, meanwhile lengthening and widening the whole of your back. Yawn as you take in a deep breath and hum on an exhalation. Release your torso so that it rests down toward your legs. Yawn on another deep breath and hum on an exhalation. On an inhalation, roll up the spine until you are standing with your arms at your sides. Look at something on the ceiling and then at something on the floor; then let your head return to a balance point, so that the neck and shoulder muscles are relaxed.
2. Put your hands on your ribs, take a deep breath, and hum a short tune. Repeat several times. Hum an *m* or *n* up and down the scale. Drop your arms; lift the shoulders an inch and drop them, releasing all tension.
3. Take a deep breath and with the palm of your hand push gently down on your stomach as you exhale. Do this several times. Exhale on sighs and then on vowels.
4. Standing, yawn with your throat and mouth open and be aware of vibrations in the front of your mouth, just behind your front teeth, as you vocalize on the vowels *ee, ei,* and *o*. Take these up and down the scales. Sing a simple song and then say it, and see if you have just as much vibration in your mouth when you are speaking as when you are singing.
5. Using a light, quick tempo, shift to a tongue twister (such as *Peter Piper picked a peck of pickled peppers*). Feel a lively touch of the tongue on the gum ridge on the *t*'s and *d*'s, and a bounce of the back of the tongue on the *k*'s and *g*'s. Feel the bouncing action on the lips on the *p*'s and *b*'s.

Source: Courtesy of Professor John Sipes of University of Tennessee-Knoxville and Emeritus Professor Barbara F. Acker of Arizona State University.

A number of key figures contributed to this movement. For example, in the second and third decades of the twentieth century, the Russian director Vsevolod Meyerhold (1874–1942) developed a program called *biomechanics* that emphasized physical exercises and full control of the body, in the manner of circus performers such as acrobats and trapeze artists. In France in the 1920s, Jacques Copeau (1878–1949) incorporated such disciplines as mime, masks, Italian commedia dell'arte, and Asian acting into his

THE FORMAL GESTURES OF ASIAN THEATRE

In most Asian theatre, acting requires careful, precise, formal gestures. The first example here is a scene from *Journey to the West*, a piece from Beijing (or Peking) opera in China (top). The second example is an actor in a performance of traditional Kathakali dance-theatre in India (bottom). Note the poses, the physical requirements, and the dexterity that are required, as well as the elaborate costumes, heavy makeup, and striking headpieces.
(top: Tianchun Zhu/TAO Images Limited/Alamy Stock Photo; bottom: lakhesis/123RF)

system of training. Beginning in mid-century and continuing for the next fifty years, Jacques Lecoq (1921–1999) ran an influential school in Paris dedicated to explaining and exploring the physical side of performance. In addition to emphasizing the elements on which Copeau concentrated, Lecoq incorporated a clown figure in his work.

ACTING TRAINING FROM OTHER DISCIPLINES
Actors' training today often involves exercises and other activities from related disciplines such as circus routines, juggling, acrobatics, and Asian martial arts. A good example is tai chi, a refined form of martial arts from China, here being practiced in a park. (Inge King)

Along with European influences, there has also been a strong global presence in the new approaches to actor training. A good example is Asian theatre. Stylization and symbolism characterize the acting of the classical theatres of India, China, and Japan. To achieve the absolute control, the concentration, and the mastery of the body and nerves necessary to carry out the stylized movements, performers in the various classical Asian theatres train for years under the supervision of master teachers. Every movement of these performers is prescribed and carefully controlled, combining elements of formal ballet, pantomime, and sign language. Each gesture tells a story and means something quite specific—contributing to a true symbolism of physical movement.

One Asian discipline, not from theatre but from martial arts, which modern acting teachers have found helpful is *tai chi chuan*, commonly called *tai chi*. Unlike some martial arts, tai chi is not aggressive: it is a graceful, gentle exercise regimen performed widely in China. It has spread to other countries, where it is sometimes practiced in conjunction with meditation or body awareness. The movements of tai chi are stylized and often seem to be carried out in slow motion. Among other things, tai chi requires concentration and control, both valuable qualities for a performer. The Japanese director Tadashi Suzuki (b. 1939) developed a training technique, again taken from classical Japanese practices, emphasizing the connection between the feet and the ground underneath. Consciousness of this connection is accomplished by exercises involving "stomping."

An approach to training that originated in the United States and has gained acceptance and wider use in our contemporary theatre is known as *viewpoints*. Based on ideas from the avant-garde choreographer Merce Cunningham (1919–2009) and the experimental director Jerzy Grotowski (1933–1999), it combines elements of dance and stage movement with concepts of time and space. The director Anne Bogart (b. 1951), one of its chief proponents, feels that viewpoints theory provides a new vocabulary for certain elements that have always been significant in performance: spatial relationships onstage, movement, and the notion of time, among others.

In the United States in the twenty-first century the emphasis on physical movement—training in the use of the voice and the body—has become more pronounced and widespread than ever. In the words of author David Bridel in an article in *American Theatre* magazine:

> Body awareness and alignment, mask work, clowning and circus skills, physical characterization, spatial relationships, ensemble work, improvisation, games, mime . . . so many forms of movement training exist today, and so many specialists work in these related fields, that the opportunity to connect the craft of acting with the movement of the body has never been richer.[6]

TRAINING FOR MUSICAL THEATRE
Along with the classics and various types of theatre from other nations, the American musical, with its physical and vocal demands, requires extensive training. A prime example is the exuberant dancing by the men in the Broadway musical *Newsies*, choreographed by Christopher Gattelli, directed by Jeff Calhoun, with music by Alan Menken and lyrics by Jack Feldman. (Sara Krulwich/The New York Times/Redux)

Today, no one approach, no one master, no one technique appears to have become universally recognized as the single authority in the field. For that matter, the belief that actors need to study many of these approaches was underscored in a 2015 *Backstage* article, "7 Movement Techniques All Actors Should Study." Rather, teachers, coaches, and directors draw on a wide variety of sources, including those mentioned earlier as well as others, to develop their individual approaches to training the voice and body. The field also goes by various names: body movement, physical theatre, and a term favored by many, *physical acting.*

As a way of integrating and unifying various approaches to body and voice training, many acting teachers emphasize a process called *centering.* This is a way of pulling everything together and allowing the performer to eliminate any blocks that impede either the body or the voice. *Centering* involves locating the place—roughly in the middle of the torso—where all the lines of force in the body come together. When performers are able to "center" themselves, they achieve a balance, a freedom, and a flexibility they could rarely find otherwise.

All this should make it clear that to master the many techniques required to play a variety of roles and to be at ease onstage—moving and speaking with authority, purpose, and conviction—performers must undergo arduous training and be genuinely dedicated to their profession.

PLAYING YOUR PART: EXPERIENCING THEATRE

1. Read a speech from Shakespeare aloud in class or to yourself. Why would this speech be difficult for an actor? What are some of the challenges an actor would face in bringing this speech to life?
2. Remember a situation recently that made you happy. Re-create the circumstances in your mind. Where were you? Whom were you with? Can you once again feel the emotions you felt during that situation? Is this similar to an acting exercise developed by Stanislavski?
3. Make a fist. Now make it tighter and tighter. Does it change how you are feeling emotionally? Does this help you understand how an actor might approach developing an emotional moment in a play physically?
4. Analyze why you felt a recent film performance was successful. Describe how the main performer brought his or her character to life.
5. Attend a rehearsal at your university or community theatre. Then attend the final performance. What changes were made between the rehearsal and the performance by one of the actors in the production? Explain how the change affected the performance.

Training for Special Forms of Theatre Certain types of theatre and theatre events require special discipline or training. For example, musical theatre obviously requires talent in singing and dancing. Coordination is also important in musical theatre: the members of a chorus must frequently sing and dance in unison. Pantomime is another demanding category of performance: without words or props, a performer must indicate everything by physical suggestion, convincingly lifting an imaginary box or walking against an imaginary wind.

Various forms of modern avant-garde and experimental theatre also require special techniques. A good example is Samuel Beckett's *Happy Days,* in which the lead character is buried onstage in a mound of earth up to her waist in the first act, and up to her neck in the second. She must carry on her performance through the entire play while virtually immobile. In some types of avant-garde theatre, the performers become acrobats, make human pyramids, or are used like pieces of furniture. In the theatres of Robert Wilson, Mabou Mines, and similar groups, the elements of story, character, and text are minimized or even eliminated. The stress, rather than being on a narrative or on exploring recognizable characters, is on the visual and ritualistic aspects of theatre, like a series of tableaux or a moving collage.

Stage movement in this approach to theatre is often closely related to dance; thus, the performers must have the same discipline, training, and control as dancers. In Wilson's work, performers are frequently called on either to move constantly or to remain perfectly still. In *A Letter to Queen Victoria,* two performers turn continuously in circles like dervishes for long periods of time—perhaps thirty or forty minutes. In other works by Wilson, performers must remain frozen like statues.

Synthesis and Integration

The demands made on performers by experimental and avant-garde theatres are only the most recent example of the rigorous, intensive training that acting generally requires. The goal of all this training—both internal and external—is to create for the performer an instrument that is flexible, resourceful, and disciplined. Above all, the actor must bring together the inner approach to acting, the work on truthfulness and believability, with the physical aspects discussed earlier. He or she must combine inner and outer into one indivisible whole. What is important to remember

THE SPECIAL DEMANDS OF ACTING
At times performing makes exceedingly strong demands, requiring performers to convey a range and depth of emotions or to transform themselves in terms of age, mood, and the like. A good example is Samuel Beckett's *Happy Days,* in which the actress playing Winnie—in this case, Fiona Shaw—must perform while buried in a mound of sand up to her waist, and later up to her neck. This production was directed by Deborah Warner at the National Theatre in London in 2006. (Robbie Jack/Corbis Entertainment/Getty Images)

is that whatever the starting point, the end result must be a synthesis of these two aspects. The inner emotions and feelings and the outer physical and vocal characteristics become one.

Only then will the character be forcefully and convincingly portrayed. This process is termed *integration.* When a performer is approaching a role in a play, the first task is to read and analyze the script. The actress or actor must discover the *superobjective* of the character being played and put together not only the *spine* of the role but the many smaller moments, each with its own objective and given circumstances. The next challenge is to begin specific work on the role. In taking this step, some performers begin with the *outer* aspects of the character—with a walk, a posture, or a peculiar vocal delivery. They get a sense of how the character looks in terms of makeup and other external characteristics, such as a mustache or hairstyle. They consider the clothes the character wears and any idiosyncrasies of speech or movement, such as a limp or a swagger. Only then will they move on to the inner aspects of the character: how the character feels; how the character reacts to people and events; what disturbs the character's emotional equilibrium; what fears, hopes, and dreams the character has.

Other performers, by contrast, begin with the *internal* aspects: with the feelings and emotions of the character. These performers delve deeply into the psyche of the character to try to understand and duplicate what the character feels inside. Only after

Chapter 4 *Acting for the Stage*

IN FOCUS: PUPPETRY AROUND THE WORLD

Puppetry in its various forms (puppets, marionettes, shadow puppets) has a long and honorable history. Remarkably, it emerged independently in widely separated parts of the world: in Indonesia, in Japan, in sections of Europe, and among Native Americans in the far northwest of what is now the United States.

In whatever form, the puppet figure is the image, reflection, and embodiment of a theatrical character and, therefore, a replacement for the actor. Puppets can run the gamut of emotions. They can be evil, demonic figures; they can be eerie, otherworldly creatures; they can be wildly comic, as in Punch and Judy shows when they biff one another across the head and knock one another down; they can be intensely human, as in the suffering characters in Japanese bunraku. In short, when puppets are onstage, audiences usually experience these silent, nonhuman characters as real people.

It should be noted as well that while puppet or marionette characters are often either comic or tragic figures, they are also frequently employed as advocates for a political point of view. The Bread and Puppet Theatre of San Francisco, founded by Peter Schuman (b. 1934), features larger-than-life, exaggerated figures made of papier-mâché. This theatre began with protests against the Vietnam War but has continued, often with the figures proceeding down city streets, in protests against all wars, including the Iraq War.

Puppet characters are created and manipulated in various ways. In Indonesia and other parts of Southeast Asia, two kinds of puppets were developed. One kind is rod puppets, so called because the movements of these puppets are controlled by rods attached to the head and limbs and operated by one or more persons from either above or below. (Though they are most often associated with Southeast Asia, rod puppets, nearly life-size, were developed as well on the island of Sicily in the Mediterranean.) The other type of puppet popular in Southeast Asia—in Java and Bali as well as Indonesia—is the shadow puppet. In this case, silhouette figures, often made of leather, are highlighted on a screen that is lit from behind.

Marionettes are puppets controlled by strings attached to the head, arms, and legs and operated from above. A unique type of puppet is the *bunraku* puppet from Japan, which will be discussed in more detail later. Originating in the late seventeenth century, it was firmly established by the eighteenth century and has continued to this day. In the early eighteenth century, one of the most famous playwrights of all time, Chikamatsu Monzaemon wrote masterful plays for *bunraku* theatre. In the case of *bunraku* figures, which today are roughly two-thirds life-size, one man operates the feet; another operates the left hand; and a third controls the face, head, and right hand.

Shown here is Christiani Pitts as Ann Darrow in the musical *King Kong* at the Broadway Theater in New York in 2018. King Kong was a one-ton, 20-foot gorilla puppet, controlled by computers and human handlers. (Sara Krulwich/The New York Times/Redux)

Probably the puppet figures most familiar to Western audiences are hand puppets, operated by a person who has one or two hands inside the puppet itself. Among the immediately recognizable hand puppets are the Muppets, featuring such popular and enduring characters as Kermit the Frog and Miss Piggy. Another example of hand puppets onstage appeared in the successful Broadway production of the musical *Avenue Q* (2003), as well as in the dark comedy *Hand to God* (2011).

More recent spectacular examples of puppetry were the horses and other animals created for the play *War Horse* (2007), as well as the gigantic ape created for the Broadway musical *King Kong* (2018). The puppet used for the great ape was the largest in Broadway history and employed ten on-stage puppeteers, computer microprocessors, and mini motors that created the creature's intricate movements and changes in facial features.

Puppetry remains, and will continue to remain, a vital art form in its own right and an important adjunct to live theatre.

UNIQUE ACTING DEMANDS OF AVANT-GARDE THEATRE
Avant-garde theatre often requires special training and techniques—acrobatics, tumbling, mime, and special control of voice and body. Here we see Michael C. Hall as Newton and Amy Lennox as Elly in David Bowie's and Enda Walsh's *Lazarus* directed by Ivo van Hove at the Kings Cross Theatre in London, England. (Robbie Jack/Corbis Entertainment/Getty Images)

doing this will they go on to develop the outer characteristics. Still other performers work on both aspects—inner and outer—simultaneously. Finally, we must realize that although a competent, well-trained performer may become a successful actress or actor, another ingredient is required in order to electrify an audience as truly memorable stage artists do. This results from intangibles—qualities that cannot be taught in acting schools—that distinguish an acceptable, accomplished actor or actress from one who ignites the stage. *Presence, charisma, personality, star quality*—these are among the terms used to describe a performer who communicates directly and kinetically with the audience. Whatever term one uses, the electricity and excitement of theatre are enhanced immeasurably by performers who possess this indefinable attribute.

EVALUATING PERFORMANCES

As observers, we study the techniques and problems of acting so that we will be able to understand and evaluate the performances we see. If a performer is unconvincing in a part, we know that he or she has not mastered a technique for truthful acting. We recognize that a performer who moves awkwardly or cannot be heard clearly has not been properly trained in body movement or vocal projection. We learn to notice how well performers play together: whether they listen to one another and respond appropriately. We also observe how well performers establish and maintain contact with the audience.

There are, therefore, some key questions we may ask ourselves about the acting in a production:

1. Were the performers believable, given the requirements of the play? If they were believable, how did they seem to accomplish this? If they were not believable, what occurred to impair or destroy their believability?
2. Identify the performers you considered most successful. Citing specifics from the production, note what they did well: particular gestures, lines, or moments. For example, how did the performer's voice sound? How did she or he interpret the role?
3. If there were performers you did not like, identify them and explain why you did not like them. Give concrete examples to explain why their performances were

IN FOCUS: ACTING IN FILM AND TELEVISION

Acting for film and television can be quite different from acting for the stage because of technical issues. One of the most significant differences between acting for stage versus acting for the electronic media is that because the camera can get extremely close to the actor, actors on film must use more subtle, controlled, and natural expressions and gestures. Emotional reactions cannot be too large.

Film and television actors do not have to worry about projecting their voices into a theatre space. In the theatre, while actors, as we noted, strive to be realistic, they must still project physically and vocally to the entire audience, requiring them to be, especially in larger spaces, somewhat bigger than real life.

Theatre actors must strive to get their performances right each night. They must know their lines, their entrances and cues, and be able to create the needed emotions on stage at each specific moment. Film and television actors can do multiple "takes" of a scene until the director feels it is right. Mistakes can be fixed. In addition, scenes are not shot in the order that they are written so film and television actors, unlike stage actors, are not building their characters through the actual sequence of events in the storyline. But film and television actors have much less rehearsal time than stage actors, so they must be prepared to immediately film their scenes.

While many film and television actors work in the theatre and vice versa, there are others who do not and, in some instances, because of the unique performance demands of each form are unable to.

---

less successful. (As you discuss this, be sure to separate the performer from the role. For example, you can dislike a character but admire the performance.)

4. Acting is more than a collection of individual performances. The entire company needs to work as a unit (as noted earlier, this is sometimes called ensemble): each member of the cast must not only perform her or his own role but also support the other performers. Discuss how the performers related or failed to relate to one another. Did they listen to each other and respond? Did anyone seem to be "showing off" and ignoring the others?

Before leaving the subject of the performer, we should note that actors and actresses have always held a fascination for audiences. In some cases this is because they portray larger-than-life characters; it can also result from the exceptional talent

PLAYING YOUR PART: THINKING ABOUT THEATRE

1. What is the most convincing performance you've seen, where you felt the actor on stage was really the person being portrayed? What was it about the performance that made it believable? In contrast, what was the least convincing and effective performance you have seen? Explain why this was so.

2. In Shakespearean and other classic plays, the actors often speak in verse. In what way are the various vocal techniques described in this chapter important to actors in preparing to play a role in this kind of play and in the performance itself?

3. Identify a scene in a play in which two, three, or four actors are locked in conflict. What can individual actors do to hold the attention of the audience and make their actions and feelings convincing? How do you think these actors can best prepare for conflict scenes?

4. Read either *Miss Julie* or *A Doll's House*, both of which are available online. What kinds of background information would the actors in these plays need to know? What are the physical attributes actors would need to create for some of the key characters? Choose one scene and one character and discuss what is motivating the character. How might you employ some of Stanislavski's concepts in order to bring the character to life?

NOTE: *A Doll's House* is also available in *Anthology of Living Theatre*, Third Edition, by Edwin Wilson and Alvin Goldfarb.

they bring to their performances. Also, of course, some performers have personal charisma or appeal. Theatre audiences have often responded to stars onstage in the same way that people tend to respond to a rock star or a film star. There is something in these personalities that audiences find immensely attractive or intriguing. Moreover, the personal lives of actors are often of great interest to the public, and some people find it difficult to separate a stage character from the offstage woman or man.

SUMMARY

1. All human beings engage in certain forms of acting; imitation and role playing are excellent examples of acting in everyday life.
2. Acting onstage differs from acting in everyday life, for several reasons—including the fact that a stage actor or actress is always being observed by an audience and the fact that acting for the stage involves playing roles with which the performer may have no direct experience in life.
3. Historically, stage performances have required exceptional physical and vocal skills: the ability to move with agility and grace and to engage in such actions as sword fights and death scenes; the ability to deal with poetic devices (meter, imagery, alliteration, etc.); the skill to project the voice to the farthest reaches of the theatre space.
4. Acting is a difficult, demanding profession. Despite its glamour, it calls for arduous training and preparation. Looking at what is called for in a role like Hamlet gives some idea of the challenges involved.
5. From the end of the nineteenth century to the present day, many plays have been written in a very realistic, lifelike style. The characters in these plays resemble ordinary people in their dialogue, behavior, etc. Presenting them requires that performers make the characters they portray believable and convincing.
6. A Russian director, Konstantin Stanislavski, developed a system or method of acting to enable performers to believe in the "truth" of what they say and do. His suggestions included applying techniques of relaxation and concentration; dealing with specific objects and feelings (a handkerchief, a glass of water, etc.); using the power of fantasy or imagination (the "magic if") to achieve a sense of inner truth in a role; using psychophysical action; developing a *spine,* or *through line,* which runs through a role from the beginning to the end of a play; and playing together as an ensemble.
7. In the later stages of his work on actor training, Stanislavski moved from an emphasis on internal elements to more external ones—to what he called *psychophysical action.* Rather than emotion leading to action, he suggested that action leads to emotion.
8. Exercises and tasks have been developed to train performers. These include numerous physical and vocal exercises and techniques taken from other disciplines such as tai chi and the circus. "Centering" is often emphasized as a part of body and voice training.
9. Avant-garde theatre and some other theatres make additional demands on the performer with regard to voice and body training. The voice is sometimes used to emit odd sounds—screams, grunts, and the like. The body must perform feats of acrobatics and gymnastics.
10. The end result must be a synthesis or integration of the inner and outer aspects of acting.
11. Audience members should familiarize themselves with the problems and techniques of acting in order to judge performances properly.

Design Elements: Audience Sitting in Theatre (theatre): Ron Chapple/Photodisc/Getty Images; Studio Light (spotlights): Exactostock/SuperStock

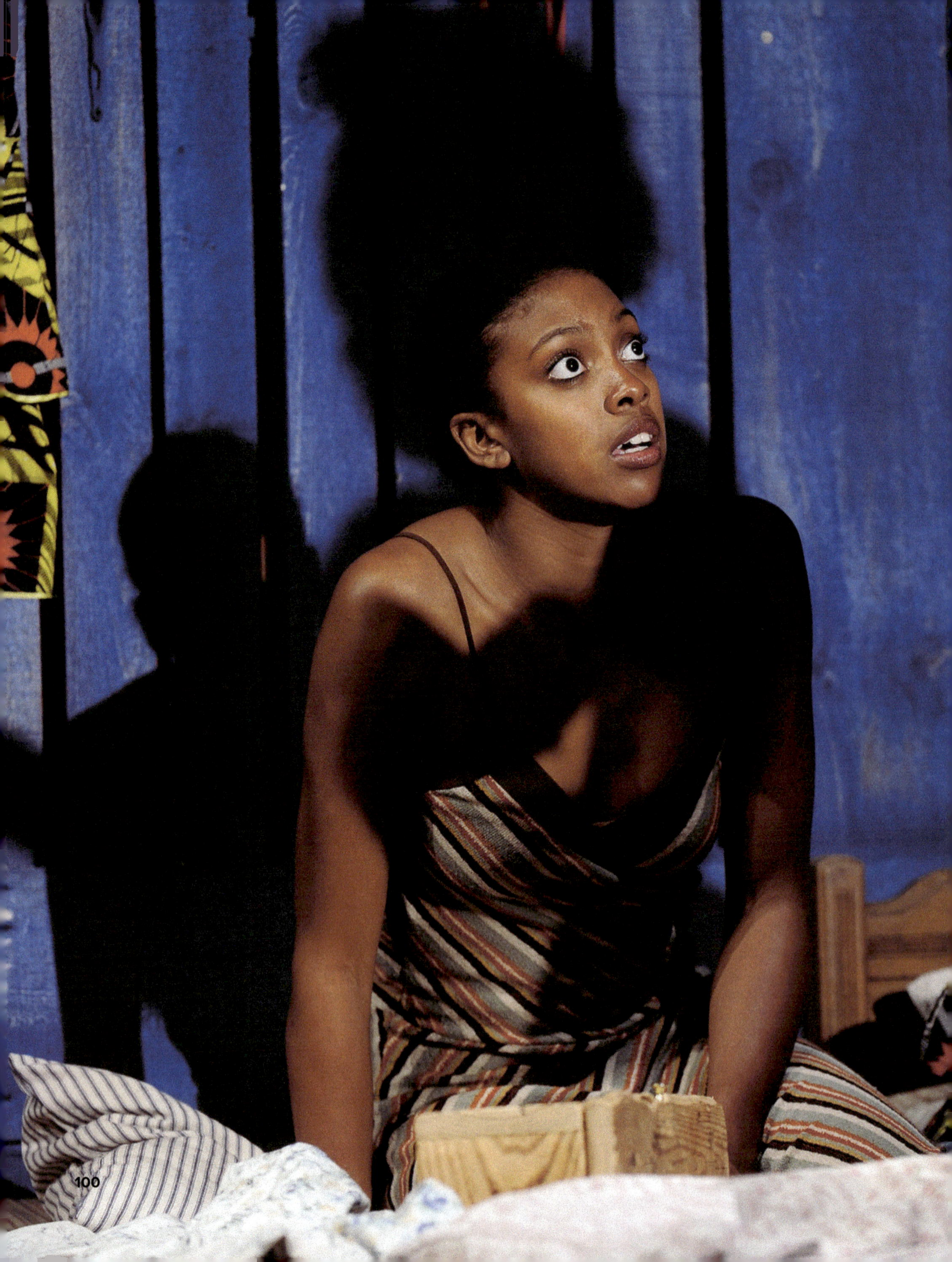

5

The Director and the Producer

When we see a theatre performance, our most immediate connection is with the actresses and actors onstage. We begin to identify with the characters they play and absorb the situations in which they find themselves. Behind the performances, however, is the work of another creative person—the ***director.*** The director, with the support of the stage manager, rehearses the performers and coordinates their work with that of others, such as the designers, to make certain the event is performed appropriately, intelligently, and excitingly. The director oversees all of the choices made for a production in order to create a unified whole under a unified vision. In this chapter, we will look at the role of the director and also at the role of the producer or manager—the person who is responsible for the management and business aspects of theatre.

director In American usage, the person responsible for the overall unity of a production and for coordinating the work of contributing artists. The American director is the equivalent of the British producer and the French *metteur-en-scène* ("meh-TURR ahn SENN").

THE THEATRE DIRECTOR

The director is the person who works most closely with performers in the theatre, guiding them in shaping their performances. When a new play is being presented, the director also works closely with the playwright. The director is responsible, as well, for coordinating other aspects of the production, such as the work of the scene, costume, lighting, and sound designers. The stage manager communicates the breadth of the director's conceptual vision daily with every production area to clarify ongoing production and rehearsal choices.

For many of us, as audience members, the director's work on a production is one of the least obvious components. Other elements, such as performers, scenery, and costumes, are onstage and immediately visible to us, and the words of the playwright are heard throughout the performance. But we are often not aware that the way performers speak and move, the way the scenery looks, and the way the lights change colors and intensity often originate with the director. After the playwright,

◀ **THE DIRECTOR SHAPES A PRODUCTION**

The director of a production works closely with the cast and the designers (scenic, costumes, lighting, and sound). The director gives shape to the arc of the play or musical and determines its style, pace, and the way the actors create their characters and interact with one another. If the production is a new play or musical, the director also collaborates with the playwright, lyricist, and composer. Seen here is Condola Phylea Rashad in the play Ruined, *produced by the Goodman Theatre of Chicago and the Manhattan Theatre Club. The play was directed by Kate Whoriskey, who has served as director of over twenty-five major plays in important regional theatres across the United States. (Liz Lauren/Richard Hein)*

the director is usually the first person to become involved in the creative process of a production, and the choices made by the director at every step along the way have a great deal to do with determining whether the ultimate experience will be satisfactory for us, the members of the audience.

While the playwright incorporates a point of view toward the material dramatized in a script—it may be, for example, a tragedy, a melodrama, or a comedy—it is crucial for the director to understand this point of view and translate it into terms relevant to the production. The director must then make both the playwright's and their point of view clear to the performers, designers, and other artists and technicians involved. Although they work together, these artists and technicians must out of necessity work on segments of the production rather than the entire enterprise. During rehearsals, for instance, the performers are much too busy working on their own roles and their interactions with each other to worry much about scenery. To take another example, a performer who appears only in the first act of a two-act play has no control over what happens in the second act. The one person who does have an overall perspective is the director. The person who aids in communicating this perspective to everyone involved on a continuing basis is the production stage manager, the only other member of the production team to experience the entire rehearsal process with the director.

Directors get their training in a variety of ways. Many of them begin as performers and find that they have a talent for working with other people and for coordinating the work of designers as well as performers. Others train in the many academic institutions that have specific programs for directors. These include large universities with theatre as part of a liberal arts focus, as well as special conservatories and institutes.

THE TRADITIONAL DIRECTOR

In this chapter we will look at three approaches to directing: traditional, auteur, and postmodern. We begin with the traditional approach, which might also be called a text-based method. The starting point, or the foundation, of the traditional director's work is the script. It might be a well-known play by Shakespeare, Ibsen, or Strindberg or a more recent work, such as one by Lorraine Hansberry, August Wilson, or Sarah Ruhl. The play might also be a new script by a very young or emerging playwright.

The Director and the Script

For the most part, we experience theatre as a unified event. But as pointed out before, theatre is a complex art involving not one or two elements but many simultaneously: script, performance, costumes, scenery, lighting, and point of view. These diverse elements—a mixture of the tangible and intangible—must be brought together into an organic whole, and that is the responsibility of the director.

Choosing a Script Frequently, the director chooses the script to be produced. Generally it is a play to which the director is attracted or for which that theatre artist feels a special affinity. If the director does not actually choose the script but is asked to direct it by a playwright or a producer, they must still understand and appreciate the material. The director's attraction to the script and basic understanding of it are important in launching a production. Once the script is chosen, the actual work on the production begins.

If the play is new and has never been tested in production, the director may see problems in the script, which must be corrected before rehearsals begin. The director will have a series of meetings with the playwright to iron out the difficulties ahead of time. The director may feel, for example, that the leading character is not clearly defined or that a clash of personalities between two characters never reaches a climax. If the playwright agrees with the director's assessment, the author will revise the manuscript. Generally there is considerable give-and-take between the director and the playwright in these preliminary sessions, as well as during the rehearsal period. The stage manager must maintain well-organized rehearsal documentation of possible script revisions for the playwright and director to discuss outside rehearsals. Ideally, there should be a spirit of cooperation, compromise, and mutual respect in this relationship.

Once the script is selected, the director begins analyzing it and preparing a production. There is no one way a director should go about this: Individual directors adopt their own personal approach. One method of undertaking this task was suggested by the work of the Russian director Konstantin Stanislavski. In this case, an initial step is to determine the *spine* of the play.

The "Spine" of the Play

The spine of the drama, also referred to as the *main action,* is determined by the goal, or the primary objective, of the characters in the play, both collectively and individually. There is nothing magical about the spine: It is a working hypothesis that gives directors a foundation and a through line on which to base their analysis and their work with the actors.

Finding a spine for a play allows the director to understand the action and provides a nerve center from which to develop it. Different directors may find different spines for the same play. With *Hamlet,* for instance, several spines are possible: Much will depend on the period in which the play is produced and on the point of view of the individual director. One spine could be simple revenge; another could be Hamlet's attempt to resolve his inner conflicts; still another could be Hamlet's attempt to locate and expose the duplicity and corruption he senses in Denmark. Such varied interpretations are to be expected and are acceptable as long as the spine chosen remains true to the spirit and action of the play.

spine Also known as *main action,* the spine is determined by the goal or primary objective of all the characters in a play, both collectively and individually.

The Style of the Production

Once a spine has been found, a second task for a director is to find the *style* in which the play is to be presented. The concept of style in a theatrical production is difficult to explain. It means the *way* a play is presented. When we speak of a "casual style" of clothing, we mean that the clothing is loose and informal; when we speak of a "1960s" style, we mean that it has the look and feel of clothing worn in that time period. In theatre, one way to consider style is in terms of realism and nonrealism, or as noted elsewhere, sometimes referred to as departures from realism. These two types can also be further subdivided.

For example, there are several types of realism. At one extreme is **naturalism,** a kind of superrealism. The term *naturalism* was originated by several nineteenth-century French writers who wanted a theatre that would show human beings—often in wretched circumstances—as products of heredity and environment. In addition to

naturalism Attempts to put onstage exact copies of everyday life; sometimes also called slice-of-life drama.

ALLEGORY

The medieval morality play *Everyman* is an excellent example of an allegory, with the title character representing all humankind. In an allegory, characters personify ideas or otherworldly characters in order to illustrate an intellectual or moral lesson. Shown here is a rehearsal for *Everyman* with performers Brigitte Grothum, Georg Preusse (in the title role), and Debora Weigert at the Berliner Dom in Berlin. (Clemens Bilan/Getty Images)

heightened realism Also known as selective realism, refers to plays in which characters and their actions resemble real life but a certain license is allowed for other elements in the play.

this special use, the term *naturalism* refers more broadly to attempts to put onstage as exact a copy of life as possible, down to the smallest detail. In a naturalistic stage set of a kitchen, for instance, a performer can actually cook a meal on the stove, the toaster makes toast, the faucet produces water, and the light in the refrigerator goes on when the door opens. Characters speak and act as if they had been caught unobserved by a sound camera. In this sense, naturalism is supposed to resemble a documentary film. Naturalism is sometimes called *slice-of-life* drama, suggesting that a section has been taken from life and transferred to the stage.

At the other extreme of realism is **heightened realism,** sometimes referred to as *selective realism.* Here the characters and their activities are intended to resemble life, but a certain license is allowed. The scenery, for example, might be skeletal—that is, incomplete and in outline—although the words and actions of the characters are realistic. Or perhaps a character is allowed a modern version of a soliloquy in an otherwise realistic play. All art calls for selectivity, and heightened realism recognizes the necessity for the artist to make choices and to inject creativity into the process. *Realism* itself occupies the middle ground between naturalism and heightened, or selective, realism, but when it is used as a broad umbrella term, it includes the extremes at each end.

Nonrealism, or departures from realism, can also be divided into types, which might include such forms as fantasy, poetic drama, musical theatre, absurdist theatre, and symbolism. Examples of two well-known types of nonrealism are *allegory* and *expressionism.*

Allegory is the representation of an abstract theme or subject through symbolic characters, actions, or other elements of a production, such as scenery. Good examples are the medieval morality plays, in which characters personify ideas in order to teach an intellectual or moral lesson. In *Everyman,* performers play parts with names such as Good Deeds, Fellowship, and Worldly Goods. In less direct forms of allegory, a relatively realistic story serves as a parable or lesson. *The Crucible* by Arthur Miller is about the witch hunts in Salem, Massachusetts, in the late seventeenth century; but it can also be regarded as dealing with specific investigations into communism by the U.S. Congress in the early 1950s that Miller and others considered modern "witch hunts."

Expressionism was at its height in art, literature, and theatre during the first quarter of the twentieth century, but traces of it are still found today, and contemporary plays using its techniques are called *expressionistic.* In simple terms, expressionism gives outward expression to inner feelings. In Elmer Rice's *The Adding Machine,* when the main character, Mr. Zero, is fired from his job, his feelings are conveyed by having the room spin around in a circle amid a cacophony of shrill sounds, such as loud sirens and whistles.

Deciding on a directorial style for a production involves giving a signature and an imprint to the entire production: the look of the scenery and lights and the way performers speak and handle their costumes and props. It also involves the rhythm and pace at which the play moves, a subject that is taken up later. When a director arrives at a style for a production, two things are essential: (1) the style should be appropriate for the play and (2) it should be consistent throughout every aspect of the production.

The Directorial Concept One way for the director to embody the spine in a production and to implement style is to develop a ***directorial concept.*** Such a concept derives from a controlling idea, vision, or point of view that the director feels is appropriate to the play. The concept should also create a unified theatrical experience for those of us in the audience.

Concept and period. To indicate what is involved for the director in developing a concept, let us begin with period and location. Take, for instance, Shakespeare's play *The Tempest*. It is set on a faraway, remote island, and an air of mystery is present throughout the play. One director might take a traditional approach and present it as it might have been performed in Shakespeare's day, with appropriate costumes and scenery. Another director might wish to set it in modern times on a secluded island in the Caribbean, with scenery and costumes reflecting a decidedly modern, Latin feeling, including calypso and other native music. A third director might take a *Star Wars* approach, placing the action at some future period in a fictional universe. In this case, performers arrive and depart by intergalactic rocket ships and wear futuristic space outfits. This kind of transposition has been carried out frequently with Greek plays, Elizabethan plays, seventeenth-century French plays, and other dramatic classics.

allegory Symbolic representation of abstract themes through characters, action, and other concrete elements of a play.

expressionism The attempt in drama to depict the subjective state of a character or group of characters through such nonrealistic techniques as distortion, striking images, and poetic language.

directorial concept The controlling idea, vision, or point of view that the director feels is appropriate for the play; it should create a unified theatrical experience for the audience.

IN FOCUS: THE EVOLUTION OF THE DIRECTOR

It is sometimes argued that the theatre director did not exist before 1874, when a German nobleman, George II (1826–1914), duke of Saxe-Meiningen, began to supervise every element of the productions in his theatre—rehearsals, scenic elements, and other aspects, which he coordinated into an integrated whole. It is true that Saxe-Meiningen was one of the first people to emerge as a separate, indispensable member of the theatrical team. Although the title may have been new, however, the *function* of the director had always been present in one way or another, usually in the person of a playwright or an actor.

We know, for example, that the Greek playwright Aeschylus directed his own plays and that the chorus in a Greek play would rehearse under the supervision of a leader for many weeks before a performance. At various times in theatre history, the leading performer or playwright of a company served as a director, though without the title. The French dramatist Molière, for instance, not only was the playwright and the chief actor of his company but also functioned as the director. In Molière's short play *The Impromptu of Versailles* he made clear his definite ideas about the way actors and actresses should perform—no doubt the same advice he offered to performers in his company when rehearsing other plays.

When Hamlet gives instructions and advice to the players who perform the play-within-the-play in *Hamlet,* he is functioning as a director. In England after the time of Shakespeare—from the seventeenth to nineteenth centuries—there was a long line of *actor-managers* who gave strong leadership to individual theatre companies and performed many of the functions of a director, although they were still not given that title. Among the most famous were Thomas Betterton (1635–1710), David Garrick (1717–1779), Charles Kemble (1775–1854), William Charles Macready (1793–1873), and Henry Irving (1838–1905).

Toward the end of the nineteenth century the term *director* came into common usage and the clearly defined role of the director was fully recognized. Perhaps significantly, the emergence of the director as a separate creative figure coincided with important changes that began to take place in society during the nineteenth century. First, there was a breakdown in established social, religious, and political concepts, resulting in part from the influence of Freud, Darwin, and Marx. Second, there was a marked increase in communication. With the advent of the telegraph, the telephone, photography, motion pictures, and—later—television, various cultures that had remained remote from or unknown to one another were suddenly made aware of each other.

The effect of these changes was to alter the monolithic, ordered view of the world that individual societies had maintained for over 2,000 years prior to that time. By the early twentieth century, societies and nations had become heterogeneous and interconnected. Previously, consistency of style in theatre had been easier to achieve. Within a given society, writers, performers, and spectators were on common ground. For example, the comedies of the English playwrights William Wycherley (1640–1716) and William Congreve (1670–1729), written at the end of the seventeenth century, were aimed at a specific audience—the elite upper class, which relished gossip, clever remarks, and well-turned phrases.

The code of social behavior in this case was well understood by performers and audiences alike, and questions of style in a production hardly arose because a common approach to style was already present in the fabric of society. The way a man took a pinch of snuff or a woman flung open her fan was so clearly delineated in daily behavior that performers had only to refine and perfect these actions for the stage. Today, however, due to the greater recognition of diversity, multiculturalism, and globalization, achieving a unity of style is much more exciting and artistically challenging and the director's task, therefore, is that much more important.

Concept and central image. Another way to implement a directorial concept is to find a *central,* or *controlling, image* or *metaphor* for a theatrical production. An example would be a production of *Hamlet* that envisioned the play in terms of a vast net or spiderweb in which Hamlet is caught. The motif of a net or spiderweb could be carried out on several levels: in the design of the stage set, in the ways the performers relate to one another, and in a host of details relating to the central

THE DIRECTORIAL CONCEPT

At times, directors create an overall image or metaphor in presenting their interpretation of a play. This can serve both to illuminate the text and to give the production unity and cohesion. Shown here are Mark Strong, Phoebe Fox, and Nicola Walker in a production of Arthur Miller's *A View from the Bridge*, at the Lyceum Theatre in New York in 2015. Director Ivo van Hove's concept was a world stripped away of material objects (costumes not connected to a specific time period, no shoes on the actors, and a minimalist set that almost seemed to be an arena) to focus on the emotional intensity of the characters and plot. (Sara Krulwich/The New York Times/Redux)

image. There might be a huge rope net hanging over the entire stage, for instance, and certain characters could play string games with their fingers. In short, the metaphor of Hamlet's being caught in a net would be emphasized and reinforced on every level.

IN FOCUS: PETER BROOK, GLOBAL DIRECTOR

The English director Peter Brook (b. 1925) presented some of the most memorable productions of the late twentieth and early twenty-first centuries, a number of which drew extensively from the theatrical traditions and source materials of many countries. His major productions include Peter Weiss's *Marat/Sade* (1964), Shakespeare's *A Midsummer Night's Dream* (1970), and his own adaptation of an Indian epic, *The Mahabharata* (1985). His best-known writings include *The Empty Space* (1968), *The Shifting Point* (1987), and *The Open Door* (1993).

As a means of escaping commercial theatre and allowing himself to address the universality of the theatrical experience, Brook founded the International Center for Theatre Research in Paris in 1970. This company was formed of actors from a variety of countries, including Algeria, Japan, England, France, America, Spain, and Portugal, with directors from Armenia, England, and Romania and a designer from Switzerland. There was much sharing of ideas and techniques, with the Japanese actor teaching daily classes in nō, for example. Brook's vision was for the actors to learn from each other and to approach a kind of universal theatrical language. A production entitled *Orghast* (1971) first allowed the company to present its experimentation with language. The text was written by Ted Hughes in an invented language influenced heavily by Latin and ancient Greek and was performed in Iran.

In 1989, Brook's continued interest in identifying a universality of language in theatre was manifest in his production of *The Mahabharata*. The source text for this play was the Indian epic of the same name, which is more than 90,000 verses long, concerns wars between the Pandavas and the Kauravas, and addresses a great number of philosophical questions. Brook's production of this epic text originally took place at the Avignon Festival in France and took a full nine hours to perform. The source text was Indian, the director English, the theatre company French, the composer Japanese, and the actors were from all over the globe. This production, which toured widely, clearly drew from a large number of different cultures.

Brook continued his onstage exploration of *The Mahabharata* in 2015 in a new work entitled *Battlefield*,

Peter Brook in Paris. (Julio Donoso/Getty Images)

using just four global actors and a musician along with minimal properties to create a production about the horrific aftermath of war.

Although Brook has been criticized for exploiting and appropriating some of his source material (such as *The Mahabharata*, which he greatly simplified), his work has shown a creative and continued interest in drawing from many different global theatrical traditions. Unlike other directors who have "borrowed" certain aspects of other theatrical traditions, Brook has sought to use them to identify a common theatre language or universality understood by all.

Prepared by Naomi Stubbs, Associate Professor, LaGuardia Community College, CUNY.

Concept and purpose. The directorial concept should serve the play. The best concept is one that remains true to the spirit and meaning of the script. A director who can translate that spirit and meaning into stage terms in an inspired way will create an exciting theatre experience; however, a director who is too intent on displaying their own originality may distort or violate the integrity of the script. For instance, a director might decide to make *Macbeth* into a cowboy play, with Duncan as a sheriff and Macbeth as a deputy who wants to kill the sheriff in order to take the job himself. In this version, Lady Macbeth would be the deputy's wife, whom he had met in a saloon. *Macbeth* could be done this way, but it might also come across as simply a gimmick—a means of calling attention to the director rather than to the script.

In most instances the best directorial concept is a straightforward one deriving from the play itself, not a scheme superimposed from outside.

THE AUTEUR DIRECTOR AND THE POSTMODERN DIRECTOR

In addition to the traditional director, there are two other types of stage directors: the auteur director and the postmodern director. There are a number of similarities between these two, but we will look at them one at a time, beginning with the auteur director.

The Auteur Director

Auteur is a French word meaning "author." Just after World War II, French critics began using this term to describe certain film directors, who, they said, were really the authors of the films they made. In these films the point of view and the implementation of that point of view came almost entirely from the director, not from a writer. The term has since been applied to a type of stage director as well. We are not speaking here of directors who alter the time or place in which the action occurs but retain the original script—the playwright's words and the sequence of scenes. We are speaking rather of directors who make more drastic alterations or transformations in the material, taking responsibility for shaping *every* element in the production, including the script.

auteur French term for "author." When used to describe a director it suggests one who makes drastic alterations and transformations to a traditional script.

Interestingly, one of the first and most important auteur directors began his work with a traditional director, Stanislavski, and then went out on his own—the Russian director Vsevolod Meyerhold (1874–1940), who developed a type of theatre in which he controlled all the elements. The script was only one of many aspects that Meyerhold used for his own purposes. He would rewrite or eliminate text in order to present his own vision of the material. Performers, too, were subject to his overall ideas. Often they were called on to perform like circus acrobats or robots. The finished product was frequently exciting and almost always innovative, but it reflected Meyerhold's point of view, strongly imposed on all the elements, not the viewpoint of a writer or anyone else.

Following in Meyerhold's footsteps, many avant-garde directors of the mid-twentieth century can also be classified as auteur directors. Each in their own way demanded that the text serve their purposes, not the other way around. In some cases, the text is only fragmentary and is one of the least important elements.

Auteur Directors in the Commercial Theatre In recent years, some auteur directors have directed successful commercial productions on Broadway and in regional theatres around the United States. These productions incorporate some of their unique directorial "authoring" techniques, while trying to stay closer to the actual texts.

One such director is Ivo van Hove (b. 1958), a Belgian-born director who enjoys reinventing the classics, though not totally veering away from the texts. In his *Streetcar Named Desire* (1996), Blanche DuBois performs a good part of the play naked in a bathtub. In his staging of Arthur Miller's *A View from the Bridge* (2014), his actors, shoeless and dressed all in casual contemporary clothing, perform on a stripped-down, rectangular, box-like white stage with no props and with the audience seated on two sides (in the traditional New York Broadway proscenium, bleacher-like seating was set up on the stage). Van Hove brought his auteur-like approach to the classic musical *West Side Story,* which opened on Broadway in 2020, just prior to the COVID-19 pandemic shutdown. Among his changes to the original, he cut the song "I Feel Pretty" and the "Somewhere" ballet so that the musical would run 90 minutes without an intermission. He also had new choreography created, the first time this was done for a Broadway revival of this musical.

Other highly regarded auteur directors who have worked commercially are Julie Taymor (b. 1952), who directed the immensely popular *The Lion King* on Broadway, and Mary Zimmerman (b. 1960), who has directed musicals for Chicago's Goodman Theatre and is a member of that city's Lookingglass Theatre.

RICHARD FOREMAN: AUTEUR DIRECTOR
Richard Foreman is one of the foremost auteur directors in today's theatre. Such directors create their own theatre pieces, providing the vision and the interpretation. They serve not only as directors but also as authors, taking elements from many sources and melding them into their own version of what we see onstage. Shown here is a scene from Foreman's *Old-Fashioned Prostitutes (A True Romance)* with Alenka Kraigher (left), and Rocco Sisto at the Public Theater in New York in 2013. (Karli Cadel/The New York Times/Redux)

The Postmodern Director

There is a great deal of overlap between the auteur director and the postmodern director. What is postmodernism? Probably the best way to answer the question is historically. The modern period in drama began in the late nineteenth century with plays like those of Ibsen and Strindberg that broke long-held taboos. The subject matter of their plays included explicit sexual content, social diseases, the subjugation of women, and the hypocrisy of religious figures. The twentieth century, therefore, was the period of *modern drama.*

At mid-century, however, there were people who felt that as advanced as theatre had become, it remained bound by the strictures of the text. In their minds, this state of affairs did not properly reflect the chaos, the confusion, and the alienation of the world around us. Two groups especially advanced these ideas: the theoreticians, who propounded the doctrine of postmodernism; and a series of stage directors who embodied postmodernism in their work with a radical, rebellious, free-form approach to theatre production.

What are the hallmarks of postmodern production? One, which began with Meyerhold and continued with Grotowski in his "poor theatre," was a taking apart of the text, often called *deconstruction,* in which portions of a text may be altered, deleted, taken out of context, or reassembled.

ELIZABETH LECOMPTE: POSTMODERN DIRECTOR
Elizabeth LeCompte is a postmodern, auteur director who creates her own theatre pieces frequently by reworking classical texts, controlling every aspect of a production and making it her own. Shown here is a scene from her version of Shakespeare's *Hamlet* staged at the Royal Lyceum Theatre as a part of the Edinburgh International Festival in 2013. (Robbie Jack/Corbis Entertainment/Getty Images)

A second hallmark is the abandonment of a narrative or linear structure in a theatre piece. We have already mentioned (and will discuss more fully later in our survey of modern theatre) that Robert Wilson and Richard Foreman, in his Ontological Hysteric Theatre, both work as auteur and postmodern directors, replacing traditional structure with the use of segments, tableaux, and other nonsequential devices. A third hallmark is unfamiliar, cross-gender, multicultural casting. Lee Breuer (1937–2021) in a Mabou Mines production of *King Lear* recast the title role as a woman ranch owner in the southern United States who has difficulty leaving her inheritance to her three "good ole boy" sons.

In addition to those discussed earlier, other postmodern directors include Anne Bogart (b. 1951), working with her SITI organization; Elizabeth LeCompte (b. 1944), working with the Wooster Group; and Simon McBurney (b. 1957), founder of Théâtre de Complicité and whose recent work is the one-person *The Encounter* (2015).

THE DIRECTOR AND THE PRODUCTION: THE PHYSICAL PRODUCTION

While developing an approach to the play, the director is also working with the designers on the physical production. At the outset—once the director's concept is established—the director confers with the costume, scene, lighting, sound designers, and possibly video designers and projection designers to give visual and aural shape and substance to the concept. It is the responsibility of designers to provide images and impressions that will carry out the style and ideas of the production. (See the chapters on the various design elements.)

During the preproduction and rehearsal period, the director meets with the designers to make certain that their work is on schedule and keeping pace with the rehearsals. Obviously, the preparation of these elements must begin long before the actual performance, just as rehearsals must, so that everything will be ready on time for the performance itself. Any number of problems can arise with the physical elements of a production. For example, the appropriate props may not be available, a costume may not fit a performer, or scene changes may be too slow. Early planning will allow time to solve these problems.

THE DIRECTOR'S WORK WITH THE PERFORMERS

Casting

casting Fitting performers into roles.

Now we come to the director's work with the performers. Along with choosing and developing a script and settling questions of concept, style, and the physical production, the director also casts the play. In theatre, *casting* means fitting performers into roles; the term is derived from the phrase "casting a mold." Generally speaking, directors attempt to put performers into the roles for which their personalities and physical characteristics are best suited. A young actress will play Juliet in *Romeo and Juliet,* a middle-aged or elderly actor with a deep voice will play *King Lear,* and so on. When a performer closely resembles in real life the character to be enacted, this is known as *typecasting.* There are times, however, when a director will deliberately put someone in a role who does not appear to be right for the part. This is called *casting against type.* For example, a sinister-looking actor might be called on to play an angelic part.

Directors are now recognizing that much of traditional casting has been based on inappropriate stereotyping, excluding actors of color, those with disabilities, and other marginalized performers, and that in order to create a more diverse, inclusive, and equitable theatre, these traditional approaches to casting by type need to be reevaluated.

In the modern American theatre, performers frequently *audition* for parts in a play, and the director casts from those performers who audition. In an audition, performers read scenes from a play or perform portions of the script to give the director an indication of how they talk and move and how they would interpret a part. From this the director determines whether or not a performer is right for a given role.

Historically, casting was rarely done by audition, because theatrical companies were more permanent. In Shakespeare's time and in Molière's, as well as in Asian theatre, certain people in a theatrical troupe always played certain parts: One person would play heroic roles while another always played clowns. Today each production begins with a fresh cast, frequently chosen through an audition process, though stars are sometimes pre-cast in commercial productions. A theatre company and/or director often also employ a *casting director* who is responsible for helping to identify actors appropriate for roles in a production.

From our standpoint as members of the audience, it is important to be aware of casting and the difference it can make to the effectiveness of a production. Perhaps a specific performer seems just right for the part being played. On the other hand, sometimes the wrong performer is chosen for a part: The voice may not be right, or the gestures or facial expressions may be stilted or inappropriate for the character. One way to test the appropriateness of casting is to imagine a different kind of actor or actress in a part while watching a performance.

Diversity and Inclusion in Directing: Inclusive Casting

While there have been many significant African American, Latinx, and Asian stage performers, there is continuing recognition that there are limited opportunities for actors and actresses from underrepresented groups in the theatres around the United States (and in other countries).

In order to address this issue, there have been productions employing what was originally referred to as *color-blind casting* (a term we shall see that is no longer in favor and has been replaced by *color conscious*), or what some now refer to more as *nontraditional casting*, which is again a problematic term because it seems to suggest that there is a traditional approach, in which roles are cast by directors without considering a performer's ethnicity, gender, transgender identity, or disability.

Such casting, for example, has been frequently employed in productions of Shakespeare across the globe, as well as in other classic dramas. Some actual examples include all-women productions of Shakespeare; an all–Asian American cast playing the Jewish family in the 1930s drama *Awake and Sing;* an African American cast performing Tennessee Williams's *Cat on a Hot Tin Roof;* and a transgender performer playing a women identifying character in Thornton Wilder's *The Matchmaker.* The acclaimed musical *Hamilton* (2015), which has African American and Latinx actors portraying many of the Caucasian founders of the United States, including those playing Alexander Hamilton, George Washington, and Thomas Jefferson, is another example.

Yet directors still rarely cast performers of color, as well as women, transgender, and non-binary actors, in multiracial and gender-bending productions of contemporary texts. For that matter, many performers from underrepresented groups point out that "whitewashing," having Caucasian actors play other races such as a white actor playing the Latinx lead in *In the Heights* or the Asians in the musicals *The King and I, Flower Drum Song,* and *Miss Saigon,* is still too common and undercuts even those limited opportunities for performers of color.

Some underrepresented theatre artists (including the playwright August Wilson), however, have argued that color-blind and nontraditional casting undermines the ongoing need to present the voices of marginalized populations and that there will be fewer dramas dealing with their social and political concerns. Instead, performers of color who are cast in these roles are often forced to erase their ethnic identities and not fully express them.

Katori Hall, who disapproved of what she considered the inappropriate "color-blind" casting of a white student actor as Martin Luther King Jr. in her play *The Mountaintop,* also questioned the nontraditional casting of *Hamilton,* echoing August Wilson's arguments: "And though I applaud *Hamilton* for its use of race-revolutionary casting, let us not forget that brown bodies are still being used to further mythologize and perpetuate the narratives of dead white men, historically and currently the most privileged group in American society."[1]

These arguments have led many to reject the terms "color blind" and "nontraditional" casting. These terms are seen as again marginalizing performers of color by erasing the importance of their identities when cast. Instead, many advocate for "color-conscious" casting, which recognizes the actor's identity and unique voice while also expecting that actors of color will be cast in roles traditionally played by white actors.

Rehearsals

Once a play is cast, the director supervises all the rehearsals. The director listens to and watches the performers as they go through their lines and begin to move about the stage. Different directors work in different ways during the early phases of rehearsal. Some directors *block* a play in advance, giving precise instructions to the performers. The term **blocking** means deciding when and where performers move and position themselves on the stage. Other directors let the performers find their own movements, their own vocal interpretations, and their own relationships. And, of course, there are directors who do a bit of both.

blocking Pattern and arrangement of performers' movements onstage with respect to each other and to the stage space, usually set by the director.

At the beginning of the rehearsal process the director often has the cast sit around a table while reading through the script and discussing individual scenes as well as the play in general. After this, the director may break down the script into segments or scenes, which will be rehearsed separately. Some scenes will involve only a few people; others, as in a Shakespearean play, may be crowd scenes. At a certain point, the actors will be expected to be "off book," meaning that they have memorized their lines. Gradually, scenes are put together, and an entire act is played without stopping. After that, individual scenes are refined, and then there is a run-through, when the play is performed straight through without stopping.

Also, some directors want the actors to become thoroughly familiar with the script while they remain seated. Others wish to get the play "on its feet" as soon as possible, meaning that the actors are moving about the rehearsal hall early in the process. Regardless of the director's approach to staging, the production stage manager keeps detailed notes of all the actors' movements and actions to help maintain consistency during rehearsals.

Throughout the rehearsal period, the director must make certain that the performers are realizing the intention of the playwright—that they are making sense of the script and bringing out its meaning. Also, the director must ensure that the performers are working well together—that they are listening to one another and beginning to play as an ensemble. The director must be aware of performers' needs, knowing when to encourage them and when to challenge or criticize them. The director must understand their personal problems and help them overcome such obstacles as insecurity about a role or fear of failure.

The Director as the Audience's Eye

One could say that there are two people in theatre who stand in for us, the audience, serving as surrogate or substitute spectators. One, the critic or reviewer (discussed earlier), does work after the event; the other, the director, does work before it. In preparing a theatrical production, the director acts as the eye of the audience. During rehearsals, only the director sees the production from our point

USING STAGE AREAS PROPERLY
One responsibility of the director is to make appropriate use of stage areas to create clarity, balance, and the proper emphasis in the visual picture on stage. The scene here is from Chekhov's *The Cherry Orchard*, in a production at the Huntington Theatre. Note how the director Nicholas Martin has arranged the performers so that Kate Burton as Madame Ranevskaya in light gray costume, the leading figure in the play, stands out in front of the other actors who surround her expertly positioned. (T Charles Erickson)

of view. For this reason, the director must help the performers to show the audience—us—exactly what they intend to show. If one performer hides another at an important moment, if a crucial gesture is not visible, if an actor makes an awkward movement, if a performer cannot be heard when delivering an emotional speech, the director points it out.

Also, the director underscores the meaning of specific scenes through *visual composition* and *stage pictures,* that is, through the physical arrangement of performers onstage. The spatial relationships of performers convey information about characters. For example, important characters are frequently placed on a level above other characters—on a platform, say, or a flight of stairs. Another spatial device is to place an important character alone in one area of the stage while grouping other characters in another area. This causes our eye to give special attention to the character standing alone. Also, if two characters are opposed to each other, they should be placed in positions of physical confrontation onstage. Visual composition is more crucial in a play with a large cast, such as a Shakespearean production, than in a play with only two or three characters.

Certain areas onstage can assume special significance. A fireplace, with its implication of warmth, can become an area to which a character returns for comfort

Chapter 5   *The Director and the Producer*

and reassurance. A door opening onto a garden can serve as a place where characters go when they want to renew their spirits or relieve a hemmed-in feeling. By guiding performers to make the best use of stage space, the director helps them communicate important visual images to us—images consistent with the overall meaning of the play.

It is important to note, too, that directors must adjust their notions of blocking and visual composition to different types of stages, discussed in our chapter on stage spaces: the arena stage, the thrust stage, and the proscenium stage. Each of these calls for different approaches to the performers' movements and to the audience's sight lines.

Movement, Pace, and Rhythm

The director gives shape and structure to a play in two ways: in *space,* as was just described, and in *time.* Since a production occurs through time, it is important for the director to see that the *movement, pace,* and *rhythm* of the play are appropriate. If a play moves too quickly, if we miss words and do not understand what is going on, that is usually the director's fault. The director must determine whether there is too little or too much time between speeches and whether a performer moves across the stage too slowly or too quickly. The director must also attempt to control the pace and rhythm within a scene and the rhythm between scenes.

One of the most common faults of directors is not establishing a clear rhythm in a production. At a performance we are often impatient to see what is coming next, and the director must see to it that the movement from moment to moment and scene to scene has enough thrust and drive to maintain our interest. Variety is also important. If a play moves ahead at only one pace, whether slow or fast, we will become fatigued simply by the monotony of that pace. Rhythm within scenes and between scenes works on us subliminally, but its effects are very real. It enters our psyche as we watch a performance and thus contributes to our overall response.

It must be borne in mind as well that although pace, rhythm, and overall effect are initially the responsibility of the director, ultimately they become the performers' responsibility. Once a performance begins, they are onstage and the director is not. In cinema, pace and rhythm can be determined in the editing room; in theatre, by contrast, they are in the hands of the performers. Then, too, the audience's reaction will vary from night to night, and that will also alter pace and rhythm. The director must therefore instill in the performers such a strong sense of inner rhythm that they develop an internal clock that tells them the pace at which they should play.

Technical Rehearsal

technical rehearsal A rehearsal that focuses on running through the production with scenery, props, lighting, costumes, and sound for the first time.

Just before public performances begin, a ***technical rehearsal*** is held. The performers are onstage in their costumes and all of the production elements are in place: scenery, props, lighting, sound, and, in some instances, videos and projections for the first time. There is a *run-through* of the show from beginning to end, with all the props and scene, lighting, and other technical changes.

The stagehands may move scenery, the crew handles the needed props, lighting technicians use computer controls to dim and raise lights as well as control other lighting effects, and technicians may also run a sound board and control intricate videos and projections that change settings and environments. The backstage crew, under the supervision of the stage manager, must coordinate its work with that of the performers.

Let us say that one scene ends in a garden and the next scene opens in a library. When the performers leave the garden set, the lighting fades, and the scenery and furniture may be removed, which can be done either by stagehands or using stage machinery, such as a revolving stage or an elevator stage, or even through lighting, projection, and video changes. Then, the scenery for the library must be brought onstage, again either by stagehands or employing stage technology. The books and other props may actually be put in place as part of the new setting or again possibly represented by projections. Next, the performers for the new scene in the library take their places as the lighting comes up.

Extensive rehearsals are required to ensure that all these changes occur smoothly, especially when there is the use of complex computer-controlled sets, lights, projections, and videos. Any mishap on the part of the technical crew or the performers would affect the illusion and destroy the aesthetic effect of the complex scene change.

Dress Rehearsal

Just after the technical rehearsal, but before the first preview or tryout with an audience, the director will hold a *dress rehearsal.* The purpose of the dress rehearsal is to put all the elements together: the full involvement of the performers as well as the technical components. The dress rehearsal is performed as if an audience were present, with no stops or interruptions and with full lights, scenery, costumes, and sound. Sometimes a few people are invited—friends of the director or cast members—to provide a token audience.

dress rehearsal The first full performances of a production before performances for the public.

One function of the dress rehearsal is to give everyone concerned—cast, crew, and director—a sense of what the finished performance will be like. The dress rehearsal also allows for any last-minute changes before the first performance in front of a full audience.

Previews

Once the technical rehearsals and the dress rehearsal are completed and remaining problems are solved, the next step is a performance in front of an audience. We have stressed from the beginning the importance of performer-audience interaction and the fact that no play is complete until it is actually enacted for an audience. It is crucial, therefore, for a production to be tried out before a group of spectators. What has gone before in terms of rehearsals and other elements must now meet the test of combining harmoniously in front of an audience.

For this purpose there is most often (but not always) a period of *previews*—also called *tryouts*—when the director and the performers discover which parts of the play are successful and which are not. Frequently, for example, the director and performers find that one part of the play is moving too slowly; they know this because the

previews Tryout performances of a production before an audience, preceding the official "opening" performance.

Chapter 5 *The Director and the Producer*

TECHNICAL REHEARSAL
Before performances begin, a technical rehearsal is held. All the technical aspects—scenery, lighting, sound, costumes, props—are employed in the same sequence and manner as in the performance. This is in order to see that everything is in proper working order and is coordinated. Shown here is a rehearsal at the Guthrie Theater in Minneapolis for a production of *When We Are Married,* directed by John Miller-Stephany. Note the tables on which computers are being used by sound, light, and scenic designers to check out the running order and the coordination of all the elements. The set was designed by Frank Hallinan. (T Charles Erickson)

audience members become restless and begin to cough or stir. Sometimes, in a comedy, there is a great deal of laughter where little was expected, and the performers and the director must adjust to this. In this preview period the audiences become genuine collaborators in shaping the play. After several performances in front of an audience, the director and the performers get the "feel" of the audience and know whether or not the play is ready.

The Director's Collaborator: The Stage Manager

A key collaborator of the director, especially during the rehearsal process and then during the run of the show, is the stage manager. During the rehearsal

> ## PLAYING YOUR PART: EXPERIENCING THEATRE
>
> 1. Have you ever had to pick someone for a team or for a job? How did you go about making your choice? Is that similar to casting in the theatre? Why? Why not?
> 2. Have one of your classmates read a short speech from a play. Ask her or him to change the pace or rhythm of delivery. What terms or phrases did you use to make this request? Were your directions understood? How did the change in pace or rhythm affect the delivery of the speech and its impact on those listening?
> 3. Observe how one of your instructors interacts with the class through his or her movement. How does this movement affect the way in which the class material is delivered? Does your observation of this provide you any insight into the importance of stage blocking?
> 4. Ask if you can attend a technical rehearsal or dress rehearsal at your university theatre. What insights did you gain from attending those rehearsals?

process the stage manager works as the right-hand person to the director, doing such tasks as taking notes, keeping track of blocking, noting decisions about visual elements, communicating with all of the designers, making sure everyone is aware of rehearsal schedules, and keeping daily reports and logs. Throughout the final stages of preparing the production, for example, the stage manager continues to give detailed notes to all actors to ensure consistency in dialogue and movement.

Once the play has opened and the director is no longer present at every performance, it is the stage manager's responsibility to maintain the consistency of the director's vision. Among their responsibilities are to make sure that actors stay true to the director's interpretation and that all technical cues are called on time during the run of the show. If understudies should go on for missing actors, it is the stage manager's responsibility to make sure they are prepared. If a performer in a long-running show is replaced, it is often the stage manager's responsibility to work with the replacement to make sure the performer works within the confines of the director's vision.

The responsibilities of the stage manager vary depending on the type of theatre in which they are working and from director to director. In commercial theatre, it is important to realize that stage managers and actors are members of the same union, Actors' Equity Association (AEA), reflecting the close work stage managers do with performers.

The Director's Collaborator: The Choreographer

The choreographer is a significant collaborator who most often works with directors in musical theatre. The choreographer develops the movement and dance steps made by performers in a musical. The choreographer works closely with the director to make certain that the dance and movement serve the text, music, and concept of the production. The choreographer will usually create notations to capture the various dances employed within the production.

The choreographer must also take into account the differing levels of dance proficiency within the cast and how the dances created help us better understand the characters and their relationships. This may be a reason, as we shall see when discussing musical theatre, why many current directors of musicals are also choreographers.

There are also times when a choreographer will collaborate with a director on a drama or comedy that has complex expectations of movement and/or dance.

The Director's Collaborators: The Fight Director and the Intimacy Director

Certain scripts have very specific demands that require a director to work with a fight director and/or an intimacy director.

A fight director will design—some would say almost choreograph—the elaborate fights that are required in some plays. Stage combat training includes unarmed combat skills such as slaps, punches, kicks, and throwing and holding techniques, as well as theatrical versions of fencing and the use of other weapons and forms of martial arts. You might think of all of the Shakespearean plays, including *Hamlet* and *Romeo and Juliet,* that require the actors to be proficient at stage combat.

Of course, the fights in the production must again help us better understand the circumstances, the characters, and the director's concept. And while they must give a sense of reality, they must always be safe.

The importance of fight direction led to the founding of the Society of American Fight Directors in 1977. Since then, organizations for fight directors have been established in many other countries, including Britain, Canada, Australia, and New Zealand. Many of these organizations offer certificates to actors and potential fight directors indicating areas of specific proficiency.

The intimacy director is someone who helps the director stage scenes that involve sexuality, nudity, or other types of intimacy. The intimacy director's function is to make sure such sensitive scenes are designed (again, some would say choreographed) correctly and that the actors involved are comfortable and understand why such scenes are necessary to the text and production.

The intimacy director makes certain that the actors also know that they have someone with whom they can discuss any concerns about intimate scenes. Intimacy Directors International was founded in 2016 to help train and support the newest of the director's collaborators.

dramaturg The individual who works on literary and historical issues with members of the artistic team mounting a theatre production.

The Director's Collaborator: The Dramaturg

A person who can be of great assistance to the director is the ***dramaturg*** (sometimes also spelled dramaturge), or literary manager, whom we mentioned earlier. The duties of the dramaturg are discovering promising new plays, working with

> ## IN FOCUS: TECHNOLOGY FOR DIRECTORS AND THEIR COLLABORATORS
>
> Technology has affected the work of directors and their collaborators, in particular, through apps that allow them to work on tablets and smartphones and to keep track of their many complex tasks.
>
> There are apps that allow directors and stage managers to document blocking and choreography. There are also specific blocking apps that let directors develop and review stage movement patterns in various stage spaces on their phones or tablets.
>
> There are also apps that allow stage managers to keep track of the running times of shows, prop lists, production checklists, and e-mail and phone number lists for contacting all members of the production teams.
>
> Rather than print up traditional call sheets, which tell cast and crew when they need to be present for production meetings and rehearsals, there is an app that allows the stage manager to share these sheets digitally and to edit them, as needed, easily.

playwrights on developing their scripts, identifying significant plays from the past that may have been overlooked, preparing material for teachers whose students will be attending performances, and writing articles for the programs that are distributed at performances. Of particular importance to directors is the work of dramaturgs in conducting research on previous productions of classic plays, as well as researching past criticism and interpretations of these plays. It is easy to see how the work of the dramaturg can be invaluable in assisting the director to arrive at decisions regarding style, approach, and concept.

THE DIRECTOR'S POWER AND RESPONSIBILITY

Any artistic event must have a unity not encountered in real life. We expect the parts to be brought together so that the total effect will enlighten us, move us, or amuse us. In theatre, the director—who has a voice in so many areas of a production—is in a unique position to bring this about. This power, however, is a double-edged sword. If a director gets too carried away with one idea, for example, or lets the scene designer create scenery that overpowers the performers, the experience for the audience will be unsatisfactory or incomplete. If, on the other hand, the director has a strong point of view—one that is appropriate for the theatre piece and illuminates the script—and if all the parts fit and are consistent with one another, the experience will be meaningful and exciting, and at times even unforgettable.

For an idea of the director's full range of responsibilities, see the following chart "Duties of a Director."

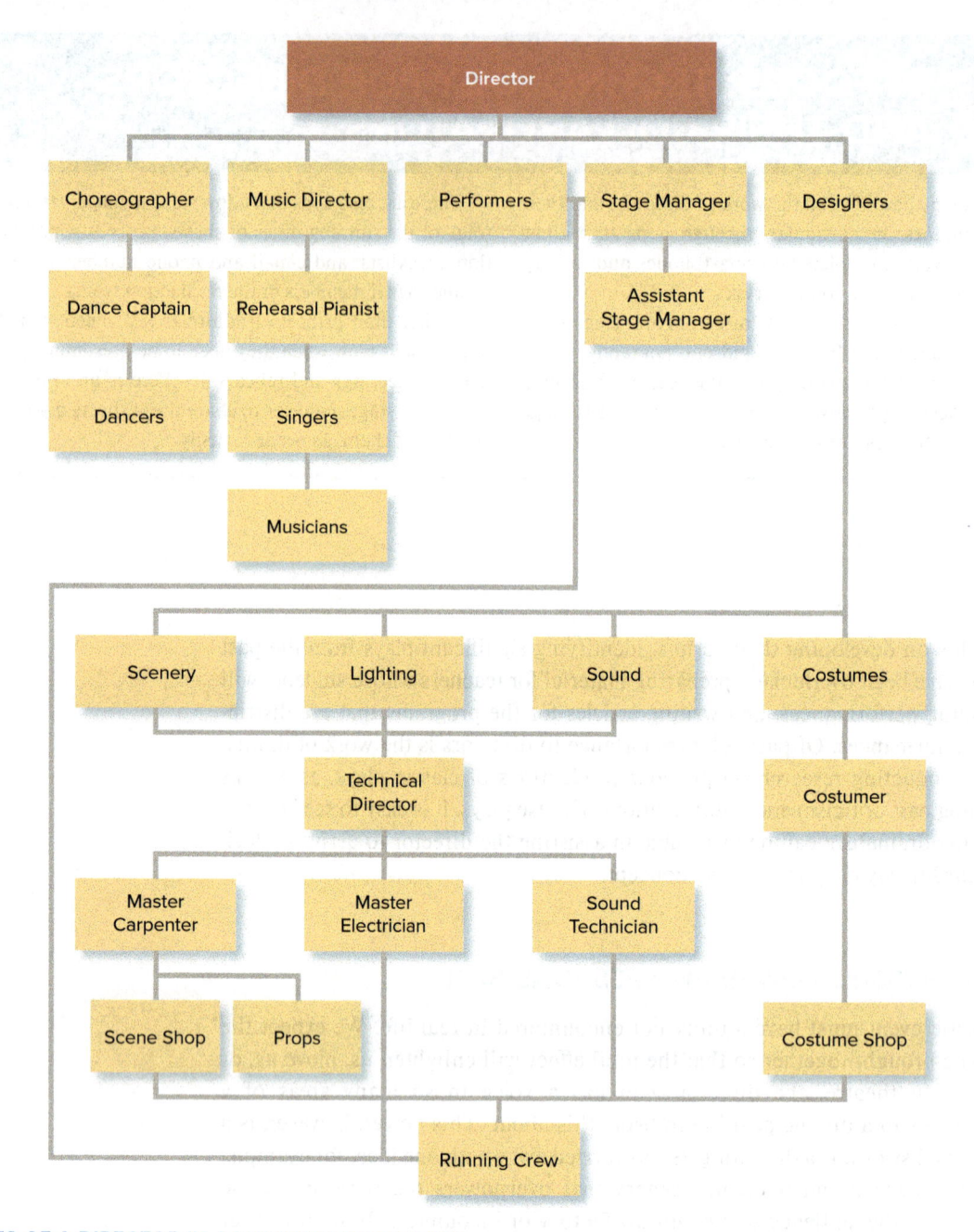

```
                                    Director
                                       │
        ┌──────────┬────────────┬──────┼──────────┬─────────────┐
   Choreographer  Music      Performers  Stage Manager    Designers
        │        Director        │          │                │
   Dance Captain   │              │    Assistant             │
        │      Rehearsal Pianist  │    Stage Manager         │
     Dancers       │              │                          │
                Singers           │                          │
                   │              │                          │
                Musicians         │                          │
                                                             
    ┌──────────┬──────────┬──────────┬──────────┐
  Scenery    Lighting    Sound              Costumes
                 │                               │
            Technical                        Costumer
            Director                             │
    ┌──────────┼──────────┐                     │
  Master    Master       Sound                  │
 Carpenter Electrician  Technician               │
    ┌────┬─────┘                            Costume Shop
 Scene Shop Props
                      Running Crew
```

DUTIES OF A DIRECTOR IN A THEATRE PRODUCTION

Once a director has decided on a script (and has worked with the playwright, if it is a new play), he or she must organize the entire artistic side of the production. This chart indicates the many people that the director must work with and the many elements that must be coordinated.

PLAYING YOUR PART: THINKING ABOUT THEATRE

1. Imagine that while you are watching a production, one performer is overacting badly, to the point that he or she is quite unbelievable. Another performer is listless and has no energy. In each case, to what extent do you think this is the director's fault and to what extent the performer's failure?
2. If you get bored or impatient when watching a performance, what do you think the director could have done in preparing the production to prevent this from happening?
3. Is it fair to say, as some critics do, when everything "clicks" in a production, that is, when the acting, the scenery and lighting, and the pace of the action all seem to be beautifully coordinated, that the director's hand is "invisible"?
4. If you have read a play this semester (or sometime in the past), what do you think the spine of that play is? What would your directorial concept be if you were directing a production of that play?

THE PRODUCER OR MANAGING DIRECTOR

As spectators, we naturally focus on the event onstage rather than on what happens behind the scenes. But no production would ever be performed for the public without a business component. Here, too, the coordination of elements is crucial, and the person chiefly responsible, known as the *producer* in the commercial theatre, or *managing director* in the noncommercial theatre, is the behind-the-scenes counterpart of the director.

The Commercial Producer

In a commercial theatre venture, the producer has many responsibilities. (See the nearby chart.) In general, the producer oversees the entire business and publicity side of the production and has the following duties:

1. Raising money to finance the production.
2. Securing rights to the script.
3. Dealing with the agents for the playwright, director, and performers.
4. Hiring the director, performers, designers, and stage crews.
5. Dealing with theatrical unions.
6. Renting the theatre space.
7. Supervising the work of those running the theatre: in the box office, auditorium, and business office.
8. Supervising the advertising.
9. Overseeing the budget and the week-to-week financial management of the production.

It is clear that the responsibilities of the commercial producer range far and wide. They require business acumen, organizational ability, aesthetic judgment, marketing know-how, and an ability to work with people. The producer in commercial theatre must have the artistic sensibility to choose the right script and hire the right director, but at the same time must be able to raise capital as well as oversee all financial and business operations in a production.

producer In American usage, the person responsible for the business side of a production, including raising the necessary money. (In British usage, a producer for many years was the equivalent of an American director.)

managing director In nonprofit theatre organizations, the individual who controls resources and expenditures.

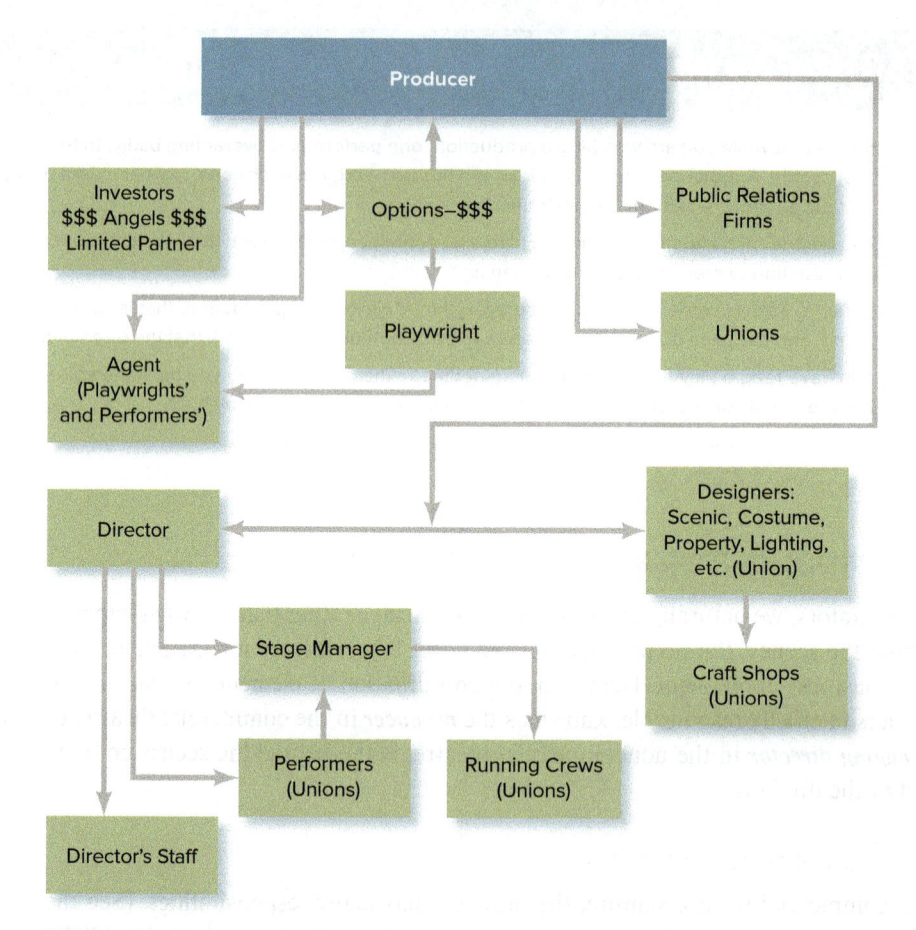

RESPONSIBILITIES OF THE COMMERCIAL THEATRE PRODUCER
When a commercial theatre production is mounted, the person responsible for organizing the full range of nonartistic activities is the producer. This chart shows the producer at the top and indicates the people the producer must deal with and the numerous elements he or she must coordinate.

Noncommercial Theatres

In a nonprofit theatre the person with many of the same responsibilities as the producer is called the *executive director* or *managing director*.

Administrative Organization of a Nonprofit Theatre

Most nonprofit theatres—including theatres in smaller urban centers as well as the large noncommercial theatres in major cities like New York, Chicago, and Los Angeles—are organized with a board of directors, an artistic director, and an executive or managing director. The board is responsible for selecting both the artistic and the managing director. The board is also responsible for overseeing the financial affairs of the theatre, for fundraising, for long-range planning, and the like. To carry out some of these tasks, the board frequently delegates authority to an executive committee.

The artistic director is responsible for all creative and artistic activities. That person selects the plays that will constitute the season and chooses directors, designers, and other creative personnel. Frequently, the artistic director also directs one or more plays during the season.

Responsibilities of a Noncommercial Managing Director The managing director in a noncommercial theatre is, in many respects, the counterpart of a producer in commercial theatre. In both a commercial production and the running of a nonprofit theatre organization, the tasks of the person in charge of administration are many and complex.

The managing director is responsible for the maintenance of the theatre building, including the dressing rooms, the scene and costume shops, the public facilities, and the lobby. The managing director is also responsible for the budget, making certain that the production stays within established limits. The budget includes salaries for the director, designers, performers, and stage crews, as well as expenditures for scenery, costumes, and music. Again, an artistic element enters the picture. Some artistic decisions—such as whether a costume needs to be replaced or scenery needs to be altered—affect costs. The managing director must find additional sources of money or must determine that a change is important enough artistically to justify taking funds away from another item in the budget. In other words, the managing director must work very closely with the director and the designers in balancing artistic and financial needs.

The managing director, often with additional staff members, is also responsible for publicity. The audience members would never get to the theatre if they did not know when and where a play was being presented. The managing director must work with staff to advertise the production and decide whether the advertisements and information should be placed in daily newspapers, magazines, on radio, on television, or in social media (such as Facebook, Twitter, and Instagram).

A host of other responsibilities come under the supervision of the managing director and his or her staff: Tickets must be ordered, the box office must be maintained, and plans must be made ahead of time for how tickets are to be sold. Securing ushers, printing programs, and maintaining the auditorium—usually called the *front of the house*—are also the responsibility of the managing director's staff.

front of the house Portion of a theatre reserved for the audience; sometimes called simply the *house*.

Once again, plans must be made well in advance. In many theatre organizations, an entire season—the plays that will be produced, the personnel who will be in charge, and the supplies that will be required—is planned at least a year ahead of time. It should be clear that coordination and cooperation are as important in this area as they are for the production onstage. (For the organization of a nonprofit theatre company, see the nearby chart.)

The Producer and Director's Collaborator: The Production Manager

In some nonprofit theatres, a production manager is employed to serve as a liaison between the design artists and technical staff and the director and producer or managing director. The production manager oversees the budgets for all of the design and technical areas, sets deadlines for completion, and makes sure that those deadlines are met. Should there be delays, possible budget overruns, or other behind-the-scenes problems, the production manager will attempt to resolve the issues, as well as communicate with the director and/or the producer to make sure that those issues do not affect the artistic quality of the production or its financial well-being. The responsibilities of the production manager may vary from theatre to theatre, depending on budgets and size of operations. If there is not a specifically designated

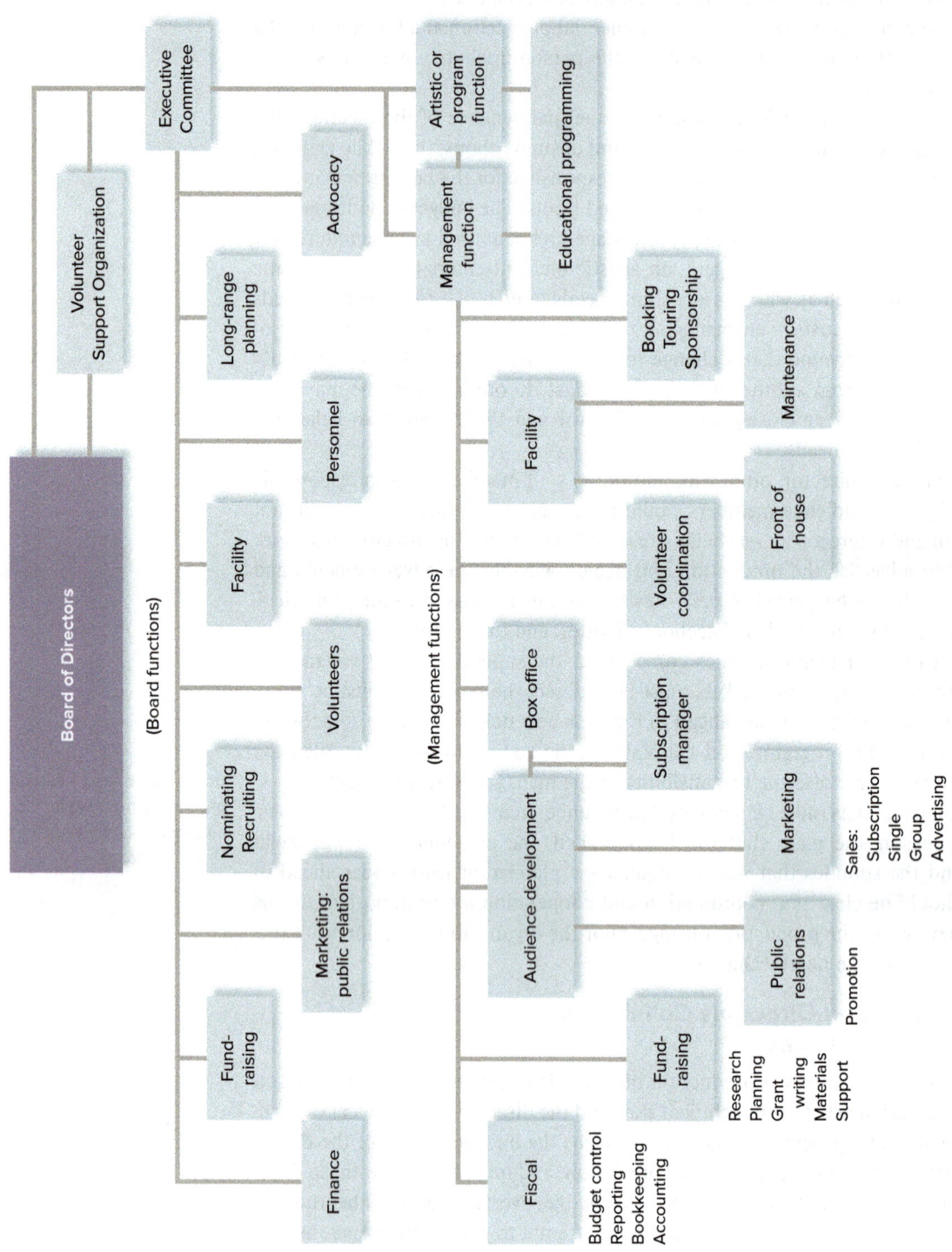

ORGANIZATIONAL STRUCTURE OF A NONPROFIT THEATRE COMPANY

A nonprofit theatre is a complex institution, with many facets. This chart shows the various activities that must be organized for the successful management of such a theatre.

production manager, then someone within the artistic or administrative staff will take on these duties.

COMPLETING THE PICTURE: PLAYWRIGHT, DIRECTOR, AND PRODUCER

A theatre presentation can be compared to a mosaic consisting of many brightly colored pieces of stone that fit together to form a complete picture. The playwright puts the words and ideas together; the performers bring them to life; the designers provide the visual and aural environment; the director integrates the artistic elements; the producer or managing director coordinates the business side of a production. The separate pieces in the mosaic must become parts of an artistic whole, providing us with a complete theatre experience.

Evaluating Directing

While watching a production or experiencing a performance, we do not have time to pause and analyze every aspect of the production, from the acting and the script to the visual and aural elements. There is even less time, perhaps, to analyze the work of the director. But the topics covered in this chapter should give us, as audience members, some idea of what might or might not be the responsibility of the director: when the director might be at fault for a failure or, on the other side, when he or she should be given credit for the successful unfolding of a theatrical event.

There are some key questions we might ask to determine whether the director was successful after we attend a production:

1. Did all the elements of the production seem to be unified and to fit together seamlessly? How was this reflected, in particular, in the visual elements—the scenery, costumes, and lighting or in the sound, video, or projection design?

IN FOCUS: DIRECTING FOR FILM AND TELEVISION

While directors in film, television, and theatre work closely with actors to help shape performances and coordinate the overall artistic work, the director in film and television controls the final artistic product in ways that are not possible in the theatre.

A film and television director, through placement of the camera and sound equipment, as well as through editing and later sound additions, can control what the audience looks at and what they hear. Film directors, through careful manipulation of the way in which a shot is framed and edited, can also manipulate the viewer's emotional response.

The film and television director also has many more technical elements than the stage director to create the world of the film, including varying locations and computer and digital technologies. In addition, the director in the electronic media can film multiple "takes" of the same scene and then pick which they prefer.

In many ways, the film and television director is responsible for helping all of the artists and technicians understand the "jigsaw puzzle" of scenes that are being shot out of sequence. And the media director finally puts that puzzle together, collaborating with the editor, in the editing process.

Editing allows the film and television director to shape performances. Sound and other elements can also be added long after the film or TV show is edited.

Many stage directors are also successful film directors, including Orson Welles, Laurence Olivier, Elia Kazan, Franco Zefffirelli, Mike Nichols, Nicholas Hytner, Sam Mendes, Julie Taymor, and Phylidia Lloyd.

2. How did the director move the actors around onstage? Were there any moments when you felt that such movement was particularly effective or ineffective? Were entrances and exits smooth?

3. Did the pace or rhythm of the production seem right for the type of play you are attending? Did it drag or move swiftly? Did one scene follow another quickly, or were there long pauses or interruptions?

4. Did there seem to be a unifying idea or concept behind the production? If so, how was it reflected in the production? How were we, as audience members, able to see it embodied in the production? Was it reflected in striking images or in the way the actors developed their performances? (Evaluating a directorial concept can be one of the most difficult aspects of a production for us to judge, even for those of us who are very experienced theatergoers.)

SUMMARY

1. The term *director* did not come into general use until the end of the nineteenth century. Certain functions of the director, however—organizing the production, instilling discipline in the performers, and setting a tone for the production—have been carried out since the beginning of theatre by someone in authority.

2. The director's duties became more crucial in the twentieth century. Because of the fragmentation of society and the many styles and cultures that now exist side by side, it is necessary for someone to provide a point of view and a single vision on individual productions.

3. The director has many responsibilities: working with the playwright, if the script is a new work; evolving a concept or approach to the script; developing the visual side of the production with the designers; holding auditions and casting roles; working with the performers to develop their individual roles in rehearsals; ensuring that stage action communicates the meaning of the play; establishing appropriate pace and rhythm in the movement of the scenes; establishing the dynamics of the production as a whole; and supervising the technical and preview rehearsals.

4. *Auteur* directors demand that a text serve their own purposes, rather than shaping their purposes to serve the text. *Postmodern* directors often "deconstruct" a text or rearrange elements to create a theatre piece.

5. Because the director has such wide-ranging power and responsibilities, the director can distort a production and create an imbalance of elements or an inappropriate emphasis. The director is responsible for a sense of proportion and order in the production.

6. The producer or manager of a production is responsible for the business aspects: maintaining the theatre, arranging publicity, and handling finances, as well as managing the ticket sales, budgets, and ushers.

Design Elements: Audience Sitting in Theatre (theatre): Ron Chapple/Photodisc/Getty Images; Studio Light (spotlights): Exactostock/SuperStock

Part Three

The Designers

6 Scenery   **7** Stage Costumes   **8** Lighting and Sound

A SETTING FOR *THE CHERRY ORCHARD*
The Russian dramatist Anton Chekhov created a type of realistic modern drama, subtle and low-key, that had a profound influence on subsequent dramatists. The scene design we see here for Chekhov's *The Cherry Orchard* has the simplicity, the openness that allows for the emphasis to be on the performers and their actions. At the same time it creates a somber mood and realistic environment appropriate to the play's tone and mood. The scene here shows Kenneth Granham as Firs, James Laurenson as Gaev, Conleth Hill as Lopakhin, and Zoe Wanamaker as Ranyevskaya. The scene designer was Bunny Christie. The production was directed by Howard Davies at London's National Theatre in 2011. (Geraint Lewis/Alamy Stock Photo)

Part Three | The Designers

Our experience of seeing a performance does not occur in a visual vacuum. We sit in the theatre watching what unfolds before us. Naturally, we focus most keenly on the performers who are speaking and moving about the stage. But the visual images of scenery, costumes, and lighting are always present. We also become aware of the elements of sound that are part of the production. The creation of these effects is the responsibility of designers.

As in other areas, there is a parallel between design elements in theatre and our experiences in everyday life. Every building or room we enter can be regarded as a form of stage set. Interior decorating, along with architectural design—the creation of a special atmosphere in a home or a public building—constitutes scene design in real life. A church decorated for a wedding is a form of stage set; so too is the posh lobby of a hotel, or an apartment interior with flowers, candlelight, and soft music. In every case the "designer"—the person who created the setting—has selected elements that signal something to us, thus making an impression.

Just as scenic design surrounds our daily lives, costumes are all around us. For instance, there are the outfits people wear in a holiday parade, at a masquerade ball, or in a pageant. Other obvious examples of the costumes we frequently see are in fashion magazines and runway shows. The dresses and other outfits created by top-name designers for haute couture shows are not what women would ordinarily wear; they are exotic, extreme, and offbeat.

In a less obvious way, costumes also play a significant role in daily life. We wear clothing not only for comfort, but also for the information we want to convey to others about ourselves. If we look around us, we are surrounded by costumes

The austere plain black robes worn by judges indicate authority and formality. Seen here are the judges of the Texas Court of Criminal Appeals in Austin. (Bob Child/AP Images)

High fashion—a model walks the runway during a show at the Paris Womenswear Fashion Week for the Spring/Summer 2010 season. (Karl Prouse/Catwalking/Getty Images)

every day: the formal, subdued uniform of a police officer; the sparkling outfits of a marching band at a football game; a judge's long black robe; the cap and gown for graduation; the dresses worn by bridesmaids at a formal wedding. In this sense, everything we wear is a form of costume.

Stage lighting, quite simply, includes all forms of illumination on the stage. The lighting designer makes decisions in every area of lighting: the color of the lights, the mixture of colors, the number of lights, the intensity and brightness of the lights, the angles at which lights strike performers, and the length of time required for lights to come up or fade out.

As with costumes and scenery, we encounter lighting design in daily life: a dance club may use varying levels of light in addition to strobes or black lights to create a party atmosphere or to encourage people to dance.

Another designer in theatre is often referred to as the aural or sound designer. This is the person who arranges the sound components. Sound, of course, is all around us: the conversations in a meeting place; trains, trucks, and automobiles that pass by; music that blares from sound systems. In theatre, the sound designer is responsible for sound effects, recorded or digitized music, and the placement and synchronization of microphones for the performers. Not only must he or she create all aural material not originating with the performers; the sound designer must also blend the sound from all sources.

In Part Three we examine the work of the scenery, costume, lighting, and sound designers, which includes the various skilled theatre technicians who assist designers in bringing their visions and sounds to life.

Fireworks are part of colorful pyrotechnic displays on many occasions, such as these starbursts for New Year's Eve in Dubai, UAE. (Patryk Kosmider/Shutterstock)

131

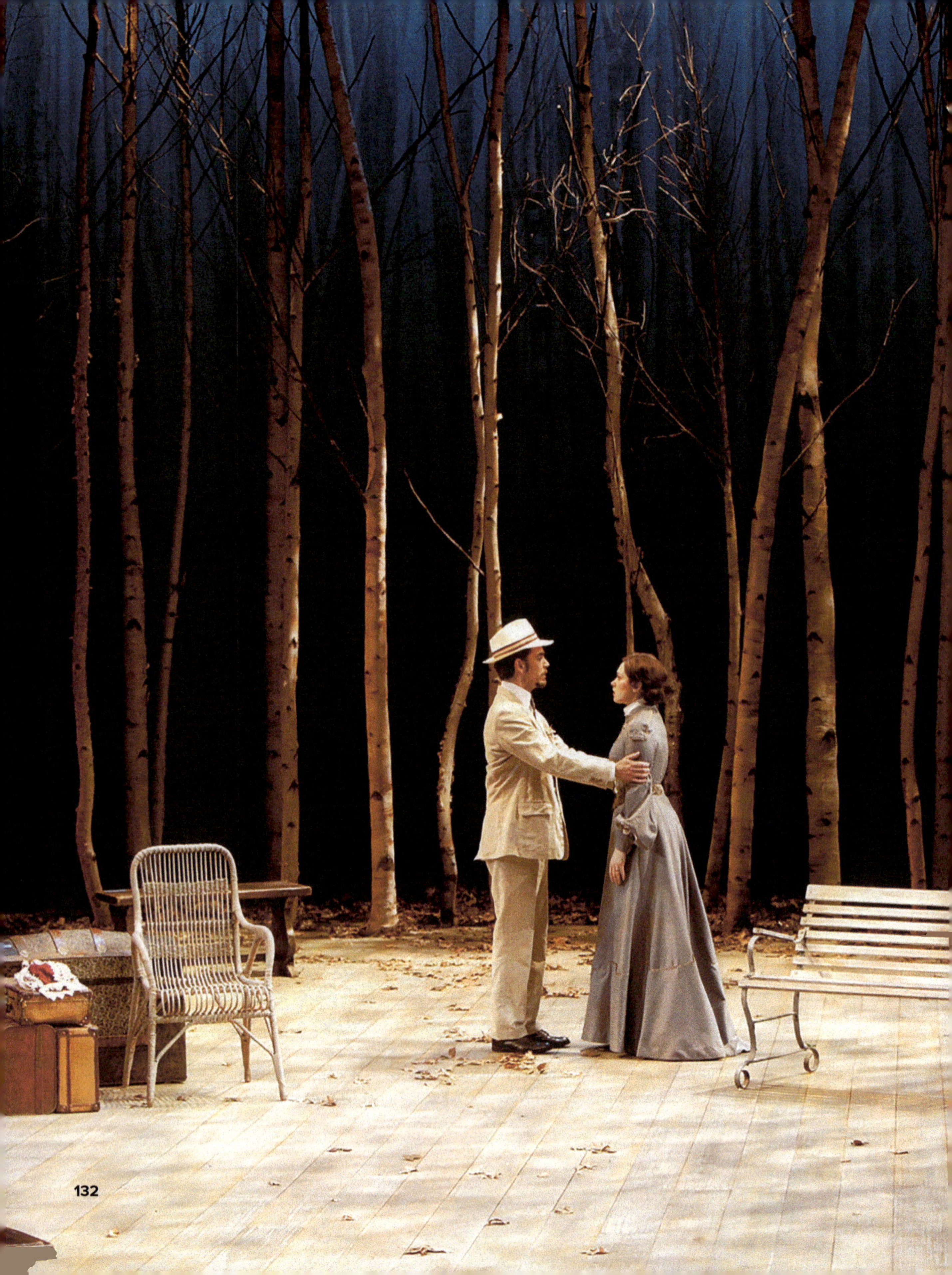

6

Scenery

When we attend a theatre production, we first encounter the environment—the look and size of the space. Is it large or small, formal or informal? Then, as the presentation begins, we become aware of the performers and the roles they are playing, as well as the story that begins to unfold.

But along with these elements, which we immediately notice, other design factors affect how we experience a production: the scenery (possibly including video and projections), costumes, lighting, and sound. In their own way, these are indispensable elements of the theatre experience.

THE AUDIENCE'S VIEW

As we begin to take in the visual elements of a performance, we should look for specifics. Is the scenery realistic, resembling a recognizable kitchen, bedroom, or office? Or is the scenery abstract: shapes, steps, levels, or platforms on a relatively bare stage? Is it futuristic or dreamlike? What about the costumes? Are they like everyday clothes, or do they suggest some period: ancient Rome, the American Revolution, the Civil War, the 1920s, the 1960s, current time? Are the costumes fanciful, like Halloween outfits, or do they resemble clothes from daily life: judges' robes, police uniforms, physicians' outfits?

As for lighting, is it what we would expect in a normal setting, coming from sunlight outdoors or lamps indoors? Or perhaps the lighting is abstract and arbitrary: beams of light cutting through the darkness, special lighting illuminating one part of the stage while the rest is dark. We must also take sound into account. Are there arbitrary sounds: a music track, special effects such as sudden eruptions of synthetic noises? Or is the sound realistic: sirens for ambulances, thunder for a storm?

In all these areas, we should be conscious of the visual and aural signals that are being sent continuously. As for who prepares these signals, they are the designers and all the technicians and others who work with them.

◀ **SCENE DESIGN PROVIDES THE VISUAL ENVIRONMENT**

Scenery provides a visual guide to the place or places in which the action of a theatre piece takes place. Is it realistic or fanciful; is it contemporary or from the past; is it elaborate or minimal? Shown here is an outdoor setting for a production of Anton Chekhov's The Three Sisters, *suggesting loneliness, among other things. Production directed by Joe Dowling with scenery by Patrick Clark. (T. Charles Erickson)*

THE SCENE DESIGNER

The scene designer creates the visual world in which a play unfolds. Together with the playwright and the director, the scene designer determines whether a scene is realistic or in the realm of fantasy. The scene designer decides on the colors, shapes, and visual style that the spectators view and the actors inhabit. The set indicates the kind of world we are in—outdoors or indoors; an affluent environment or a humble one; a time period long ago, today, or in the future. When different locales are called for—in a play with an episodic structure, for instance—the scene designer must ensure that we move smoothly and quickly from one locale to another.

Designers and lead technicians in their respective areas must deal with practical as well as aesthetic considerations. A scene designer must know in which direction a door should open onstage and how high each tread should be on a flight of stairs. A lighting designer must know exactly how many feet above a performer's head a particular light should be placed and whether it requires a 500- or 750-watt lamp. A costume designer must know how much material it takes to make a certain kind of dress and how to "build" clothes so that performers can wear them with confidence and have freedom of movement. A sound designer must know about acoustics, be familiar with echoes, and understand digital sound systems.

As in other elements of theatre, symbols play a large role in design. A single item onstage can suggest an entire room—a bookcase, for instance, suggests a professor's office or a library; a stained-glass window suspended in midair suggests a church or synagogue. A stage filled with a bright yellow-orange glow suggests a cheerful sunny day, whereas a single shaft of pale blue light suggests moonlight or an eerie graveyard at night. How designers deal with the aesthetic and practical requirements of the stage will be clearer when we examine the subject in detail: scene design in this chapter, costumes and lighting and sound in the following chapters.

A BRIEF HISTORY OF STAGE DESIGN

At the beginnings of both Western and Asian theatres there was little of what we now call scene design. The stage itself was the background for the action. In Greek theatre, for instance, the facade of the stage house usually represented a palace or some other imposing edifice. In medieval theatre, "mansions" were set up in town squares. These were small set pieces representing such things as Noah's ark, the whale that swallowed Jonah, and the manger in which Christ was born.

The Elizabethan and Spanish theatres of the Renaissance had bare stages in which the facade of the stage house functioned as the background for the action, just as it had in Greece. In Elizabethan England and Spain, set pieces as well as furniture such as thrones were used, but there was still little scenery as we know it. Very often the language of the plays helped set the place and time of the action.

More elaborate settings began to appear along with the proscenium theatres in Italy and later in France and England in the seventeenth and eighteenth centuries. These were the theatres (described in our chapter *"Theatre Spaces"*) where designers such as the Bibiena family came to the forefront.

Since then, theatre has experienced improved stage machinery (that is, the means by which scenery is shifted), as well as increasing realism in depicting scenes, along with the use of videos and projections and the use of computers and handheld devices to assist in creating designs. This growing emphasis on mechanization, technology, and realism has been the basis of much modern stage scenery.

SCENIC DESIGN TODAY

We are accustomed to "stage settings" in everyday life; but as with other elements in theatre, there is an important difference between interior decoration in real life and set designs for the stage. For example, the stage designer must deal with scale: the relationship of the performer in the set to his or her surroundings. This must in turn correspond to the scale of settings we experience in the world outside the theatre. The scale in a stage set may be different from that of a living room or a courtroom in real life. Robert Edmond Jones, who is widely considered an outstanding American scene designer of the first half of the twentieth century, put it in these terms:

> A good scene should be, not a picture, but an image. Scene-designing is not what most people imagine it is—a branch of interior decorating. There is no more reason for a room on a stage to be a reproduction of an actual room than for an actor who plays the part of Napoleon to be Napoleon or for an actor who plays Death in the old morality play to be dead. Everything that is actual must undergo a strange metamorphosis, a kind of sea change, before it can become truth in the theater.[1]

A stage set signals an atmosphere to us in the same way as a room in real life, but the scene designer must go a step further. As has been pointed out many times, theatre is not life: It resembles life. It has, as Jones suggests, both an opportunity and an obligation to be more than mere reproduction.

The special nature of scenery and other elements of scene design will be clearer when we examine the objectives and functions of scene design.

The Scene Designer's Objectives

In preparing scenery for a stage production, a scene designer has the following objectives:

1. Help set the tone and style of the production.
2. Establish the locale and period in which the play takes place.
3. Develop a design concept consistent with the director's concept.
4. Provide a central image or metaphor, where appropriate.
5. Ensure that scenery is coordinated with other production elements.
6. Solve practical design problems.

Establishing Tone and Style   A stage setting can help establish the mood, style, and meaning of a play. In the arts, style refers to the manner in which a work is done: how scenery looks, how a playwright uses language or exaggerates dramatic elements, how performers portray characters. (A realistic acting style, for example,

SCENERY: AN ENVIRONMENT FOR A PLAY
Scenery provides the visual world in which a performance takes place. It indicates whether a play is realistic, expressionistic, or fantastic and where the action takes place: inside a home, at various locations, in some exterior setting and also whether the story occurs in a past era or at the present time. For *The Curious Incident of the Dog in the Night-Time*, the scene designer, Bunny Christie, created a visual environment filled with mathematical formulas, equations, diagrams—some indicated in silhouette, others in falling papers covered with formulas—to indicate the world in which the main character, Christopher Boone, exists. The production shown here at the National Theatre in London was directed by Marianne Elliott. Christopher was played by Graham Butler. (Geraint Lewis/Alamy Stock Photo)

resembles the way people behave in everyday life; in contrast, the lofty quality of traditional tragedy calls for formal, larger-than-life movements and gestures.)

A slapstick farce might call for a design style involving comic, exaggerated scenery, like a cartoon, and perhaps for outrageous colors, such as bright reds and oranges. Such scenery would match the acting, which would also be exaggerated,

MOOD AND STYLE
The designers should establish the mood, tone, and style of a production, a challenge that is accomplished with architectural shapes, colors, fabrics, furniture, and other elements. Note here the stage setting of the facade of a house with projections of ominous lighting on a rear screen and the stage floor. (Chris Selby/Alamy Stock Photo)

with lots of physical comedy—people tripping over carpets, opening the wrong doors, and so forth. A satire would call for a comment in the design, like the twist in the lines of a caricature in a political cartoon. A serious play could call for less exaggerated or less comic scenery.

Scene design is especially important in indicating to us whether a play is realistic or departs from realism. *Realism* in theatre means that everything connected with a production conforms to our observation of the world around us. This includes the way characters speak and behave, the clothes they wear, the events that occur in the play, and the physical environment. Characters presented in a living room or a bar, for example, will look and act as we expect people in those settings to look and act.

On the other hand, *nonrealism,* or *departures from realism,* means all types of theatre that depart from observable reality. A musical in which characters sing and dance departs from realism because we do not ordinarily go around singing and dancing in public places. A play like Shakespeare's *Macbeth* departs from realism because it has witches and ghosts—two types of creatures not encountered in

realism Broadly, an attempt to present onstage people, places, and events corresponding to those in everyday life.

nonrealism (or departures from realism) All types of theatre that depart from observable reality.

Chapter 6 *Scenery*   137

REALISTIC AND NONREALISTIC SCENERY

Generally, realism and departures from realism call for different design elements, underscoring the difference in style between these two types of theatre. Here (top), we see an extremely realistic set, designed by James Noone for a production of William Inge's *Bus Stop* at the Huntington Theatre, directed by Nicholas Martin. Lighting design: Philip Rosenberg; costume design: Miranda Hoffman. The bottom scene is a surrealistic landscape designed by the avant-garde director Robert Wilson for his rock opera *POEtry,* about Edgar Allan Poe. There is no attempt to portray reality; rather, there is a surrealistic presentation of images and ideas.
(top: T Charles Erickson; bottom: David Baltzer/Zenit/laif/Redux)

our everyday existence. Also, the language of the play is poetry, and there are soliloquies in which characters speak thoughts out loud—again, these are elements that depart from the reality we see in our daily lives. Nonrealistic elements are, of course, highly theatrical and can increase our interest and excitement. Moreover, they often indicate a deeper reality than we see on the surface. Thus "departures from realism" does not imply that something is not genuine or not true; it simply means that something is a departure from what we see in the world around us.

The terms, then, are simply ways of categorizing aspects of theatre and are not mutually exclusive; they can be a helpful starting point in evaluating scene design, because scenery can quickly signal to an audience the type of world we are viewing.

Establishing Locale and Period Whether realistic or not, a stage set should tell us where and when the play takes place. Is the locale a bar? A bedroom? A courtroom? A palace? A forest? The set should also indicate the time period. A kitchen with old-fashioned utensils and no electric appliances sets the play in the past. An early radio and an icebox might tell us that the period is the 1920s. A spaceship or the landscape of a faraway planet would suggest that the play is set in the future.

In addition to indicating time and place, the setting can tell us what kinds of characters a play is about. For example, the characters may be neat and formal or lazy and sloppy. They may be kings and queens or members of an ordinary suburban family. The scenery should suggest these things immediately.

Developing a Design Concept In order to convey information, the scene designer frequently develops a *design concept*. Such a concept should be arrived at in consultation with the director and should complement the directorial concept, as discussed previously. The design concept is a unifying idea carried out visually.

A strong design concept is particularly important when the time and place of a play have been shifted. Modern stage designs for Shakespeare's *A Midsummer Night's Dream* illustrate this point. In most productions, this play is performed in a palace and a forest, as suggested by the text. But the director Peter Brook, in his landmark production, wanted to give the play a clean, spare look so that the audience would see its contemporary implications. Accordingly, the scene designer, Sally Jacobs (1932–2020), fashioned a single set consisting of three bare white walls, rather like the walls of a gymnasium. This single set was used as the background for all the scenes in the play, giving visual unity to the production and also creating a modern, somewhat abstract atmosphere. As part of the action, trapezes were lowered onto the stage at various times, and in some scenes the performers actually played their parts suspended in midair.

A more recent example of a distinctive design concept was that of director Daniel Fish's and scenic designer Laura Jellinek's revival of *Oklahoma* staged off-Broadway in 2018 and on Broadway in 2019. The goal was to immerse the audience in the world of *Oklahoma*, make the setting of the musical more contemporary, and present a bleaker version of this classic work. Jellinek transformed the theatre spaces in which the musical was staged into a social hall, with colorful streamers and Christmas lights dangling from the ceiling. Rather than the usual and ornate settings,

SCENE DESIGN SETS THE TONE
Good scene design sets the tone and style of a production, letting the audience know where and when the action takes place and whether the play or musical is a serious, a comedy, or some other type of drama. Also, it harmonizes with other elements of the production—script, acting, costuming, and direction—to create a unified whole. The setting for the musical *Hadestown*, along with the costumes and lighting indicates the eerie, supernatural, mythological elements of the text and its connections to the contemporary world. Shown here is Reeve Carney and the cast of the musical performing at the 73rd annual Tony Awards at Radio City Music Hall in New York on June 9, 2019 (Sara Krulwich/The New York Times/Redux)

the setting for this revival was simply a large wooden stage floor (much like a gym or social hall floor), long tables (on which the actors sometimes performed), and wooden panels with guns hung on them surrounding the audience.

Providing a Central Image or Metaphor   The design concept is closely related to the idea of a central image or metaphor. Stage design not only must be consistent with the play; it should have its own integrity. The elements of the design—lines, shapes, and colors—should add up to a complete visual universe for the play. Often, therefore, the designer tries to develop a central image or metaphor. In a 2013 production of *The Color Purple*, designed by John Doyle, who was also the director, the set was an abstract re-creation of a single room, a wooden house, with a number of straight-back chairs hanging on the back wall as the central image. Company members would take chairs from the wall and create various spaces that represented the constant change of environment as the lead character went on her journey.

The 2018 revival of *Oklahoma* discussed earlier also created a strong central image for the audience, immersing them in the world of the musical with the surrounding wooden walls, gun racks, and wooden stage floor.

140   Part Three   The Designers

A CENTRAL DESIGN IMAGE
For a production of the musical *The Color Purple*, director and designer John Doyle created a central design concept consisting of a bare wooden wall on which chairs were hung. To create different locales and scenes, performers would take chairs off the wall and place them on stage. They could thus indicate a wide variety of spaces in a very novel and economic way. Based on the novel by Alice Walker, the play was by Marsha Norman and the music by Brenda Russell. Shown here in the role of Harpo is Adebayo Bolaji. (Geraint Lewis/Alamy Stock Photo)

Coordinating Scenery with the Whole   Because scenic elements have such strong symbolic value and are so important to the overall effect of a production, the designer needs to provide scenery consistent with the playwright's intent and the director's concept. If the text and acting are highly stylized, the setting should be stylized too. If the text and acting are realistic, the setting should also be realistic, rather than, say, a fantastic or overpowering spectacle. As with other elements, the setting should contribute to the overall effect of a production.

Solving Practical Design Problems   Finally, the scene designer must deal with practical problems of design. Many of these involve physical elements of stage design, to which we will now turn.

Elements of Scene Design

Five Elements of Scene Design   As the scene designer proceeds, he or she makes use of the following elements:

1. *Line,* the outline or silhouette of elements onstage; for example, predominantly curved lines versus sharply angular lines.

2. *Mass,* the overall bulk or weight of scenic elements; for example, a series of high, heavy platforms or fortress walls versus a bare stage or a stage with only a single tree on it.
3. *Composition,* the balance and arrangement of elements; the way elements are arranged; for example, mostly to one side of the stage, in a vertical or horizontal configuration, or equally distributed onstage.
4. *Texture,* the "feel" projected by surfaces and fabrics; for example, the slickness of chrome or glass versus the roughness of brick or burlap.
5. *Color,* the shadings and contrasts of color combinations.

The designer will use these elements to affect us, in conjunction with the action and other aspects of the production.

ground plan A blueprint or floor plan of the stage indicating the placement of scenery, furniture, doors and windows, and the various levels of the stage, as well as the walls of rooms, platforms, and the like.

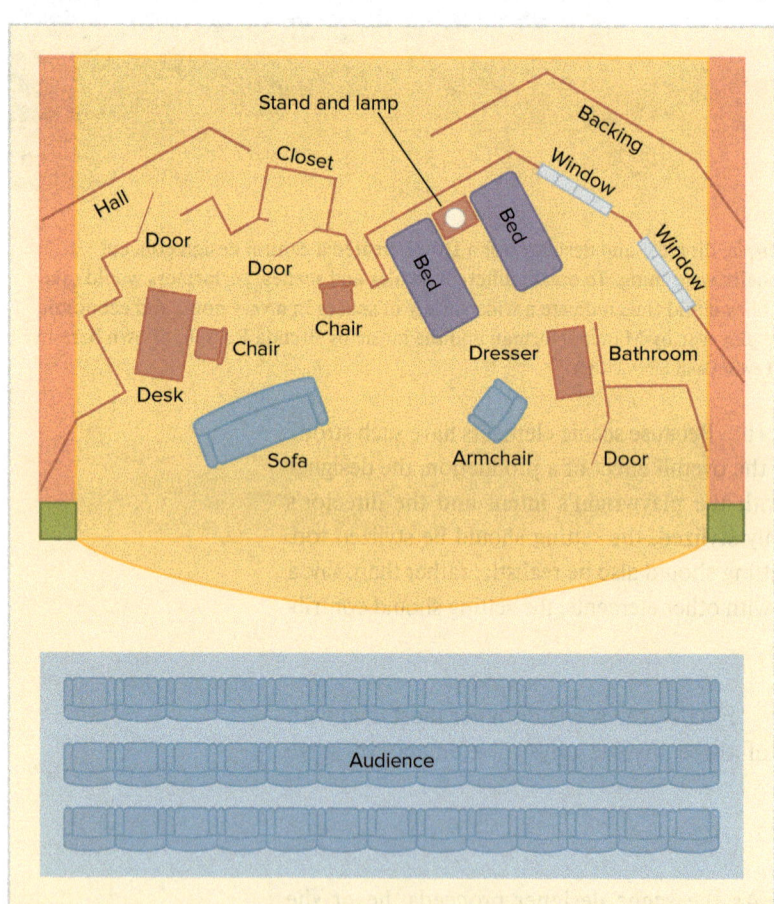

Physical Layout: The Playing Area

A playing area must, obviously, fit into a certain stage space and accommodate the performers. A designer cannot plan a gigantic stage setting for a theatre where the proscenium opening is only twenty feet wide and the stage is no more than fifteen feet deep. By the same token, to design a small room in the midst of a forty-foot stage opening might be ludicrous.

The designer must also take into account the physical layout of the stage space. If a performer must leave by a door on the right side of the stage and return a few moments later by a door on the left, the designer must obviously provide space for crossing behind the scenery. If performers need to change costumes quickly offstage, the scene designer must make certain that there is room offstage for changing. If there is to be a sword fight, the actors must have space in which to make their turns, to advance and retreat.

Any type of physical movement requires a certain amount of space, and the scene designer must allow for this in the ground plan. A *ground plan* is a floor plan outlining the various levels on the stage and indicating the placement of all scenery, furniture, doors, windows, and so on. The designer, working in conjunction with the director, is chiefly responsible for ensuring a practical ground plan.

GROUND PLAN
To aid the director, performers, and stage technicians, the designer draws a ground plan, or blueprint of the stage, showing the exact locations of furniture, walls, windows, doors, and other scenic elements.

142   Part Three   The Designers

IN FOCUS: THE TECHNOLOGICAL INNOVATIONS OF THE GLOBAL DESIGNER JOSEF SVOBODA

The Czech scene designer Josef Svoboda (1920–2002) developed a number of significant techniques in stage design, which have since been adopted and utilized by designers in countries around the globe. Svoboda's work centered on his understanding of the kinetic stage and scenography. The term *kinetic stage* refers to his belief that the set should not function independently of the actors, but rather should develop and adapt as a performance progresses. *Scenography* was what he called his art, conveying the sense that he created a whole physical space, not just designs on paper intended for the back of the stage. His experiments with these ideas led to many significant concepts in modern stage design, most notably the *polyekran*, *diapolyekran,* and *laterna magika*.

Polyekran literally means multiscreen and was the practice, devised by Svoboda, of using multiple screens at multiple angles and heights. Although real people and objects were projected, the aim was to convince the spectators not that they were looking at the real object, but rather that they were looking at a projection or a collage of projections. A later development of this technique was *diapolyekran*, which employed whole walls of small, square screens making up a composite image. The wall of screens could be used to present one unified image, cubist images, or a collage.

Laterna magika, the best-known of his innovations, used screens in conjunction with actors; the actors were part of the film, and the film was part of the action. The projections used in this form were not simply for decoration or for communicating images independent of the action; rather, the projections and action functioned together, creating a new manner of performance.

These developments were introduced to the global community in 1958 at the Brussels World's Fair, where they instantly commanded attention from the wider theatrical community. Svoboda had been the chief designer at the National Theatre in Prague at the time of the World's Fair, and a showcase of the work of the theatre was displayed to the global audience, winning him three medals.

What was seen as ingenious in 1958 was quickly adopted and adapted by numerous practitioners in many countries, and the effect of these means of design can still be witnessed in contemporary theatre, in performance art, and on Broadway, as well as at rock concerts and sporting events. This incorporation of screens and projections as well as video into onstage action has infiltrated the world of the theatre to the extent that it has become one of the conventional tools of theatre design worldwide.

MICHAL (KRUMPHANZL/AFP/Newscom)

Prepared by Naomi Stubbs, Associate Professor, LaGuardia Community College, CUNY.

How doors open and close, where a sofa is placed, at what angle steps will lead to a second floor—all these are important. Performers must be able to execute stairs easily and to sit in such a way that the audience can readily see them, and they must have enough space to interact with each other naturally and convincingly. If a performer opens a door onstage and is immediately blocked from the view of the audience, this is obviously an error on the part of the scene designer.

wagon Low platform mounted on wheels or casters by means of which scenery is moved on- and offstage.

turntable A circle set into the floor of a stage that is rotated mechanically or electronically to bring one set into view as another disappears.

Materials and Machinery of Scene Design There are some long-used materials and machinery for scene design that continue to be used even in our increasingly technologically advanced theatre world.

In creating a stage set, a designer begins with the stage floor. At times, trapdoors are set into the floor; through them, performers can enter or leave the stage. For some productions, tracks or slots are set into the stage floor, and set pieces or wagons are brought onstage in these tracks. A *wagon* is a low platform set on wheels. Wagon stages are brought onstage electronically using computer assistance or by stagehands hidden behind them. This type of scene change is frequently used in musical theatre. Another device used along the stage floor is a *treadmill*, which can carry performers, furniture, or props from one side of the stage to the other. Sometimes the stage floor includes a *turntable*—a circle, set into the floor, which is rotated mechanically or electronically to bring one set into view as another disappears.

Formerly, equipment such as turntables, wagons, and treadmills would be moved mechanically or by hand. However, these operations have been computerized. Complicated scene changes can be controlled by computer so that they take place efficiently and simultaneously. Computers can also control the turning and shifting of scenic elements. In addition, safety features are built into the new computerized equipment. When performers are on a moving treadmill, for example, light beams or pressure-sensitive plates can detect a malfunction and shut the system down before anyone is hurt. More recently, scene shifting can even be controlled by handheld devices.

SPECIAL SCENIC EFFECTS: THE SCRIM
Scene designers use various materials and devices to achieve their effects. One popular scenic element is the scrim, which can be transparent when light comes from behind it and opaque when light comes from the front. It is especially effective for scenes of memory and fantasy. Shown here is the use of a scrim in the Broadway musical *An American in Paris*. (Nigel Norrington/Camera Press/Redux)

SCENIC PROJECTIONS
An increasingly popular scenic resource is projections: rear-screen and front-screen projections produced on an opaque surface or on a scrim. Projections allow rapid changes of locale, panoramic views, and abstract designs. Shown here is a scene from 2016 production of *The Tempest* by William Shakespeare at the Royal Shakespeare Company, directed by Gregory Doran, with Jennifer Wilton. Projections create a supernatural environment. (Geraint Lewis/Alamy Stock Photo)

Instead of coming from the sides, scenery can be dropped from the ***fly loft;*** *to fly* is the term used when scenery is raised into the area above the stage, out of sight of the audience.

From floor level, ramps and platforms can be built to any height desired. To create walls or divisions of other kinds, for many years the most commonly used element was the ***flat,*** so named because it is a single flat unit, consisting of canvas stretched on a wood frame. The side of the flat facing the audience was painted to look like a solid wall, and flats connected together were made to look like a complete room.

Today scene designers and shop technicians have turned increasingly to the *hard flat*, sometimes called a *movie* or *Hollywood flat;* it consists of a thin, solid material, called *lauan,* mounted on a wooden or hollow metal frame. A hard flat can be painted, and three-dimensional plastic moldings can be attached to it, creating cornices, chair rails, and other interesting features. Other vertical units are cutouts—small pieces made like flats or cut out of plywood. These, too, can be painted.

A special type of scenery is the ***scrim***—a gauze or cloth screen. A scrim can be painted like a regular flat; however, the wide mesh of the cloth allows light to pass through. When light shines on a scrim from the front—that is, from our point of

fly loft Space above the stage where scenery may be lifted out of sight by ropes and pulleys.

flat A scenic unit consisting of canvas stretched on a wooden frame often used with similar units to create a set.

scrim Thin, open-weave fabric that is nearly transparent when lit from behind and opaque when lit from the front.

Chapter 6 *Scenery*   145

SPECIAL EFFECTS

All manner of stage spectacle, from the eerie to the comic, come under the heading of special effects. An ancient tradition in the theatre, these effects can include fog, ghosts, and swords that appear to run through victims. The play *The Thirty-Nine Steps* calls for fog when we see the characters Pamela (Jennifer Ferrin) and Hannay (Charles Edwards) running for their lives, hoping to escape danger by climbing up a ladder. The play, which had its American premiere with the Huntington Theatre Company, is based on the Alfred Hitchcock film of the same name. The scenic and costume designer was Peter McKintosh. (T. Charles Erickson)

view in the audience—it is reflected off the painted surface, and the scrim appears to be a solid surface. When light comes from behind, the scrim becomes transparent and, as audience members, we can see performers and scenery behind it. Scrims are particularly effective in scenes where ghosts appear or when eerie effects are desired. Scrims are also useful in memory plays or plays with flashbacks: The audience sees the scene in the present in front of the scrim; then, as the lights in front fade and the lights behind come up, a scene with a cloudy, translucent quality appears through the gauzelike scrim, indicating a scene taking place in someone's memory or in the past.

Another scenic device is *screen projection*. An image can be projected on a screen either from in front—as in an ordinary movie theatre—or from behind. The advantage of projection from behind is that the performers will not be in the beam of light, and thus there will be no shadows or silhouettes. And today, projections can be projected onto three-dimensional objects and manipulated through the use of computers.

Obviously, projections offer many advantages: images can change with the rapidity of cinema, and vast scenes can be presented onstage in a way that would otherwise require tremendously elaborate scene painting. Two recent productions that used projections extensively and successfully in London and then on Broadway were *War Horse* and *The Curious Incident of the Dog in the Night-Time*.

The use of video and projection has led to scene designers either becoming proficient with the new technology (since in some instances, video and projections literally replace scenery) or with video and projection designers being employed as part of the design team.

prop Properties; objects that are used by performers onstage or are necessary to complete a set.

Special Effects   Scrims and projections bring us to a consideration of special effects. These are effects of scenery, lighting, sound, and props that seem unusual or even miraculous. (The term ***prop*** comes from the word property; it refers to any object that will be used onstage but is not a permanent part of the scenery or costumes. Props are such things as smartphones, lamps, mirrors, computers, walking sticks, umbrellas, and fans.) Special effects include fog, ghosts, knives, or swords that appear to stab victims, walls and windows that fall apart, and so forth.

146   Part Three   The Designers

> ## IN FOCUS: NEW DESIGN MATERIALS: VIDEO AND PROJECTION DESIGN
>
> Video design and projection design are burgeoning areas of stage design. While early on, video and projection design consisted of integrating film and static images onto the stage of live theatre events, with the advent of greater computer control, the introduction of tablets and other handheld devices, high-definition video, more sophisticated projection technology, and digital downloads, designers in these areas have become more significant contributors to the creation of an overall stage design, not just special effects. In some instances, they have become equal partners with the set designer.
>
> The design process itself has changed due to the development of three-dimensional animation software in which the set design can be manipulated and presented without the need to create a series of traditional models. Projection mapping allows projections to be designed and viewed on a computer and then projected on various three-dimensional objects of varying sizes on stage, not just on a two-dimensional surface, as was true in the past.
>
> But even more significantly, the designs themselves incorporate these new technologies. Today, enhanced projectors, three-dimensional projections, and high-definition video can be employed to create onstage, for example, avatars that seem to interact with live actors. Actors can walk through projections or become part of a projection, creating magical effects. Entire sets can be replaced by high-tech videos and projections. Gaming technology allows live actors to initiate moments of special effects on stage themselves.
>
> One of the most spectacular recent uses of projections was in the Broadway and roadshow productions of the Disney musical *Frozen* (2018). When Anna covers her entire kingdom in ice, the entire effect was created through projections.
>
> Some critics worry that the emphasis on technology in design is an ultimately unsuccessful attempt by theatre artists to compete with film and television and unfortunately undercuts what theatre does best: creating live interaction between the actor and the audience. However, others point out that throughout theatre history, all the way back to the Greeks and Romans, there have been experiments with special effects and new technologies. Our theatre will continue to explore the ways in which the innovations of this digital age can be incorporated in live performances.

Today, films and television—because of their technical capabilities—have very realistic special effects, like burning buildings and exploding cars. Also, computers can create the world of dinosaurs, supernatural universes, or all forms of catastrophes.

However, the use of special effects onstage is almost as old as theatre itself. From the Greeks on, theatre has tried to create the illusion of the miraculous or extraordinary. With the enhanced use of computer and handheld technologies, along with all of the ways in which new media can be employed, theatrical productions frequently incorporate sophisticated effects.

An example of the use of an onstage special effect occurs in the internationally popular musical *The Phantom of the Opera*, when a huge chandelier falls from the top of the auditorium onto the stage. In the musical *Matilda* (2010), a child seemingly writes on a chalkboard using her eyes. Unbeknownst to the audience, the chalkboard is plastic and has the letters projected on it from a screen behind it.

We will see in a later discussion that there are also many special effects using lighting and sound.

PLAYING YOUR PART: EXPERIENCING THEATRE

1. Think about your residence hall room or your home as a set design. What does it reveal about you? Why?
2. Set your classroom up as a proscenium theatre, if possible, with the audience facing in one direction. Using stage directions (stage right, stage left, upstage, downstage), direct a classmate around the stage area.
3. If a designer was going to create a play with you as a character, what props would be most central to representing you on stage?
4. Watch a recent film that employs significant special effects. Why are such special effects so popular? Is there any way that the same effects could be created in the theatre?
5. Visit your university or community theatre scene shop. What types of equipment are found in the shop? Is there a set under construction? Ask if there are drawings, elevations, or ground plans that you might review.
6. Visit a technical rehearsal at your university or community theatre. Ask if you can walk around the setting prior to or after the rehearsal. What elements make up the set? Is any machinery being employed for set changes?

The Process of Scene Design

In meeting the objectives described earlier, how does the scene designer proceed? Although every designer has his or her own method, usually the same general pattern is followed.

The designer reads the script and develops ideas about scene designs and a design concept. They may even make a few rough sketches to illustrate thoughts about the designs. Meanwhile, the director also has ideas about the scenery. These ideas may vary considerably, depending on the director: They may be vague, or they may be an exact picture of what the scenery should look like.

Director and designer meet for a preliminary conference to exchange ideas about the design. During these discussions, they will develop and discuss questions of style, a visual concept for the production, and the needs of the performers.

Next, the designer develops preliminary sketches, called *thumbnail sketches*, and rough plans to provide a basis for further discussions about the scenic elements.

As the designer proceeds, attempts are made to fill out the visual concept with sketches, drawings, models, and the like. Sometimes the designer will bring the director sketches showing several possible ideas, each emphasizing different elements to achieve different results.

When the director and the designer have decided on an idea and a rough design, the designer will make a more complete sketch, usually in color, called a ***rendering***. If the director approves of the rendering, the designer will make a small-scale three-dimensional model that the director can use to help stage the show. There are two types of models. One shows only the location of the platform and walls, with perhaps some light detail drawn in; it is usually all white. The other is a complete, finished model: Everything is duplicated as fully as possible, including color and perhaps moldings and texture.

Today, designers increasingly use computers, handheld devices, and digital media to develop not only ground plans but also their renderings, thumbnail sketches, and three-dimensional models of what a set will look like. Computerized design, known technically as ***computer-assisted design (CAD),*** is very flexible. The designer can make instantaneous changes in what appears on the screen and can

rendering A complete drawing of a set, usually in color.

Computer-assisted design (CAD) Designs created by computer. All features of a set design, including ground plans, elevations, and walls, can be indicated by computer, and variations and alternations can be easily created and displayed.

STEPS IN THE SCENE DESIGN PROCESS

In designing a production, the scenic, costume, lighting, and sound designers look closely at the script and work cooperatively with the director and with one another. Scene designers often make sketches, computer-generated designs, and models in preparing for the scenic aspect of a production. Here we see three stages in the scene design for the musical *In the Heights,* which originated off-Broadway at the 37 Arts Theatre in New York and later moved to Broadway. The scene designer Anna Louizos carefully scouted out the Washington Heights neighborhood in Manhattan where the play takes place and made many rough pencil sketches, one of which is shown here at the top. The second photo shows one of various set models she built and the bottom photo shows the completed set with actors onstage. (Top-left and top-right: Anna Louizos; Bottom: Sara Krulwich/The New York Times/Redux)

Chapter 6 *Scenery*

IN FOCUS: APP TECHNOLOGY FOR SCENE DESIGN

As we have noted, app technology for mobile devices has greatly affected the work of actors and directors. The same is true for scene designers and their collaborators.

A variety of apps are available that allow designers to create drawings and sketches (including two-dimensional and three-dimensional versions) on handheld devices. Various AutoCad apps allow for the sharing and editing on mobile devices of computer-assisted drawings of settings.

There are apps that allow designers to view and choose paint colors and match them to each other.

The app Technical Theatre Assistant saves time for stage carpentry projects. It produces lists for all of the materials needed for creating scene pieces, as well as diagrams for constructing set pieces.

All of these applications allow set designers and their collaborators to work on the go and interact digitally.

---

easily indicate to the director and others alternative plans and features of a stage set. Not only ground plans but also the three-dimensional look of a set can be instantaneously rearranged to let both director and designer see what various configurations would look like. In this way, the scene can be shown in three dimensions; it can also be looked at from various perspectives: from the right or left, from above, from the front.

These digital renderings and models can be created and shared on tablets and other handheld devices as well as on computers. Designs can be sent immediately to directors and other collaborators via e-mail or on the "digital cloud."

THE SCENE DESIGNER'S COLLABORATORS AND THE PRODUCTION PROCESS

As with every element of theatre, there is a collaborative aspect to scene design: In addition to the director, there are a number of other important people with whom the scene designer works. In fact, any scene design would be little more than a creative idea without the input of the following collaborators: technical directors, property designers, scenic charge artists, stage managers, design assistants, and skilled technicians working in every one of these areas, often with expanded new technologies. These scenic collaborators are essential at every level of production, from university theatre to regional professional theatre to Broadway.

A few definitions are in order. The **technical director** is responsible for solving overall technical problems; the technical director is in charge of scheduling, constructing and painting scenery, and in general making certain that all designs are executed as conceived by the scene designer. The *property designer* creates and executes all props; this work may include building special pieces of furniture, finding or devising magical equipment, and selecting items such as lamps and other accessories. *Scenic charge artists* are responsible for seeing that sets are built and painted according to the specifications of the scene designer. In the case of painting the set, the person in charge is referred to as the *paint charge artist*. As noted earlier in

technical director Staff member responsible for scheduling, construction, and installation of all equipment; he or she is responsible for guaranteeing that designs are executed according to the designer's specifications.

this chapter, projection design is becoming a more common feature of the scenic environment, also requiring additional skilled technicians to bring the world of the play to life.

Realizing the design typically begins with drafting (predominantly with CAD these days, including the use of tablets and other handheld digital devices) all production ground plans, also known as floor plans, which are detailed layouts of each scenic location drafted within the context of a specific theatre space. Drawings that show all exact scenic details from the point of view of the audience are known as *designer/front elevations*. The drafting of the designer/front elevations is completed either by the scene designer or by various design assistants. These drawings are then used to construct accurate scenic models or perspective renderings that are useful visual tools for anyone involved in the production. Once they have been given final approval by the director, the floor plans are delivered to the stage manager, who will tape on the floor of the rehearsal spaces an accurate, full-scale version of all platforms, ramps, staircases, and entrances and exits to be used by the director and the actors in rehearsal.

The use of CAD (which, as noted, includes the use of handheld digital devices as well as computers) is now commonplace to create almost all of these representations of settings, since designers and their associates, assistants, and collaborators are now using advanced CAD skills. The flexibility of CAD allows designers to make changes very quickly and to share designs electronically with all collaborators. Designs can be sent via e-mail, by placing them in the "digital cloud," or viewed on tablets or other handheld devices. Such technological flexibility in the design process, along with the use of projection and video technology, have made all forms of computer-assisted design the norm in almost all theatres today.

The technical director uses the floor plans to determine where all the construction elements will go, as well as to determine backstage escapes for actors. The technical director then completes construction drawings for all those floor plan elements. The technical director also converts the complete set of designer/front elevations into a complete set of rear elevations or working drawings for construction purposes. Without this critical engineering and drafting step, the scenery could never be built accurately or safely. The technical director and scenic designer work together in much the same way an engineer will work with an architect in completing the blueprints to plan construction of a building.

The visual world of many production designs is so complex that a property designer typically works as an essential collaborator with the scenic designer. The property area is also broken down into areas: (1) functional props used by actors, and (2) set dressing, which fills out the visual stage reality. Once the scene designer has approved all of the property designer's research, solutions, and drawings, those are also forwarded to the technical director to be worked into the construction schedule. It is also frequently the property designer who completes the mechanical special effects used in theatrical production.

Due to developments in computer and electronic technology, special effect solutions are frequently, as noted earlier, crafted by projection designers as well. Although not many productions utilize the intense level of scenic projection noted previously, projection technology solutions are finding their way into many

> ## PLAYING YOUR PART: THINKING ABOUT THEATRE
>
> 1. What production that you have attended had the most elaborate scenery and special effects? What effect did these visual elements have on you? Were you captivated by the visual elements, or did you think they were overdone?
> 2. What production that you have seen had the least amount of scenery and visual effects? Did you miss seeing an elaborate scene design, or did you enjoy using your imagination to create the setting in your mind?
> 3. Have you seen a production that has many changes of setting? How efficiently and effectively were the scene changes carried out? What types of stage machinery were employed to create smooth transitions?
> 4. It is often argued that film and television can employ more realistic scenery and special effects than the theatre. Is there any way in which theatrical scenery and special effects compete with those in the media?

production designs for special visual effects requiring the presence of yet another essential scenic collaborator.

The scene designer and assistants also complete a full series of paint elevations that are delivered to the scenic charge artist, who works with a group of scenic artists in completing the painting of the actual scenery. Paint charge and scenic artists require both talent and technique, for instance, to create the feeling of rare old wood in a library, or of bricks, or of a glossy, elegant surface in an expensive living room.

In commercial theatre, construction drawings and paint elevations are sent to scenic houses separate from the theatre that specialize in both construction and painting. In regional theatres and university settings there are typically support spaces and support staff for scenic, property, painting, and costume construction on-site. In these settings the entire production team is typically present at all times, allowing for convenient tracking of the construction and painting process. In Broadway and other professional producing theatres without technical support spaces and staff, it is necessary for the designer or the assistant designers (or both) to visit the scenic houses and paint studios to check on progress and to ensure consistency with the original design intent.

When the time comes for technical rehearsals, dress rehearsals, and the actual performances after the official opening, a production requires backstage leadership by the stage management team. The members of this team call all the cues for lights, sound, projections, scenic shifts, and actors' entrances. An entire crew of stagehands will work together to coordinate every change, no matter how small, in the visual world of the play. These changes may involve a fly crew for flown scenery; a shift crew for either automated, computerized, or manual shifting of entire settings; and a property crew for any preparation or movement of furniture and properties onstage or offstage. Meanwhile, a crew of dressers, whose work will be covered in more detail in the next chapter, will work backstage with the actors helping them prepare for the upcoming scene. As noted earlier in our discussion of directing, once a production moves beyond opening night, it is controlled by the stage manager, who is also responsible for maintaining the director's artistic intent, as well as maintaining consistency in cue placement and the visual world of the play.

DESIGNING A TOTAL ENVIRONMENT
For some productions designers go beyond scenery and special effects to design an entire theatre space, reimagining the relationship of the stage area to the audience. Shown here is a scene from the 2018 Broadway revival of *Oklahoma*, at the Circle in the Square Theatre, in which designer and director tried to place the audience in the environment of the musical. At intermission, for example, the audience became fully immersed in and part of the total environment of the production when they were served chili and cornbread, just as the homesteaders in the musical might have eaten, on the stage set. (Sara Krulwich/The New York Times/Redux)

Designing a Total Environment

Sometimes a designer goes beyond scenery and special effects to design an entire theatre space, rearranging the seating for spectators and determining the relationship of the stage area to the audience. For instance, in an open space such as a gymnasium or warehouse, a designer might build an entire theatre, including the seats or stands for the audience and the designated acting areas. In this case, the designer considers the size and shape of the space, the texture and nature of the building materials, the atmosphere of the space, and the needs of the play itself. This is also true of multifocus theatre.

Even in Broadway theatres some designers change the architecture of the theatre space in creating the world of the play; we noted in the previous chapter that a recent example was *Natasha, Pierre & the Great Comet of 1812*.

Another example was the 2018 revival of *Oklahoma* that we discussed earlier in this chapter. At intermission, the audience became fully immersed in and part of the total environment of the production when they were served chili and cornbread, just as the homesteaders in the musical might have eaten, on the stage set.

IN FOCUS: SCENE DESIGN IN FILM AND TELEVISION

The scene designer in the theater, unlike those working in film and television, has some key limitations. The set designer for a theatre production must create a design for a specific theatre space and its technical capabilities. Scene changes must be designed keeping the space in mind. Often scene shifting must be done in full view of the audience. Multiple environments may have to be placed on stage at the same time, requiring the designer to not create fully realistic settings. The theatre designer often relies on the audience's imagination and the play's language to help fill out the setting. Even with new computer technology and media, scene designers' work is confined to the spaces for which they design.

Given the complexity of film and television designs, some projects hire both a production designer and a set designer. While these terms have been frequently used interchangeably, in recent years the functions of each have become distinct. Production designers, who are unique to film and television, oversee sets, costumes, lighting, and makeup. Set designers in film and television, as does a theatre scene designer, focus on creating the needed environments for the script.

The only thing that might stand in the way of a film set designer is the budget. For large-budget films, few limitations are placed on the scene designer. Locales can be filmed in actual locations or created within studios. Digital and computer enhancements can bring to life remarkable places and design effects.

Evaluating Scene Design

After we attend a production, there are many questions we should ask ourselves as we try to evaluate the scene design and its success in supporting the play presented. Among those questions are:

1. What information was conveyed by the scenery about time, place, characters, and situation? How was this information conveyed to you?
2. What was the overall atmosphere of the setting? How was that atmosphere created?
3. Did any colors dominate the design? How did colors affect your impression of the theater event?
4. Was the setting a specific place, or was it no recognizable or real locale? Did that choice seem appropriate for the play?
5. If the setting was realistic, how effectively did it reproduce what the place would actually look like?
6. Were there symbolic elements in the scenery? If so, what were they? How did they relate to the play?
7. Were there many scene changes? Were they handled effectively? Could you tell how they were done?
8. Were projections or video used in the production? If so, what was their function: to create scenery, for special effects, for both? Did you feel the use of these media was appropriate? Why or why not?
9. Were there any special effects? Were you able to ascertain how they were done?

We have been examining the work of the scene designer. We turn in the next chapter to someone whose work is closely related: the costume designer.

SUMMARY

1. We encounter forms of scene design in everyday life: in the carefully planned decor of a restaurant, in a hotel lobby, or in a decorated apartment.
2. Scene design for the stage differs from interior decorating in that it creates an environment and an atmosphere that is not complete until occupied by performers and that is able to meet the practical needs of the script.
3. In addition to creating an environment, the scene designer has the following objectives: to set tone and style, distinguish realism from nonrealism, establish time and place, develop a design concept, provide a central design metaphor, coordinate scenery with other elements, and deal with practical considerations.
4. As in other aspects of theatre, in scene design there has been more and more crossover and interaction between theatre design and design for many types of popular entertainment.
5. In practical terms the scene designer must deal with the limits of the stage space and the offstage area. For example, ramps must not be inclined too steeply, and platforms must provide an adequate playing area for the performers. In short, the stage designer must know the practical considerations of stage usage and stage carpentry, as well as the materials available, in order to achieve desired effects. Close work with the technical director allows the scene designer to push the limits of construction in creating a unique visual world while maintaining a safe environment for performers.
6. In theatrical productions that stress visual elements over the play or the acting, the scene design must constantly engage and entrance the spectator.
7. Special effects are elements of scenery, lighting, costumes, props, or sound that appear highly unusual or miraculous. Technical expertise is required to develop them properly.
8. Elements of design include line, mass, composition, texture, color, rhythm, and movement.
9. The scene designer works closely with the director and other designers and creates a series of drawings (sketches and renderings) and models of what the final stage picture will look like.
10. In dealing with created or found space, the designer must plan the entire environment: the audience area as well as the stage area.
11. The technical director, with staff, supervises the construction of scenery, special effects, and the like in order to meet the designer's specifications.
12. A scenic charge artist and additional scenic artists must translate the look shown in models, renderings, and paint elevations into the full-scale version of the design.
13. Working with the technical director and the scenic charge artist are the property designer and the paint charge artist.

Design Elements: Audience Sitting in Theatre (theatre): Ron Chapple/Photodisc/Getty Images; Studio Light (spotlights): Exactostock/SuperStock

156

7

Stage Costumes

Clothes have often indicated or signaled a number of things regarding the wearer, including the following:

- Position and status
- Occupation
- Relative flamboyance or modesty
- Degree of independence or regimentation
- Whether one is dressed for work or leisure, for a routine event or for a special occasion

As soon as we see what clothing people are wearing, we receive visual messages about them and form impressions of them. We instantaneously relate those messages and impressions to our past experience and our preconceptions, and we make judgments, often including value judgments. Even if we have never before met someone, we feel we know a great deal when we first see what that person is wearing.

COSTUMES FOR THE STAGE

In theatre, clothes send us signals similar to those in everyday life, but as with the other elements of theatre, there are significant differences between the costumes of everyday life and theatrical costumes. Stage costumes often communicate the same information as ordinary clothes with regard to position, status, and occupation, but onstage this information is magnified because every element in theatre is a focus of attention. Also, costumes on a stage must meet other requirements not normally imposed in everyday life. These requirements will be clearer after we look at the objectives of costume design.

Objectives of Costume Design

Stage costumes should meet the following seven requirements:

1. Help establish the style of a production.
2. Indicate the historical period of a play and the locale in which it occurs.

◀ **STAGE COSTUMES: AESTHETIC, SYMBOLIC, AND SUITED TO THE CHARACTER**
In addition to being stylish and beautiful, costumes can convey a wealth of information to the audience. Seen here are characters in colorful, formal, historic attire in the Broadway production of the musical Hamilton, *written by Lin-Manuel Miranda. The colors of the costumes also help the audience differentiate between the characters in the musical. The costume designer was Paul Tazewell. Seen here are Daveed Diggs (left), as Thomas Jefferson and Lin-Manuel Miranda as Hamilton. (Sara Krulwich/The New York Times/Redux)*

3. Indicate the nature of individual characters or groups in a play—their stations in life, their occupations, and their personalities.
4. Show relationships among characters—separating major characters from minor ones and contrasting one group with another.
5. Where appropriate, symbolically convey the significance of individual characters or the theme of the play.
6. Meet the needs of individual performers, making it possible for a performer to move freely in a costume, perhaps to dance or engage in a sword fight, and (when required) to change quickly from one costume to another.
7. Be consistent with the production as a whole, especially other visual elements.

The Process of Costume Design

In order to achieve these objectives, the costume designer goes through a process similar to that of the scene designer. The costume designer reads the script, taking particular note of the characters: their age, physical qualities, and special traits, as well as their roles in the play.

Early in the process, the costume designer also meets with the director and other designers to discuss the "look" that the show will have and how the various elements will be coordinated. The costume designer may make preliminary sketches or use computer-assisted design to show the director and other designers. These may include not only suggestions about style (for example, historical, modern, futuristic) but also ideas for colors and fabrics. Once agreed upon, these designs will move from sketches to renderings (which again may be done by hand or on computers or handheld devices) of what the costumes will look like in their final form. Swatches of material may be attached to these designs, indicating the texture and color of the fabrics to be used.

As part of this process, the costume designer will meet with the members of the cast, measuring each performer and making certain that the costumes will be workable and appropriate for the individual performers.

The following sections discuss how the various objectives of costume design are realized by the designer in this process.

Setting Tone and Style Along with scenery and lighting, costumes should inform us about the style of a play. For a production set in outer space, for instance, the costumes would be futuristic. For a Restoration comedy, the costumes could be quite elegant, with elaborate gowns for the women and lace at the men's collars and cuffs. For a tragedy, the clothes might be formal and dignified—seeing them, we would know immediately that the play itself was serious.

Indicating Time and Place Costumes indicate the period and location of a play: whether it is historical or modern, whether it is set in a foreign country or the United States, and so on. A play might take place in ancient Egypt, in seventeenth-century Spain, or in modern Africa. Costumes should tell us when and where the action occurs.

For most historical plays, the director and the costume designer have a range of choices, depending on the directorial concept. For a production of Shakespeare's *Julius Caesar,* for instance, the costumes could indicate the ancient Roman period when Caesar actually lived; in this case, the costumes would include Roman togas and soldiers' helmets. Or the costumes could be Elizabethan. We know that in Shakespeare's day costumes were heightened versions of the English clothes worn at the time, regardless of the period in which a play was set. As a third option, the designer could create costumes for an entirely different period, even our own day—with the men in business suits, modern military uniforms, and perhaps even tuxedos. Whatever the choice, the historical period should be clearly indicated by the costumes.

A Girl *Dumas* *Benoit*

Cyrano de Bergerac costume for Coquelin *Eleonora Duse* *Sarah Bernhardt*

COSTUME DESIGN: THE PROCESS
Costume designers often make preliminary sketches of costumes as they begin to design a production. Shown here are sketches for *The Ladies of the Camellias* by the costume designer Jess Goldstein for a production at the Yale Repertory Theatre. (Jess Goldstein)

Identifying Status and Personality   Like clothing in everyday life, costumes can tell us whether people are from the aristocracy or the working class, whether they are blue-collar workers or professionals. But in theatre, these signals should usually be clear and unmistakable. For example, in real life a person in a long white coat could be a doctor, a laboratory technician, or a hairdresser. A costume onstage must indicate the occupation exactly—by giving the doctor a stethoscope, for instance.

Costumes also tell us about the personalities of characters: A flamboyant person could be dressed in flashy colors; a shy, retiring person might wear subdued clothing.

Costumes also indicate age. This is particularly helpful when an older performer is playing a young person, or vice versa. A young person playing an older character, for instance, can wear padding or a beard.

Indicating Relationships among Characters   Characters in a play can be set apart by the way they are costumed. Major characters, for example, will be dressed differently from minor characters. Frequently, the costume designer will distinguish the major characters by dressing them in distinctive colors, in sharp contrast to the other characters. Consider, for instance, Shaw's *Saint Joan,* a play about Joan of Arc. Obviously, Joan should stand out from the soldiers surrounding her. Therefore, her costume might be bright blue while their costumes are steel gray. In another play of Shaw's, *Caesar and Cleopatra,* Cleopatra should stand out from her servants and soldiers.

Chapter 7   *Stage Costumes*   **159**

photo essay

Stage Costumes Make a Strong Visual Statement

On these pages are three examples of striking costumes. Costume designers, using colors, fabric, intricate cuts and shapes of cloth, accessories, and other elements, create a special look for each production. The costumes must fit the actor and allow for easy movement, as well as be visually appealing. They must also be appropriate for the play and communicate to the audience the period, the social status, and the financial level of the characters wearing the costumes.

Seen in the first photo are John Scherer (Hysterium) and Beth McVey (Domina) in vividly colorful costumes designed by Matthew Hemesath for *A Funny Thing Happened On The Way To The Forum,* at the Papermill Playhouse.

(T Charles Erickson)

160

For this African-themed production of Shakespeare's *The Tempest* directed by Janice Honeyman at the Royal Shakespeare Company in collaboration with the Baxter Theatre Centre of Cape Town, South Africa, Illka Louw designed the spectacular scenery and costumes worn by Antony Sher as Prospero and Atandwa Kani as Ariel.

(Geraint Lewis/Alamy Stock Photo)

Deborah Hay (Celimene) sinks to the floor in exasperation in Chicago Shakespeare Theater's *The School for Lies,* adapted from Molière's *The Misanthrope.* Directed by CST Artistic Director Barbara Gaines, written by David Ives, with hilarious costumes designed by Susan E. Mickey.

(Liz Lauren/Richard Hein)

161

COSTUMES INDICATE SOCIAL RELATIONSHIPS
Along with their many other properties, costumes can signal the relationships and contrasts among characters in a production. Not only can costumes indicate the time period when a drama takes place and the locale where it occurs, but they can, and should, indicate occupations and relative social positions. Who, for example, is a laborer or tradesman and who is a professional businessperson? In this scene from August Wilson's *Radio Golf* at the Goodman Theatre, we see John Earl Jelks as Sterling Johnson and Hassan El-Amin as Harmond Wilks in costumes designed by Susan Hilferty. The man on the right is a successful businessman; the man on the left is a laborer. (Peter Wynn Thompson)

Costumes underline important divisions between groups. In *Romeo and Juliet,* the two feuding families, the Montagues and the Capulets, would be costumed in different colors. In a modern counterpart of *Romeo and Juliet,* the musical *West Side Story,* the two gangs would be dressed in contrasting colors.

Creating Symbolic and Nonhuman Characters In many plays, special costumes are called for to denote abstract ideas or give shape to fantastic creatures. Here the costume designer must develop an outfit that conveys the appropriate imaginative and symbolic qualities. In *Macbeth,* for instance, how does one clothe the witches or the ghost of Banquo? For the musical *The Lion King,* the director Julie Taymor, who was also the costume designer, used puppets, masks, and other devices to create outfits for numerous animal characters, such as lions, tigers, giraffes, and elephants.

THE COSTUME DESIGNER MEETS PERFORMERS' NEEDS
Costume designer Stefano Nicolao, a prodigious designer for theatre and film, works in his Venice studio on the creation of an elegant gown for a performer who is standing at a mirror. (Stefano Rellandini/Reuters/Alamy Stock Photo)

Meeting Performers' Needs Virtually every aspect of theatre has practical as well as aesthetic requirements, and costume design is no exception. No matter how attractive or how symbolic, stage costumes must work for the performers. A long, flowing gown may look beautiful, but if it is too long and the performer wearing it trips walking down a flight of steps, the designer has overlooked an important practical consideration. If performers are required to duel or engage in hand-to-hand combat, their costumes must stand up to this wear and tear, and their arms and legs must have freedom of movement. If they are to dance, they must be able to turn, leap, and move freely.

Quick costume changes are also frequently called for in theatre. Tear-away seams and special fasteners are used so that one costume can be ripped off quickly and another put on (often with the assistance of dressers). A recent example of a seemingly magical onstage costume change occurred in the Disney musical *Frozen*. Costume designer Christopher Oram designed a tear-away costume for Elsa, which then made it possible for her to spontaneously change into the new, more elaborate costume when she sang "Let it Go" before freezing her kingdom.

Unlike scenery, which stays in place until it is moved, a costume is always in motion, moving as the performer moves. This provides an opportunity for the designer to develop grace and rhythm in the way a costume looks as it moves across the stage, but with that goes the great responsibility of making the costume workable for the performer.

Each of these specific costuming needs points to the absolute importance of skilled *stitchers* (technicians who sew all the costumes) and *drapers* (technicians who pattern, pin, and drape the fabric to fit individual actors perfectly) in a costume shop.

At times it is important for the costume designer to work closely with individual performers, who must know how to use the accessories and costumes provided for them. This is particularly true for historical costumes that re-create elements unique to that time period; such costumes often require the performer to work closely with

stitchers Technicians who sew all of the costumes for a production.

drapers Technicians who pattern, pin, and drape the fabric to fit the actors in a production perfectly.

Chapter 7 *Stage Costumes* **163**

SPECTACULAR COSTUME CHANGES
Shown here is costume designer Christopher Oram's tear-away costume for princess Elsa for Disney's Broadway production of *Frozen*, which made it possible for the performer to spontaneously change into the new, more elaborate costume when she sang "Let it Go" before freezing her kingdom. (Sara Krulwich/The New York Times/Redux)

pull To choose a costume from an inventory owned by a theatre company or costume warehouse.

build To create a costume from scratch in a costume shop.

the director and the costume designer and frequently with a movement specialist as well.

Maintaining Consistency Finally, costumes must be consistent with the entire production—especially with the various other visual elements. A realistic production set in the home of everyday people calls for down-to-earth costumes. A highly stylized production requires costumes designed with flair and imagination.

The Costume Designer at Work

The Costume Designer's Responsibilities
As noted earlier, the person who puts all these ideas into effect is the costume designer. Every production requires someone who takes responsibility for the costumes. This is true whether the costumes are *pulled* or *built*.

Pulling is a term used when costumes are rented (or maintained in an extensive costume collection in, for example, a university or regional theatre) and the designer goes to a costume house or storeroom and selects outfits that are appropriate for the production. The designer must already know about period, style, and the other matters discussed earlier. The costumer must also have the measurements of all the performers for whom costumes are to be pulled. Seldom will pulled or rented costumes fit perfectly, and it is the responsibility of stitchers, often with tailoring experience, to complete the necessary alterations.

When costumes are ***built***, they are created in a costume shop under the direction of the shop supervisor, who works closely with a costume designer in much the same way the technical director and scene designer work together. Before making a costume out of expensive fabrics, well-staffed costume shops will make *muslin mock-ups* of the costumes first, and those are then fitted to the actor. Next, the mock-ups are taken apart and used as patterns for the actual costume fabric.

In these shops, costumes are built in two different ways. Some are drafted as flat patterns based on the performer's measurements, and some are draped. Draping involves pinning and tucking the fabric directly to a dress form of the proper size and marking the fabric while it is on the dress form in preparation for stitching, detailed finish work, and closures.

Today, technology has also made it possible to create mock-ups on a computer or handheld device, and cutting and draping can be completed with digital assistance.

The Costume Designer's Resources
Among the elements a costume designer works with are (as discussed next): (1) line, shape, and silhouette; (2) color; (3) fabric; and (as discussed later) (4) accessories.

Line Of prime importance is the cut or line of the clothing. Do the lines of an outfit flow, or are they sharp and jagged? Does the clothing follow the lines of the body, or is there some element of exaggeration, such as shoulder pads or a bustle at

One of the most active costume designers of recent times is William Ivey Long. Like many costume designers, he often sketches the costumes of the characters in the play, indicating the style of the clothes, the fabrics, the colors, and the silhouette. Long developed a collage board for all the characters in the "grand finale" of the musical *Hairspray*, not only sketching the costumes themselves but—below the sketches—adding swatches of fabric indicating colors and other qualities of the fabrics. Shown here are several of the costumes taken from the full cast of the finale, giving an indication of how the final costumes were developed. (Courtesy of William Ivey Long Studios)

Shown here is famed designer William Ivey Long in front of a display of his costume sketches for *The Lost Colony,* the nation's longest-running historical drama, presented annually on Roanoke Island, on the outer banks of North Carolina. (Chris Curry/AP Images)

Chapter 7 *Stage Costumes*   165

the back of a dress? The outline or silhouette of a costume has always been significant. There is a strong visual contrast, for instance, between the line of an Egyptian garment for a woman, flowing smoothly from shoulder to floor, and that of an empire gown of the early nineteenth century in Europe, which featured a horizontal line high above the waist, just below the breasts, with a line flowing from below the bosom to the feet. The silhouettes of these two styles would stand in marked contrast to an outfit for a woman in the United States during the early 1930s: a short outfit with a prominent belt or sash cutting horizontally across the hips.

Undergarments are an aspect of costume design often overlooked by audiences. For costumes for women, one example is the hoopskirt. In *The King and I,* a musical of 1951 that was revived at Lincoln Center in New York in 2015, Anna, an English schoolteacher in Siam, wears dresses with hoopskirts several feet in diameter, which were in fashion in England in the mid-nineteenth century, the time of the play.

Other undergarments include bustles, which exaggerate the lines in the rear, and corsets, which can greatly alter posture and appearance. For example, some corsets pull in the waist and cause the wearer to stand very straight. But in the first decade of the twentieth century, women in society often bent forward because they wore a curved corset that forced them to thrust their shoulders and upper body forward.

A costume designer will be aware of the importance of undergarments and will use them to create the appropriate silhouette and line. During the nineteenth century there were times when men wore corsets to achieve the fashionable posture of the day.

Color A second important resource for costume designers is color. Earlier, we saw that leading characters can be dressed in a color that contrasts with the colors worn by other characters and that characters from one family can be dressed in colors different from those of a rival family. Color also suggests mood: bright, warm colors for a happy mood; dark, somber colors for a more serious mood.

Beyond these applications, however, color can indicate changes in character and changes in mood. Near the beginning of Eugene O'Neill's *Mourning Becomes Electra,*

COSTUMES CONVEY A MESSAGE
Costume designers for musicals, fantasies, and historical plays have the opportunity to create costumes that are highly decorative as well as eye-catching but also tell a story. In the musical *Hamilton,* nontraditionally cast contemporary performers wear elaborate costumes from the Revolutionary period in American history, thus presenting an interesting juxtaposition of time and events. Shown here are two stars of the original production, Lin-Manuel Miranda (also the author) and actress Phillipa Soo, with costume design by Paul Tazewell. (Theo Wargo/Getty Images)

General Manon, who has recently returned from the Civil War, dies, and his wife and daughter wear dark mourning clothes. Lavinia, the daughter, knows that her mother was involved in her father's death, and she and her brother conspire to murder the mother. Once they have done so, Lavinia adopts characteristics of her mother, and as an important symbol of this transformation, she puts on brightly colored clothes of the same shades her mother had worn when she was young.

Fabric Fabric is a third tool of the costume designer. In one sense, this is the costume designer's medium, for it is in fabric that silhouette and color are displayed. Just as important as those qualities are the texture and bulk of the fabric. What is its reflective quality? Does it have a sheen that reflects light? Or is it rough, so that it absorbs light? How does it drape on the wearer? Does it fall lightly to the floor and outline physical features, or does it hide them? Does it wrinkle naturally, or is it smooth? Ornamentation and trim can also be used. Fringe, lace, ruffles, feathers, beads—all these add to the attractiveness and individuality of a costume.

Beyond its inherent qualities, fabric has symbolic values. For example, burlap and other roughly textured cloths suggest people of the earth or of modest means. Silks and satins, on the other hand, suggest elegance and refinement—perhaps even royalty.

The connotations of fabrics may change with passing years. Two or three generations ago, blue denim was used only for work clothes, worn by laborers or by ranch hands who rode horseback. Today, denim is the fabric of choice in informal clothes for people of all incomes and all ages.

Using the combined resources of line, color, fabric, and trims, the costume designer arrives at individual outfits, which tell us a great deal about the characters who wear them and convey important visual signals about the style and meaning of the play as a whole.

The Costume Designer's Collaborators

Once again, it is important to recognize that a number of collaborators aid in the process of costume design. Remember that the *costume shop supervisor* is the lead costume technician, and there are other, very specific job responsibilities in a typical costume shop.

Often young professionals beginning a career will start as *buyers* for professional shops that have copies of the designers' renderings. They will scour garment districts to find fabrics that best match the designer's renderings. After fabric comes back to the shop and the muslin mock-ups are made, it will go to a *cutter-draper*. A costume designer's "firsthand" (see later) will often build the initial costume and complete the fitting with the designer and the actor.

It is important to note that the stage manager is typically responsible for scheduling all actors' fittings to work out times that coordinate with rehearsals and the designer's shop schedule. Once the fitting has been completed, the costume will proceed to the costume designer's *firsthand,* or a *lead stitcher,* who completes the detailed sewing. Once construction is completed, in cases where costumes should not look brand-new, they are turned over to design assistants for the purpose of *distressing*, to make them look weathered and worn.

distressing Making a costume look weathered or worn.

IN FOCUS: TECHNOLOGY AND COSTUME DESIGN

As in the practice of scene design, costume designers also have had their work transformed by new technologies.

Costume research is now more easily done through the Web. Designers can review historical costumes by browsing museum sites through the Internet. Photographs and images of people in period clothing can be found through web browser searches. Newspapers and magazines from different time periods are also accessible.

Designers can use software to create their sketches on their computers or tablets. Designers who still sketch by hand can also scan and save their drawings digitally, as well as manipulate them in this fashion. This also makes all of their designs mobile so that they can have them on their laptop or handheld device. In addition, designs can be e-mailed or shared through the "cloud." (This is also true for set design sketches.)

Technology has also affected the types of fabrics available and the ways in which designers and their collaborators work with them. Computers can now be used to assist in cutting and embroidering of costume materials, and technology has allowed the production of fabrics that in the past might have been too expensive to use or too difficult to re-create. And laser cutting can allow for easier construction of very intricate designs.

Technology has also affected costume designs that require ornamentation and special effects. 3D printing can be used to create hats, helmets, and other ornamental elements. A character who needs lights in his costume, such as in the Disney musical *Beauty and the Beast*, can have LED lights embedded in what he is wearing, and the actor can control them with an unseen small switch. Fiber optics can be sewn into a fabric to create a costume that can be illuminated.

Many other cutting-edge costume technologies are still being explored, including robotics (in which mechanized, computer-controlled elements are used by the performer wearing the costume) and "intelligent" costumes that allow offstage personnel to communicate with the costumes via a wireless network in order to create special effects.

There are also apps available for costume designers that allow them to work on their mobile devices. As noted, a variety of sketch apps allow designers to draw on their smartphones or tablets. Wardrobe Journal allows designers to keep track of costumes for each of the characters in the production. DH Costume is an app that allows the designer to match the scenes with the specific costumes needed, as well as any complex costume changes.

When costumes are completed and ready for dress rehearsals and performances, they become the responsibility of the *wardrobe supervisor,* who makes all decisions related to costume organization and preparation in the theatre. The wardrobe crew's responsibilities begin with backstage preparation before every performance and end when the laundry is completed following every performance. In an elaborate production, there are numerous dressers from the wardrobe crew assigned to actors, especially lead actors, during rehearsals and performances. There are other areas of specialty and artisans integral to costume design, discussed in the next section.

RELATED ELEMENTS OF COSTUME DESIGN

Makeup

A part of costume is makeup—the application of cosmetics (paints, powders, and rouges) to the face and body. With regard to age and any other special facial features, an important function of makeup is to help the performer personify and embody a character.

Theatrical makeup used to be more popular than it is today. In a modern small theatre, performers playing realistic parts will often go without makeup of any consequence, in which case, they can handle their own makeup. Anything beyond the most simple makeup, however, demands an accomplished makeup designer to plan specifically what makeup performers will wear. Historical figures are frequently incorporated into realistic plays and may demand extensive use of extremely realistic

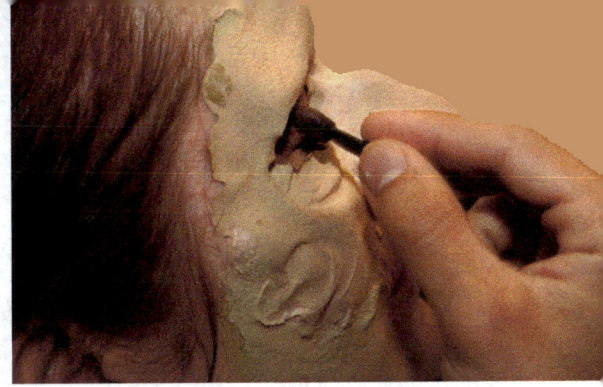

MAKEUP: CHANGING A FACE OR CREATING A NEW ONE

Makeup is an ancient theatre tradition. Makeup can highlight features of the face or parts of the body that might be washed out under the glare of stage lights. It can also be used to alter the appearance of the face altogether. In the first photograph, makeup artist Suhyun Kang applies Day of the Dead makeup on actress Morwynna Cambridge for a performance mounted in London. The second photo shows a makeup artist altering the skin and eyes of a performer who is to play a witch. (left: Terence Mendoza/Alamy Stock Photo; right: Paul Wood/Alamy Stock Photo)

prosthetic makeup. An example on Broadway was William Gibson's one-woman play *Golda's Balcony*. Nine prosthetic noses, cast in foam latex, were required each week for the show's star who played Israeli Prime Minister Golda Meir. Prosthetics were also needed for the musicals *Shrek* and *Beauty and the Beast* to create the creatures.

Makeup has a long and important history in theatre, and sometimes it is a necessity—one good example being makeup to highlight facial features that would not otherwise be visible in a large theatre. Even in a smaller theatre, bright lights tend to wash out cheekbones, eyebrows, and other facial features.

Makeup is often essential because the age of a character differs from that of the performer. Suppose that a nineteen-year-old performer is playing a sixty-year-old character. Through the use of makeup—a little gray in the hair or simulated wrinkles on the face—the appropriate age can be suggested. Another situation calling for makeup to indicate age is a play in which the characters grow older during the course of the action. The musical *I Do! I Do!* with book and lyrics by Tom Jones and music by Harvey Schmidt is based on the play *The Fourposter* by Jan de Hartog. In the musical, a husband and wife are shown in scenes covering many years in their married life, from the time when they are first married until they are quite old. In order to convey the passing years and their advancing age, the actress and actor must use makeup extensively.

Makeup is also a necessity for fantastic or other nonrealistic creatures. Douglas Turner Ward (1930–2021), a Black playwright, wrote *Day of Absence* to be performed by Black actors in whiteface. The implications of this effect are many, not the least being the reversal of the nineteenth-century minstrel performances in which white actors wore blackface to create stereotypical and racist depictions of African Americans. Ward was not the first to put Black actors in whiteface; French dramatist Jean Genet had part of the cast of his play *The Blacks* wear white masks.

MAKEUP FOR PERFORMERS IN KATHAKALI

Kathakali is a traditional form of theatre that has been practiced for many years in India. It combines song, dance, and dramatic action. It also features elaborate costumes and makeup. The makeup is extremely colorful and often takes a great deal of time to apply. In the first of these two photos, we see the makeup for a character being applied. In the second photograph, we see the performer in full makeup, as well as in costume. (top: Huw Jones/Alamy Stock Photo; bottom: Huw Jones/Alamy Stock Photo)

A popular musical on Broadway and on tour, Stephen Schwartz's *Wicked* portrays a green witch named Elphaba from birth until she becomes better known as the Wicked Witch of the West. Perhaps even more amazing in *Wicked* is the makeup on the numerous flying monkeys in the production.

Asian theatre frequently relies on heavy makeup. For instance, Japanese *kabuki*, a highly stylized theatre, uses completely nonrealistic makeup. The main characters must apply a base of white covering the entire face, over which bold patterns of red, blue, black, and brown are painted. The colors and patterns are symbolic of the character. In Chinese theatre, too, the colors of makeup are symbolic: All white suggests treachery, black means fierce integrity, red means loyalty, green indicates demons, and yellow stands for hidden cunning.

When using makeup, the human face becomes almost like a canvas for a painting. The features of the face may be heightened or exaggerated, or symbolic aspects

170 Part Three The Designers

of the face may be emphasized. In either case, makeup serves as an additional tool for the performer in creating an image of the character.

Hairstyles and Wigs

Another important component of costume design includes hairstyles and wigs. When costume designers create their renderings, they include characters' hairstyles as a part of the design, which will later require a hair and wig specialist as a part of the crew.

Hairstyles can sometimes denote period and social class. In the middle of the nineteenth century, for example, women often wore ringlets. A few decades later, in the 1890s, women wore their hair piled on top of the head in a pompadour referred to as the Gibson girl look. In the 1920s, women wore their hair marcelled, a hairstyle with waves made by a heated curling iron, sometimes slicked down close to the head. In the modern period, women wear their hair in more natural styles. But again there is tremendous variety—some women have short, curly hair; others have long hair, perhaps even down to the waist. The musical *Hairspray* featured young women in the bouffant hairdos of the 1960s.

For men, too, hairstyles are significant and can denote period and social class. A military brush cut, an Elvis Presley-style pompadour, and a ponytail each point to a certain lifestyle, but each may be interpreted in several ways.

Audiences would actually be surprised to know how often wigs are used in theatrical productions. They may not even recognize a performer outside the theatre because such a complete visual transformation can be accomplished with the use of wigs made from real hair. For a production, hair designers fashion the wigs in the shop before dress rehearsals. A hair and wig specialist is also required backstage to care for the wigs throughout the performance process to keep the hair looking exactly as the designer envisioned it.

Wigs can also help differentiate characters. One of the most amazing uses of a wig on Broadway was the extraordinary design by Paul Huntley for the musical *Jekyll & Hyde*. The actor could manipulate the character's wig instantaneously, allowing him to shift back and forth between Jekyll and Hyde within the same song. In the Broadway musical *A Gentleman's Guide to Love & Murder*, the lead actor played eight different roles, and wigs helped differentiate those characters.

Masks

Masks appear to be as old as theatre, having been used in ancient Greek theatre and in the drama developed by primitive tribes. In one sense, the mask is an extension of the performer—a face on top of a face. Theatre masks remind us, first of all, that we are in a theatre, that the action going on before our eyes is not real in a literal sense but is a symbolic or an artistic presentation. For another thing, masks allow a face to be frozen in one expression: a look of horror, perhaps, which we see throughout

WIGS
Wigs can help audience members differentiate characters and also give clues to the characters' personalities. Shown here is Jefferson Mays in the musical *A Gentleman's Guide to Love and Murder* at the Walter Kerr Theater in New York on October 21, 2013. Mays had to play eight different characters and his wigs (one of which seen here) helped differentiate those characters.
(Sara Krulwich/The New York Times/Redux)

photo essay

Masks

Masks are as old as theatre—they were part of ancient Greek theatre and early Asian theatre, and of ceremonial costumes in Africa and elsewhere. Masks can have a variety of uses: They can be highly decorative, but they can also convey the character and temperament of the actor wearing them. Here we see a variety of masks in old and new plays.

(Andrew Watson/Getty Images)

Khon dancers during the Phimai festival in Thailand. Khon is a traditional Thai masked dance-drama based on stories from the national epic, the *Ramakian*.

The Asaro "mud men" from the Asaro Valley in Papua New Guinea's eastern highlands are known for the ghoulish clay masks they use in many rituals. Here they perform for visitors at the Australian Museum in Sydney in 2016.

(Peter Parks/Getty Images)

Venetian carnival masks are worn by actors in Shakespeare's *The Merchant of Venice,* a production by the Habima National Theatre, in Hebrew, at Shakespeare's Globe in London, as part of the World Shakespeare Festival and the London Olympics, 2012.

(Leon Neal/AFP/Getty Images)

Tristano (Pedro Pascal) and Don Bertolino Fortunato (Dick Latessa) perform the commedia play, *Pulcinella Goes to Hell*, in the Huntington Theatre Company's production of *The Miracle at Naples*, by David Grimm, directed by Peter DuBois, with costumes and masks designed by Anita Yavich.

(T Charles Erickson)

U.S. theatrical producer and director Harold Prince (R) and Russian actors Yelena Bakhtiyarova (C) as Christine Daaé, Dmitry Yermak (L) as the Phantom during a rehearsal of Andrew Lloyd Webber's *The Phantom of the Opera* at the Moscow Youth Palace. Yermak is shown wearing the iconic Phantom mask.

(Vyacheslav Prokofyev/TASS/Alamy Stock Photo)

173

> ### PLAYING YOUR PART: EXPERIENCING THEATRE
>
> 1. How might what you are wearing today reveal your personality, your station in life, your character? What would lead someone to make those observations?
> 2. If you were a character in a play, what costume would you design for yourself to tell us the most about you? What are the key elements? Why?
> 3. Have you ever commented on a friend's makeup, hair, or accessories? What did your comments suggest about how you characterized your friend due to these "costume" elements?
> 4. Find photos of famous film stars in publications or online. What does the clothing they are wearing tell you about them? Why?
> 5. Visit the costume shop of your university or community theatre. Are there costumes available to be pulled? Are there renderings of costumes that are under construction? What types of equipment can you find in the shop?

a production. Masks can also make a face larger than life, and they can create stereotypes, in which one particular feature—for example, cunning or haughtiness—is emphasized to the exclusion of everything else.

Masks offer other symbolic possibilities. In his play *The Great God Brown*, Eugene O'Neill calls for the performers at certain times to hold masks in front of their faces. When the masks are in place, the characters present a facade to the

WIGS AND HAIRSTYLES
Hairstyle indicates social status and other facts about a character; it provides information about when and where a play is taking place. Beyond that, hairstyles and wigs can make a comment. Shown here is a scene from Rodgers & Hammerstein's *Cinderella*. The actors are Harriet Harris, standing, as Cinderella's stepmother, with, from left, Laura Osnes as Cinderella, and Ann Harada and Marla Mindelle, who play the stepsisters, wearing elaborate wigs in hairstyles that exaggerate the norm even for the period. The hair and wig designs are by veteran Broadway designer Paul Huntley. (Sara Krulwich/The New York Times/Redux)

public, withholding their true selves. When the masks are down, the characters reveal their inner feelings. The long run London and Broadway musical *The Phantom of the Opera* uses an iconic mask for the title character.

Neutral masks are also frequently used in actors' training, to prompt them to use more dynamic physical movement without the benefit of facial expression to express character. More often today, audiences will see half masks, like those used in the *commedia dell'arte* of the Italian Renaissance, as these allow for stylized character expressions but also give the actor more freedom to speak clearly and effectively.

Characters' mask designs are also incorporated into the costume renderings and are typically built by a makeup or crafts specialist in the costume shop.

Millinery, Accessories, and Crafts

A number of the seven objectives of costume design noted at the beginning of this chapter are actually achieved through the design and use of accessories to the costumes. Accessories include items such as hats, walking sticks, jewelry, purses, and parasols. All these items instantly refer to various historical periods and also make visual statements about character and locale. Virtually every major costume shop will have a technician who specializes in millinery and crafts. Each of these pieces must be carefully designed and constructed to connect visually to the costumes and to other areas of design. It is hard to imagine a production of Shakespeare's *A Midsummer Night's Dream* without some kind of delightful donkey's headpiece or mask made specifically for the character Bottom. Theatre design and execution in all areas, including millinery, accessories, and craft, rely heavily on extensive details to make the visual world of the play compelling for audiences.

IN FOCUS: COSTUME DESIGN IN FILM AND TELEVISION

The film and television costume designer must take into account specific differences in the ways in which the costumes will be seen and used. The primary difference between designing costumes for the stage and for film and television is that costumes designed for the stage are meant to be seen by the live audience, while those for film and television are designed to be captured by a camera. Depending on how a scene is shot, certain elements of the costume may be highlighted. A costume can be zoomed into or seen as larger than life on the screen.

The film and television costume designer must, therefore, take all of this into account and realize that minute details might need to be a greater focus because of the camera's position. In the theatre, because of the distance between the audience and the stage, costumes may be more exaggerated or stylized and very minute details are often not as significant.

Film and television costume designers must also have costumes (and accessories) available for when specific scenes are filmed, so they must be prepared to costume the performers in whatever order the scenes are being shot.

Film and television costumes are used for only as long as it takes to successfully complete the specific scene or scenes in the film. Stage costumes may have to last for eight shows a week over a long run. Film and television costumes (like the other elements) can be digitally enhanced during the editing process. In the theatre, intricate and elaborate costume changes must be designed to happen in real time with the audience waiting or watching, while in film many "takes" and editing can make magical costume transformations occur.

IN FOCUS: INCLUSIVITY: TOUCH TOURS AND AUDIO DESCRIPTION

In an attempt to make theatre more accessible to visually impaired audience members, many theatres have scheduled *touch tours* that provide audio descriptions through headsets so that those audience members can experience the visual elements of a production.

Touch tours take place before a performance and allow visually impaired audience members to have a tactile exploration of scenery, properties, and costumes. In this fashion, those audience members can have a sensory experience of all of the design elements and be aware all of the visual changes that will occur in sets, costumes, and properties. Actors also describe themselves and their characters during such tours.

The audio description then allows visually impaired audience members to hear, through headphones (which will be discussed in the next chapter), a spoken description of sets, costumes, and lights and the changes as well as actors' movements throughout the production.

As we mentioned in the opening chapter, the theatre today reflects the diversity of our society, and theatre companies that schedule touch tours and provide audio descriptions are striving for greater inclusivity.

COORDINATION OF THE WHOLE

Performers would have great difficulty creating a part without costumes and accessories, and in some cases without makeup or a mask. These elements help the performer define the role and are so closely related to the performer that we sometimes lose sight of them as separate entities. At the same time, costumes, makeup, hairstyles, and masks must be integrated with other aspects of a production, and each demands special technical skills in order to complete the visual design.

These elements are essential in carrying out a point of view in a production. Masks, for instance, are clearly nonrealistic and signal to the audience that the character wearing the mask and the play itself are also likely to be nonrealistic. Costumes suggest whether a play is comic or serious, a wild farce or a stark tragedy. Costumes, makeup, hairstyles, and masks must also be coordinated with scenery and lighting. The wrong kind of lighting can wash out or discolor costumes and makeup. It would be self-defeating, too, if scenery were in one mood or style and the costumes in another. Ideally, these elements should support and reinforce one another, and spectators should be aware of how essential it is for them to work together.

PLAYING YOUR PART: THINKING ABOUT THEATRE

1. Think back to the last play or film you attended. How did the costume designer use color, fabric, and/or other elements to set up visual coordination and contrast among the characters?
2. Watch a historical film, like Steven Spielberg's *Lincoln* or *The Current War*, about the battle between early inventors of electricity Edison and Tesla. Are any unique accessories employed to help establish time period? What about the hairstyles? Are wigs used?
3. Watch the film version of the musical *Hamilton*. How do the costumes differentiate the characters? How do they tell us about the differences between the Schuyler sisters?
4. How are Halloween masks like theatre masks? How are they different?
5. If you have been required to read a play this semester, how might you use color and line to define one of the leading characters?

Evaluating Costume Design

There are key questions we should ask ourselves about costume design after we attend a production. By doing so, we can then assess how successful we believe the costume designer was in helping support the director's concept, the actors, and the other designers. Among these questions are:

1. What information was conveyed by the costumes about time, place, characters, and situation? How was this information conveyed to you?
2. What was the period of the costumes? What was the style? Were the costumes from a period other than the one in which the play was written or originally set? If so, how did this affect the production? Why do you think this choice was made?
3. How was color used to give you clues to the personalities of the characters and the relationships between them?
4. Did each character's costume or costumes seem appropriate for his or her personality, social status, occupation, etc.? Why or why not?
5. Did the costumes help you understand conflicts, differing social groups, and interpersonal relationships? If so, how?
6. Were makeup, wigs, unique hairstyles, masks, millinery, ornamentation, and/or special effects used with the costuming? How integrated were these elements into the overall design? Did these elements help you better understand the characters and the play?

SUMMARY

1. The clothes we wear in daily life are a form of costume. They indicate station in life, occupation, and a sense of formality or informality.
2. Onstage, costumes—like clothes in real life—convey information about the people wearing them; more than that, these costumes are chosen consciously and are designed to give the audience important information.
3. The objectives of costume design are to set tone and style, indicate time and place, characterize individuals and groups, underline personal relationships, create symbolic outfits when appropriate, meet the practical needs of performers, and coordinate with the total production.
4. The designer works with the following elements: line and shape, color, fabric, and accessories.
5. Costumes can be pulled or built. When they are pulled, they are drawn from a preexisting costume collection. Building costumes means creating the complete costume: sewing and constructing the outfit in a costume shop.
6. Those working with a costume designer include a firsthand (or lead stitcher) and other assistants.
7. Makeup and hairstyles are also important to the appearance of the performers and are part of the designer's concern.
8. Where called for, masks, too, are under the direction of the costume designer.
9. Often, costume, makeup, and wig assistants work with actors during a performance.

Design Elements: Audience Sitting in Theatre (theatre): Ron Chapple/Photodisc/Getty Images; Studio Light (spotlights): Exactostock/SuperStock

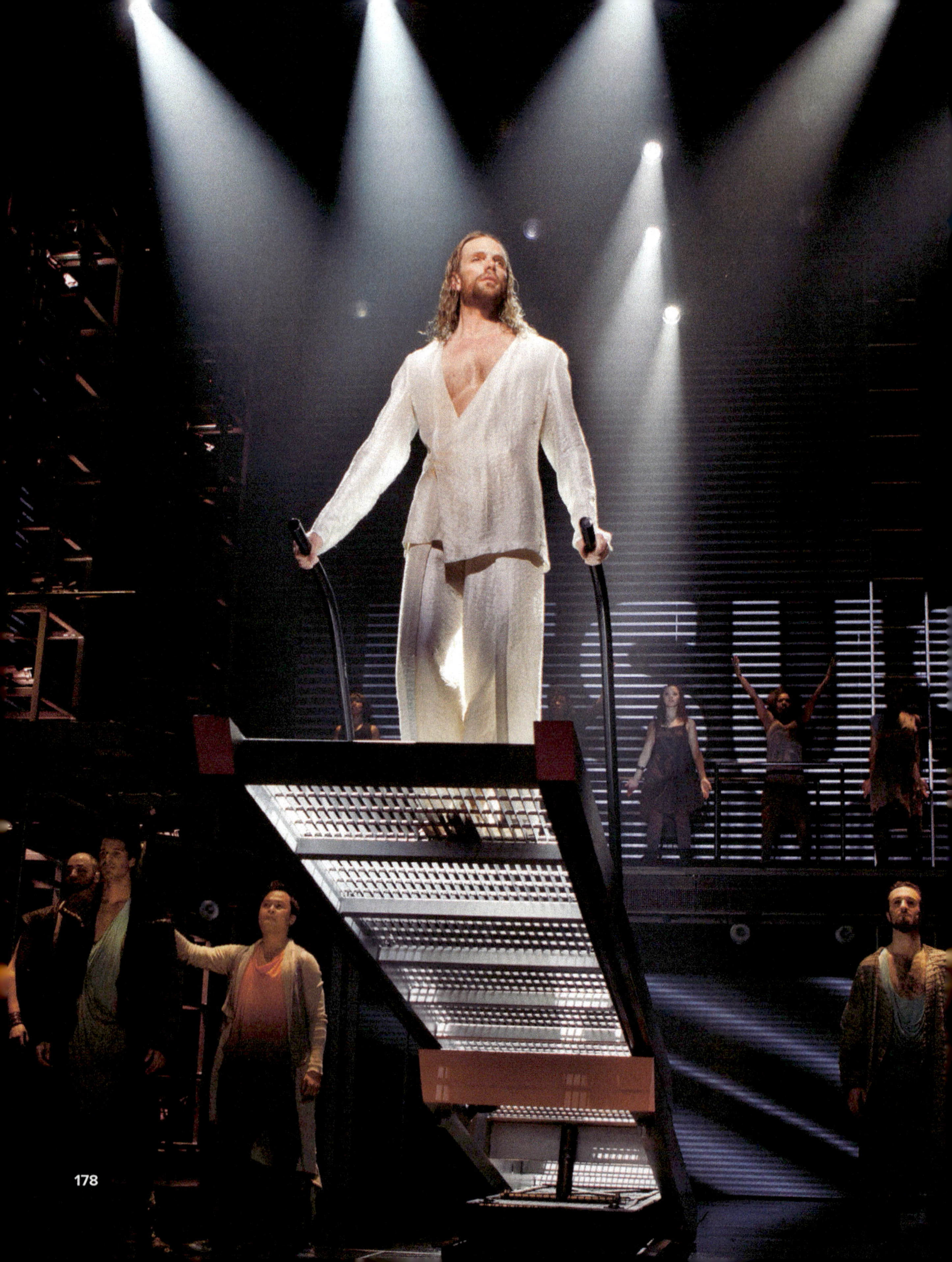

Lighting and Sound

Like scenery, costumes, and other elements of theatre, stage lighting and sound have counterparts in everyday life. For example, in real life the basic function of lighting is, of course, illumination—to allow us to see at night and indoors. But there are also many theatrical uses of light in daily life. Advertising signs often have neon lights or brightly colored bulbs. Restaurants feature soft lights, candles, and background music to help establish mood and atmosphere.

In our homes, we put spotlights on special parts of a room, such as a dining-room table. Also, in our homes we frequently use a rheostat so that we can dim lights to create a mood. What home does not have projected images available through a flat-screen high-definition (HD) or new organic light-emitting diode (OLED) television or the ability to change digital images in picture frames? And today some of us can control all of the lighting and sound throughout our residence with our computers, tablets, or smartphones.

With the explosion of such handheld devices as digital music players, smartphones, and tablets, all of us carry our own sound tracks each day.

STAGE LIGHTING

Lighting was historically the last element of visual design to be incorporated into theatre production—and, ironically, it is perhaps the most advanced in terms of equipment, technology, and techniques. Most of the advances have occurred in the past 100 years. Before we look at theatre lighting today, it will be helpful to have a short historical view of its development.

A Brief History of Stage Lighting

For the first 2,000 years of its recorded history, theatre was held mostly outdoors during the day. A primary reason was the need for illumination. The sun, after all, is an excellent source of light. Since sophisticated lighting was unavailable, playwrights used imagination—the handiest tool available—to suggest nighttime or shifts

◀ **LIGHTING AND SOUND: INDISPENSABLE ELEMENTS**
Illuminating the stage and the performers is essential to theatre, as is indicating such things as the time of day, indoors or outdoors, realism or nonrealism. Seen here is a scene from the musical Jesus Christ, Superstar *written by Andrew Lloyd Webber, directed by Des McAnuff, with the lighting designed by Howell Binkley, who has used down lighting and back lighting to isolate actor Paul Nolan in the title role. (Sara Krulwich/The New York Times/Redux)*

in lighting. Performers brought on torches or a candle, as Lady Macbeth does, to indicate night. Playwrights also used language to indicate lighting.

In *The Merchant of Venice,* Shakespeare has Lorenzo say, "How sweet the moonlight sleeps upon this bank"; this is not just a pretty line of poetry but also serves to remind us that it is nighttime. The same is true of the eloquent passage when Romeo tells Juliet that he must leave because dawn is breaking.

> Look, love, what envious streaks
> Do lace the severing clouds in yonder East:
> Night's candles are burnt out, and jocund day
> Stands tiptoe on the misty mountain tops.

Around 1600 CE, theatre began to move indoors. Candles and oil lamps were used for illumination, and the chief refinements were more sophisticated uses of these basic elements, such as those achieved in the 1770s by David Garrick, the actor-manager of the Drury Lane Theatre in London, and Philippe Jacques DeLoutherbourg (1740–1812), a French designer whom Garrick brought to the Drury Lane. DeLoutherbourg, for example, installed lighting above the stage and used gauze curtains and silk screens to achieve subtle effects with color. In 1785 an instrument known as the Argand lamp (after its inventor, Aimé Argand of Geneva) was introduced. It made use of a glass chimney and a cylindrical wick to create a steadier, brighter light.

Not until 1803, however, when a theatre in London installed gaslights, was there a genuine advance in stage lighting. With gas, which was the principal source of illumination during the nineteenth century, lighting was more easily controlled and managed. Lighting intensity, for example, could be raised or lowered. Its effectiveness, however, remained limited. In addition, the open flames of gas and other earlier lighting systems posed a constant threat of fire. Through the years there were several tragic and costly fires in theatres, both in Europe and in the United States.

In 1879 Thomas Edison invented the incandescent lamp (the electric lightbulb), and the era of imaginative lighting for the theatre began. Not only are incandescent lamps safe, but they can also be controlled. Brightness or intensity can be increased or decreased: The same lighting instrument will produce the bright light of noonday or the dim light of dusk. Also, by putting a colored film over the light or by other means, color can be controlled.

Beyond the power and versatility of electric light, there have been numerous other advances in controls and equipment over the past fifty years. Lighting instruments have been continually refined to become more powerful, as well as more subtle, and to throw a more concentrated, sharply defined beam. Also, lighting has lent itself more successfully than other theatre elements to miniaturization and computerization.

When applied to lighting, technological developments have allowed for increasingly complex and sophisticated controls. For a large college theatre production, 200 to 300 lighting instruments may be hung around and above the stage, whereas for a large Broadway musical, there may be 800 or many more. (The Broadway musical *Wicked,* for example, uses 650 instruments.) Each of these instruments can be hooked up to a central computer board, and light settings can be stored in the computer. By pushing a single button, an operator can, in a split second, bring about a shift in literally dozens of instruments, changing, for example, focus, color, and intensity. The resulting flexibility and control are remarkable tools for achieving stage effects. And even more remarkably, today lighting can also be controlled by handheld devices as well as computers.

Objectives and Functions of Lighting Design

Adolphe Appia (1862–1928), a Swiss scene designer, was one of the first to see the vast artistic possibilities of light in the theatre. He wrote: "Light is to the production what music is to the score: the expressive element in opposition to the literal signs; and, like music, light can express only what belongs to the inner essence of all vision's vision." Norman Bel Geddes (1893–1958), an imaginative American designer who was a follower of Appia, put it in these words: "Good lighting adds space, depth, mood, mystery, parody, contrast, change of emotion, intimacy, fear." Edward Gordon Craig (1872–1966), an innovative British designer, spoke of "painting with light." The lighting designer can indeed paint with light, but far more can be done. On the deepest sensual and symbolic level, the lighting designer can convey to us something of the feeling, and even the substance, of a play.

It is intriguing that today's leading lighting designers still speak of the artistic potential and aesthetics of light in precisely the same way as these early innovators did. In a sense the art of lighting has not changed, but the innovation continues, and the technology has exploded in the last twenty years. In fact, the most serious problem in lighting for the theatre today is to prevent the technology from taking over the aesthetics of the design, which is where the greatest distinction exists between contemporary lighting technicians and earlier lighting designers.

The following are the primary functions and objectives of stage lighting:

1. Provide visibility.
2. Reveal shapes and forms.
3. Provide a focus onstage and create visual compositions.
4. Assist in creating mood and reinforcing style.
5. Help establish time and place.
6. Establish a rhythm of visual movement.
7. Reinforce a central visual image, establish visual information, or both.

An experienced lighting designer will be capable of accomplishing all these functions simultaneously and will emphasize various objectives at various times during a production to help maintain a strong physical and emotional connection between audience members and the world of the play on stage.

Visibility   On the practical side, the chief function of lighting is illumination or visibility. We must be able, first and foremost, to see the performers' faces and their actions onstage. Occasionally, lighting designers, carried away with atmospheric possibilities, will make a scene so dark that we can hardly see what is happening. Mood is important, but seeing the performers is obviously even more important. It is true that unless you can see the performers, the lighting designer has not carried out their assignment; however, the accomplished designer will establish a balance that allows for visibility while meeting other design objectives effectively.

Shape and Form   The lighting designer must enhance the visual world of the play by revealing the objects in that world as interestingly as possible. Lighting objects from the front, with lights above the audience illuminating the stage, visually wash out all three-dimensional objects onstage, making them look flat and uninteresting. The designer must therefore enhance the actors and other visual elements of the world of the play with lighting and color from the side, top, and behind.

Focus and Composition In photography, the term *focus* means adjustment of the lens of a camera so that the picture recorded on the film is sharp and clear. In theatre lighting, *focus* refers to the fact that beams of light are aimed at—focused on—a particular area. In stage action the director and lighting designer collaborate in creating a continually moving visual composition that always keeps the audience focused on the central action of the play. This kind of collaboration and compositional focus also allows a character to slip into position without those of us in the audience ever realizing how he got there until it is time to reveal him. Careful focus of light is integral to successful visuals onstage. Adjacent lighting and acting areas must be overlapped in focus to allow actors to move across the stage without going into and out of the edges of light beams. At the same time, the designer must control the *spill* of the light in front of and behind the actor so that it will not distract us as we watch the action of the play.

By means of focus and changes in light cues, the lighting designer and director keep the audience focused on the essential action. These compositions, or *looks,* can vary from turning the stage into one large area to creating small, isolated areas, all intended to take the audience on an interesting visual journey through the world of the play.

Mood and Style Theatre, as a collaborative art form by definition, combines all areas of a production to establish the mood and world of the play. Once that predominant mood is established for an audience, the individual production areas can manipulate mood throughout the play, especially through lighting and sound. A production can also effectively manipulate our reaction. For example, early in a play we may see two or three romantic moments when the stage is filled with blue moonlight; then, in a later scene the look may seem the same until the action starts and we realize that the mood has changed to a cold, dark, evil situation. Action, scenery, and words, in conjunction with light, tell us exactly what the mood is. Experienced playwrights and designers know how we can be manipulated and will often take advantage of our expectations to make our journey more interesting.

In terms of style, lighting can indicate whether a play is realistic or departs from realism. In a realistic play, the lighting will simulate the effect of ordinary sources—table lamps, say, and outside sunlight. In a nonrealistic production or a highly theatrical musical, the designer can be more imaginative: Shafts of light can cut through the dark, sculpturing performers onstage; a glowing red light can convey a scene of damnation; a ghostly green light can cast a spell over a nightmare scene; a hard-edged spotlight can let the audience members know that what they are now seeing is not a realistic moment in a character's life.

Time and Place By its color, shade, and intensity, lighting can suggest the time of day, giving us the pale light of dawn, the bright light of midday, the vivid colors of sunset, or the muted light of evening. Lighting can also indicate the season of the year, because the sun strikes objects at very different angles in winter and summer.

LIGHTING CREATES MOOD AND STYLE
Along with scenery and costumes, lighting is a key element in creating the mood and style of a production. Shown here is a scene where light criss-crosses the stage, creating abstract shapes and illuminating the performers, as well as projecting colors that contrast the top section with that below. The scene is from a production of *Eurydice* by Sarah Ruhl, directed by Geoff Elliott at A Noise Within Theatre. The lighting was designed by Meghan Gray. (Craig Schwartz)

Lighting can also suggest place by showing indoor or outdoor light. In this manner, lighting helps reinforce the story being told.

Rhythm   Since changes in light occur on a time continuum, they establish a rhythm running through a production. It is absolutely imperative that the seemingly simple lighting changes from scene to scene help establish the kind of rhythm and timing that the director needs for us to be drawn into the action. Abrupt, staccato changes with stark blackouts might unsettle us if that is called for, and languid, slow fades and

photo essay

The Many Uses of Stage Lighting

(Sara Krulwich/The New York Times/Redux)

Stage lighting can be used for many purposes: to illuminate, to highlight characters or stage areas, and to create mood.

In this scene, lighting designer Justin Townsend has used lights to highlight the couple in the center (Dashiell Eaves and Amanda Quaid) and also the single figure at the right (Eisa Davis) in a different color and mood. The lights above add framing and atmosphere. The play is Kirsten Greenidge's *Luck of the Irish* directed by Rebecca Taichman.

A scene from a production of *Desire Under the Elms* by Eugene O'Neill, directed by Dámaso Rodriguez at A Noise Within Theatre, in Pasadena, California, shows a skillful use of local front lighting: The oil lamp illuminates Abbie (Monette Magrath). Lighting by James P. Taylor; costumes by Julie Keen.

(Craig Schwartz)

Shown here is actor Lynn Japjit Kaur, center, as Jyoti Singh Pandey, a woman who died in 2012 after she was gang-raped and tortured in New Delhi, in the play *Nirbhaya*. The testimony of five Indian women describing their experiences of sexual abuse is used by South African playwright and director Yael Farber to create the drama. Note how spotlights are used to focus the audience's attention on the women on stage.

(Sara Krulwich/The New York Times/Redux)

Lighting designer Elizabeth Harper has used lighting to create a crimson sky in the dust bowl area of the Midwest in a production of *The Grapes of Wrath* by John Steinbeck, adapted by Frank Galati, directed by Michael Michetti at A Noise Within Theatre. Note the effective use of the light to silhouette the silent actors.

(Craig Schwartz)

gradual cross-fades can allow us a more thoughtful transition between scenes. Does the designer fade out the previous scene slowly while the next scene is beginning, thus prompting us to think about the connection? Or does the designer make the lights fade in very slowly, prompting us to ask what is to come and pulling our attention in? Either way these changes in rhythm have an effect on our interaction with and understanding of the world of the play.

Since many lighting changes are coordinated with scene changes and changes in other production elements, it is a challenge for the lighting designer to make artistic choices that will support the director's vision, whether a change is pragmatic or solely aesthetic. Either way, the importance of this synchronization is recognized by directors and designers, who take great care to ensure the proper changes—"choreographing" shifts in light and scenery like dancers' movements.

Reinforcement of the Central Image Lighting—like scenery, costumes, and all other elements—must be consistent with the overall style and mood of a production. Over the past thirty years there has been a dramatic change in the style of writing plays. Long, extended scenes taking place in a single location are less and less common. Today's audiences are most accustomed to film and television editing and to shorter scenes with multiple locations. Most of our contemporary plays tend to be written in a style that also cuts frequently from location to location; the actors may be on a bare stage with only the most essential props or suggested props to support the action. These kinds of changes in writing style prompt the lighting designer to provide more visual information than ever before about place and locale to allow for such simple staging. The wrong choices in lighting can distort or even destroy the effect of a play. At the same time, because lighting is the most flexible and the most atmospheric visual element of theatre, it can aid enormously in creating our theatre experience.

The Lighting Designer

The person responsible for creating, installing, and setting controls for stage lighting is the lighting designer, who also works with collaborators. It is important for the lighting designer to have a background in the technical and mechanical aspects of lighting, as well as a broad, creative visual imagination. The ability to translate words and actions and feelings into color, direction, and intensity comes only after much training and experience.

The Process of Lighting Design In creating the lighting design for a production, the lighting designer first reads the script and begins to form some rough ideas and develop some feelings about the play. He or she meets with the director and other designers to discuss visual concepts. The lighting designer receives from the set designer copies of all the scenery plans and usually consults with the costume designer to learn the shape and color of the costumes.

The lighting designer will do a great deal of visual research and will also see one or perhaps several rehearsals to get the feel of the production, to see the exact location of various pieces of furniture and stage business, and to consult with the director about possible effects. Following this, the lighting designer draws a plan called a *light plot*. This includes the location and color of each lighting instrument. Also indicated is the kind of instrument called for and the area of the stage on which it is focused. When lighting instruments are moved into the theatre and hung (that is, placed on pipes and other supports), the designer supervises the focusing.

During technical rehearsals, the lighting designer works with the director to establish light cues; that is, instructions about when the lights go on and off. The designer also sets the length of time for light changes and the levels of intensity on the computer-controlled light board, which sends a digital signal to the actual dimmers to adjust the lighting instrument levels. (The actual dimmers, which allow lighting intensities to be changed smoothly and at varying rates, are located in a remote offstage location.)

Properties of Stage Lighting   When working on the design for a production, the lighting designer knows what controllable properties of light will achieve the objectives discussed earlier. The lighting designer can manipulate four different properties of light for any visual change onstage: intensity, color, distribution, and movement.

Intensity   The first property of light is brightness, or intensity. Intensity can be controlled (as noted earlier) by devices called dimmers, which make the lights brighter or darker. A dimmer is an electric or electronic device that can vary the amount of power going to the lights. This makes it possible for a scene at night to take place in very little light and a daylight scene to take place in bright light. Since the advent of computer control systems, lighting intensities can be set at any level between 1 percent and 100 percent of full, as opposed to levels 1 through 10 on older manual controls.

Color   The second property of light is color. Color is a very powerful part of lighting, and theatre lights can very easily be changed to one of several hundred colors simply by placing colored material in slots at the front of the lighting instruments. This material is usually called a gel—short for gelatin, of which it was originally made. Today, however, these color filters are generally made of plastic, such as Mylar, or acetate.

Also in recent years, color *scrollers* have been introduced. These devices typically make it possible to change up to fifteen colors for each lighting, and the scrollers are also programmed into each light cue along with intensity and timing. Color is often mixed so that the strong tones of one shade will not dominate, since such dominance would give an unnatural appearance. Colors are most often selected to support choices made by the scenic and costume designers while still including sufficient dramatic color to support the varied action of the play. Quite often scenes will call for special effects; we expect stark shadows and strange colors, for example, when Hamlet confronts the ghost of his father.

Distribution   The third property of light that the lighting designer can use is distribution: the position and type of lighting instrument being used and the angle at which the light strikes the performers onstage. (Another term for this property could be *direction,* that is, the source from which the light comes, the type of instrument used, and the points on the stage at which a light beam is aimed.) In earlier days, footlights—a row of lights across the front of the stage floor—were used, primarily because this was almost the only location from which to light the front of the

THE USE OF COLOR IN LIGHTING

One of the prime elements in stage lighting is color: It can alter and transform a stage set, changing and establishing different moods. Here we see the same set with different lighting from *The Underpants* by Carl Sternheim, adapted by Steve Martin, presented at the Alley Theatre, Houston. Note the stark white of the first photograph and the pink and purple hue of the second, contrasting the mood and the tone from one visual picture to another. All this is done with light. The director was Scott Schwartz, with lighting design by Pat Collins, costume design by David C. Woolard, and set design by Anna Louizos. (both: T Charles Erickson)

performers. However, footlights, which were below the performers, had the disadvantage of casting ghostly shadows on their faces. Footlights also created a kind of barrier between performers and audience. With the development of more powerful, versatile lights, footlights have been eliminated and they are now used only when a production is trying to re-create the look and style of a classic play of the eighteenth or nineteenth century.

Today, most lighting hits the stage from above, coming from instruments in front of the stage and at the sides. The vertical angle of light beams from the *front of the house* is typically close to 45 degrees; this is an excellent angle for lighting the actor's face without creating harmful shadows, and it also gives a sense of sunlight or an overhead light source found in most locations.

A wide variety of lighting instruments are available today, both conventional instruments and automated moving light fixtures. They all have distinctive features, and each instrument is selected for the quality of light and the design options it allows. What visual qualities or "texture" does the light produce on stage? Is it a single shaft of light, like a single beam of moonlight through the trees, or a spotlight in a nightclub?

Or is the light in a pattern, such as dappled sunlight through the leaves of trees in a forest? Are the edges of the light sharp or soft and diffused? In conventional ellipsoidal lighting instruments, light can be shaped by special shutters that close in at the edges (very few moving lights even have that capability). All these are additional tools for the designer.

Movement The last property of light the designer can work with is movement, and in fact this is where the lighting design comes to life. On one level, the eye is carried from place to place by the shifting focus of lights: follow spots moving from one person or one area to another, automated lights changing directions, a performer carrying a candle or flashlight across the stage. The subtlest and often the most effective kind of movement of light comes with shifting the audience's focus when lights go down in one area and come up in another. Lighting cross-fades like this can shift the focus from location to location and from color to color, but even within single scenes a good lighting design will force the audience members to change their focus without even realizing it. Also, time of day, sunsets, and so on can help provide visual information for the audience.

For an example of how these properties function, consider the lighting for a production of *Hamlet*. To emphasize this play's eerie, tragic quality, with its murders and graveyard scene, the lighting would generally be cool rather than warm, but it could also have a slash of red cutting through the otherwise cool light. As for angles, if the production took place on a proscenium stage, there would be more dramatic down lighting and back lighting to give the characters a sculptured, occasionally unreal quality. In terms of movement, the lights would change each time there was a shift in locale, or a low-angle special could come on diagonally from behind the ghost of Hamlet's father. This would give a rhythm of movement throughout the play and would also focus the audience's attention on particular areas of the stage, as well as support the thematic elements of the play.

The Lighting Designer's Resources
Among the resources of the lighting designer are various kinds of lighting instruments and other kinds of technical and electronic equipment.

Types of stage lights Most stage lights have three main elements: a lamp that is the source of the light, a reflector, and a lens through which the beams pass. The two basic categories of lighting fixtures are conventional lighting instruments and automated or moving light fixtures. Conventional lights are fixed instruments with a single focus and design purpose. Intelligent moving light fixtures are able to alter focus, change color, project multiple patterns, rotate the patterns at varying speeds, change the size of the beam, and give a sharp or diffused focus.

Philips Selecon Pacific 2350 Ellipsoidal.
Philips Selecon

Philips Selecon Rama Fresnel.
Philips Selecon

Examples of common conventional lights are the ellipsoidal reflector spotlights, Fresnel spotlights, strip/cyc/flood/border lights, PAR floodlights, and followspots:

1. *Ellipsoidal reflector spotlight or ERS.* This is the most widely used conventional fixture. It creates a bright, hard-edged spot. However, the edge can be softened with focus adjustment or with a different fusion filter. Lenses of different focal lengths allow for eight different standard-size beams depending on the distance from the theatre's hanging positions to the stage; this instrument is therefore useful from almost any position in the theatre. Clearly, it is the "workhorse" of contemporary lighting practice. It also has a special *gobo* slot for pattern projection. A *followspot* is another typically hard-edged spotlight controlled by an operator that is designed to follow the leading performer across the stage. Originally, this type of light was created by igniting the mineral lime in front of a reflector in the back end of a long metal tube. The chemical reaction created a bright but slightly green light, which led to the common expression for someone who likes attention as "liking to be in the limelight."

2. *Soft-edged spotlights.* The most popular soft-edged spotlight is the Fresnel (pronounced "fruh-NEL"). It is a high-wattage spot, and the Fresnel lens helps dissipate the heat, but it can create only a soft-edged beam of light that can be focused down to a small spot or flooded to cover a larger stage area. The lens is named for Auguste Fresnel, who designed for lighthouses the first lenses that would not crack with intense heating and cooling. The concentric rings he cut into the lens allowed it to function properly while preventing the buildup of heat from cracking the lens after the light was turned off. Many lighting designers use this instrument for top lighting and back lighting and to cover a large stage area with a wash of color. The Fresnel is generally used in positions near the stage—behind the proscenium opening or mounted close to the action on an arena or thrust stage. Another common soft-edged lighting instrument is the parabolic aluminized reflector (PAR), which emits an oval beam. *Barn doors,* with flaps that can cut off an edge of the beam, and *color changers/scrollers,* which increase the options from one color to fifteen colors on a single instrument, are common accessories used on both PARs and Fresnels.

3. *Floodlights, strip lights, and border lights.* These lights bathe a section of the stage or scenery in a smooth, diffused wash of light. Floodlights are used, singly or in groups, to provide general illumination for the stage or scenery. The light from floods can be blended in acting areas or used to "tone" settings and costumes. They are most often used to illuminate cycloramas at the rear of the stage or ground rows along the floor of the stage.

4. *Automated or moving light (also referred to as intelligent fixtures).* The moving light is the newest and most versatile instrument of the group. Automated light

Philips Selecon Hui Flood. (Philips Selecon)   Vari-Lite VL6 spot luminaire (Philips Vari-Lite)

fixtures are able to alter focus, change color using dichroic—or two-beam—color mixing, project multiple patterns, rotate the patterns at varying speeds, change the size of the beam, and give a sharp or diffused focus. One moving light fixture used as a special can replace numerous conventional fixtures. Most contemporary lighting designers use a combination of both types of instruments. Automated fixtures are particularly useful in elaborate musical productions and are widely used in rock concerts.

Lighting controls Lighting design is clearly the most technologically developed element of theatre. We have already considered some of the advances in this area in terms of lighting instruments. These fixtures can now be hung all over a performance space and aimed at every part of the stage. In addition, one person sitting at a console can control the elements of these lighting instruments. New technologies have also prompted a great deal of change in the design of control systems, which now allow for remarkable computer-controlled lighting along with the ability to employ traditional methods of cue changes. Lighting control systems are extremely expensive, so the change to systems that continue to evolve technologically happens only gradually for most theatre operations.

Lighting changes—or *cues,* as they are called—are usually arranged ahead of time. Sometimes, in a complicated production (a musical, say, or a Shakespearean play), there will be from 75 to 150 or more light cues. A cue can range from a *blackout* (in which all the lights are shut off at once), to a *fade* (the lights dim slowly, changing the scene from brighter to darker), to a *cross-fade* (one set of lights comes down while another comes up) or a split cross-fade (the lights that are coming up are on a different fade count from the lights that are coming down). Thanks to computerized control, the split cross-fade is the most common.

Although light board programming is complicated and somewhat time-consuming, the actual running of a show has become a fairly simple task because of well-designed computer control systems. The most critical aspect of the lighting design is the ability of the stage manager to fully understand the pacing and design aesthetic

cues Any prearranged signal—such as the last words in a speech, a piece of business, or any action or lighting change—that indicates to a performer or stage manager that it is time to proceed to the next line or action.

> ## IN FOCUS: ROCK CONCERT AND THEATRE LIGHTING
>
> As we mentioned in the chapter "Theatre Is Everywhere," rock music and theatre have strong connections. One of those connections is the influence theatre has had on rock concert lighting design and vice versa.
>
> In the early days of touring rock performers, particularly in the 1950s and 1960s, many of the designers for their concerts were theatre trained and had the same aesthetic goals as theatre lighting design: clear illumination, mood, and slight changes of color. This was particularly true because available lighting instruments had to be hung in multi-use spaces on preexisting grids and put up and taken down quickly.
>
> Beginning in the 1970s, with the development of computer-assisted technology and new lighting technology, rock concerts began to become performance events with lighting design becoming almost another onstage performer. Lighting designers for rock concerts used cutting edge computer-assisted controls, new software and lighter materials to create poles for hanging multiple instruments as well as lighter instruments, more intense floodlights for color, intelligent instruments that could move, and the use of projections and media.
>
> A recent example of rock performance using cutting edge technology to create lighting effects was Lady Gaga's 2017 Super Bowl performance. Besides the intricate light plot that employed 84 intelligent Philips Vari-Lites, 300 Intel Shooting Star drones flew over Lady Gaga during her opening number creating a mechanized and computer-controlled light show. The drones were outfitted with colored LEDs, and the unmanned aerial vehicles (UAVs) were remotely controlled in order to create stunning images including the American flag.
>
> Many of the technological innovations used to create spectacular lighting designs for rock musicians were later incorporated into large-scale commercial productions. For example, some Broadway rock and juke box musicals have re-created the visual aesthetic of rock concerts. *Natasha, Pierre & the Great Comet of 1812*, which opened on Broadway in 2016, uses spectacular lighting that frequently mimics a rock concert.

in calling the lighting and sound cues. Even the process of calling cues has been simplified in some ways by technology. In lighting for dance or for large-scale musicals, it is critical to merge the lighting and sound cues. Through the use of new digital sound technology, a computer-controlled sound program can interface with a computer light board, and both light and sound cues can be run simultaneously with one tap of the keyboard space bar.

For instance, Strindberg's *A Dream Play* has numerous and complex scene changes—like a dream, as the title implies—in which one scene fades into another before our eyes. At one point in the play, a young woman, called the Daughter, sits at an organ in a church. In Strindberg's words, "The stage darkens as the Daughter rises and approaches the Lawyer. By means of lighting the organ is transformed into a wall of a grotto. The sea seeps in between basal pillars with a harmony of waves and wind." At the light cue for this change, a button is pushed, and all the lights creating the majesty of the church fade as the lights creating the grotto come up. In many ways stage lighting technology has finally started to catch up with, and serve, the creative ideas that artists like Strindberg and Appia had at the start of the twentieth century.

The Lighting Designer's Collaborators

As in every aspect of theatre, in lighting, too, there is collaboration. Those who work with the lighting designer include assistant designers and people who help create the light plot, as well as a master electrician responsible for the preparation, hanging, and focusing of the lights and all accessories (often, if not always, electricians must climb on catwalks and ladders to remote areas above, behind, and in front of the stage). One of the newer jobs is that of the moving light programmer. Until the advent of moving lights, programming light cues had always fallen to either the lighting designer or the lead associate designer. More recently, however, the complexity of programming has grown exponentially with automated fixtures and other digital accessories, thus requiring another technical specialty.

Large-scale musical productions, for example, are often so complex that even calling all the cues is impossible for one person to do. For that reason, all followspot cues (usually three or four followspots in a design) are typically called by the lead spot operator. In the concert industry, this gets even more complex, as there are usually a minimum of eight followspots and often as many as sixteen or more on a major tour of a rock musical production in addition to almost unimaginably complex moving light packages.

SOUND IN THE THEATRE

Scenery, costumes, and lighting can all be described as the visual elements of theatre. Another major design element is sound. In recent years, sound has become an increasingly important aspect of theatre, with its own artistry, technology, and designers.

In 2007, the Tony Awards voted to include sound design as a category for plays and musicals beginning with the 2008 awards. However, in 2014, the Tony Administration Committee eliminated the awards. Even though the committee stated it could give a special award to a production with extraordinary sound design, there was great protest by many members of the profession reflecting how significant sound design has become in so many Broadway productions. The committee therefore reinstated the award for both a play and a musical for the 2017–2018 season. In other cities, sound design is recognized as a separate theatre awards category; for example, Chicago's Joseph Jefferson Award Committee recognizes sound design in Equity and non-Equity productions.

Sound Reproduction: Advantages and Disadvantages

Amplification   In the past few decades, sound reproduction has become increasingly prominent in theatre. For some audience members, it has sometimes proved to be controversial as well. The intense amplification at popular music concerts along with the availability of inexpensive personal audio systems—now in digital formats—are just two of the reasons we now expect widespread sound reproduction in the theatre. As a result, large musicals, whether presented in Broadway houses or in spacious performing art centers across the country, are now extensively amplified. Most of us, accustomed to amplified sound in many other settings, take such amplification for granted.

Some critics charge, however, that amplification in theatre is sometimes overdone, with the sound too loud, as well as too mechanical and artificial. In opera the objections are even stronger. In today's theatre, those continuing to oppose amplification appear to be "purists" who want a return to past theatrical practice. It may be difficult for us in the twenty-first century to imagine, but the

THE SIGNIFICANCE OF SOUND

There are times when sound takes over in a production. Of course, in most musical productions, all the voices, as well as the instruments of the orchestra, are enhanced by sound equipment. But in many productions there are certain moments when sound is crucial. An example is the scene shown here from a production of *Uncle Vanya* by Anton Chekhov. Derek Jacobi, as Vanya, fires a gun at a professor he finds unbearable. The gunshot goes astray (perhaps on purpose), but the sound of the firing is central to the scene, underscoring Vanya's rage. Sound design was by David Van Teighem. (Sara Krulwich/The New York Times/Redux)

great American musicals of the 1940s and the 1950s were all produced without any sound amplification whatsoever. Today, however, electronic amplification is a way of life in theatre, and sound design has become an indispensable part of any production.

We are speaking here of larger spaces: college or university theatres of approximately 400 or 500 seats and professional theatres that might range from 800 to 2,000 seats. The issue of amplification is less pressing in smaller venues: in "black boxes," for example, or fringe theatres in lofts, warehouses, or storefronts, that seat perhaps 100 spectators. In such spaces, sound amplification is likely to be less used. (It should be noted, however, with the advent of less expensive computer-assisted sound design, such theatres may still have intricate sound effects for their productions.)

Sound Effects Aside from the argument about the volume or pervasiveness of voice amplification, we should recognize that sound has always been an important, and necessary, component of theatre production. One aspect of this is sound effects. In earlier years—for several centuries, in fact—various devices were developed to create such sounds.

Historically, for example, a wooden drum made from slats was used to produce the sound of wind. The drum was usually two or three feet in diameter and covered with a muslin cloth. When the drum was turned, by means of a handle, it made a noise like howling wind. Thunder was suggested by hanging a large, thick metal sheet backstage and gently shaking it. For the sound of a door slamming, a miniature door or even a full-size door in a frame was placed just offstage and opened and shut. Two hinged pieces of wood slammed shut also simulated the sound of a closing door.

Part Three   The Designers

A gunshot sound could also be created with these hinged pieces of wood, as well as by firing a gun loaded with blank cartridges. Live ammunition could not be used safely onstage. In some states, blank guns were (and still are) illegal. As we shall see, recorded sound, now easily digitized, makes this issue irrelevant in the contemporary theatre.

Today, of course, the developments in computer technology and digitization, which support sound design and its playback on stage, are extensive. Many programs are available on the Internet for free download as well, so it is not difficult to get started using simple sound programs. Most often these same programs have more advanced and complex capabilities that are available for purchase. You can record and play back a myriad of sound cues; if you want to interface those sound cues through a lighting control board or projection system for creation and alteration, you may use sophisticated software packages such as Pro Tools, Final Cut Pro, or Garage Band. Also available are SFX and CueLab computer playback systems.

The Sound Designer

The person responsible for arranging and orchestrating all the aural aspects of a production is the sound designer. Like his or her counterparts in visual design, the sound designer begins by reading the script, noting all the places where sound might be needed. For a large-scale musical, the designer also decides on the number and type of microphones to be used, the placement of speakers throughout the theatre, and all other aspects of sound reproduction.

After reading the script, the sound designer consults with the director to determine the exact nature of the sound requirements, including sound effects and amplification. The designer then sets about preparing the full range of components that constitute sound for a production. Encompassing anything from preshow and intermission music, to any and all microphones, to special pre-recorded sound effects, to preshow announcements about cell phones, to live voice-overs, sound is an essential component of every theatre production.

Understanding Sound Reproduction and Sound Reinforcement

One way to classify sound design is as *sound reproduction* and *sound reinforcement*. Sound *reproduction* is the use of motivated or environmental sounds. ***Motivated sounds*** would be, for instance, the noise of a car crunching on gravel, a car motor turning off, and a door slamming—a sequence that would announce the arrival of a character at a house where a scene is taking place. Motivated sounds, then, are those called for by the script. ***Environmental sounds*** are noises of everyday life that help create verisimilitude in a production: street traffic in a city, crickets in the country, loud rock music coming from a stereo in a college dormitory. Such sounds are usually heard as background.

Sound effects are one form of sound reproduction. A sound effect can be defined as any sound produced by mechanical or human means to create for us a noise or sound associated with the play. Today, as we noted previously, sound effects are most often digitally downloaded to computers and even handheld devices. Virtually every sound imaginable—from birds singing, to dogs barking, to jet planes flying—is available

motivated sounds Sounds called for by the script.

environmental sounds Noises of everyday life that help create a sense of reality in a production.

> ## PLAYING YOUR PART: EXPERIENCING THEATRE
>
> 1. How do you use lighting in your room or home for different circumstances? How do you change the lighting for those occasions? How is this similar to what is done in the theatre?
> 2. What sound technology do you use in your everyday life? How might this also be employed in the theatre?
> 3. If someone asked, "What is the soundtrack for your life?" What would your response be? How does that sound reflect who you are? How is that similar to the use of sound accompanying the production of a play?
> 4. On a sunny day, observe how the light shines through the leaves of a tree on your campus or near your home. What mood does the light evoke in you? Why? How?
> 5. What is the lighting like in your favorite restaurant? What mood does it evoke in you? Why? How?
> 6. Watch a film and discuss how the sound enhances the film. How is underscoring used?
> 7. Attend a technical rehearsal at your university or community theatre. Observe the light changes. Do you see who is operating the light and sound boards? Can you identify any of the lighting instruments and where they are hung in the theatre? Ask if you may see the computer boards that operate lighting and sound.

reinforcement The amplification of sounds produced by a performer or a musical instrument.

for digital download from the Internet, not only for expensive commercial, professional productions but also for small noncommercial companies, college, university, and community theatres.

Sound *reinforcement* is the amplification of sounds produced by a performer or a musical instrument. With the growth of electronics and computerization in music, more and more instruments have been amplified. At any rock concert, you can see wires coming out of the basses and guitars. In an orchestra pit in a theatre, the quieter acoustic instruments such as the guitar are miked to achieve a balance of sound with the louder instruments. In today's Broadway theatres it is not unusual to have some members of the orchestra in a separate room in another part of the building with a television monitor showing the conductor. In most cases, the audience would never know about this seating arrangement. The total sound can overwhelm a singer, especially one who has not been trained—as opera singers are—to project the voice into the farther reaches of a theatre. As a result, we have body mikes on the performers.

At first, a body mike was a small microphone attached in some way to the performer's clothing. A wire ran from the mike to a small radio transmitter concealed on the performer; from the transmitter, the sound was sent to an offstage listening device that fed it into a central sound-control system. In today's large musical productions, the microphone worn by a performer is frequently a small instrument, hardly larger than a piece of wire, worn over one ear alongside the temple or placed elsewhere near the performer's head, that carries the sound to the body transmitters.

It is now very common in large musical theatre playhouses for performers to wear this very tiny, almost unnoticeable microphone around the ear; it is also most commonly used by rock performers in concerts. Head microphones are used so that they will be as close as possible to the performer's mouth and at a constant distance away from it. (How many of us attending a musical realize that the tap dancers are frequently wearing wireless microphones near their feet, inside their dance tights?)

Still another kind of sound that must be added to the final mix is musical or other *underscoring,* which one hears between scenes or acts, and sometimes during spoken sections of a performance, to add emphasis or create mood.

196   Part Three   The Designers

Sound Creates the Environment

In recent years, sound has become an even more integral element in the overall design of a production. In some productions, sound has become almost, if not as, important as scene design in helping to create place, time, and set changes.

A recent production of *Macbeth* in Austin, Texas, staged by Past Is Prologue Productions and the Filigree Theatre, was done in a completely darkened space, with the actors surrounding the audience and four audio speakers delivering sounds that helped create the changes in time and place. In *Encounter,* a production by the English company Complicité that toured the world and was presented on Broadway in 2016, audience members were each given their own headphones so that they could hear intimately the voice of the solo actor as well as sounds that were recorded in the Amazon, immersing them in and creating for them the setting of the show.

Such experiments are becoming more commonplace in the contemporary theatre as sound is more easily created and controlled through digital technologies and, in some cases, becoming the most important design element in a production.

Sound Technology

Microphones and Loudspeakers   In preparing the sound for a production, the designers and engineers not only must assemble all the necessary sounds but also must be certain that the appropriate microphones are used correctly and must place the speakers effectively onstage and in the auditorium.

Several types of microphones are used. A *shotgun mike* is highly directional and is aimed from a distance at a specific area. A *general mike* picks up sounds in the general area toward which it is aimed. A *body mike,* as we described earlier, is a wireless microphone attached to a performer's body or clothing. Microphones not worn by performers are placed in various locations. One position is alongside the downstage edge of the stage. Another position is hanging in the air above the stage. Any type of microphone must be hooked up to an amplifier that increases the electronic energy of the sound and sends it through the speakers.

The placement of loudspeakers is both an art and a science. It is necessary to determine the correct speakers, which have become smaller due to advances in digital sound, for the size and shape of the theatre and to position them so that they carry sound clearly and evenly into the auditorium—to the upper reaches of the balcony, to the side seats, and to areas underneath the balcony as well as the first few rows in the orchestra. Also, live sound from the performers must reach the sides and back of the theatre at the same time that it reaches those of us seated in the front. One problem in this regard is that sound travels much more slowly than light.

The speed of sound is only 1,100 feet per second—which means that for those of us seated at the back of a large theatre, sound from a speaker at the rear of the auditorium will be heard before the human voice from the stage. Developments in digital electronics have led to devices that process, sample, and synthesize sound for various effects, including delaying the electronic sound so that it arrives through a loudspeaker at the same time as the much slower live sound.

Sound Recordings   The process of assembling sound recordings is similar for professional and nonprofessional productions. First, a list is made of all sound

IN FOCUS: INCLUSIVITY AND SOUND TECHNOLOGY

As we discussed in the previous chapter, theatre companies are striving to make productions more accessible to all audience members. Just as technology has been employed to make theatre more accessible for visually impaired audience members, it has also been used to allow hearing-impaired audience members to better experience a production.

New sound technology has improved the theatre experience for audience members with hearing issues through assistive listening devices (ALDs). An ALD consists of a small wireless radio receiver and either an independent earpiece or an earpiece compatible with certain hearing aids. ALDs transmit amplified sound from the stage through a sophisticated set of tiny microphones. These devices allow those audience members who need assistance to hear the dialogue spoken by performers, sound effects, and songs and music. The ALDs also eliminate a significant amount of the ambient noise, thereby enhancing the hearing experience.

Some theatres, like the National Theatre in London, have introduced "smart caption" glasses for hearing-impaired audience members so that they can attend any performance. The glasses allow the hearing-impaired audience members to watch the production and see the dialogue captions in real time.

Most theatres also offer some captioned and/or signed performances for those audience members with hearing loss.

---

required. This list is usually developed by the sound designer in consultation with the director, and possibly with a composer: For a show with a great deal of sound or music, there may be both a sound designer and a music composer.

Once the list is drawn up, a master recording is made and the sounds are arranged in their order of appearance in the script. This process is called *editing* and is now done with computer assistance. In addition, sound designers and music composers can have their digital sounds and new music captured on their tablets, smart devices, or stored online, so that they can share with the director and other collaborators.

When the production moves into the theatre, there is a technical rehearsal without performers, during which each sound cue is listened to and the volume is set. When rehearsals with the performers start in the theatre, more changes will be made. Depending on the action and the timing of scenes, some cues will be too loud and others too soft; some will have to be made shorter and others made longer.

During an actual performance of a production using sound reinforcement, an operator must sit at a complex sound console *mixing* sound or, as is becoming the norm, use a computerized playback system such as SFX or CueLab. In this way the operator blends all elements from the many microphones and from the master sound recording so that there is a smooth, seamless blend of sound. Also, the operator must make certain not only that all sound is in balance but also that sound does not intrude on the performance or call attention to itself, away from the stage and the performers.

New Technologies in Sound As with lighting, in recent years we have seen frequent advances and breakthroughs in sound equipment and technology. The new body microphones and tiny head microphones, as well as a device that delays the delivery of electronic sound, have already been mentioned. There are other developments as well.

Analog reel-to-reel tape decks, which were standard, have given way to digital technology such as direct playback from a computer's hard drive. Sound is now

IN FOCUS: LIGHTING AND SOUND DESIGN IN FILM AND TELEVISION

While the functions of lighting in film and television are very similar to stage lighting, including illumination, creating mood, and adding special effects, the lighting designer in film and television has to deal with differing sources and instruments for light than the designer in the theatre.

Lighting designers in film frequently have to make use of and compensate for natural lighting. They may be shooting in outdoor locations during the day, and they then have to factor in the actual light of shoot time along with the need for artificial lighting to supplement or enhance. Also, the film and television lighting designer must take into account the changes in natural lighting during the course of the day's filming.

Film and television lighting designers also have to frequently use a more focused light (or what is known as a "key" light) to illuminate a specific actor or object in a scene. Unlike a spot light in the theatre, which is highly theatrical, the "key" light is usually not meant to detract from the reality of the scene.

The types of lighting instruments and techniques in film are also different from those in the theatre because of the way in which the camera captures light. Unlike in theatre where the lighting designer is designing for the eyes of audience members, the film and television lighting designer is creating lighting effects to be captured by the camera and eventually to be projected in a movie theatre or seen on a TV screen or on another other digital device.

Sound design in film and television also serve the same functions as in the theatre, but the film and television sound designers have more technical means at their disposal. Sound can be added after filming is completed. Dialogue can be redubbed, if needed, after shooting. Background music can be added and changed throughout the editing process, as can sound effects.

Unlike the theatre, where the sounds must be created for the appropriate moment during a live performance and there is limited ability to fix any mistakes, film and television sound is carefully controlled throughout production and can be enhanced, fixed, changed, or added to in postproduction.

---

recorded and edited at digital audio workstations and housed on personal computers, as well as on tablets and even smartphones. Such stations allow easier editing of sound, more complex effects, and higher-quality sound. Digital playback systems allow very easy and precise cueing of shows, as well as greatly improved sound quality.

SPECIAL EFFECTS IN LIGHTING AND SOUND

As in scene design, some effects of lighting and sound, separately or in combination, can seem unusual or even miraculous and add to the magic of live theatre.

Several special lighting effects can be used to create interesting visual pictures. One simple effect is to position a source of light near the stage floor and shine the light on the performers from below. This creates shadows under the eyes and chin and gives performers' faces a ghostly or horrifying quality. Another common special effect is ultraviolet light, a very dark blue light that causes phosphorus to glow; when the stage is very dark or completely dark, costumes or scenery that have been painted with a special phosphorus paint will "light up."

The effect of slow motion—where the performers seem to be moving in jerks—is created by a strobe light, a very powerful, bright gas-discharge light that flashes at rapid intervals. As we saw earlier, technological advances in lighting

> ## PLAYING YOUR PART: THINKING ABOUT THEATRE
>
> 1. During the last play you attended, what did you notice about the lighting? Were there lighting instruments throughout the theatre aimed at the stage? When the performance began, where did the beams of light appear to come from?
> 2. During that same production, what colors were created on the stage by lighting? Did you think the colors were appropriate for the production? How did the color of the lights affect your overall experience?
> 3. Again, during that same production, were you able to spot sound speakers? Where were they located? During the performance, did you notice if microphones were attached to the actors? Do you think there were microphones elsewhere on stage? Can you speculate as to where they were?

have made it possible to create even more spectacular effects and to enhance these effects as well.

There are also a number of special sound effects. Sometimes speakers are placed completely around the audience so that the sound can move from side to side. Echoes can be created by a machine that causes reverberations in sound waves. Expanding audio technology also allows for more complex sound effects. Computerized noises and electronic music can be used to create special sounds for various situations, and digitization gives instantaneous access to any element of the sound design. Also, with computerized synthesizers, a few musicians can now replace a large orchestra.

Lighting and sound, therefore, like scenery and costumes, are means to an end: They implement the artistic and aesthetic aspects of a production. The colors, shapes, and lines of lighting and the qualities of sound design interact with other elements of theatre and contribute to the overall experience.

Evaluating Lighting and Sound Design

As with the other design elements, there are key questions we should ask ourselves as we try to determine how successful the lighting and sound designers were in supporting the production we have attended. These include:

1. What information was conveyed by the lighting about time, place, characters, and situation? How was this information conveyed to you?
2. Describe the mood of the lighting. How was color and intensity used to affect your mood? What other characteristics of light were used to affect mood? Was the lighting appropriate for the mood of each scene? Why or why not?
3. Was the lighting realistic or nonrealistic? What was the direction of the light? Did it seem to come from a natural source, or was it artificial? Did this choice seem appropriate for the text?
4. Were the performers properly lit? Could their faces be seen?
5. Were light changes made slowly or quickly? How did this affect the play? Did it seem right for the type of play you attended?
6. Were there any lighting special effects? What were they? How were they used to support the play?

IN FOCUS: APP TECHNOLOGY FOR LIGHTING AND SOUND DESIGN

Lighting and sound designers are now also able to use apps on their mobile devices in order to be able to more easily work away from the theatre and to revise and share their designs online.

A lighting handbook is available online that has information on conventional lighting fixtures, moving instruments, dimmers, and effects that can be downloaded into an app and is a remarkable resource for designers. There are apps that allow lighting designers to calculate the illumination and other qualities of lighting instruments onto a stage. There are other mobile applications that allow designers to review gel and filter colors and to then plug their choices into the computer that will run light color changes. There are even apps that allow designers to control all of the stage lighting from their mobile devices.

Mobile technology has given sound designers similar app tools. There are smartphone and tablet apps that allow the designer to record, edit, and share audio design. Music and sound effects can also be played from these apps, which can be played through a theatre's sound system by connecting a mobile device. There are applications that allow the entire audio design for a production to be controlled from a smartphone or tablet.

---

7. Were sound effects used in the production? How did they help support your understanding of the play?
8. Were the sound effects realistic or nonrealistic?
9. Were the performers amplified? Was that a distraction, or did it seem well integrated into the production?
10. Was there original music? How did it help set the mood or help you better understand the action of the play?

SUMMARY

1. Stage lighting, like other elements of theatre, has a counterpart in the lighting of homes, restaurants, and other environments in our everyday life.
2. Lighting was historically the last visual element to be fully developed for the stage but is today the most technically sophisticated. Once the incandescent electric lamp was introduced, it was possible to achieve almost total control of the color, intensity, and timing of lights. Lighting controls have also benefited from computerization, with extensive light shifts being controlled by an operator at a computerized console.
3. Lighting design is intended to provide illumination onstage, to establish time and place, to help set the mood and style of a production, to focus the action, and to establish a rhythm of visual movement.
4. Lighting should be consistent with all other elements.
5. The lighting designer uses a variety of instruments, colored gels, special accessories, and advanced dimmer controls, as well as computerized control consoles, to achieve effects. Electronic developments and computers have greatly increased the flexibility and control of lighting instruments and equipment.

6. Sound is taking its place alongside scenery, costumes, and lighting as a key design element.
7. Rapid advances in technology allow for sophisticated delivery of both sound reproduction—sound effects and such—and sound reinforcement of both musical instruments and the human voice.
8. The sound designer and engineer must (1) prepare the sound track, (2) place microphones and speakers appropriately, and (3) mix recorded and live sounds during the performance to achieve the desired effects.

Design Elements: Audience Sitting in Theatre (theatre): Ron Chapple/Photodisc/Getty Images; Studio Light (spotlights): Exactostock/SuperStock

Part Four

The Playwright and the Play

9 Creating the World of the Play

10 Dramatic Structure and Dramatic Characters

11 Theatrical Genres

12 Alternative and Experimental Dramatic and Theatrical Forms

13 Diverse and Inclusive Plays, Playwrights, and Theatrical Forms

CREATING THE PLAY: THE PLAYWRIGHT

Historically, the subject, the tone, the structure, and the point of view of a dramatic script are the creation of the playwright. The plays of Henrik Ibsen, who was an innovator in realistic drama at the end of the nineteenth century, continues to be produced today because of his focus on truthful, universal human circumstances. Shown here is a scene from Ibsen's *Hedda Gabler,* with Roxanna Hope in the title role in the Hartford Stage Company production directed by Jennifer Tarver. (T Charles Erickson)

Part Four | The Playwright and the Play

It begins with an impulse, a story, an event, an inspiration: a composer has an idea for a song or a symphony, a choreographer conceives of a ballet, a playwright has a story for a drama or a musical, an architect conceives of a building. Following that beginning, the person who envisions the artwork sets about putting the idea into a form that will be recognizable to those with whom that person will be collaborating. What emerges is the musical score, the script, the blueprint that others can bring alive as an orchestral concert, a theatrical production, an imaginative piece of architecture. The finished script, musical score, or blueprint establishes guidelines that point everyone toward the ultimate realization of the idea.

A theatre production is a collaboration, not only between the audience and the performers but also among a whole range of people who work together to make it happen: performers, directors, designers, technicians. All these are essential, but like any enterprise, a theatre production must begin somewhere, and in most cases that starting point is the script. For more than 2,000 years, in both the West and Asia, the script of a play has been created by the dramatist or playwright, the person who chooses the story to be told, selects the characters, determines the sequence of dramatic episodes, and composes the dialogue for the characters to speak. Like theatre, other forms of art also involve collaboration. For instance, in architecture a team of engineers, designers, and contractors will work to create the finished structure. It is the vision of the architect, however, that drives the project.

In recent years, architects have used computer diagrams to render their plans, allowing the architect to create and be

Choreographer Christopher Wheeldon (right) rehearsing *Carousel (A Dance)* with dancers Kathryn Morgan and Andrew Veyette of the New York City Ballet. (Paul Kolnik)

An often-repeated story is akin to a drama, with words, characters, and a plot. Here we see a storyteller repeating a folk legend to a group of Native American children on the Barona Indian Reservation. (Bob Rowan/Corbis Documentary/Getty Images)

involved in many variations of the original idea. In the end, however, one plan is decided on—the equivalent of the blueprint, the script, the score, the scenario. During the past 100 years, theatre artists other than the playwright have sometimes assumed the work of creating a script. One is the auteur director, who not only conceives and originates the work but also directs and controls what happens onstage. Others creating scenarios—outlines for performances that are sometimes developed through improvisation—include ensemble theatre groups and performance artists.

It is important to understand, however, that these alternative approaches have not eliminated the playwright; rather, these other artists have taken the place of the playwright and become "theatre authors." The creation of a blueprint, a scenario, or script remains an essential element of creating a theatrical event.

Anyone who creates a theatre piece faces the same challenge: how to turn nontheatrical material into a viable work for the stage. At what point in the story does the dramatic action begin? Who are the characters; what actions are they given; what words do they speak? How are interest and excitement developed and maintained? How is suspense created and increased? Will the work be serious or comic, funny or sad? In the process of answering these questions, a script emerges—a script that is both the embodiment of a vision and a blueprint for a production. Through the centuries, certain principles and strategies have emerged in creating a dramatic work. In Part Four, we look at some of these principles and strategies, as well as the point of view that is adopted by a dramatist that might make the work tragic, comic, or some other dramatic type.

An architect conceives and designs a building in the way that a composer or dramatist creates a composition or a drama. The acclaimed architect Frank Gehry is shown here with his models for the new business school at the University of Technology in Sydney, Australia. (Renee Nowytarger/Newspix/Getty Images)

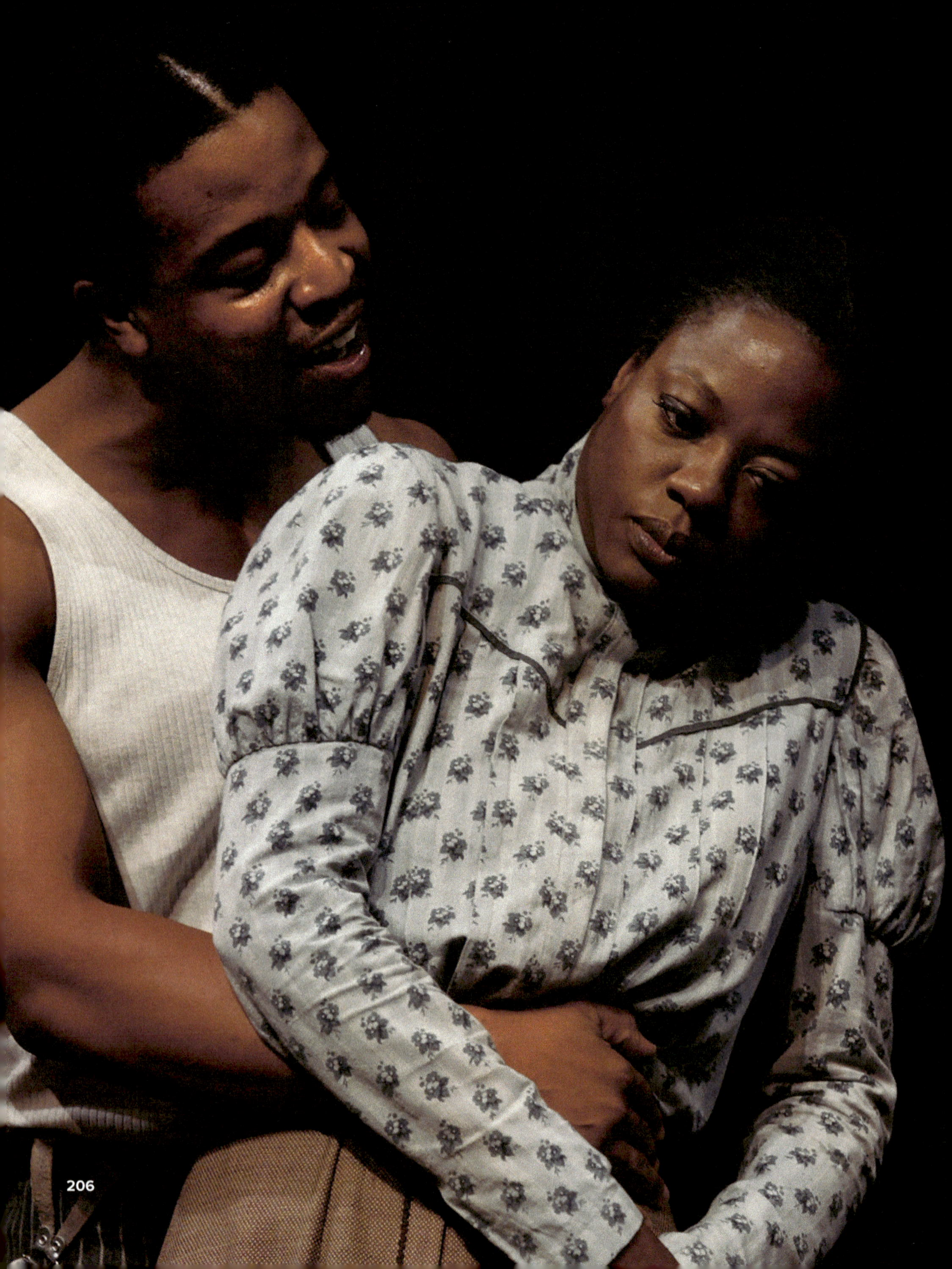

Creating the World of the Play

Beginning in ancient times, in virtually every culture, there have been storytellers: a person who recounted tales to people gathered together, describing heroic figures, daring deeds, frightening encounters, and humorous episodes. These chroniclers told stories of adventure, ghost stories, tall tales, horror stories, legends and histories, and fantastic fables.

In the theatre many people work together to present a story—actors and directors, designers and technicians—but it all begins with the theatre's storyteller: the playwright. Consciously or unconsciously the playwright makes a number of decisions that will determine exactly what kind of event audiences will see onstage. Among those decisions are what story will be told, the time and place of the story, the characters who will take part, the tone and emphasis of the story (will it be serious and tragic, or comic and humorous?), the way the story is told (the structure of the drama), and how it unfolds and ends. In the next chapter we will focus on decisions concerning the structure of the play and the characters who are featured. In the chapter after that we will turn to the question of whether the play is funny or sad, comic or tragic.

Before those decisions, however, there are other choices the playwright makes. For example, the playwright or dramatist determines what subject matter to present and which characters to include. Will the work be based on history—for example, an episode or incident from the American Civil War, from World War II, from the Vietnam War, the Civil Rights movement, or from the war in Iraq or Afghanistan? Perhaps the play will be based on biography—on the life of Eleanor Roosevelt or Martin Luther King Jr or Cesar Chavez. Perhaps it will be an exploration of the creator's own life—facing the problems of growing up or facing a personal crisis as an adult. Still another possibility would be an imaginary story, either resembling everyday life or based on a fantasy or a nightmare.

◀ **THE PLAYWRIGHT CREATES THE TEMPLATE**

In undertaking to write a script, the playwright makes a number of decisions. The intention may be to entertain; to raise timeless questions, as is often the case in tragedy; or to make a political or social comment. In any case, the person or persons who create a theatre script set the tone, the agenda, and the approach to be followed by director, actors, designers, and others. Seen here are Viola Davis. who plays Esther, resisting the advances of George, played by Russell Hornsby in Lynn Nottage's Intimate Apparel *at Los Angeles's Mark Taper Forum. The play, set in 1905, is about a Black woman Esther who makes intimate apparel for a rich woman and a call girl. She saves her money hoping to fall in love. (Anne Cusack/Contributor/Getty Images)*

Along with the subject to be dramatized, there is also the question of whom and what to focus on. For example, a playwright can emphasize a particular character trait in one play and its opposite in another. This is what Henrik Ibsen often did. In his *Brand,* the leading character is a stark, uncompromising figure who will sacrifice everything—family, friends, love—for his principles. In contrast, the leading character in Ibsen's *Peer Gynt* is just the opposite: always compromising, always running away. In creating a theatre piece there is great leeway in making a number of such decisions.

The playwright must also determine the order of events in a play. A good example is the way the myth of Electra was treated by three prominent tragic dramatists in Greece in the fifth century BCE. The story concerns Electra's revenge on her mother, Clytemnestra, and her stepfather, Aegisthus, for having murdered her natural father, Agamemnon. In carrying out her revenge, Electra enlists the help of Orestes, her brother, who has just returned from exile. In the versions by Aeschylus and Euripides, the stepfather is murdered first, and the mother, Clytemnestra, is murdered last. This puts emphasis on the terror of murdering one's own mother.

Sophocles, however, saw the story differently. He wanted to emphasize the idea that Electra and her brother were acting honorably and to play down the mother's murder. And so he reversed the order of the murders: he had the mother killed first; then he built up to the righteous murder of the stepfather as the final deed. The change made by Sophocles indicates the latitude writers, directors, and performance artists have in altering events to suit their artistic purposes.

There is also the question of why use the subject matter? What does the dramatist want the story to tell us? Contemporary playwrights, for example, have taken Greek tales and reworked them to deal with current sociopolitical issues. For example, Luis Alfaro (b. 1963), a Chicano playwright, has adapted Sophocles' *Electra* into *Electricidad: A Chicano Take on the Tragedy of 'Electra',* in which the protagonist, living in Los Angeles, wants to avenge her father by plotting to kill her mother, who had him murdered. There is also a chorus of three women who speak a combination of Spanish and English. The playwright's Greek adaptations, also including versions of *Oedipus Rex* and *Medea,* speak to issues confronting Mexican immigrants in the United States.

FOCUS AND EMPHASIS

A playwright can choose to emphasize a particular character trait in one play and its opposite in another. Henrik Ibsen, in his *Brand*, presents the leading character as a stark, uncompromising figure who will sacrifice everything—family, friends, love—for his principles. The leading character in Ibsen's *Peer Gynt*, however, is always compromising, always running away. Here we see actor Barret O'Brien in the role of Peer Gynt in a production at the Yale School of Drama directed by Mike Donahue. (T Charles Erickson)

CONFLICT: THE CRUCIBLE OF DRAMA
Theatre requires conflict. This conflict might be between people; among family members; between opposing nations, differing ideologies, or distinct political agendas. Here, in a scene from Lynn Nottage's play *Sweat* at the Public Theatre in New York City, we see steelworkers in Reading, Pennsylvania, whose jobs are being threatened by changes in the global economy, turning on one another out of desperation. The actors from left are: Michelle Wilson, James Colby and Johanna Day. (Sara Krulwich/The New York Times/Redux)

Still another choice open to a dramatist is what degree of seriousness to convey, or what point of view to take toward the subject of the drama: will it be comic or tragic, sympathetic or satiric, cynical or celebratory?

THE SUBJECT AND VERB OF DRAMA: PEOPLE AND ACTION

Before turning to the specifics of creating a dramatic work, we should note an important point about the nature of drama. The subject of theatre is always people—their hopes, their joys, their foibles, their fears. In other words, if we were to construct a "grammar of theatre," the *subject* would be people: that is, dramatic characters. In grammar, every subject needs a verb; so, in the grammar of theatre, dramatic characters need some form of action that defines them.

The terms *to act* and *to perform* are used in theatre to denote the impersonation of a character by an actor or an actress, but these words also mean "to do something," or "to be active." The word *drama* derives from a Greek root, the verb *dran*, meaning "to do" or "to act." At its heart, theatre involves action. One way to provide action is to create a test or challenge for the characters. The American dramatist Arthur Miller named one of his plays *The Crucible.* Literally, a *crucible* is a vessel in which metal is tested by being exposed to extreme heat. Figuratively, a crucible has come to stand for any severe test of human worth and endurance—a trial by fire. In a sense, every play provides a crucible: a test devised by the playwright to show how the characters behave under conditions of stress. Through this test, the meaning of the play is brought out.

STRUCTURAL CONVENTIONS: THE RULES OF THE GAME

Despite the options open to a dramatist with regard to the focus of the drama and the characters involved, there is one thing every dramatist is compelled to do if the work is to succeed as a theatre piece, and that is to transform the raw material of the drama into a viable work for the stage. In order to make certain that the events onstage will be dynamic and that the characters will face a meaningful test, conventions or "ground rules" have evolved for dramatic structure. A good analogy would be the rules in games such as card games, board games, video games, and sports. In each case, rules are developed to ensure a lively contest.

Consider, for example, how theatre can be compared to sports. Theatre is more varied and complex than most sports events, and theatrical rules are not so clearly defined or so consciously imposed as rules in sports. Nevertheless, there are similarities that highlight the ways a play makes its impact.

Limited Space

Most sports have a limited playing area. In some cases this consists of a confined space: a boxing ring, a basketball court, a baseball field. The playing area is clearly defined, and invariably there is some kind of "out of bounds."

Theatre, of course, is usually limited to a stage; but there is also a limit within the play itself. The action of a play is generally confined to a "world" of its own—that is, to a fictional universe that contains all the characters and events of the play—and none of the characters or actions moves outside the orbit of that world. Sometimes the world of a play is restricted to a single room.

In his play *No Exit,* Jean-Paul Sartre (1905–1980), a French existentialist, confines three characters to one room from which, as the title suggests, there is no escape. The room is supposed to be hell, and the three characters—a man, Garcin, and two women, Estelle and Inez—are confined there forever. Estelle loves Garcin, Garcin loves Inez, and Inez (a lesbian) loves Estelle. Each one, in short, loves the one who will not reciprocate, and by being confined to a room, they undergo permanent torture. There are numerous modern plays in which the action takes place in a single room, a good example being *'Night, Mother* by Marsha Norman (b. 1947), about a mother and daughter in crisis, which takes place in their rural home.

Limited Time

Sports events put some limit on the duration of action. In football and basketball, there is a definite time limit. In golf, there is a given number of holes; in tennis, there is a limited number of sets. Theoretically, some sports, such as baseball, are open-ended and could go on forever; but spectators tend to become impatient with this arrangement. Tennis, for instance, was originally open-ended but now

LIMITED SPACE
In his play *No Exit*, Jean-Paul Sartre presents three characters involved in an impossible love triangle confined to one room, from which, as the title suggests, there is no escape. Karen MacDonald as Estelle, Will Lebow as Garcin, and Paula Plum as Inez are shown in this scene, directed by Jerry Mouawad at the A.R.T. in Boston. (T Charles Erickson)

Part Four   The Playwright and the Play

has a "sudden death" or tiebreaker play-off when a set reaches six-all. A time limit or score limit ensures that the spectators can see a complete event, with a clear winner and loser and no loose ends. The time limit in theatre can be looked at in two ways: first, as the length of time it takes a performance to be completed; second, as the time limit placed on the characters within the framework of the play itself.

Most theatrical performances last from one to three hours. In the drama festivals of ancient Greece, plays were presented for several days in a row. On a single day there might be a trilogy of three connecting plays followed by a short comic play. Still, even if we count a Greek trilogy as one play, it lasted only the better part of a day. In the theatre today, there are also plays that last the better part of a day, such as Matthew Lopez's *The Inheritance* (2018), which deals with gay men in contemporary New York and consists of two parts, each over three hours. However, such plays are the exception not the norm.

More important than the actual playing time of a performance is the time limit or deadline *within* the play. This means the time that is supposed to elapse during the events of the play, the time covered by those events—a few hours, a few days, or longer. Frequently, we find in a play a fixed period within which the characters must complete an action. For instance, at the end of the second act of Ibsen's *A Doll's House,* the heroine, Nora, is trying desperately to persuade her husband to put off until the following evening the opening of a letter that she fears will establish her as a forger and will threaten their marriage. When he agrees, Nora says to herself, "Thirty-one hours to live." The playing time within *'Night Mother*, mentioned earlier, matches the exact amount of time the audience is in the theatre.

Strongly Opposed Forces

Most sports, like many other types of games, involve two opposed teams or individuals. This ensures clear lines of force: the old guard versus the young upstarts, the home team versus the visitors. The musical *West Side Story* (based on Shakespeare's *Romeo and Juliet*) features two opposed gangs, not unlike opposing teams in sports. In the simplest dramatic situations, one character directly opposes another. The man and woman, Julie and Jean, in Strindberg's *Miss Julie* are a perfect example of characters bound to clash. Julie, an aristocrat, is the daughter of the owner of an estate. She has had an unhappy engagement and is deeply suspicious of men, but at the same time sexually attracted to them. Jean is a servant, an aggressive man who dreams of escaping his life of servitude and owning a hotel. These two characters experience strong forces of repulsion and attraction and are drawn together on a midsummer eve in a climactic encounter.

One device frequently used by dramatists to create friction or tension between forces is restricting the characters to the members of one family. Relatives have built-in rivalries and affinities: parents versus children, sisters versus brothers. Being members of the same family, they have no avenue of escape. Mythology, on which so much drama is based, abounds in familial relationships.

Shakespeare frequently set members of one family against one another: Hamlet opposes his mother; Lear opposes his daughters; Othello kills his wife, Desdemona. In modern drama, virtually every writer of note has dealt with close family situations: Ibsen, Chekhov, Williams, Miller, Edward Albee (b. 1928), and August Wilson, to

STRONGLY OPPOSED FORCES

Traditional plot structure calls for strongly opposing forces: the antagonist opposes the protagonist; one group opposes another. Here we see two characters in conflict in Arthur Miller's play *The Price* in a 2019 Theatre Royal Bath production directed by Jonathan Church. David Suchet (on the left) portrays Gregory Solomon and Brendon Coyle performs the role of Victor Franz. (Geraint Lewis/ Alamy Stock Photo)

mention a few. The American dramatist Eugene O'Neill wrote what many consider his finest play, *Long Day's Journey into Night,* about the four members of his own family.

A Balance of Forces

In most sports, there are rules designed to ensure that the contest will be as equal as possible without coming to a draw. We all want our team to win, but we would rather see a close, exciting contest than a runaway. And so rules are set up, with handicaps or other devices to equalize the forces. In basketball or football, for instance, as soon as one team scores, the other team gets the ball so that it will have an opportunity to even the score. In theatre, a hard-fought and relatively equal contest is implicit in what has been said about opposing forces.

Even in the somewhat muted, low-key plays of Anton Chekhov, there is a balance of forces among various groups. In *The Cherry Orchard,* the owners of the orchard are set against the man who will acquire it; in *The Three Sisters,* the sisters are opposed in the possession of their home by their acquisitive sister-in-law.

In August Wilson's *Ma Rainey's Black Bottom* (1982), the Black jazz singer protagonist attempts to exert a balance of power against her white recording producers, even in the midst of the highly racist and segregated 1920s.

Incentive and Motivation

In sports, as in other kinds of games, a prize is offered to guarantee that the participants will give their best in an intense contest. In professional sports it is money; in amateur sports, a trophy, such as a cup. In addition, there is the glory of winning, as well as the accolades of television and the press and the plaudits of family and friends. In the same way, good drama never lacks incentive or motivation for its characters: Macbeth wants desperately to be king in *Macbeth,* and Blanche DuBois must find protection and preserve her dignity in *A Streetcar Named Desire.* Troy Maxson, in *Fences,* wants to be the driver of his garbage truck, a position denied to a Black man in Pittsburgh in the 1950s.

CREATING STRUCTURE

Applying the principles and conventions outlined earlier, the dramatist sets about developing a dramatic structure for the theatre piece. Every work of art has some kind of structure, or framework. It may be loosely connected or tightly knit; the important thing is that the framework exists. In theatre, structure usually takes the form of a *plot,* which is the arrangement of events or the selection and order of scenes in a play. Plot, in turn, is generally based on a *story.*

plot As distinct from story, patterned arrangements of events and characters in a drama, with incidents selected and arranged for maximum dramatic impact.

Plot versus Story

Stories—narrative accounts of what people do—are as old as the human race, and they form the substance of daily conversation, of newspapers and television, of novels and films. But every medium presents a story in a different form. In theatre, the story must be presented in a limited period of time by living actors and actresses on a stage, and this requires selectivity.

It is important for us to recognize that the plot of a play differs from a story. A story is a full account of an event, or series of events, usually told in chronological order. Plot is a selection and arrangement of scenes taken from a story for presentation onstage. It is what actually happens onstage, not what is talked about. The story of Abraham Lincoln, for example, begins with his birth in a log cabin and continues to the day he was shot at Ford's Theater in Washington. To create a play about Lincoln, a playwright would have to make choices. Would the dramatist include scenes in Springfield, Illinois, where Lincoln worked as a lawyer and held his famous debates with Stephen Douglas? Or would everything take place in Washington after Lincoln became president? Would there be scenes with Lincoln's wife, Mary Todd, or would the other characters be only government and military officials? The plot of a play about Abraham Lincoln and Mary Todd would have scenes and characters related primarily to their lives. The plot of a play about the Lincoln-Douglas debates would consist mostly of scenes relating to the debates.

Even when a play is based on a fictional story invented by the playwright, the plot must be more restricted and structured than the story itself: characters and scenes must still be selected and the sequence determined.

The Opening Scene

The first scene of a drama starts the action and sets the tone and style for everything that follows. It tells us whether we are going to see a serious or a comic play and whether the play will deal with fantasy or with affairs of everyday life. The opening scene is a clue or signal about what lies ahead. It also sets the wheels of action in motion, giving the characters a shove and hurtling them toward their destination.

The playwright poses an initial problem for the characters, establishing an imbalance of forces or a disturbance in their equilibrium that compels them to respond. Generally, this imbalance has occurred just before the play begins, or it develops immediately after the play opens. In *Antigone,* for example, two brothers have killed each other just before the opening of the play. In *Hamlet,* "something is rotten in the state of Denmark," and early in the play the ghost of Hamlet's father tells Hamlet to seek revenge. At the beginning of *Romeo and Juliet,* the Capulets and the Montagues are at one another's throats in a street fight.

IN FOCUS: GLOBAL CONNECTIONS

The Asian Influence on the Playwrights Brecht and Wilder

During the past 100 years, many European and U.S. playwrights have been influenced by the structures, styles, and subject matter of traditional theatres of other continents. Two mid-twentieth-century dramatists from the West who were strongly influenced by Asian theatre were the German playwright Bertolt Brecht (1889–1956) and the American playwright Thornton Wilder (1897–1975). Brecht, for example, drew from Asian legends, and used techniques and styles borrowed from Chinese, Japanese, and Indian theatre. Chinese theatre and literature were to prove particularly important for his *Good Woman of Setzuan* (1938–1949), which was set in China; and *The Caucasian Chalk Circle* (1944–1945), based on a Chinese play, *The Story of the Chalk Circle*.

Bertolt Brecht. (Hulton Deutsch/Corbis/Getty Images)

Thornton Wilder. (Bettmann/Getty Images)

Both Brecht and Wilder had seen Beijing opera and adopted certain features of this dramatic style into their own work. Beijing opera (also called *jingju* and Peking opera) blends song, dance, martial arts, theatre, acrobatics, and dance and uses much symbolism. Beijing opera takes place on an almost bare stage (often with just a table and a few chairs onstage throughout) and uses simple props brought on by stage attendants, and symbolic movements by the actors. For example, an actor walking in a circle around the stage indicates a long journey; a banner with a fish design indicates water, although rolled up on a tray, the same banner would represent a fish. Brecht used such symbolic props and actions to achieve his alienation or distancing effect, which prevented the audience from identifying emotionally with the drama. In 1935, Brecht saw a performance by the Beijing opera star Mei Lanfang (1894–1961) in Moscow, and the following year he wrote his essay "Alienation Effects in Chinese Acting," which noted aspects of Beijing opera conducive to the distancing effect he desired.

Similarly, Wilder had been exposed to Chinese theatre first at an early age, when his father's work took him to Hong Kong and Shanghai; and then as an adult, when he saw Mei Lanfang perform in New York in 1930. Aspects of Beijing opera that Wilder adopted can best be seen in his Pulitzer Prize–winning *Our Town* (1938). In this play, Wilder uses an almost bare stage with just two tables and six chairs positioned by the stage manager (who also acts as a narrator), and other locales are suggested by very simple alterations; in the third act, for example, the cemetery is suggested by just ten or twelve people sitting in chairs. Both playwrights illustrate the increasing prevalence of Asian influences in twentieth-century playwriting.

Prepared by Naomi Stubbs, Associate Professor, LaGuardia Community College, CUNY.

THE OPENING SCENE
The first scene of a play is crucial, usually setting the location; establishing mood and tone; and introducing characters, themes, and action. A famous opening scene is that in Shakespeare's *Romeo and Juliet,* in which the Capulet and Montague families confront each other in a street fight. Shown here is the opening scene in a production directed by Dominic Dromgoogle at Shakespeare's Globe, with Ukweli Roach as Tybalt and Philip Cumbus as Mercutio in the foreground. (Geraint Lewis/Alamy Stock Photo)

Obstacles and Complications

Having met the initial challenge of the play, the characters then move through a series of steps—alternating between achievement and defeat, between hope and despair. The moment they seem to accomplish one goal, certain factors or events cut across the play to upset the balance and start the characters on another path. In theatre these may be *obstacles,* which are impediments put in a character's way; or they may be *complications*—outside forces or new twists in the plot introduced at an opportune moment.

Shakespeare's *Hamlet* provides numerous examples of obstacles and complications. Hamlet stages a "play within the play" in order to confirm that his uncle Claudius has killed his father. Claudius reacts to the play in a manner that makes his guilt obvious. But when Hamlet first tries to kill Claudius, he discovers him at prayer. An obstacle has been thrown into Hamlet's path: If Claudius dies while praying, he may go to heaven rather than to hell. Since Hamlet does not want Claudius to go to heaven, he does not kill him.

Later, Hamlet is in his mother's bedroom when he hears a noise behind a curtain. Surely Claudius is lurking there, but when Hamlet thrusts his sword through the curtain, he finds that he has killed Polonius, the father of Ophelia, the young lady he is close to. This provides Claudius with an excuse to send Hamlet to England with Rosencrantz and Guildenstern, who carry with them a letter instructing the king of England to murder Hamlet. Hamlet escapes that trap and returns to Denmark. Now, at last, it seems that he can carry out his revenge. But, on his return, he discovers that Ophelia has killed herself while he was away, and her brother, Laertes, is seeking revenge on him. This complicates the situation once again, as Hamlet is prevented from meeting Claudius head-on because he must also deal with Laertes. In the end Hamlet does carry out his mission, but only after many interruptions.

obstacle That which delays or prevents the achieving of a goal by a character. An obstacle creates complication and conflict.

complication Introduction, in a play, of a new force, which creates a new balance of power and entails a delay in reaching the climax.

Crisis and Climax

As a result of conflicts, obstacles, and complications in a play, the characters become involved in a series of *crises.* A play usually builds from one crisis to

crisis A point in a play when events and opposing forces are at a crucial moment, and when the course of further action will be determined. There may be a series of crises leading to the definitive climax.

Chapter 9 *Creating the World of the Play* 215

another. The first crisis will be resolved only to have the action lead to a subsequent crisis. The final and most significant crisis is referred to as the *climax.* In the climax the issues of the play are resolved, either happily or, in the case of tragedies, unhappily, often with the death of the protagonist.

It should be noted that a series of crises leading to a climax in a drama applies most readily to traditional plays—that is, works created before the modern period. During the past 100 years, a number of variations of classic plot structure have appeared in which the notion of a climax has been either eliminated or minimized. These approaches to structure will be looked at in detail in the chapter "Dramatic Structure and Dramatic Characters."

POINT OF VIEW

In addition to structure and character portrayal, the person or persons creating a dramatic work must determine the point of view represented in the work: will it be tragic or comic, humorous or sad, or perhaps a mixture of the two? People and events can always be interpreted in widely different ways. How we perceive them depends on our point of view. There is a familiar story of two people looking at a bottle that is partly full of wine. The optimist will say that the bottle is half-full, the pessimist that it is half-empty.

Anyone familiar with the presentation of evidence in a courtroom—in a trial involving an automobile accident, for instance—knows that different witnesses, each of whom may be honest and straightforward, will describe the same incident differently. One will say that she saw a minivan go through a stoplight and hit a blue car; another will say that he remembers clearly that the blue car pulled out before the light had changed and blocked the path of the van. The same variation in viewpoint affects our assessment of politicians and other public figures. To some people, a certain politician will be a dedicated, sincere public servant, interested only in what is best for the nation. But to others, the same politician will be a hypocrite and a charlatan.

Point of view is particularly important in the arts. Under ordinary circumstances, those who attempt to influence our point of view, such as advertisers and politicians, frequently disguise their motives. They use subtle, indirect techniques to convince us that they are not trying to impose their views on us, though people who understand the process know that this is exactly what an advertiser or a politician is trying to do. In the arts, on the other hand, the imposition of a point of

PLOT COMPLICATIONS IN *HAMLET*
In conventional plot structure, the action is prolonged and tension is increased by a series of problems confronting the characters. The twists and turns in the plot of Shakespeare's *Hamlet* are an example. Shown here is Michael Benz as Hamlet, preparing to kill King Claudius (Dickon Tyrrell), who he thinks has murdered his father. But Hamlet hesitates because he does not want to send Claudius to heaven, as he fears might happen if he kills Claudius at prayer. This scene is from a production at The Broad Stage in Santa Monica, California. (Noel Vasquez/WireImage/Getty Images)

climax The highpoint in the development of a dramatic plot.

view is direct and deliberate. The artist makes it clear that he or she is looking at the world from a highly personal and perhaps unusual angle, possibly even turning the world upside down.

In films, for example, we have become familiar with the various points of view, angles of vision, and perspectives that the camera selects for us. In a close-up, we do not see an entire room or even an entire person—we see one small detail: hands on a computer keyboard or a finger on the trigger of a gun. In a medium shot we see more—a couple embracing, perhaps—but still only part of the scene. In an exterior scene we might have a panorama of the Grand Canyon or a military parade. The camera also predetermines the angle from which we see the action. In a scene emphasizing the strength of a figure, the camera might look up from below to show a person looming from the top of a flight of stairs. In another scene we might look down on the action. In still other instances the camera might be tilted so that a scene looks off balance; a scene might be shot out of focus so that it is hazy or blurred, or it might be filmed through a special filter.

Similarly, the viewpoint of the theatre artist tells us how to interpret the words and actions of the characters we see onstage; it provides a key to understanding the entire experience.

The Dramatist's Point of View

"There is nothing either good or bad, but thinking makes it so," Shakespeare wrote in *Hamlet*. To this could be added a parallel statement: "There is nothing either funny or sad, but thinking makes it so." One's point of view determines whether one takes a subject seriously or laughs at it, whether it is an object of pity or of ridicule. Horace Walpole (1717-1797), an English author, wrote: "This world is a comedy to those that think, a tragedy to those that feel." Walpole's epigram underlines the fact that people see the world differently.

It is difficult to say just why some people look at the world and weep while others look at it and laugh, but there is no question that they do. In theatre, point of view begins when a dramatist, a director, or a performance artist takes a strong personal view of a subject, deciding that it is grave, heroic, or humorous. As in other art forms, opportunities for selectivity are greater than in everyday life; hence a point of view can be adopted in drama consciously and deliberately. In the case of a play, point of view is incorporated by the playwright into the script itself, with characters being given words to speak and actions to perform that convey a certain attitude. In a serious work the writer will choose language and actions suggesting sobriety and sincerity. Take the lines spoken by Shakespeare's Othello:

> Oh, now for ever
> Farewell the tranquil mind! Farewell content!
> Farewell the plumed troop and the big wars
> that make ambition virtue!

These words express unmistakably Othello's profound sense of loss.

Another writer might take what is ordinarily a serious subject and treat it humorously. A good example is Arthur Kopit (b. 1937), who gave a comic twist to a dead body in his play *Oh, Dad. Poor Dad. Mama's Hung You in the Closet, and I'm Feelin' So*

THE INDIVIDUAL POINT OF VIEW
In addition to the social and cultural climate, the individual artist's outlook also determines whether a work will be serious or comic. Even two people writing in the same country at the same time will view the world differently. In seventeenth-century France, Racine wrote mostly tragedies, such as *Phèdre*. Shown at left is a London production at the National Theatre featuring Helen Mirren in the title role with Dominic Cooper as Hippolytus, directed by Nicholas Hytner. However, in the same period Racine's contemporary, Molière, wrote comedies like *The Bourgeois Gentleman*, with French actor Pascal Reneric (left) as Monsieur Jourdain and French actor Francis Leplay as Maitre de Philosophie, shown here in a 2015 production at the Château de Chambord in France. (left: Geraint Lewis/Alamy Stock Photo; right: Guillaume Souvant/AFP/Getty Images)

Sad. The title itself, with its mocking tone and its unusual length, makes it clear from the beginning that Kopit wants us to laugh at his subject.

Jeremy O' Harris's *Slave Play* deals with interracial relationships and white society's unwillingness to hear Black voices by using broad stereotypes of enslavement to make the audience uncomfortable, not knowing how to react. His sardonic tone clearly wants to create discomfort in his audience members.

Once the playwright's intentions are known, the director and the performers transmit them to the audience.

> # PLAYING YOUR PART: EXPERIENCING THEATRE
>
> 1. If you were to write a play about your life, what would you choose as your opening scene? What would some of your complications be? Would there be a climactic moment?
> 2. If you were to write a play about a family you know (your own or another), what point of view would you take? Why? Are there strongly opposed forces or balanced forces in this family?
> 3. If you were told you were going to have to attend a play that lasted over four hours, what would your reaction be? Why? What are your traditional expectations about the space and time of a play?
> 4. After watching a popular film, describe how the opening scene aids in setting the action. Describe one or two of the complications in the film. Can you discuss the film's point of view?

Society's Point of View

In discussing point of view, we cannot overlook the role that society plays in the viewpoint adopted by an artist such as a playwright. As discussed in the chapter "Background and Expectations of the Audience," there is a close relationship between theatre and society. This relationship manifests itself particularly in the point of view artists adopt toward their subject matter.

Tragedy, for example, generally occurs in periods when society as a whole assumes a certain attitude toward people and toward the universe. Two periods conducive to the creation of tragedy were the golden age of Greece in the fifth century BCE and the Renaissance in Europe during the fourteenth, fifteenth, and sixteenth

A CLIMATE FOR TRAGEDY
The worldview of a society is one factor that determines whether it will embrace and encourage tragedy. Some cultures, such as Athens in the fifth century BCE and Elizabethan England, were particularly conducive to the creation of tragic drama. Shakespeare's *King Lear* is a good example. Shown here are John Lithgow (left) and Clarke Peters (right) in a production of the Elizabethan tragedy, directed by Daniel Sullivan at the Delacorte Theater in New York in 2014. (Sara Krulwich/The New York Times/Redux)

centuries CE. Both periods incorporated two ideas essential to tragic drama: on the one hand, a concept of human beings as capable of extraordinary accomplishments; and on the other, the notion that the world is potentially cruel and unjust. A closer look at these two periods will demonstrate how they reflect these two viewpoints.

In both the fifth century BCE in Greece and the Renaissance in continental Europe and England, human beings were exalted above everything else. The gods and nature were given a much less prominent place in the scheme of things. The men and women of those periods considered the horizons of human achievement unlimited. In the fifth century BCE, Greece was enjoying its golden age in commerce, politics, science, and art; nothing seemed impossible in the way of architecture, mathematics, trade, or philosophy. The same was true in Europe and England during the centuries of the Renaissance. Columbus had reached the new world in 1492, and the possibilities for trade and exploration appeared infinite. Science and the arts were on the threshold of a new day as well.

In sculpture during the two periods, the human figure was glorified as it rarely had been before or has been since, and the celebration of the individual was apparent in all the arts as well, including drama. The Greek dramatist Sophocles exclaimed:

> Numberless are the world's wonders, but none
> More wonderful than man.

And in the Renaissance, Shakespeare has Hamlet say:

> What a piece of work is man! How noble in reason! How infinite in faculty! In form, in moving, how express and admirable! In action how like an angel! In apprehension how like a god!

The credo of both ages was expressed by Protagoras, a Greek philosopher of the fifth century BCE:

> Man is the measure of all things.

But there is another side to the tragic coin. Along with this optimistic, humanistic view, there was a faculty for admitting, unflinchingly, that life can be—and frequently is—cruel, unjust, and even meaningless and that these societies also oppress and marginalize people because of race, gender, religion, and socioeconomic position.

Shakespeare put it this way in *King Lear:*

> As flies to wanton boys, are we to the gods;
> They kill us for their sport.

In *Macbeth,* he expressed it in these words:

> Out, out brief candle!
> Life's but a walking shadow, a poor player
> That struts and frets his hour upon the stage
> And then is heard no more; it is a tale
> Told by an idiot, full of sound and fury,
> Signifying nothing.

These periods of history—the Greek golden age and the Renaissance—were expansive enough to encompass both strains: the greatness of human beings on the one hand, and the cruelty of life and society on the other.

> ## PLAYING YOUR PART: THINKING ABOUT THEATRE
>
> 1. Think of a play you have read or seen where the main character encounters one impediment or roadblock after another. Describe the various obstacles that must be overcome before the end of the play.
> 2. Think of a play or musical you have seen or read where two major characters are in conflict with one another. Describe the two characters and explain the source of their conflict. How does it play out?
> 3. Think of a situation some people saw as very serious, but another person viewed as humorous. Explain what you believe led different people to see it so differently. What was your own feeling—was the incident funny or sad?

To clarify the distinction between the tragic point of view and other points of view, we need only examine periods in history when one or both of the attitudes forming the tragic viewpoint were absent or were expressed quite differently. In continental Europe and Great Britain, the eighteenth century was known as the *age of enlightenment,* and the nineteenth century as the *century of progress.* Enlightenment and progress: together they express the philosophy that people can analyze any problem—poverty, violence, disease, injustice—and, by applying their intelligence, solve it. An age of unbounded optimism in which no problem is thought insurmountable, and a sense of moral justice runs strong, is not one in which tragic drama can easily emerge and also does not truly reflect that society.

We should also always recognize that the optimistic viewpoints during the Enlightenment and age of progress reflected only the lives of those who were privileged at the time. During those eras, Africans were enslaved and parts of the world colonized. For the most part, the privileged optimism of those eras did not reflect honestly or tragically on those peoples or their concerns.

Before we examine tragedy, comedy, and other dramatic forms in detail, we will look first at dramatic structure and dramatic characters—the way a playwright moves the action from scene to scene to develop a plot and creates individual stage characters.

SUMMARY

1. Drama is written and produced for different purposes: to move us, to involve us, to amuse us, to entertain us, to inform us, to shock us, to raise our awareness, to inspire us. The dramatist must determine which of these purposes the work being created will serve.
2. The action of a play frequently consists of a test, or crucible, for the characters, in which their true nature is defined. This test involves some form of conflict.
3. Dramatic conventions, ensuring a strong plot and continuation of tension, are analogous to rules in sports. In both sports and theatre there are limited spaces or playing areas, time limits imposed on the action, strongly opposing forces, evenly matched contestants, and prizes or goals for the participants.
4. A play generally begins with an imbalance of forces or a loss of equilibrium by one of the characters; this propels the characters to action.

Chapter 9 *Creating the World of the Play*

5. As a play progresses, the characters encounter a series of obstacles and complications in attempting to fulfill their objectives or realize their goals. These encounters produce the tension and conflict of drama.
6. Generally, every work of art, including theatre, has some kind of structure. In theatre, structure usually takes the form of a plot.
7. A dramatic plot is not the same as a story. A story is a complete account of an episode or a sequence of events, but a plot is what we see onstage. In a plot the events have been selected from a story and arranged in a certain sequence.
8. Point of view is the way we look at things: the perspective, or angle of vision, from which we view people, places, and events.
9. In the arts, the establishment of a point of view is direct and deliberate; it is an integral part of a performance or work of art, giving the audience a clue about how to interpret and understand what is being seen and heard.
10. Whether a theatre piece is serious, comic, or some combination of the two depends on the point of view of the artists who create it.
11. The viewpoint of society also affects the outlook of individual artists in terms of whether they create tragedy, comedy, or other genres.

Design Elements: Audience Sitting in Theatre (theatre): Ron Chapple/Photodisc/Getty Images; Studio Light (spotlights): Exactostock/SuperStock

224

10

Dramatic Structure and Dramatic Characters

DRAMATIC STRUCTURE

Throughout theatre history, we find basic dramatic forms reappearing. In Western civilization, a form adopted in Greece in the fifth century BCE emerges, somewhat altered, in France in the seventeenth century. The same form shows up once more in Norway in the late nineteenth century, and is repeated throughout the twentieth century and into the twenty-first century. This form can be referred to as *climactic*. Another, contrasting form, best illustrated by the plays of Shakespeare, can be called *episodic*. Through most of the history of Western theatre, one or the other of these two forms—or some combination of the two—has predominated.

In addition, there are other forms. An approach in which dramatic episodes are strung together without any apparent connection has emerged in a new guise in recent times. Structure based on a ritual or pattern is both old and new. And musical theatre has a structure of its own. The characteristics of the basic types will be clearer when we look at each separately, beginning with climactic form. We then turn to the episodic structure, and then take up additional forms.

Characteristics of Climactic Structure

Climactic structure which, as we noted above began with the Greek classic theatre, follows specific guidelines and tenets that have always defined this dramatic structure. In the section below, we enumerate and explain the characteristics of climactic structure that have been employed by playwrights during successive periods of theatre history.

◀ **EPISODIC DRAMATIC STRUCTURE**

In different periods and different countries, various approaches to dramatic structure have been followed. Climactic structure was created by the Greeks and adopted by many cultures in the years after that. Another structure is episodic, found in the plays of Shakespeare and his contemporaries as well as modern playwrights such as Bertolt Brecht. Here we see a scene from Shakespeare's The Tempest *with Antony Sher (right) as Prospero and Atandwa Kani (left) as Ariel in the joint Baxter Theatre and Royal Shakespeare Company production, directed by Janice Honeyman at the Courtyard Theatre, Stratford-upon-Avon, in 2009. (Robbie Jack/Corbis/Getty Images)*

CLIMACTIC STRUCTURE
In climactic structure time, place, action, and characters are restricted: The action occurs in a brief time, in limited locations, and with very few characters involved. Climactic structure, first developed in Western theatre by the Greek dramatists of the fifth century BCE. in Athens, was also used by the realists in the late 1800s and early 1900s. This is a scene from Henrik Ibsen's *A Doll's House,* in a version by Tanika Gupta, with Anjana Vasan as Niru and Elliot Cowan as Tom staged at the Lyric Theatre, Hammersmith in 2019 and directed by Rachel O'Riordan. This adaptation employs the climactic structure and places the play in colonial India.
(Tristram Kenton/Eyevine/Redux)

The Plot Begins Late in the Story

The first hallmark of climactic drama is that the plot begins quite late in the story. Ibsen's *Ghosts*, written in 1881, is a clear example. Before *Ghosts* begins, a number of events have already occurred: Mrs. Alving has married a dissolute man who fathers an illegitimate child by another woman and contracts a venereal disease. When she discovers her husband's infidelity early in their marriage, Mrs. Alving visits the family minister, Pastor Manders, telling him she wishes to end the marriage. Although Manders is attracted to her and realizes that she has been wronged, for religious reasons, he sends her back to her husband with whom she stays out of a sense of duty. She does, however, send her son, Oswald, away to escape his father's influence. When her husband dies, Mrs. Alving builds an orphanage in his honor to camouflage his true character. At this point—as is typical with climactic plot structure—the play itself has still not begun. It begins later, when the son returns home and the facts of the past are unearthed, precipitating the crisis.

In climactic structure the play begins when all the roads of the past converge at a crucial intersection in the present, at the *climax,* a situation that has two important consequences. First, it is frequently necessary to explain what has happened earlier by having one or more characters report the information to others. The technical term for this background information is *exposition.* A second consequence of the plot beginning late is that the time span covered within a climactic play is usually brief—in many cases a matter of a few hours, and at the most a few days. Some

---

climax The highpoint in the development of a dramatic plot.

exposition Information necessary for an understanding of the story but not covered by the action onstage; events or knowledge from the past, or occurring outside the play, that must be introduced so that the audience can understand the characters or plot.

playwrights, attempting to push events as near the climax as possible, have stage time (the time we imagine is passing when we are watching a play) coincide with real time (that is, clock time). An example is Tennessee Williams's *Cat on a Hot Tin Roof*: the events depicted in the story last the same time as the play itself—a little over two hours; as we noted the same is true of Marsha Norman's *'Night Mother*.

Scenes, Locales, and Characters Are Limited

Climactic drama typically has a limited number of long segments, or acts. In Greek plays there are generally five episodes separated by choral interludes. The French neoclassicists invariably used five acts. For much of the nineteenth and twentieth centuries, three acts were standard. Today, the norm is two acts, though the long one-act play performed without intermission is also frequently presented.

Limiting the scenes in a play usually entails restricting the locale as well, sometimes to one room or one house. Along with restriction of locale, there is a restriction of characters. Greek drama generally has four or five principal characters. Many modern plays have no more than a similar number of main characters or even fewer.

Construction Is Tight

Because it is carefully constructed, a climactic play fits together tightly, with no loose ends. It is like a chain linked in a cause-and-effect relationship. As in a detective story, event A leads to event B; B leads to C, causing D; D leads in turn to E; and so on. Just as the time frame and the restricted space afford no exit, so the chain of events is locked in. Once the action begins, there is no stopping it. Because climactic dramas are so carefully and tightly constructed, they are frequently referred to as *well-made plays*. In this form the aim is always to make events so inevitable that there is no escape—at least not until the very last moment, when a *deus ex machina* may intervene to untangle the knot. (*Deus ex machina* means "god from the machine," referring to the apparatus in Greek theatre when gods were brought down from the top of the stage house at the end of a play to resolve the action. The term has since become used to describe any outside intervention at the end of a play to bring the play to a close.)

Clearly, the method of climactic drama is compression. All the elements—characters, locale, events—are severely restricted. As if by centripetal motion, everything is forced to the center, in a tighter and tighter nucleus, making the ultimate eruption that much more explosive.

Characteristics of Episodic Structure

When we turn to episodic structure, we see a sharp contrast to climactic structure. Episodic drama begins relatively early in the story and does not compress the action but expands it. The forces in episodic drama are centrifugal, moving out to embrace additional elements. Also, unlike climactic drama, episodic plays do not necessarily follow a close cause-and-effect development.

People, Places, and Events Proliferate

In a typical episodic play the action begins relatively early in the story and covers an extensive period of time—sometimes many years. It also ranges over a number of locations. In one play we can go anywhere: to a small antechamber, a large banquet hall, the open countryside, a mountaintop.

Short scenes (some only half a page or so in print) alternate with longer ones. Two examples of episodic dramas are Shakespeare's *Antony and Cleopatra,* which has thirty-four characters and forty-plus scenes; and the Spanish playwright Lope de Vega's *The*

---

well-made plays Type of play popular in the nineteenth century and early twentieth century that combines apparent plausibility of incident and surface realism with a tightly constructed, highly causal, and contrived plot.

deus ex machina ("DEH-oos eks MAH-kih-nah") Literally, "god from a machine," a resolution device in classic Greek drama; hence, intervention of supernatural forces—usually at the last moment—to save the action from its logical conclusion. In modern drama, an arbitrary and coincidental solution.

King Lear by William Shakespeare

I-1 Lear's Palace. Kent and Gloucester discuss the division of the kingdom and Gloucester's sons. Lear comes. The division of kingdom: first Goneril and then Regan praise Lear. Kent intercedes and is banished. Gloucester enters with Burgundy and France. Burgundy will not have Cordelia without a dowry. France takes her. Goneril and Regan begin plotting. (305 lines)

I-2 Gloucester's Castle. Edmund's soliloquy and scheme. Letter and plan against Edgar begins. Gloucester leaves, Edgar comes, scheme furthered. (173 lines)

I-3 Albany's Palace. Goneril and Oswald scheming. (26 lines)

I-4 The Same. Kent enters disguised; Lear comes, then Oswald, Kent trips him. Fool enters and talks to Lear. Goneril comes, chides Lear. He curses her and leaves. Goneril, Albany, and Oswald conspire further, then leave. (336 lines)

I-5 In Front of Palace. Lear, Kent, Fool. Lear sends letters to Gloucester, starts to Regan. (46 lines)

II-1 A Court in Gloucester's Castle. Edmund and Curan. Edgar comes, then leaves. Edmund stabs himself; Gloucester comes, Edmund blames Edgar, Gloucester finds letter. Cornwall and Regan enter. (The forces of evil join.) (129 lines)

II-2 Before Gloucester's Castle. Kent confronts Oswald, Cornwall comes; Kent put in stocks. (168 lines)

II-3 The Open Country. Edgar's soliloquy: he will disguise and abase himself. (21 lines)

II-4 Before Gloucester's Castle. Lear comes, sees Kent; confronts Regan. She is stubborn too. Goneril comes. He sees a league. Begs; leaves as storm begins. (306 lines)

III-1 A Heath. Kent with a Gentleman. (55 lines)

III-2 Another Part of Heath. Lear comes with Fool. Storm and insanity begin. Kent comes. (95 lines)

III-3 Gloucester's Castle. Gloucester tells Edmund of divisions between dukes and of letter from France. (23 lines)

III-4 The Heath before a Hovel. Lear, Kent, Fool—storm. Lear's madness and beginning self-realization. Edgar joins them, then Gloucester with a torch. (172 lines)

III-5 Gloucester's Castle. Cornwall and Edmund scheming. (22 lines)

III-6 A Farmhouse Near Gloucester's Castle. The mock trial for Lear. Kent, Gloucester, Fool, Edgar. All leave but Edgar. (112 lines)

III-7 Gloucester's Castle. Cornwall, Regan, Goneril, Edmund. They send for Gloucester (the "traitor"), prepare to blind him. Servant is killed; they pluck out Gloucester's eyes. (106 lines)

IV-1 The Heath. Edgar. Enter Gloucester, blind. Edgar prepares cliff scene. (79 lines)

IV-2 Before Albany's Palace. Goneril and Edmund. Enter Oswald. Intrigue of Goneril and Edmund. Albany comes; Goneril chides him. Servant comes telling of Cornwall's death. (979 lines)

IV-3 French Camp Near Dover. Kent and Gentleman report Lear ashamed to see Cordelia. (55 lines)

IV-4 French Camp. Cordelia and Doctor enter, plan to go to England. (29 lines)

IV-5 Gloucester's Castle. Regan and Oswald. She says Edmund is for her. (40 lines)

IV-6 Country Near Dover. Gloucester and Edgar—jumping scene. Lear comes, mad. The two wronged madmen together. Gentleman comes, then Oswald attacks him. Edgar kills Oswald, finds letters to Edmund—Goneril is plotting Albany's death in order to marry Edmund. (283 lines)

IV-7 Tent in French Camp. Cordelia and Kent. Lear brought in. The awakening and reconciliation. (96 lines)

V-1 British Camp Near Dover. Edmund, Regan, etc. Goneril comes, also Albany. Edgar enters, leaves. (69 lines)

V-2 A Field between Camps. Cordelia and Lear cross. Edgar and Gloucester come. (11 lines)

V-3 British Camp. Edmund comes, Lear and Cordelia are prisoners; are sent away. Edmund sends note with guard. Enter Albany, Goneril, and Regan, who quarrel. Edgar comes; challenges Edmund and wounds him. Truth about Goneril's plan comes out; she leaves. Edgar talks. Goneril and Regan are brought in dead. Edmund dies. Lear enters with the dead Cordelia; then he dies. Kent and Albany pronounce the end. (326 lines)

EPISODIC STRUCTURE IN *KING LEAR*

Shakespeare's play sets up a juxtaposition of scenes. Note how the scenes move from place to place and alternate from one group of characters to another. Note, too, that the scenes move back and forth from intimate scenes to those involving a number of characters (an alternation of public and private scenes) and that the length of the scenes varies, with short scenes followed by longer ones, and so forth. This structure gives the play its dynamics, its rhythm, and its meaning.

Chapter 10 *Dramatic Structure and Dramatic Characters* 229

EPISODIC STRUCTURE: MANY CHARACTERS, PLACES, AND EVENTS
A good example of the typically wide-ranging episodic structure is *Measure for Measure* by William Shakespeare. Shown here is a 2015 production directed by Dominic Dromgoole at Shakespeare's Globe in London. In this scene are the actors (from left to right): Paul Rider as Escalus, Kurt Egylawan as Angelo, Dean Nolan as Elbow/Barnadine, Petra Massey as Mistress Overdone, Dennis Herdman as Froth, and Trevor Fox as Pompey. (Nigel Norrington/Camera Press/Redux)

Sheep Well, which has twenty-six characters and seventeen scenes. Tony Kushner's two-part *Angels in America* (1991) has many short sections, people, and differing scenes.

There May Be a Parallel Plot or Subplot In place of compression, episodic drama offers other techniques. One is the *parallel plot,* or **subplot.** In *King Lear,* by Shakespeare, Lear has three daughters, two evil and one good. The two evil daughters have convinced their father that they are good and that their sister is wicked. In the subplot—a counterpart of this main plot—the Earl of Gloucester has two sons, one loyal and one disloyal, and the disloyal son has deceived his father into thinking he is the loyal one. Both old men have misunderstood their children's true worth, and in the end both are punished for their mistakes: Lear is bereft of his kingdom and his sanity; Gloucester loses his eyes. The Gloucester plot, with complications and developments of its own, is a parallel and reinforcement of the Lear plot.

Subplot Sometimes referred to as parallel plot, a secondary plot that reinforces or runs parallel to the major plot in an episodic play.

Juxtaposition and Contrast Occur Another technique of episodic drama is *juxtaposition* or *contrast.* Rather than moving in linear fashion, the action alternates between elements. Short scenes alternate with longer scenes, public scenes alternate with private scenes, we move from one group to an opposing group, and comic scenes alternate with serious scenes.

An example of this last alternation comes in Shakespeare's *Macbeth.* Just after Macbeth has murdered King Duncan, there is a knock on the door of the castle. This is one of the most serious moments of the play, but the man who goes to open the

IN FOCUS: COMPARING CLIMACTIC AND EPISODIC STRUCTURES

Comparing Climactic and Episodic Forms

Climactic

1. Plot begins late in the story, toward the very end or climax.
2. Covers a short space of time, perhaps a few hours or at most a few days.
3. Contains a few solid, extended scenes, such as three acts with each act comprising one long scene.
4. Occurs in a restricted locale, such as one room or one house.
5. Number of characters is severely limited—usually no more than six or eight.
6. Plot is linear and moves in a single line with few subplots or counterplots.
7. Line of action proceeds in a cause-and-effect chain.
8. The characters and events are closely linked in a sequence of logical, almost inevitable development.

Episodic

1. Plot begins relatively early in the story and moves through a series of episodes.
2. Covers a longer period of time: weeks, months, and sometimes many years.
3. Has many short, fragmented scenes; sometimes an alternation of short and long scenes.
4. May range over an entire city or even several countries.
5. Has a profusion of characters, sometimes several dozen.
6. Is frequently marked by several threads of action, such as two parallel plots, or scenes of comic relief in a serious play.
7. Scenes are juxtaposed to one another. An event may result from several causes; or it may have no apparent cause, but arises in a network or web of circumstances.

The table outlines the chief characteristics of climactic and episodic forms and illustrates the differences between them. It is clear that the climactic and episodic forms differ from each other in their fundamental approaches. One emphasizes constriction and compression on all fronts; the other takes a far broader view and aims at a cumulative effect, piling up people, places, and events.

COMIC SCENES ALTERNATE WITH SERIOUS SCENES

One device possible in episodic drama is the juxtaposition and alternation of serious and comic scenes. Shakespeare often incorporates this technique in his plays. In the grave-digging scene in *Hamlet,* comedy interrupts very serious scenes involving the death of Ophelia and other tragic events. Shown here is Joshua McGuire as Hamlet with the skull of Yorick, in Shakespeare's Globe production, directed by Dominic Dromgoole.
(Geraint Lewis/Alamy Stock Photo)

COMBINING CLIMACTIC AND EPISODIC STRUCTURES
Though we often separate the episodic and climactic structures, there have been a number of times when the two forms were combined, joining together characteristics from each. Good examples are plays from the English Restoration and, 200 years later, the plays of the Russian dramatist Anton Chekhov. Shown here is a scene from a Restoration comedy *The Way of the World* by William Congreve and directed in 2012 by Rachel Kavanaugh at the Chichester Festival Theatre, with Penelope Keith as Lady Wishfort and Robin Pearce as Waitwell. The play has some of the economy of climactic drama but features a number of elements typical of the episodic form. (Nigel Norrington/Camera Press/Redux)

door is a comical character, a drunken porter, whose speech is a humorous interlude in the grim business of the play. In other words, comedy alternates with tragedy.

The Overall Effect Is Cumulative With regard to cause and effect in episodic drama, the impression created is of events piling up: a tsunami, a tidal wave of circumstances and emotions sweeping over the characters. Rarely does one letter, one telephone call, or one piece of information determine the fate of a character. Time and again, Hamlet has proof that Claudius has killed his father; however, what eventually leads him to kill Claudius is not a single piece of hard evidence but a rush of events. In modern theatre both climactic form and episodic form have been adopted, sometimes by the same playwright. This is characteristic of the diversity of our age. Ibsen, for example, wrote not only a number of "well-made" or climactic plays—*Ghosts, A Doll's House,* and others—but also several episodic plays, such as *Brand* and *Peer Gynt.*

Combinations of Climactic and Episodic Form

There is no requirement that a play be exclusively episodic or exclusively climactic. It is true that during certain periods one form or the other has been predominant.

Also, it is not easy to mix the two forms because—as we have seen—each has its own laws and its own inner logic. In several periods, however, they have been successfully integrated.

A group of plays that combine elements of the climactic and episodic forms are the comedies of the Restoration period in England (from 1660, when the English monarchy was restored, to 1700). These comedies usually had a large cast, a subplot as well as a main plot, and several changes of scene. They did not, however, cover extended periods of time or move rapidly from place to place as the plays of Shakespeare did.

The climactic and episodic forms have frequently been combined successfully in the modern period. The Russian playwright Chekhov, who generally wrote about one principal action and set his plays in one household, usually has more characters than is customary in climactic drama. For instance, there are fifteen in *The Cherry Orchard*. Frequently, too, Chekhov's plays cover a period of several months or years.

August Wilson, in his ten play cycle about Black life in the United States in the twentieth century, also frequently combined climactic drama with episodic elements. His play *Fences,* for example, is set in one place but covers an extended period of time.

RITUAL IN MODERN THEATRE
Many avant-garde playwrights and groups use ceremonies and rituals. Ceremonies and rituals are also used in many contemporary dramas. Paula Vogel's *Indecent,* which focuses on an early twentieth-century Yiddish play that, because of its treatment of a lesbian relationship, resulted in the arrest of the Broadway actors performing in it. Vogel and director Rebecca Taichman employed many ritualistic Jewish dances and accompanying music throughout its staging, as seen here in a moment from the off-Broadway production at the Vineyard Theatre in 2016. (Sara Krulwich/The New York Times/Redux)

Rituals as Dramatic Structure

Like acting, ritual is a part of everyday life of which we are generally unaware. Basically, ***ritual*** is a repetition or reenactment of a proceeding or transaction that has acquired special meaning. It may be a simple ritual like singing the national anthem before a sports contest, or a deeply religious ritual such as the Roman Catholic mass or the Jewish *kaddish,* a prayer for the dead. All of us develop rituals in our personal or family life: a certain meal we eat with the family once a week, for example, or a routine we go through every time we take an examination in school. Occasions like Thanksgiving, Christmas, and Ramadan become family rituals, with the same order of events each year, the same menu, and perhaps even the same conversation. Rituals give us continuity, security, and comfort. Often, as in the case of primitive tribes, people assume that if they perform a ritual faithfully, they will be blessed or their wishes will be granted. Conversely, they assume that failure to follow a ritual to the letter will lead to punishment.

In theatre, ritual is an activity where the old and new come together. Traditional plays are full of rituals: coronations, weddings, funerals, and other ceremonies. And in modern theatre, ritual has been discovered and given new life. Certain avant-garde theatre groups, for example, have made a conscious attempt to develop new rituals or revive old ones. Many of these artists incorporate Afrocentric and Asian ritual traditions into their work. Ritual has structure. Actions are repeated in a set fashion; these actions have a beginning, a middle, and an end; and there is a natural progression of events.

ritual Ceremonial event, often religious, that takes place in a prescribed sequence.

Patterns as Dramatic Structure

Related to ritual is a pattern of events. In Samuel Beckett's *Waiting for Godot,* the characters have no personal history, and the play does not build to a climax in the ordinary way. But if Beckett has sacrificed traditional plot structure, he has replaced it with a repeated sequence of events containing its own order and logic. The play has two acts, and in each act a series of incidents is duplicated. Each act opens with the two chief characters coming together on a lonely crossroads after having been separated. Then, in both acts, a similar sequence of events occurs: they greet each other; they despair of Godot ever coming; they attempt to entertain themselves. Two other men, Pozzo and Lucky, appear and, following a long scene, disappear. The first two men are left alone once more. The two acts continue to follow the same sequence: a small boy comes to tell the men that Godot will not come that day, the boy leaves, and the men remain together for another night. There are important differences between the two acts, but the identical sequence of events in each act achieves a pattern, which takes on a ritualistic quality.

Serial Structure

Another kind of structure is a series of acts or episodes—individual theatre events—offered as a single presentation. In this case, individual segments are strung together like beads on a necklace. Sometimes a central theme or common thread holds the various parts together. Sometimes there is little or no connection between the parts.

The musical *revue* is a case in point. In a revue, short scenes, vignettes, skits, dance numbers, songs, and possibly even vaudeville routines are presented on a single program. There may be an overall theme, such as political satire or the celebration of a past event or period. Sometimes a master of ceremonies provides continuity between the various segments. Also, in today's theatre we frequently see a program of short plays. Sometimes there will be a bill of one-act plays by the same author; at other times there will be two or three plays by different authors. On some occasions an attempt is made to relate the separate plays to a central theme; but sometimes the plays are chosen simply to complete an evening's entertainment.

Structure in Experimental and Avant-Garde Theatre

In the second half of the twentieth century, a number of theatre groups in Europe and the United States experimented with forms such as ritual. These included the Polish Laboratory Theater, headed by Jerzy Grotowski, and the Living Theater, the Open Theater, the Performance Group, Mabou Mines, and the Wooster Group in the United States. These groups had two things in mind. On one hand, they felt that the theatre of the past was no longer relevant to the problems of the present and that new forms had to be found to match the unique challenges and aspirations of the modern world. On the other hand, they wanted to look back beyond the traditions of the past 2,500 years to the beginning of theatre, to scrape off the layers of formality and convention that have accumulated through the centuries, and to rediscover the roots of theatre.

From the experiments of this radical theatre movement, several significant departures from traditional theatre practice were developed. Among them were the following: (1) emphasis on *nonverbal theatre,* that is, theatre in which gestures, body movements, and sounds without words are stressed rather than logical or intelligible

SEGMENTS AND TABLEAUX IN AVANT-GARDE THEATRE
The works of many modern experimental theatre directors consist of separate segments, almost like pictorial tableaux. The emphasis is on the visual aspect, and also on images, sounds, music, and dancelike movement. An example of segments and tableaux can be seen in this scene from Robert Wilson's interpretation of the Brecht-Weill *Threepenny Opera,* a Berliner Ensemble production, with Stefan Kurt (center) as Macheath (Mack the Knife). (David Baltzer/Zenit/Laif/Redux)

language; (2) reliance on improvisation or a scenario developed by performers and a director to tell the story, rather than a written text; (3) interest in ritual and ceremony; and (4) stress on the importance of the physical environment of theatre, including the spatial relationship of the performers to the audience. The theatre groups that developed these ideas were referred to as *avant-garde,* a French term that literally means "advance guard in a military formation." The term has come to mean an intellectual or artistic movement in any age that breaks with tradition and therefore seems ahead of its time.

Segments and Tableaux as Structure

The experimental pieces of the directors Robert Wilson (noted in the chapters "Acting for the Stage" and "The Director and the Producer") and Richard Foreman (b. 1937), like other types of avant-garde theatre, often stress nonverbal elements. At times they include non sequitur as well. In spite of this, their work does have structure. Often the various elements are united by a theme, or at least by a pronounced point of view on the part of the director. Also, the material is organized into units analogous to the frames of film and television, or to the still-life tableaux of painting or the moving tableaux of dance. (In theatre, a *tableau*—plural, *tableaux*—is a static scene onstage featuring performers in costume.)

Robert Wilson, in productions such as *A Letter to Queen Victoria, Einstein on the Beach,* and *CiVil WarS: A Tree Is Best Measured When It Is Down,* begins a segment with a visual picture—like a large painting, but three-dimensional. The performers move from this static image into the activities of the segment. When one segment has concluded, another picture or tableau will be formed to initiate the next segment. Frequently directors like Foreman and Wilson will use rapid movements—as in silent films—or slow-motion movements. At times several activities will occur simultaneously. All of these, however, relate both to an image and to a tableau or frame.

For many years Foreman, under the banner of his Ontological-Hysteric Theatre, presented new work almost annually. In 2013 he directed a piece that many considered a retrospective of his career titled *Old-Fashioned Prostitutes (A True Romance).*

Structure in Musical Theatre

In musical theatre, structure often involves alternation and juxtaposition. Musical numbers alternate with spoken scenes; solos and duets alternate with choral numbers; singing alternates with dance numbers; and sometimes comic songs and scenes alternate with serious ones. An example of structural principles in musicals is found

THE KING AND I: A MUSICAL WITH A CLEAR DRAMATIC STRUCTURE
Musicals, like other forms of theatre, require a definite form and structure. In *The King and I* by Rodgers and Hammerstein II (which was based on the novel *Anna and the King of Siam*), scenes of dialogue alternate with musical and dance numbers; solos alternate with duets and choral numbers. Here we see Kelli O'Hara, as Anna the British school teacher, and Ken Watanabe, as the king, as well as other cast members in the family prayer scene from the 2015 Lincoln Center revival directed by Bartlett Sher. (Sara Krulwich/The New York Times/Redux)

in *My Fair Lady,* with book and lyrics by Alan Jay Lerner and music by Frederick Loewe. The story is based on George Bernard Shaw's play *Pygmalion.*

My Fair Lady concerns a speech teacher, Henry Higgins, who claims that the English judge people by how they speak. He bets his friend Colonel Pickering that he can take an ordinary cockney flower girl, Eliza Doolittle, and by teaching her correct diction, pass her off as a duchess. The comic subplot of *My Fair Lady* deals with Eliza's father, Alfred P. Doolittle, a ne'er-do-well who doesn't want to achieve middle-class respectability, because if he does he will have to marry the woman he lives with.

The first song in the show is sung by Higgins—"Why Can't the English Learn to Speak?" The next song shifts to Eliza and her dreams of luxury as she sings "Wouldn't It Be Loverly?" The action now shifts to the subplot, and Alfred Doolittle is joined by two buddies to sing of how he hopes to avoid working, "With a Little Bit of Luck." We then move back to a scene with Higgins, who is pushing Eliza very hard to learn to speak properly. After a song by Higgins, "I'm an Ordinary Man," Eliza vows revenge on him in her next song: "Just You Wait."

The musical proceeds in this manner, moving from one character to another, from a solo to a trio to a dance routine to an ensemble. There is variety in these numbers—some are serious; some are comic; some explain the characters' feelings; some describe a situation. It is on such alternation that structure in musical theatre is based. Always, too, it must be remembered, spoken scenes are interspersed with musical numbers, and ballet or modern dance routines with other numbers.

The musical *Hamilton*, as another example, contains serious and comic rap numbers, as well as traditional musical numbers, to help identify characters, circumstances, and emotions. For example, to satirize and characterize King George III, who is too self-absorbed to understand the American Revolution, author-composer Lin-Manuel Miranda (b. 1980) gives him three comic solo songs, including "You'll Be Back," which has silly lyrics and a musical composition that sounds like a campy 1960s British invasion pop song. But when his choral refrain goes from the comical "da da das' to "die, die, die," we hear the character transform from comic to evil.

Diversity and Inclusion in Dramatic Structure: Feminist Structure

As a result of the women's movement of the 1970s, some feminist theatre critics examined Aristotle's *Poetics* and suggested that his concept of the ideally structured tragedy, which had been the template for Western drama for centuries, reflected the West's dominant male culture. Feminist theorists, for instance, saw the plot complications, crisis, and denouement in tragedy as a duplication of the male sexual experience of foreplay, arousal, and climax. Other feminist critics viewed traditional linear, cause-and-effect plot development as a reflection of the step-by-step approach that men have traditionally used to empower their lives and control society. The leading figures, or subjects, of these plays, according to feminist critics, were invariably male.

To counter this Aristotelian tradition, feminist theatre critics and practitioners aimed to create what Professor Sue-Ellen Case, in her groundbreaking book *Feminism and Theatre* (1988), called a "new poetics." The idea was to explore a "women's form" of drama, and also to construct new, feminist ways of analyzing and responding to theatrical texts and performance.

Among the pioneers was the French feminist and playwright Hélène Cixous (b. 1937), who, in her famous essay "The Laugh of the Medusa," called for women to create a new language that would be suggestive and ambiguous. Other feminists called for a dramatic form that stressed "contiguity," a form, writes Case, that is "fragmentary rather than whole" and "interrupted rather than complete." This form is often cyclical and without the single climax. It is frequently open-ended and offers woman as subject. One example is *Fefu and Her Friends,* written and directed in 1977 by the Cuban-born American dramatist Maria Irene Fornés (b. 1930). Instead of a plot, there is a cyclical, physical action; and in place of logical cause and effect, Fornés writes each scene as though it were a new event. There is no hero; the subject of the play is a group of educated women sharing thoughts and ideas.

Not all women have embraced the new poetics. But increasingly, feminists have experimented with dramatic structure and theatrical styles to confront, expose, and rewrite what they see as centuries of male cultural privilege.

DRAMATIC CHARACTERS

Along with structures, the playwright creates dramatic characters. These can range from fully rounded human beings to so-called ***stock characters*** who are two-dimensional.

stock characters Two-dimensional, stereotypical characters.

Extraordinary Characters

In most important dramatic works of the past, the heroes and heroines are extraordinary in some way. They are larger than life. Historically, major characters have been kings, queens, bishops, members of the nobility, or other figures clearly marked as holding a special place in society. In drama, as in life, a queen is accorded respect because of her authority, power, and grandeur; a high military official is respected because of the position he holds. Dramatists go one step further, however, in depicting extraordinary characters. In addition to filling prestigious roles, dramatic characters generally represent men and women at their best or worst—at some extreme of human behavior. Lady Macbeth is not only a noblewoman; she is one of the most ambitious women ever depicted onstage. In virtually every instance, with extraordinary characters, we see men and women at the outer limits of human capability and endurance.

Comic characters can also be extremes. The chief character in *Volpone* by Ben Jonson (1572–1637) is an avaricious miser who gets people to present him with expensive gifts because they think he will remember them in his will. Characters may also be extraordinary because of their exceptional personalities or achievements. A good example is Joan of Arc, the heroine of George Bernard Shaw's *Saint Joan,* a simple peasant who rises to become commander of an army that triumphs in the name of the king of France.

Some characters are mixtures, combining extreme virtue and extreme vice. Faustus, treated by Christopher Marlowe in *The Tragical History of Doctor Faustus* and by Johann Wolfgang von Goethe in *Faust,* is a great scholar but becomes so bored with his existence and so ambitious that he makes a compact with the devil, forfeiting his soul in return for unlimited power. Cleopatra, an exceedingly vain, selfish woman, also has "immortal longings." Queen Elizabeth I of England and Mary Queen of

Scots, rivals in real life, have made admirable dramatic characters—women of strong virtues and telling weaknesses.

In sum, larger-than-life characters become the heroes and heroines of drama not only because of their station in life but also because they possess traits common to us all—ambition, generosity, malevolence, fear, and achievement—in such great abundance.

In the eighteenth century, ordinary people began taking over from royalty and the nobility as the heroes and heroines of drama—a reflection of what was occurring in the real world. But despite this move away from royalty and the nobility, the leading figures of drama continued in many cases to be exceptional men and women at their best and worst.

Representative or Quintessential Characters

When characters from everyday life replaced kings and queens as the leading figures in drama, a new type of character emerged alongside the extraordinary character. Characters of this new type

THE TRAGIC FIGURE: AN EXCEPTIONAL CHARACTER
A good example of an extraordinary figure in tragedy is Tamburlaine, a larger-than-life character who through terror and cunning conquered much of the known world in central Asia and was the hero of two plays by Christopher Marlowe in the late 1580s. Shown here is John Douglas Thompson, as the lead character, in a Theater for a New Audience production of *Tamburlaine, Parts I and II* at the Polonsky Shakespeare Center in New York in 2014. (Sara Krulwich/The New York Times/Redux)

are in many respects typical or ordinary, but they are significant because they embody an entire group. Rather than being notable as "worst," "best," or some other extreme, they are important as *representative* or *quintessential* characters. A good example of such a character is Nora Helmer, the heroine of Henrik Ibsen's *A Doll's House*. A traditional wife and mother, she has secretly forged a signature to get money for her husband when he was very ill and needed medical attention. All her life, first by her father, then by her husband, she has been treated like a doll or a plaything, not as a mature, responsible woman.

In the last act of the play, Nora rebels against this attitude; she makes a declaration of independence to her husband, slams the door on him, and walks out. It has been said that Nora's slamming of the door marks the beginning not only of modern drama but also of the emancipation of modern women. Certainly Nora's defiance—her demand to be treated as an equal—has made her typical of all housewives who refuse to be regarded as pets. In one sense, Nora is an ordinary wife and mother, but she is unusual in the way she sums up an entire group of women. *A Doll's House* was written

photo essay
Extraordinary Characters

In dramas of the past, the leading characters are often people who are exceptional in some way. Shown here is a gallery of exceptional characters from a range of dramas.

(Geraint Lewis/Alamy Stock Photo)

Christopher Marlowe's *Dr. Faustus* contains a quintessential tragic character, Faustus, who trades his soul to the devil in order to gain the knowledge and power of supernatural magic. Seen here are Sandy Grierson (left) as Mephistophilis (Lucifer's servant) and Oliver Ryan as Doctor Faustus in a 2016 production at The Swan theatre, Stratford-upon-Avon, Britain.

(Donald Cooper/Alamy Stock Photo)

Frances Barber as Cleopatra, the powerful, alluring queen of Egypt with whom Antony fell in love in Shakespeare's *Antony and Cleopatra,* in a production at Shakespeare's Globe in London.

Anne-Marie Duff as the exceptional historical figure Joan of Arc in George Bernard Shaw's *Saint Joan*, directed by Marianne Elliott at the National Theatre, London.

(Kevin Cummins)

Greek actor Grigoris Valtinos as the quintessentially extraordinary figure of Oedipus in the National Theatre of Greece's *Oedipus Rex* by Sophocles presented in Rome's Colosseum.

(Pier Paolo Cito/AP Images)

241

QUINTESSENTIAL CHARACTERS
Certain key characters in drama, especially in modern drama, are not extraordinary or exceptional in the same way as royalty or military leaders, but become important because they embody qualities of an entire group of people. Included in this description would be the lead characters in Arthur Miller's *Death of a Salesman*. Shown here are: Brian Dennehy (center) as Willy Loman, the salesman of the title, Mark Bazeley (left) as Happy Loman, one of Willy's sons, and Douglas Hensall as Biff Loman, his other son, in a 2005 revival directed by Robert Falls at the Lyric Theatre, London. This revival was first produced at the Goodman Theatre in Chicago and was also staged on Broadway. (Donald Cooper/Photostage)

in 1879; but today, well over a century later, Nora is still a symbol of modern women, and the play is revived year after year.

In *Who's Afraid of Virginia Woolf?* by Edward Albee, the main characters are a husband and a wife who are in many ways quite commonplace. He is a somewhat ineffectual college professor; she is the daughter of the college president. They argue and attack each other almost to the point of exhaustion. Another unhappily married couple? Yes. But again, they are quintessential. To Albee, they represent an American type: a bitter, alienated couple, bored with themselves and each other. To underline this point, he names them Martha and George—the same first names as Martha and George Washington, America's "first couple." Another example is Willy Loman, in Arthur Miller's *Death of a Salesman,* who sums up all salesmen, traveling in their territories on a "smile and a shoeshine." Willy has lived by a false dream: the idea that if he puts up a good front and is "well liked," he will be successful and rich.

Still another example is Troy Maxson in *Fences* by August Wilson. Maxson epitomizes the proud, headstrong man who in order to survive in a world of oppression and systemic racism has developed firmness and resolution, which serve him well but take their toll on his wife and son.

> # PLAYING YOUR PART: EXPERIENCING THEATRE
>
> 1. If you were to dramatize your life, how might you use a climactic structure? Describe the moments you would dramatize.
> 2. How might you use an episodic structure to structure a play about your life? What events would you dramatize?
> 3. Have you seen a movie or television show that uses stock characters? Describe the characters? Have you seen a film that employs quintessential characters? Describe them.
> 4. Describe a family ritual. What are the elements of the ritual?
> 5. Are there any films or television shows that present nonhuman characters? Describe them.

Nora Helmer, Martha and George, Willy Loman, and Troy Maxson: all are examples of characters who stand apart from the crowd, not by standing above it but by summing up in their personalities the essence of a certain type of person.

Stock Characters

The characters we have been describing, whether extraordinary or representative, are generally fully rounded figures. Many characters in drama, however, are not three-dimensional; rather, they exemplify one particular characteristic to the exclusion of virtually everything else. Frequently they are known by their station in life, their sex, and their occupation along with some tendency of personality: the clever

STOCK CHARACTERS OF COMMEDIA DELL'ARTE

Italian Renaissance comedy developed stereotyped characters who were always the same: each of them was famous for a certain trait—greed, boastfulness, gullibility, or the like—and was always easily identifiable by his or her costume. Here we see examples of those characters and their masks, including the wily servant Harlequin (left) and the pompous supposedly educated Dottore (right), in a 2006 comedia performance in Piazza San Marco during Carnival in Venice.
(PjrTravel/Alamy Stock Photo)

Chapter 10 *Dramatic Structure and Dramatic Characters*

servant, for instance, or the absentminded professor. They are referred to as *stock characters*, and they appear particularly in comedy and melodrama, though they can be found in all kinds of drama and also today in films and television shows.

Some of the most famous examples of stock characters are found in **commedia dell'arte.** This is a form of popular comedy that flourished in Italy during the sixteenth and seventeenth centuries. In commedia dell'arte, there was no script but rather a scenario that gave an outline of a story. The performers improvised or invented words and actions to fill out the play. The stock characters of commedia were either straightforward or exaggerated and were divided into servants and members of the ruling class. In every character, however, one particular feature or trait was stressed.

Whenever such a character appeared, he or she would have the same propensities and would wear the same costume. The bragging soldier, called *Capitano,* always boasted of his courage in a series of fictitious military victories. *Pantalone,* an elderly merchant, spoke in clichés and chased girls; and a pompous lawyer called *Dottore* spoke in Latin phrases and attempted to impress others with his learning. Among servants, *Harlequin* was the most popular; displaying both cunning and stupidity, he was at the heart of most plot complications. These are but a few of a full range of commedia characters, each with his or her own peculiarities. As for examples of stock characters in melodrama, we are all familiar with such figures as the all noble hero opposed by the evil villain, lurking in the shadows, twirling his moustache. In today's television, the familiar figures on weekly situation comedies are examples of stock or stereotypical characters.

commedia dell'arte Form of comic theatre, originating in Italy in the sixteenth century, in which dialogue was improvised around a scenario involving a set of stock characters, each with a traditional costume, name, and often mask.

CHARACTERS WITH A DOMINANT TRAIT
Many comic plays feature characters with one predominant trait—greed, ambition, self-importance, hypocrisy, and so forth. The extremes of the character are one of the elements that create the comic effect. The French playwright Molière often named his plays for such characters. Shown here are Elsa Poivre, Didier Sandre, and Michel Vuillermoz in a Comédie-Française production of *Tartuffe'* directed by Galin Stoev. The play's title character is a religious hypocrite who undermines a family. (Raphael Gaillarde/Getty Images)

Closely related to stock characters are characters with a *dominant trait,* that is, a single excess or "humor." The French playwright Molière and the English dramatist Ben Jonson wrote a number of comedies in which the chief character's excesses—avarice, self-importance, greed, pride, pomposity—lead to wildly humorous results. To further point up the one-sided nature of these characters, Jonson often named his characters for their single trait: his play *The Alchemist,* for example, includes characters with names like Subtle, Face, Dapper, Surly, Wholesome, and Dame Pliant.

Minor Characters

Stock characters or characters with a dominant trait are not to be confused with *minor characters.* Minor characters are those—in all types of plays—who play a

244 Part Four The Playwright and the Play

small part in the overall action. Generally they appear briefly and serve chiefly to further the story or to support more important characters. Typical examples of minor characters are servants and soldiers; but even figures such as generals, bishops, judges, dukes, and duchesses are considered minor if they play only a small role in the action. Since we see so little of these characters, the dramatist can usually show only one facet of their personalities; but this is a different case from that of a main character who is deliberately portrayed as one-sided.

A Narrator or Chorus

A special type of character is a narrator or the members of a chorus. Generally, a *narrator* speaks directly to the audience. He or she may or may not assume a dramatic persona as the other characters do. In Tennessee Williams's *The Glass Menagerie* and Thornton Wilder's *Our Town*, for instance, a performer appears both as a narrator and as one or more characters in the play. The chorus in ancient Greek drama, in song and dance, commented on the action of the main plot and reacted to events in the story. Use of a chorus or narrator creates a *dialectic* or *counterpoint* between a party outside the play and characters in the central action. (*Counterpoint* is a term from music denoting a second melody that accompanies or moves in contrast to the main melody.)

The dramatist Bertolt Brecht used a narrator, and sometimes singers, in a pointed way: to startle the audience by making a sudden shift from the main story to the presentation of a moral or political argument. In *The Caucasian Chalk Circle,* for instance, Grusha—an innocent, peace-loving peasant woman—steps out of character at one point to sing a song extolling the virtues of a general who loves war. Grusha, in other words, momentarily becomes a sort of chorus when she is asked to sing a song with a point of view opposite to her own. This wrenching of characters and attitudes is deliberate on Brecht's part: it is meant to make us think seriously about some issue, such as war and the ravages of war.

Some playwrights will have characters talk directly to the audience, acting as a narrator or choral leader for a short time. For example, in *Fairview* (2018) Jackie Sibblie Drury has an actor break out of her character and speak as herself directly to a Black audience member to illustrate how racism is inherent in the "views" of privileged white audience members. The actor says: "You, I've been trying to talk to You.

THE NARRATOR OR CHORUS
A role in drama in which a performer or group steps out of character to address the audience directly is a narrator or a chorus. In Thornton Wilder's *Our Town,* the character of the Stage Manager is the narrator of the piece, and also plays small roles such as the preacher who marries the young couple. Here we see Helen Hunt, the first woman to portray that role, in a production directed by David Cromer at the off-Broadway Barrow Street Theatre in 2010. (Chester Higgins Jr./ The New York Times/Redux)

Chapter 10   *Dramatic Structure and Dramatic Characters*

THE CHORUS: A TIME-HONORED DEVICE

The Greeks were the first to use a chorus. It extended the range and sweep of their plays, which otherwise adhered closely to the climactic form. Here we see the chorus in the London production of *Bacchai* by Euripides, directed by Peter Hall at the National Theatre. (Donald Cooper/Photostage)

This whole time. Have you heard me? Do I have to keep talking to the white people? Do I have to keep talking to them, and keep talking to them, and keep talking only to them, only to them, only to them, until I have used up every word? . . . Do I have to tell them that I want them to make space for us for them to make space for us? Do I really have to tell them that?"

Nonhuman Characters

In Greece in the fifth century BCE, and in many earlier cultures, performers portrayed birds and animals, and this practice has continued to the present. Aristophanes, the Greek comic dramatist, used a chorus of actors to play the title parts in his plays *The Birds* and *The Frogs*. In the modern period, Eugene Ionesco has men turn into animals in *Rhinoceros;* and the French playwright Edmond Rostand wrote a poetic fable called *Chantecler*, about a rooster.

Occasionally performers are called on to play other nonhuman roles. Karel Čapek (1890–1938) wrote a play, *R.U.R.,* in which people enact robots. (The initials in the title stand for "Rossum's Universal Robots," and it is from this play that the word *robot* derives.) In the medieval morality play *Everyman,* characters represent ideas or concepts, such as Fellowship, Good Deeds, Worldly Possessions, and Beauty.

Dramatic characters in the guise of animals or robots are the exception rather than the rule, and when they do appear, it is usually their human qualities that are emphasized.

NONHUMAN CHARACTERS

Sometimes characters are nonhuman, although they usually have human characteristics. This tradition goes back at least as far as the comedies of the Greek writer Aristophanes in the fifth century BCE in Greece. Frequently they are animals of some sort. Shown here is a scene from Edward Albee's *Seascape*, in which the characters are lizards, directed in 2002 by Mark Lamos at the Hartford Stage Company, with costumes by Constance Hoffman. (T Charles Erickson)

The Audience and Character Types

Classifying characters in categories is neither artificial nor arbitrary. Different types of characters are part of the fabric of various dramatic forms, and being aware of them is a helpful tool in appreciating and understanding those forms. It should also be remembered that not every character fits neatly into a single category, and that various character types are not necessarily mutually exclusive. For example, an extraordinary or quintessential character might also be a character with a dominant trait. At the same time, knowledge of the character types we have been studying can greatly help audiences understand how characters function in a drama and enhance their experience when seeing a performance.

When a playwright in ancient Greece or Elizabethan England wrote a tragedy, the dramatist did not think of the central figure in the drama as an extraordinary character. In nineteenth-century France, when a dramatist composed a bedroom farce, there was not a conscious employment of stock characters. And when a twentieth-century playwright wrote a serious drama, the focus was not on developing quintessential figures as the play's chief characters. Dramatists create characters, not labels. In the same way, we as audience members attending a performance should not be preoccupied with assigning characters onstage to a specific category. During a theatre event we should let the action onstage unfold, taking it in as a whole, and observing particular elements only when they appear evident or are especially striking. Focusing on character types should be undertaken in studying a play before seeing it, or in analyzing it afterward.

Juxtaposition of Characters

We turn now from single characters to the way characters interact with and relate to one another. Often in the creation of a dramatic work, characters are combined in important, significant ways to bring out certain qualities.

Protagonist and Antagonist From Greek theatre we have the terms *protagonist* and *antagonist*. The *protagonist* in a play is the main character—Othello, for instance—and the *antagonist* is the main character's chief opponent. In *Othello*, the antagonist is Iago. It is through the contest between these two characters that their individual qualities are developed.

protagonist Principal character in a play, the one whom the drama is about.

antagonist Opponent of the protagonist in a drama.

Contrasting Characters Another way characters are contrasted is by setting them side by side rather than in opposition. Sophocles created two exceptionally strong-willed, independent women characters—Antigone and Electra—each one the title character in a play. Both are women intent on defying an older person and willing to risk death to fight for a principle. But unlike other dramatists who had told the same story, Sophocles gave each of them a sister with a sharply contrasting personality. To Antigone he gave Ismene, a docile, compliant sister who argues that Antigone should obey the law and give in to authority. To Electra he gave Chrisothemis, who protests that women are powerless to act. Sophocles strengthened and heightened Antigone and Electra by providing them with contrasting characters to set off their own determination, agency, and courage.

Chapter 10 *Dramatic Structure and Dramatic Characters*

CONTRASTING CHARACTERS

Playwrights often set two characters beside each other, or against each other, so that they stand in sharp contrast. In Henrik Ibsen's *Hedda Gabler,* the frustrated, volatile, reckless Hedda is juxtaposed with her friend Mrs. Elvsted, a calmer, wiser, quieter person. In this scene Roxanna Hope as Hedda is on the left and Sara Topham as Mrs. Elvsted is on the right, under the direction of Jennifer Tarver at the Hartford Stage Company. (T Charles Erickson)

Orchestration of Characters

Anton Chekhov, the Russian dramatist, is said to have "orchestrated" his characters. The same is true for August Wilson whose characters frequently search for their "songs" and are brought together as is if they are part of a larger musical work.

This reference to "orchestrated" characters is to a musical composition in which the theme is played first by one section of the orchestra, such as the violins, and then by another, such as the brasses or woodwinds. Not only is the theme taken up by various sections, but it can be played in different ways as well—first in a major key, for instance, and then in a minor key. Beyond that, there is the way the various segments of the orchestra—strings, brass, woodwinds, percussion—are blended together, how they play with one another or in counterpoint to one another. In a similar fashion, Chekhov created his characters, giving each a distinctive voice. But his real genius was in the way he blended his characters, creating differences, similarities, subtle shadings, and contrasts.

In each of their plays, both Chekhov and Wilson drew a series of characters with a common problem, and each character represents some aspect of the central theme. In *Uncle Vanya,* for example, Chekhov's theme of disillusionment and frustration with life is reflected by virtually every character in the play, each of whom longs for a love that cannot be fulfilled. The same is true in Wilson's *Fences,* with every character constrained by the systemic racism in the United States in the 1950s. In Chekhov's play practically everyone embodies the theme of unrequited love and in *Fences* everyone's life is circumscribed by racist oppression. But in both plays all of this is done subtly and carefully brought out through gradations and shadings of meaning and characterizations, orchestrated like a stirring symphony.

ORCHESTRATION OF CHARACTERS

Characters in a play serve as contrasts, counterparts, or foils to each other; sometimes one group of characters is set in opposition to another, sometimes they complement one another. In every case, the playwright should make the relationships among characters serve the aims of the drama. Anton Chekhov was a master at combining and contrasting characters, sometimes a great many characters in one play. A good example is his work *The Three Sisters*. Shown here is a historical re-enactment of the Vladimir Nemirovich-Danchenko production of the play originally staged in 1940, produced at the Gorky Moscow Art Theatre in 2020. (Stanislav Krasilnikov/Tass/Getty Images)

Chekhov and Wilson were masters at orchestrating their characters, but they were not the only dramatists to use the technique. In one way or another, most dramatists try to arrange their characters so as to produce a cumulative effect. It is not what one character does or says but what all the characters do together that creates the effect.

PLAYING YOUR PART: THINKING ABOUT THEATRE

1. During the last performance you attended, did the action take place in one locale (one room, for instance) or, instead, in three or four locations? Did the action move frequently, returning at times to a former location? What effect did these elements of place or location have on your experience of the play?

2. Look at the cast of characters in a Shakespearean play you have seen or read. Place each character in a category: major character; minor character; or a character in between—that is, a character with a clear personality but not a large role. Which characters are in opposition to one another? Which characters in the play dominate in the struggle? Is there a reversal of their fortunes?

3. While you are watching a modern play or drama involving a small group of characters locked in a struggle for dominance or control, how does the action usually play out? Is first one person in the ascendency and then another? What do shifts of power and control have to do with revealing the personalities of the characters? What do these changes have to do with the meaning of the play?

Chapter 10 *Dramatic Structure and Dramatic Characters*

SUMMARY

1. There are several basic types of dramatic structure. *Climactic* form was adopted by the ancient Greeks and has been used frequently ever since. Its characteristics are a plot beginning quite late in the story, a limited number of characters, a limited number of locations and scenes, little or no extraneous material, and tight construction, including a cause-and-effect chain of events.

2. *Episodic* form involves a plot covering an extended span of time, numerous locations, a large cast of characters, diverse events (including mixtures of comic and serious episodes), and parallel plots or subplots. Shakespeare's plays are good examples of episodic form.

3. The climactic and episodic forms can be combined, as they have been in the Restoration period and in the modern period, in the works of Anton Chekhov and others.

4. Ritual or pattern is often used as the basis of dramatic structure. Words, gestures, and events are repeated; they have a symbolic meaning acquired both through repetition and through the significance invested in them from the past.

5. Theatre events are sometimes strung together to make a program. Examples are a group of unrelated one-act plays and a group of skits and songs in a revue. In this case, structure is within the individual units themselves; among the units the only structure might be the unfolding of the separate elements; or there can be a common theme uniting them.

6. Avant-garde theatre sometimes arranges events in a random way to suggest the random or haphazard manner in which life unfolds in everyday situations.

7. Experimental groups in the modern period have often used radical forms, including nonverbal and improvisational structures.

8. Segments and tableaux have also been used as structure.

9. Structurally, musical theatre consists of different elements put together in a sequence, in which solo musical numbers alternate with group numbers and dances and these musical elements alternate with dramatic scenes.

10. Dramatic characters symbolize people and fall into several categories. Frequently the chief characters of theatre are extraordinary characters: men and women at the outer limits of human behavior. Also, these characters often hold important positions: king, queen, general, admiral, duchess.

11. In modern serious theatre we frequently find typical or ordinary characters—complete, fully rounded portraits of people—who embody a whole group or type. An example is Willy Loman, the salesman in *Death of a Salesman*.

12. Some characters are stereotypes. Stock characters, for instance, are predictable, clearly defined types. Other characters have one dominant trait, which overshadows all other features.

13. A special type of character in drama of many periods is a narrator or the members of a chorus.

14. Occasionally performers are asked to play nonhuman parts—animals, birds, and so on—but these parts generally have a strong human flavor.

15. Characters are placed together by the playwright in certain combinations to obtain maximum effectiveness. A protagonist may be opposed by an antagonist; minor characters support major characters; and individual characters are orchestrated into a whole.

Design Elements: Audience Sitting in Theatre (theatre): Ron Chapple/Photodisc/Getty Images; Studio Light (spotlights): Exactostock/SuperStock

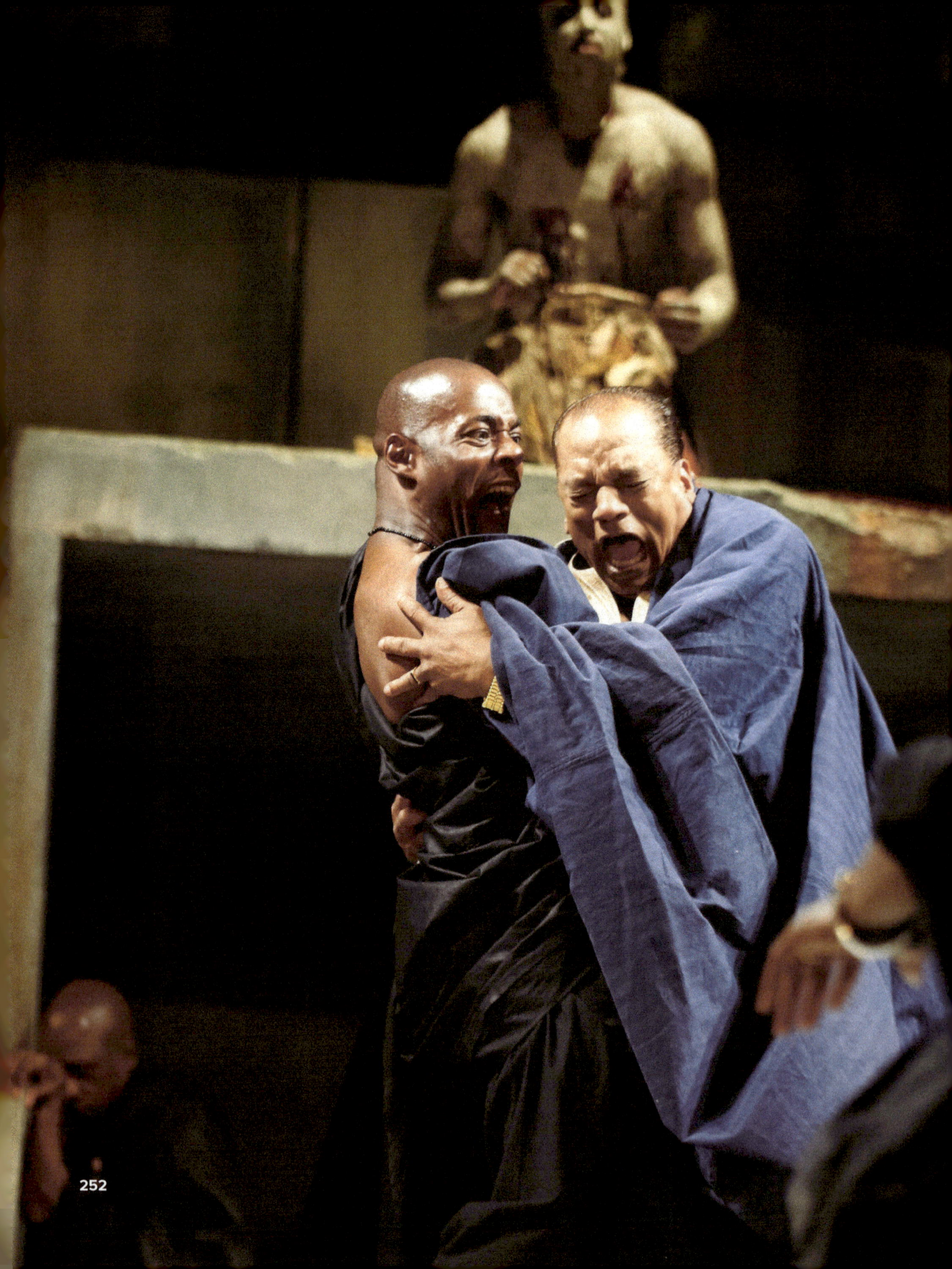

11

Theatrical Genres

When we attend a theatre performance, within the first fifteen minutes or so, we sense a tone and a mood that are being communicated. We become aware that those presenting the play—the playwright, the actors, the director—are signaling to the audience that they have adopted a definite point of view and attitude toward what is to follow. For example, in the opening scene of Shakespeare's *Hamlet,* the ghost of Hamlet's father appears to men on guard at the castle. It is an ominous, eerie scene that tells us this will be a serious play, perhaps even a tragedy. On the other hand, at the beginning of Shakespeare's *A Midsummer Night's Dream,* Theseus, the Duke of Athens, says: "Stir up the Athenian youth to merriment, awake the pert and nimble spirit of mirth," a clear sign that this will be a comedy.

TYPES OF DRAMA

In Greece in the fifth century BCE, where Western theatre began, the actors wore masks covering their faces when they performed. The Greeks took the idea of the mask to create symbols of the two kinds of plays presented at their dramatic festivals—the mask of tragedy and the mask of comedy—symbols that are still used today. Similarly, in Japan in the fourteenth century CE, a theatre called nō had become established as the serious form of drama. Alongside nō, however, was a comical, farcical type of drama called kyōgen.

In other words, wherever theatre has appeared, there has been a tendency to divide it into categories or types, often referred to by the French term *genre* (JAHN-ruh). In addition to tragedy and comedy, additional genres have developed: farce, melodrama, tragicomedy, and a number of others.

This tendency to divide dramatic works into categories is not confined to theatre. We find it widespread, not only in the arts, but in many aspects of life. Not only do those who create theatre adopt different points of view toward events and toward life in general; all of us do. Depending on our perspective, we can see the same subject as funny or sad, take it seriously or laugh at it, make it an object of pity or of

genre A French word meaning category. In theatre, genre denotes the category into which a play falls: for example, tragedy, comedy, or tragicomedy.

◀ **THEATRICAL GENRES**

Drama is often divided into categories or types, referred to as genres. The Greeks separated tragedy and comedy. To those two genres have been added tragicomedy and many others. Shown here is a scene from Shakespeare's tragedy Julius Caesar, *set in modern-day Africa with an all-Black cast. In this scene we see Paterson Joseph (left) as Brutus and Jeffery Kissoon as Caesar in a production by the Royal Shakespeare Company. (Geraint Lewis/Alamy Stock Photo)*

ridicule. Just why we look at events from different points of view is difficult to say, but there is no question that we do. The English author Horace Walpole (1717–1797) wrote: "This world is a comedy to those that think, a tragedy to those that feel."[1]

In theatre, this question of viewpoint—looking at people or events from a particular perspective—becomes crucial. Viewpoint is not taken for granted, as it is in everyday life; rather, it is a conscious act on the part of whoever creates the text. To take an example, in most cases death is considered a somber matter; but in *Arsenic and Old Lace* (1941), the dramatist Joseph Kesselring (1902–1967) makes it clear that we are to regard death in his play as comic. Kesselring presents two elderly women who kill no fewer than 12 old men by serving them arsenic in glasses of wine. But because the dramatist removes from the play any feeling that the deaths are to be taken seriously, he engenders in the audience the notion that it is all in fun.

Sometimes a playwright takes a serious subject matter and makes the audience uncomfortable through the humor generated. Jeremy O. Harris in *Slave Play* presents three interracial couples who, as a form of outrageous therapy, act out enslavement-era sexual fantasies to try to resolve their intimacy issues. Harris makes audiences constantly uncomfortable as they react to the exaggerated comedy in those scenes while at the same time recognizing the serious issues of race relations both intimate and societal and systemic racism.

Before examining genre, we should note that often a play does not fit neatly into a single category. Those who create a text do not write categories or types of plays; they write individual, unique works—and preoccupation with genre may distract us from the individuality of a play or a production. Still, if we keep these reservations in mind, we will find that it is helpful to understand the traditional genres into which much of Western dramatic literature has fallen.

TRAGEDY

Serious drama takes a thoughtful, sober attitude toward its subject matter. It puts the spectators in a frame of mind to think about what they are seeing and to become involved with the characters onstage: to love what these characters love, fear what they fear, and suffer what they suffer. The best-known form of serious drama, to which we turn first, is *tragedy*. Other forms of serious theatre are *heroic drama, domestic drama,* and *melodrama*.

tragedy A serious drama in which there is a downfall of the primary character.

Tragedy asks very basic questions about human existence. Why are people sometimes cruel to one another? Why is the world unjust? Why are human beings called on to endure suffering? What are the limits of human suffering and endurance? In the midst of cruelty and despair, what are the possibilities of human achievement? To what heights of courage, strength, generosity, and integrity can human beings rise? Tragedy assumes that the universe is indifferent to human concerns and often cruel and malevolent. Sometimes the innocent appear to suffer, whereas the evil prosper. In the face of this, some humans are capable of despicable deeds, but others can confront and overcome adversity, attaining a nobility that places them "a little lower than the angels." We can divide tragedy into two basic kinds: traditional and modern. *Traditional tragedy* includes works from several significant periods of the past. *Modern tragedy* generally includes plays from the late nineteenth century to the present day.

Traditional Tragedy

Tragic Protagonists Generally, the lead character, the protagonist, of a tragedy is an extraordinary person—a king, a queen, a general, a noble person—in other words, someone of stature. In Greek drama, Antigone, Electra, Oedipus, Agamemnon, Creon, and Orestes are members of royal families. In the plays of Shakespeare, Hamlet, Claudius, Gertrude, Lear, and Cordelia are also royal; Julius Caesar, Macbeth, and Othello are generals; and others—Ophelia, Romeo, and Juliet—are members of the nobility.

Tragic Circumstances The central figures of the play are caught in a series of tragic circumstances: Oedipus, without realizing it, murders his father and marries his mother; Antigone must choose between death and dishonoring her dead brother; Phaedra falls hopelessly and fatally in love with her stepson, Hippolytus; Othello is completely duped by Iago; and Lear is cast out by the daughters to whom he has given his kingdom. In traditional tragedy, the universe seems determined to trap the hero or heroine in a fateful web and for that character to suffer a tragic fall.

MAJOR CHARACTERS CAUGHT IN A TRAGIC WEB
In traditional tragedy the fall of a hero or heroine has a special significance because of the combination of his or her personality and position. An example of a tragic heroine is the Duchess of Malfi in the play of the same name by John Webster. Despite her title and station in life, the duchess is taunted and destroyed by her evil brothers when she marries someone of a lower social rank. Seen here are Ursina Lardi in the title role and Robert Beyer as Bosola, one of the brothers, in a production at the Schaubuehne Theatre in Berlin, Germany. (Ullstein Bild/Getty Images)

Tragic Irretrievability The situation becomes irretrievable: There is no turning back. The tragic figures are in a situation from which there is no honorable avenue of escape; they must go forward to meet their fate.

Tragic Flaw The tragic character is also flawed, which leads to the tragic circumstances and heightens the tragic irretrievability. In Greek, the term used by the philosopher Aristotle was *hamartia,* a human weakness in the tragic character. That weakness leads to the tragic character's eventual downfall. In most tragedies, the flaw is *hubris* or excessive pride. Oedipus thinks he can outwit his fate. Phaedra believes that she can have her inappropriate lover, her stepson.

Acceptance of Responsibility The heroic characters accept responsibility for their actions, recognizing their tragic flaws, and also show an immense capacity for suffering. Oedipus puts out his own eyes; Antigone faces death with equanimity; Othello kills himself. King Lear suffers immensely, living through personal humiliation, a raging storm on a heath, temporary insanity, and the death of his daughter, and finally confronts his own death. A statement by Edgar in *King Lear* applies to all tragic figures: "Men must endure their going hence even as their coming hither."[2]

hamartia ("hah-MARH-tee-ah") Ancient Greek term usually translated as "tragic flaw." The literal translation is "missing the mark," which may suggest that hamartia is not so much a character flaw as an error in judgment.

hubris ("HEW-brihs") Ancient Greek term usually defined as "excessive pride" and cited as a common tragic character flaw.

Tragic Verse The language of traditional tragedy is verse. Because it deals with lofty and profound ideas—with human beings at the outer limits of their lives—tragedy soars to the heights and descends to the depths of human experience, and many feel that such thoughts and emotions can best be expressed in poetry. Look at Cleopatra's lament on the death of Mark Antony. Her sense of admiration for Antony, and her desolation, could never be conveyed so tellingly in less poetic terms:

> Oh, wither'd is the garland of war,
> The soldier's pole is fall'n! Young boys and girls
> Are level now with men. The odds is gone,
> And there is nothing left remarkable
> Beneath the visiting moon.[3]

These words have even more effect when heard in the theatre spoken by an eloquent actress.

The Effect of Tragedy   When the elements of traditional tragedy are combined, they appear to produce two contradictory reactions simultaneously. One is pessimism: The tragic characters are "damned if they do and damned if they don't," and the world is a cruel, uncompromising place, a world of despair. And yet, in even the bleakest tragedy—whether *Hamlet, Medea, Macbeth,* or *King Lear*—there is affirmation. One source of this positive feeling is found in the drama itself. Sophocles, Euripides, Shakespeare, and the French dramatist Jean Racine, although telling us that the world is in chaos and utterly lost, at the same time affirmed just the opposite by creating brilliant, carefully shaped works of art.

There is another positive element, which has to do with the tragic characters themselves. They meet their fate with such dignity and such determination that they defy the gods. They say: "Come and get me; throw your worst at me. Whatever happens, I will not surrender my individuality or my dignity." In Aeschylus's play *Prometheus Bound* the title character—who is one of the earliest tragic heroes—says: "On me the tempest falls. It does not make me tremble." In defeat, the men and women of tragedy triumph.

The Greek philosopher Aristotle in *The Poetics* (c. 335 BCE) attempted to describe the effect traditional tragedy had on the audience. He suggested that tragedy arouses pity and fear in the audience and that this genre purges the audience of those emotions. Spectators feel pity for the tragic hero caught in irretrievable circumstances and fear that if characters of noble stature can suffer falls, so could they. The purgation of these emotions, however, again reflects a positive outcome of tragedy.

As for the deeper meanings of individual tragedies, there is a vast literature on the subject, and each play has to be looked at and experienced in detail to obtain the full measure of its meaning. Certain tragedies seem to hold so much meaning, to contain so much—in substance and in echoes and reverberations—that one can spend a lifetime studying them.

Modern Tragedy

Tragedies of the modern period—that is, beginning in the late nineteenth century—do not have queens or kings as central figures, and they are written in prose rather than poetry. For these as well as more philosophical reasons, purists argue that modern tragedies are not true tragedies.

In answer to this, it should be pointed out that today we have few kings or queens—either in mythology or, except in certain places like Great Britain, in real life. At the same time, we may ask: Do we not have characters today who can stand as symbolic figures for important segments of society? Many would answer that we still do. In attempting to create modern tragedy, the question is not whether we view

A MODERN TRAGIC FAMILY
In Federico García Lorca's play *The House of Bernarda Alba,* a widow who has grown to hate and distrust men keeps her daughters confined as virtual prisoners in their own home, preventing them from going out. In this production, directed by Elizabeth Huddle at the Madison Repertory Theatre, we see four of the daughters, with the mother in the center. Left to right, the performers are Jamie England, Monica Lyons, Elisabeth Adwin, Margaret Ingraham, and Diane Robinson. (Zane Williams)

the human condition in the same way as the French did in the seventeenth century or the Greeks did in the fifth century BCE—those two societies did not view life in the same way either—but whether our age allows for a tragic view on its own terms.

The answer seems to be yes. Compared with either the eighteenth or the nineteenth century—ages of enlightenment, progress, and unbounded optimism—our age has its own tragic vision. Modern tragic dramatists probe the same depths and ask the same questions as did their predecessors: Why do men and women suffer? Why do violence and injustice exist? And perhaps most fundamental of all: What is the meaning of our lives?

On this basis, many commentators would argue that writers like Henrik Ibsen, Eugene O'Neill, Tennessee Williams, Arthur Miller, and August Wilson can lay claim to writing legitimate modern tragedy. The ultimate test of a play is not whether it meets someone's definition of tragedy, but what effect it produces in the theatre and how successful it is in standing up to continued scrutiny. Eugene O'Neill's *Long Day's Journey into Night* takes as bleak a look at the human condition with, at the same time, as compassionate a view of human striving and dignity as it seems possible to take in our day. The same could be said of Arthur Miller's *Death of a Salesman* and August Wilson's *Fences.*

HEROIC DRAMA

The term **heroic drama** is not used as commonly as *tragedy* or *comedy,* but there is a wide range of plays for which *heroic drama* seems an appropriate description. We use the term specifically to indicate serious drama of any period that incorporates heroic or noble figures and other features of traditional tragedy—dialogue in verse, extreme situations, and the like—but differs from tragedy in having a happy ending, or in assuming a basically optimistic worldview even when the ending is sad.

heroic drama Serious but basically optimistic drama written in verse or elevated prose, with noble or heroic characters in extreme situations or unusual adventures.

photo essay

Modern Domestic Drama

Serious drama in America came of age in the twentieth century, with plays by Eugene O'Neill, Lillian Hellman, Tennessee Williams, Arthur Miller, and August Wilson, among others. Though all four experimented with nonrealistic dramatic devices, much of their strongest work was realistic domestic drama. Included here are examples in photographs from recent productions.

Long Day's Journey Into Night by Eugene O'Neill with Paul Nicholls as the younger son, Edmund; Jessica Lange as Mary Tyrone; and Paul Rudd as James Tyrone, Jr.

(Rune Hellestad/Corbis/Getty Images)

Gillian Anderson as Blanche Dubois and Vanessa Kirby as her sister Stella in Tennessee Williams's *A Streetcar Named Desire* in a production at the Young Vic in London, directed by Benedict Andrews.

(Robbie Jack/Corbis/Getty Images)

A scene from *All My Sons* by Arthur Miller at the Old Vic in London in 2019, directed by Jeremy Herrin with Bill Pullman (Joe Keller) and Sally Field (Kate Keller)

(Guardian/eyevine/Redux)

John Benjamin Hickey, left, and Patrick Breen in Peter Parnell's *Dada Woof Papa Hot (2015)* at New York's Lincoln Center. The play explores the gay domestic life and parenthood.

(Sara Krulwich/The New York Times/Redux)

Several Greek plays ordinarily classified as tragedies are actually closer to heroic drama. In Sophocles's *Electra,* for instance, Electra suffers grievously, but at the end of the play she and her brother Orestes triumph. Another example is *The Cid,* written by Pierre Corneille (1606-1684) in France. It has a hero who leads his men to victory in battle but who is not killed; in the end, he wins a duel against his rival. In the late seventeenth century in England, a form of drama that was called *heroic drama,* or sometimes *heroic tragedy,* was precisely the type about which we are speaking: a serious play with a happy ending for the protagonist.

Many Asian plays—from India, China, and Japan—though deviating from the usual Western classifications by including, for example, a great deal of traditional dance and music, bear a close resemblance to heroic drama. Frequently, for example, a hero goes through a series of dangerous adventures, emerging victorious at the end. The vast majority of Asian dramas end happily.

A second type of heroic drama involves the death of the heroic protagonist, but the overall effect is not considered tragic. Several of the plays of Johann Wolfgang von Goethe (1749-1832) follow this pattern. (Many of Goethe's plays, along with those of his contemporaries in the late eighteenth century and early nineteenth century, form a subdivision of heroic drama referred to as *Romantic drama.* **Romanticism,** a literary movement that took hold in Germany at the time and spread to France and throughout much of Europe, celebrated the spirit of hope, personal freedom, and natural instincts.)

Romanticism Nineteenth-century dramatic movement that imitated the episodic structure of Shakespeare, and thematically focused on the gulf between human beings' spiritual aspirations and physical limitations.

A number of plays in the modern period fall into the category of heroic drama. *Saint Joan,* by George Bernard Shaw, is a good example: Although Joan is burned at the stake, her death is actually a form of triumph. As if that were not enough, Shaw provides an epilogue in which Joan appears alive again.

In the history of theatre, the plays we are discussing as *heroic drama* occupy a large and important niche, cutting across Asian and Western civilizations and across periods from the Greek golden age to the present.

BOURGEOIS OR DOMESTIC DRAMA

With the changes in society that resulted from the rise of the middle class and the shift from kings and queens to more democratic governments, we move from classic tragedy to modern tragedy. In the same way, during the past 150 years heroic drama has largely been replaced by **bourgeois or domestic drama.** *Bourgeois* refers to people of the middle or lower middle class rather than the aristocracy, and *domestic* means that the plays often deal with problems of the family or the home rather than great affairs of state. In the Greek, Roman, and Renaissance periods, ordinary people served as main characters only in comedies; they rarely appeared as heroes or heroines of serious plays. Beginning in the eighteenth century, however, as society changed, there was a call for serious drama about people with whom members of the audience could identify and who were like themselves.

bourgeois or domestic drama Drama dealing with problems—particularly family problems—of middle- and lower-class characters. There are serious and comic domestic dramas.

In England in 1731, George Lillo (1693-1739) wrote *The London Merchant,* a story of a merchant's apprentice who is led astray by a prostitute and betrays his good-hearted employer. This play, like others that came after it, dealt with recognizable people from the daily life of Britain, and audiences welcomed it.

From these beginnings, bourgeois or domestic drama developed through the balance of the eighteenth century and the whole of the nineteenth, until it achieved a

DOMESTIC DRAMA OF EVERYDAY LIFE
Domestic drama concerns itself with family problems: parents and children, husbands and wives, growing up, growing old. The characters in it are recognizable people, and it has long been a mainstay of modern drama. Shown here in a recent Broadway revival of Lorraine Hansberry's *A Raisin in the Sun* are Denzel Washington, Sophie Okonedo, Latanya Richardson Jackson, Bryce Clyde Jenkins, and Anika Noni Rose (from left to right). (Sara Krulwich/The New York Times/Redux)

place of prominence in the new realistic works of Ibsen, Strindberg, and Chekhov. In the mid-twentieth century, three major American playwrights of domestic drama emerged: Eugene O'Neill, Arthur Miller, and Tennessee Williams. O'Neill, in such plays as *The Iceman Cometh* and *Long Day's Journey into Night,* probed the depth of his characters' anguish as realistically as any dramatist of modern times. Miller, in *The Crucible* and *Death of a Salesman,* combined the tragic lives of its characters with political and moral investigations. Williams, the most lyrical of the three, in *The Glass Menagerie* and *A Streetcar Named Desire,* explored the limits of human sorrow and endurance.

These three were followed in the decades to come by other important American playwrights such as Lorraine Hansberry, Edward Albee, August Wilson, and Paula Vogel. Problems with society, struggles within a family, dashed hopes, and renewed determination are typical characteristics of domestic drama. When sufficiently penetrating or profound, domestic drama achieves the level of modern tragedy.

In one form or another, bourgeois or domestic drama has become the predominant form of serious drama throughout Europe and the United States during the past hundred years.

Chapter 11 *Theatrical Genres*

MELODRAMA

During the eighteenth and nineteenth centuries, one of the most popular forms of theatre was **melodrama.** The word, which comes from Greek, means "music drama" or "song drama." Its modern form was introduced by the French in the late eighteenth century and applied to plays that had background music of the kind we hear in movies: ominous chords underscoring a scene of suspense and lyrical music underscoring a love scene.

Among the effects for which melodrama generally strives is fright or horror. It has been said that melodrama speaks to the paranoia in all of us: the fear that someone is pursuing us or that disaster is about to overtake us. How often do we have a sense that others are ganging up on us or a premonition that we have a deadly disease?

Melodrama brings these fears to life; we see people stalked or terrorized, or innocent victims tortured. Murder mysteries and detective stories are almost invariably melodramas because they stress suspense, danger, and close brushes with disaster. This type of melodrama usually ends in one of two ways: Either the victims are maimed or murdered (in which case our worst paranoid fears are confirmed) or, after a series of dangerous episodes, they are rescued (in which case the play is like a bad dream from which we awaken to realize that we are safe in bed and everything is all right).

Probably the easiest way to understand melodrama is to look at film and television examples. Among the kinds of popular melodramas we are familiar with are *westerns, science fiction films, horror films, superhero films,* and *detective* or *spy films.* All of these emphasize heroes and villains, other stock characters such as sidekicks and love interests, and spectacular events and special effects. But the key to the melodramatic form, on stage and in film and television, is that good is almost always victorious over evil. These characteristics are also present in melodramatic plays.

Still another form of melodrama argues a political or moral issue. Melodrama invariably shows us good characters against bad characters. Therefore, a playwright who wants to make a strong political case will often write a melodrama in which the good characters represent the dramatist's point of view.

Traditional melodrama, with its moral outlook, happy ending, stock characters, use of background music, and emphasis on spectacle, developed in the nineteenth century. Still, a list of significant melodramas could range over most of theatre history and could include writers from Euripides through

melodrama Dramatic form made popular in the nineteenth century that emphasized action and spectacular effects and also used music to underscore the action; it had stock characters, usually with clearly defined villains and heroes.

MELODRAMA INTO MUSICAL
A popular nineteenth-century melodramatic character was Sweeney Todd who appeared in a number of plays. The villainous barber murders customers, and his partner Mrs. Lovett uses their bodies to make meat pies for sale. Stephen Sondheim, composer and lyricist, and Hugh Wheeler, book author, in their musical *Sweeney Todd,* transformed the villainous barber into a more sympathetic character seeking revenge against those who had harmed him, his wife, and his daughter. Shown here is 2018 production of *Sweeney Todd,* at the Coyoacanense Forum, Mexico City. (Valente Rosas/GDAPhoto/AP Images)

262 Part Four The Playwright and the Play

Shakespeare and his contemporaries to modern dramatists throughout Europe and the Americas because many types of serious drama, tragic and nontragic, frequently have strong melodramatic elements as well.

Aside from those taking a basically serious point of view, there are two other fundamental approaches to dramatic material. One is *comedy,* with its many forms and variations; the other is a mixture of the serious and the comic, called *tragicomedy.*

COMEDY

People who create *comedy* are not necessarily more frivolous or less concerned with important matters than people who create serious works; they may be extremely serious in their own way. Writers of comedy like Aristophanes, Molière, and George Bernard Shaw cared passionately about human affairs and their problems. But those with a comic view look at the world differently: with a smile or a deep laugh or an arched eyebrow. Writers like these perceive the follies and excesses of human behavior and develop a keen sense of the ridiculous, with the result that they show us things that make us laugh.

comedy In general, a play that is light in tone, is concerned with issues that point out the excesses and folly of human behavior, has a happy ending, and is designed to amuse.

It should also be noted that there are many kinds of laughter. They range all the way from mild amusement at a witty saying or a humorous situation, to a belly laugh at some wild physical comedy, to cruel, derisive laughter. Theatre, which reflects life and society, encompasses comedies that display a similar range, from light comedies to outrageous farces.

Characteristics of Comedy

If we cannot fully explain comedy, we can at least understand some of the principles that make it possible.

Suspension of Natural Laws One characteristic of most comedy is a temporary suspension of the natural laws of probability, cause and effect, and logic. Actions do not have the consequences they do in real life. In comedy, when a haughty person walking down the street steps on a child's skateboard and goes sprawling on the sidewalk, we do not fear for their safety or wonder if they have any bruises. The focus in comedy is on the person being tripped up and getting appropriate comeuppance.

In burlesque, a comic character can be hit on the backside with a fierce thwack, and we laugh, because we know that it does not hurt anything but the character's pride. At one point in stage history a special stick consisting of two thin slats of wood held closely together was developed to make hitting someone more frightening. The stick was known as a *slapstick,* a name that came to describe all kinds of raucous, physical, knockabout comedy.

slapstick Type of comedy, or comic business, that relies on ridiculous physical activity—often violent in nature—for its humor.

Prime examples of the suspension of natural laws in comedy are found in film and television cartoons. In animated cartoons, characters are hurled through the air like missiles, are shot full of holes, and are flattened on the sidewalk when they fall from buildings. But they always get up, with little more than a shake of the head. In the audience, there are no thoughts of real injury, of cuts or bruises, because the cause-and-effect chain of everyday life is not operating.

Under these conditions, a significant accident, resulting in physical harm, itself can be viewed as comic. In the 2015 award-winning London backstage comedy *The Play That Goes Wrong,* created by members of the Mischief Theatre Company, a cast member of a disaster-prone fictional production is knocked unconscious but miraculously revives only

SUSPENSION OF NATURAL LAWS IN COMEDY

Frequently in various kinds of comedy, particularly in farce, our natural reaction to events is reordered to achieve a comic effect, and the audience accepts this. An excellent example is the play *Arsenic and Old Lace* by Joseph Kesselring, in which two elderly women, who appear to be helpless and harmless, actually murder a number of old men by giving them elderberry wine laced with poison. Because we have accepted the comic premise of the play; however, we do not condemn their acts, as we might in a melodrama, but rather become amused. Shown here is a German production of the play staged in 2001 with Michael von Rospatt, Gerda Gmelin, and Eva Maria Bauer (from left). (Ullstein Bild/Getty Images)

to find that her replacement, a technician, will not give up the role. We do not really think of the character as being rendered unconscious, and we have none of the feelings one usually has for an accident victim. The idea of suffering and harm has been suspended, and we are free to laugh at the irony and incongruity of the situation.

The Comic Premise The suspension of natural laws in comedy makes possible the development of a *comic premise*. The comic premise is an idea or concept that turns the accepted notion of things upside down and makes this upended notion the basis of a play. The premise can provide thematic and structural unity and can serve as a springboard for comic dialogue, comic characters, and comic situations.

Aristophanes, the Greek satiric dramatist, was a master at developing a comic premise. In *The Clouds,* Aristophanes pictures Socrates as a man who can think only when perched in a basket suspended in midair. In *The Birds,* two ordinary men persuade a chorus of birds to build a city between heaven and earth. The birds comply, calling the place Cloudcuckoo Land, and the two men sprout wings to join them. In another play, *Lysistrata,* Aristophanes has the women of Greece agree to go on a sex strike to end a

comic premise Idea or concept in a comedy that turns the accepted notion of things upside down.

264 Part Four The Playwright and the Play

war: They will not make love to their husbands until the husbands stop fighting and sign a peace treaty with their opponents.

Techniques of Comedy

The suspension of natural laws and the establishment of a comic premise in comedy involve exaggeration and incongruity. **Incongruity** usually refers to a character's inappropriate behavior or actions for a specific circumstance resulting in our laughter. The contradictions that result from these show up in three areas—verbal humor, characterization, and comic situations.

Verbal Humor
Verbal humor can be anything from a pun to the most sophisticated discourse. A *pun*—usually considered the simplest form of wit—is a humorous use of words with the same sound but different meanings. Someone who says they are going to start a bakery if they can "raise the dough" is making a pun.

Close to the pun is the *malaprop*—a word that sounds like the right word but actually means something quite different. The term comes from Mrs. Malaprop, a character in *The Rivals* by the English playwright Richard Brinsley Sheridan (1751-1816). Mrs. Malaprop wants to impress everyone with her education and erudition but ends up doing just the opposite because she constantly misuses long words. For example, she insists that her daughter is not "illegible" for marriage, meaning that her daughter is not "ineligible," and when asked to explain a situation, she says that someone else will provide the "perpendiculars" when she means the "particulars."

A sophisticated form of verbal humor is the *epigram*. Oscar Wilde (1854-1900), a playwright devoted to verbal humor, often turned accepted values upside down in his epigrams. "I can resist anything except temptation," says one of his characters, and "A man cannot be too careful in the choice of his enemies," says another.[4]

VERBAL HUMOR
One key element of comedy is verbal wit. No one was more the master of wit than playwright Oscar Wilde, whose epigrams and clever word play are still quoted today. Shown here is a scene from his play *The Importance of Being Earnest* in a production at the Aldwych Theatre in London featuring Maggie Smith and Richard E. Grant. (Robbie Jack/Corbis/Getty Images)

Comedy of Character
In comedy of character the discrepancy or incongruity lies in the way characters see themselves or pretend to be, as opposed to the way they actually are. A good example is a person who pretends to be a doctor—using obscure medicines, hypodermic needles, and Latin jargon—but who is actually a fake. Such a person is the chief character in Molière's *The Doctor in Spite of Himself*. Another example of incongruity of character is Molière's *The Would-Be Gentleman*, in which the title character, Monsieur Jourdain, a man of wealth but without taste or refinement, is determined to learn courtly behavior. He hires a fencing master, a dancing master, and a teacher of literature to teach him these skills, but in every case Jourdain is ridiculed.

incongruity In comedy, incongruity usually refers to a character's inappropriate behavior or actions for a specific circumstance resulting in our laughter.

Comedy of character is also a basic ingredient of Italian *commedia dell'arte* and all forms of comedy where stock characters, stereotypes, and characters with dominant traits are emphasized.

We can also find examples of comedies of characters today in film and on television. The popular TV show *Schitt's Creek* focuses on a quirky family members who have lost their wealth and the rural townspeople they now live with; much of the comedy is created by their unusual exaggerated behaviors and relationships.

Plot Complications Still another way the contradictory or the ludicrous manifests itself in comedy is in plot complications, including coincidences and mistaken identity. A time-honored comic plot is Shakespeare's *The Comedy of Errors,* based on *The Menaechmi,* a play of the late third century BCE by the Roman writer Titus Maccius Plautus (c. 254–184 BCE). *The Comedy of Errors* in turn was the basis of a successful American musical comedy, *The Boys from Syracuse,* with songs by Richard Rodgers (1902–1979) and Lorenz Hart (1895–1943). In *The Comedy of Errors,* identical twins and their identical twin servants were separated when young. As the play opens, however, both masters and both servants—unknown to one another—are in one place. The confusion among the twin brothers and the twin servants leads to an endless series of comic encounters.

A classic scene of plot complication occurs in Sheridan's *The School for Scandal,* written in 1777. Joseph Surface, the main character in the play, is thought to be upstanding but is really a charlatan, whereas Charles, his brother, is mistakenly considered a reprobate. In a famous scene called the "screen scene," both Lady Teazle, a married woman visiting Surface, and her husband, Sir Peter Teazle, are hidden, one behind a screen, one in a closet. When the honest Charles suddenly appears he discovers both of them, exposing their deceptions at a single moment.

farce A subclass of comedy with emphasis on exaggerated plot complications and with few or no intellectual pretensions.

Forms of Comedy

Comedy takes various forms, depending on the dramatist's intent and on the comic techniques emphasized.

Farce Most plays discussed in the section earlier on plot complications are *farces*. Farce thrives on exaggeration—not only plot complications but also broad physical humor and stereotyped characters. It has no intellectual pretensions but aims rather at entertainment and provoking laughter. In addition to excessive plot complications, its

PLOT COMPLICATIONS: A HALLMARK OF FARCE
Frequently used devices of comedy include twists and turns in the plot, mistaken identity, unexpected developments, and ridiculous situations. Michael Frayn's comedy *Noises Off* contains an abundance of these elements. The production shown here was directed by Lindsay Posner in London. (Geraint Lewis/Alamy Stock Photo)

266 Part Four The Playwright and the Play

> ### PLAYING YOUR PART: EXPERIENCING THEATRE
>
> 1. What recent event in everyday life has been described as a "tragedy"? Would that event meet the traditional definition of tragedy? Does it have the elements of traditional tragedy?
> 2. Is there a contemporary figure whose life you believe could be dramatized as a "modern tragedy"? Describe.
> 3. Have you seen a film or television show that could be categorized as "domestic drama"? What are its characteristics that lead you to that categorization?
> 4. Have you seen a recent film that you would categorize as a "melodrama"? What are its characteristics that lead you to that categorization?
> 5. Have you seen films or television shows that could be categorized as farce, burlesque, satire, domestic comedy, comedy of manners, or comedy of characters?
> 6. Can you describe any current events that might be dramatized as tragicomedy? Why?

humor results from ridiculous situations, as well as pratfalls and horseplay, not on the verbal wit found in more intellectual forms of comedy. Mock violence, rapid movement, and accelerating pace are hallmarks of farce. Marriage and sex are the objects of fun in *bedroom farce,* but farce can also poke fun at medicine, law, and business.

Burlesque

Burlesque also relies on knockabout physical humor, as well as gross exaggerations and, occasionally, vulgarity. Historically, burlesque was a ludicrous imitation of other forms of drama or of an individual play. An example was the take-off of the hit musical *Hamilton*, entitled *Spamilton*. In the United States, the term *burlesque* came to describe a type of variety show featuring low comedy skits and attractive women.

burlesque A ludicrous, comic imitation of a dramatic form, play, piece of literature, or other popular entertainment.

Satire

A form related to traditional burlesque, but with more intellectual and moral or political content, is *satire.* Satire uses wit, irony, and exaggeration to attack or expose evil and foolishness. Satire can attack specific figures; for example, the frequently updated and revised revue *Forbidden Broadway* makes fun of the more flamboyant or excessive stars as well as plots and storylines of Broadway musicals. It can also be more inclusive, as in the case of Molière's *Tartuffe*, which ridicules religious hypocrisy generally.

satire Comic form, using irony and exaggeration, to attack and expose folly and vice.

Domestic Comedy

The comic equivalent of domestic or bourgeois drama is *domestic comedy.* Usually dealing with family situations, it is found most frequently today in television situation comedies—often called *sitcoms*—which feature members of a family or residents of a neighborhood caught in a series of complicated but amusing situations. Television shows such as *The Simpsons, Modern Family, Black-ish,* and *Schitt's Creek* are examples. This type of comedy was once a staple of theatre and can still be found onstage in the often revived plays by Neil Simon (1927–2018).

Comedy of Manners

Comedy of manners is concerned with pointing up the foibles and peculiarities of the upper classes. Against a cultivated, sophisticated background, it uses verbal wit to depict the cleverness and expose the social pretensions

comedy of manners Form of comic drama that became popular in the English Restoration, that is set within sophisticated society, while poking fun at its characters' social pretensions, usually through verbal wit.

Chapter 11 *Theatrical Genres*

photo essay

Forms of Comedy

(Donald Cooper/Photostage)

Comedy takes a number of forms, depending on whether the emphasis is on verbal wit, plot complications, or the characters' eccentricities. It can range all the way from intellectual comedy, to high comedy (dealing with the upper classes), to domestic comedy (similar to sitcoms on TV), to slapstick farce. Shown here is a variety of types of comedy.

Shown here is Owain Arthur as Francis Henshall in *One Man, Two Guvnors,* a farce by Richard Bean after Goldoni's *The Servant of Two Masters,* in a production directed by Nicholas Hytner at the National Theatre, London.

Shown here are David Shiner, left, and Bill Irwin performing in *Old Hats,* a slapstick comedy they created at the Pershing Square Signature Center, directed by Tina Landau.

(Sara Krulwich/The New York Times/Redux)

268

of its characters. Rather than horseplay, it stresses witty phrases. In comedy of manners, pointed barbs are always at a premium. In England a line of comedies of manners runs from William Wycherley, William Congreve, and Oliver Goldsmith (1730–1774) in the seventeenth and eighteenth centuries to Oscar Wilde in the nineteenth century and Noël Coward (1899–1973) in the twentieth.

Comedy of Ideas Many of George Bernard Shaw's plays could be put under a special heading, *comedy of ideas,* because Shaw used comic techniques to debate intellectual propositions and to further his own moral and social point of view. Though witty and amusing, Shaw's plays frequently include provocative discussions of controversial social issues. *Mrs. Warren's Profession,* for example, about a woman who runs a house of prostitution, deals with hypocrisy in society and *Arms and the Man* is not only an amusing story of a pompous soldier but also a treatise on war and heroism.

COMEDY OF MANNERS
Comedy of manners usually deals with the upper class in a given society. It stresses verbal humor, repartee, and irony. The precursors of modern comedy of manners were the Restoration comedies popular in London in the late seventeenth century. In the nineteenth century, Oscar Wilde was a master of comedy of manners, and in the twentieth century it was Noël Coward. One of Coward's best-known plays is *Private Lives,* about two upper-class couples whose marriages become comically entangled. Seen here is a 2013 Chichester Festival Theatre production directed by Jonathan Kent, with Anna-Louise Plowman as Sibyl Chase, Toby Stephens as Elyot Chase, Anna Chancellor as Amanda Prynne, Anthony Calf as Victor Prynne (Geraint Lewis/Alamy Stock Photo)

In all its forms, comedy remains a way of looking at the world in which basic values are asserted but natural laws are suspended in order to underline human follies and foolishness—sometimes with a rueful look, sometimes with a wry smile, and sometimes with an uproarious laugh.

TRAGICOMEDY

In twentieth-century theatre a new genre came to the forefront—*tragicomedy.* In this section, we examine this form that has proved so important in the modern period.

What Is Tragicomedy?

In the past, comedy has usually been set in opposition to tragedy or serious drama: Serious drama is sad, comedy is funny; serious drama makes people cry, comedy makes them laugh; serious drama arouses anger, comedy brings a smile. True, the comic view of life differs from the serious view, but the two are not always as clearly separated as this polarity suggests. Many comic dramatists are serious people; "I laugh to keep from crying" applies to many comic writers, as well as to certain clowns and comedians. A great deal of serious drama contains comic elements.

comedy of ideas A comedy in which the humor is based on intellectual and verbal aspects of comedy rather than physical comedy or comedy of character. A drama whose emphasis is on the clash of ideas, as exemplified in the plays of George Bernard Shaw.

tragicomedy During the Renaissance, a play having tragic themes and noble characters but a happy ending; today, a play in which serious and comic elements are integrated. Many plays of this type present a comic or ironic treatment of a serious theme.

Chapter 11 *Theatrical Genres*

Shakespeare, for instance, included comic characters in several of his serious plays. The drunken porter in *Macbeth,* the gravedigger in *Hamlet,* and Falstaff in *Henry IV, Part 1* are examples.

In medieval plays, comic scenes are interpolated in the basically religious subject matter. One of the best-known of all medieval plays, *The Second Shepherds' Play,* concerns the visit of the shepherds to the manger of the newborn Christ child. While they stop in a field to spend the night, Mak, a comic character, steals a sheep and takes it to his house, where he and his wife pretend that it is their baby. When the shepherds discover what Mak has done, they toss him in a blanket, and after this horseplay the serious part of the story resumes.

The alternation of serious and comic elements is a practice of long standing, particularly in episodic plays; but *tragicomedy* does not refer to plays that shift from serious to comic and back again. It is a view in which one eye looks through a comic lens and the other through a serious lens, and the two points of view are so intermingled as to be one, like food that tastes sweet and sour at the same time. In addition to his basically serious plays and his basically comic plays, Shakespeare wrote others that seem to be a combination of tragedy and comedy, such as *Measure for Measure* and *All's Well That Ends Well.* Because they do not fit neatly into one category or the other, these plays have proved troublesome to critics—so troublesome that they have been officially dubbed *problem plays.*

The "problem," however, arises largely because of the difficulty in accepting the tragicomic point of view, for these plays have many of the attributes of the fusion of the tragic and the comic. A sense of comedy pervades these plays, the idea that all will end well and that much of what happens is ludicrous or ridiculous; at the same time, the serious effects of a character's actions are not dismissed. Unlike true comedy, in which a fall on the sidewalk or a temporary danger has no serious consequences, these plays contain actions that appear quite serious. And so we have tragicomedy.

Modern Tragicomedy

In the modern period—during the past hundred years or so—tragicomedy has become the primary approach of many of the best playwrights. As suggested in the chapter "The Audience," these writers are not creating in a vacuum; they are part of the world in which they live, and ours is an age

COMBINING TRAGEDY AND COMEDY
Tragicomedy has become more and more prominent in the modern period and has taken its place alongside traditional tragedy, comedy, and other genres as a major form of our time. In several of Shakespeare's so-called problem plays, comic and serious elements are intermixed in the manner of contemporary tragicomedy. A good example is *All's Well That Ends Well,* which features a strange, almost bizarre, mixture of fairy-tale elements with cynical realism. Shown here is James Garnon as Parolles in a London production at Shakespeare's Globe Theatre, directed by John Dove. (Geraint Lewis/Alamy Stock Photo)

270 Part Four The Playwright and the Play

COMEDIES OF MENACE
Comedies range widely, from the pure entertainment of farce and light comedy to more substantive and probing comedies with a strong serious component. The playwright Harold Pinter calls many of his plays comedies of menace, meaning that they can provoke laughter but also have a deeper, more disturbing, sometimes frightening element. One of Pinter's best-known plays exemplifying this is *The Birthday Party*. Shown here are Timothy West as Goldberg and Nigel Terry as McCann in a production of the play at the Piccadilly Theatre in London. (Sean Dempsey/PA Images/Alamy Stock Photo)

that has adopted a tragicomic viewpoint more extensively than most previous ages. As if to keynote this attitude and set the tone, the Danish philosopher Søren Kierkegaard (1813-1855) in 1842 wrote: "Existence itself, the act of existence, is a striving and is both pathetic and comic in the same degree."[5]

The plays of Anton Chekhov, written at the turn of the twentieth century, reflect the spirit described by Kierkegaard. Chekhov called two of his major plays *comedies,* but Stanislavski, who directed them, called them *tragedies*—an indication of the confusion arising from Chekhov's mixture of the serious and the comic.

An example of Chekhov's approach is a scene at the end of the third act of *Uncle Vanya* (1899). The lives of Vanya and his niece, Sonya, have been ruined by Sonya's father, a professor. At the moment where Sonya tells her father how cruel and thoughtless he is, Vanya comes in, waving a pistol in the air, and shoots twice at the

Chapter 11 *Theatrical Genres*   271

professor, but misses both times. There is some doubt that Vanya honestly means to kill the professor, and the scene itself is both tragic and comic: The two elements are inextricably joined together.

Theatre of the absurd (discussed later) is an example of modern tragicomedy. It probes deeply into human problems and casts a cold eye on the world, and yet it is also imbued with a comic spirit. The plays of Harold Pinter (1930–2008), a writer associated with theatre of the absurd, have been called *comedies of menace,* a phrase suggesting the idea of a theatre simultaneously terrifying and entertaining.

As we have noted earlier, many contemporary domestic dramas mix the serious and comic. Tracy Letts's *August: Osage County* (2007) and the previously discussed *Slave Play* by Jeremy O. Harris are examples of tragicomic plays that deal with domestic relationships mixing serious subject matter and comic circumstances in a seamless fashion.

THEATRE OF THE ABSURD

theatre of the absurd
Twentieth-century plays expressing the dramatists' sense of absurdity and futility of human existence through the dramatic techniques they employ.

After World War II, a new type of theatre emerged in Europe and the United States, which the critic Martin Esslin called **theatre of the absurd.** Although the dramatists whose work falls into this category do not write in identical styles and are not really a "school" of writers, they do have enough in common to be considered together. Esslin took the name for this form of theatre from a quotation in *The Myth of Sisyphus* by the French writer, dramatist, and philosopher Albert Camus (1913–1960). In *The Myth of Sisyphus,* Camus says that in the modern age there is a separation between "man and his life, the actor and his setting," and that this separation "constitutes the feeling of Absurdity."[6]

Plays falling into the category of absurdism convey humanity's sense of alienation and its loss of bearings in an illogical, unjust, and ridiculous world. Although serious, this viewpoint is generally depicted in plays with considerable humor; an ironic note runs through much of theatre of the absurd.

A prime example of theatre of the absurd is Beckett's *Waiting for Godot.* In this play Beckett has given us one of the most telling expressions of loneliness and futility ever written: two tramps on a barren plain waiting every day for a supreme being called "Godot," who they think will come but who never does. At the same time, they themselves are comic. They wear baggy pants like burlesque comedians and engage in any number of vaudeville routines. Also, the characters frequently say one thing and do just the opposite. One says to the other, "Well, shall we go?" and the other says, "Yes, let's go." But having said this, they don't move.

Absurdist plays suggest the idea of absurdity both in what they say—that is, their content—and in the way they say it, their form. Their structure, therefore, is a departure from dramatic structures of the past.

Absurdist Plots: Illogicality

Traditional plots in drama proceed in a logical way from a beginning through the development of the plot to a conclusion, an arrangement that suggests an ordered universe. In contrast, many absurdist plays not only proclaim absurdity but also embody it.

THEATRE OF THE ABSURD
Non sequitur, nonsensical language, existential characters, ridiculous situations—these are hallmarks of theatre of the absurd, which can also be viewed as a type of tragicomedy. One classic example is Samuel Beckett's *Waiting for Godot.* Shown here are Patrick Stewart as Vladimir and Ian McKellan as Estragon in a 2009 London production that came to Broadway in 2013 and was directed by Sean Mathias. (Bruce Glikas/FilmMagic/Getty Images)

TRAGICOMEDY: FUNNY AND SAD AT THE SAME TIME
Several plays by the Russian writer Anton Chekhov could be described as tragicomedies containing elements of both comedy and tragedy mixed together in a profound way. The scene here is from Chekhov's *Uncle Vanya* with June Watson as Marina, Ken Stott as Vanya, Paul Freeman as Serebryakov, and Anna Friel as Yelena. Directed by Lindsay Posner, the production was at the Vaudeville Theatre in London. (Robbie Jack/Corbis/Getty Images)

PLAYING YOUR PART: THINKING ABOUT THEATRE

1. A play by Henrik Ibsen, Anton Chekhov, Tennessee Williams, Lorraine Hansberry, or August Wilson might be set in a time fifty years ago or a hundred years ago. What do you think it is about these dramas that allow audience members in the twenty-first century to identify strongly with the characters and the situations in the play?

2. Which kind of play do you prefer: a classic tragedy, a serious contemporary drama, a knockabout farce, a comedy, a musical? Can you explain why you prefer one type over the others?

3. Do you favor a play with a strong storyline, a tight plot, and unexpected twists and turns? Or do you prefer a looser play that reflects the randomness of everyday life? What do you think attracts you to these characteristics?

An example is *The Bald Soprano* by Eugène Ionesco. The very title of the play turns out to be nonsense; a bald soprano is mentioned once in the play, but with no explanation, and it is clear that the bald soprano has nothing whatever to do with the play as a whole. The absurdity of the piece is manifest the moment the curtain goes up. A typical English couple are sitting in a living room when the clock on the mantle strikes seventeen times; the wife's first words are, "There, it's nine o'clock."

Absurdist Language: Nonsense and Non Sequitur

Events and characters are frequently illogical in theatre of the absurd, and so, too, is language. *Non sequitur* is a Latin term meaning "it does not follow"; it implies that something does not follow from what has gone before, and it perfectly describes the method of theatre of the absurd. Sentences do not follow in sequence, and words do not mean what we expect them to mean.

An example of the irrationality or debasement of language is found in Beckett's *Waiting for Godot*. The character of Lucky does not speak for most of his time onstage, but at the end of the first act he delivers a long speech consisting of incoherent religious and legalistic jargon. The opening lines offer a small sample:

> Given the existence as uttered forth in the public works of Puncher and Wattmann of a personal God quaquaquaqua with white beard quaquaquaqua outside time without extension who from the heights of divine apathia divine athambia divine aphasia loves us dearly with some exceptions for reasons unknown but time will tell. . . .[7]

Numerous examples of such language appear not only in Ionesco's and Beckett's plays but in plays written by many other absurdist writers.

Absurdist Characters: Existential Beings

A significant feature of absurdist plays is the handling of characters. Not only is there an element of the ridiculous in the characters' actions, but they frequently exemplify an *existential* point of view. In theatre, existentialism suggests that characters have no personal history and therefore no specific causes for their actions. The two main characters in *Waiting for Godot,* for example, are devoid of biography and personal motivation; we know nothing of their family life or their occupations. They meet every day at a crossroads to wait for Godot, but how long they have been coming there, or what they do when they are not there, remains a mystery.

In addition to the plays of the absurdists, other modern plays incorporate the tragicomic spirit with a mixture of absurdism and realism. In *The Visit,* by Friedrich Dürrenmatt (1921–1990), a Swiss dramatist, a wealthy woman returns to her birthplace, a small, poverty-stricken village. She offers a huge sum of money to the village on the condition that the citizens murder a storekeeper who wronged her when she was young. The townspeople express horror at the idea, but at the same time they begin buying expensive items on credit—some from the man's own store. There is a comic and almost absurdist quality to these scenes, but the conclusion is not funny, for the man is eventually murdered by his greedy neighbors. There is also a recognizable reality to the evil committed.

In tragicomedy, a smile is frequently cynical, a chuckle may be tinged with a threat, and laughter is sometimes bitter. In the past, the attitude that produced these combinations was the exception rather than the rule. In our day, it seems far more prevalent, not to say relevant. As a result, tragicomedy has taken its place as a major form alongside the more traditional approaches.

MUSICAL THEATRE

Musical theatre is a contemporary popular form that developed in the United States but is now a global phenomenon. As we shall see, musical theatre combines a text (the book), music (sometimes original, sometimes previously composed), lyrics (words set to the music), and dance to tell a story on stage. The seamless integration of all of these elements is what makes the musical theatre unique and popular.

At one time, musical theatre was frequently referred to as musical comedy because so many of the early books were comedic; however, musicals also frequently deal with serious or tragicomic subjects. And some book musicals are based on melodramatic plays and films. This popular form, therefore, borrows from many of the genres we have previously discussed.

Antecedents

A close relative and predecessor to musical theatre is opera. Opera can be defined as a drama set entirely to music. With rare exceptions, every part of the performance is sung, including not only the *arias,* long solo songs with orchestral accompaniment, but also the transitional sections between them, known as *recitatives.* Having begun in Florence, Italy, around 1600 as drama set to music, operas have been written to the present day in continental Europe, the United Kingdom and the United States. In the later fifteen century and early sixteenth century, another dramatic art form, ballet, also began in Italy, especially in the Italian Courts of that time. These two art forms have continued to develop and flourish through the centuries since then.

In the nineteenth century, melodrama used music to accompany the action of plays. Singing and dancing also played a key role in other forms of nineteenth-century theatrical entertainment, such as vaudeville and burlesque. Another form that developed in the late nineteenth century was operetta—a romantic musical piece featuring melodic solos, duets, and choruses interspersed with spoken dialogue. Examples of operetta include the works from Great Britain of W. S. Gilbert (1836-1911) and Arthur Sullivan (1842-1900), such as *The Pirates of Penzance* (1879) and *The Mikado* (1885). The American composer Victor Herbert (1859-1924) also composed operettas, such as *Naughty Marietta* (1910).

At the turn of the twentieth century, the popular syncopated rhythms of ragtime had a strong influence on the emerging musical theatre and served as a bridge for several talented African Americans. Bob Cole (1864-1912) and William Johnson (1873-1954) conceived, wrote, produced, and directed the first Black musical comedy, *A Trip to Coontown* (1898). The comedians Bert Williams (c. 1876-1922) and George Walker (1873-1911) and their wives joined composers and writers to produce musicals and operettas such as *In Dahomey* (1902) and *Abyssinia* (1906), in which Americans for the first time saw Blacks on the Broadway stage without burnt-cork makeup, speaking without dialect, and costumed in high fashion.

In the early twentieth century, the musical shows of George M. Cohan (1878-1942), such as *Little Johnny Jones* (1904) and *Forty-Five Minutes from Broadway* (1906), had songs with an American flavor and more realistic dialogue and better plot development

OPERETTA: A FORERUNNER OF MUSICAL THEATRE
In the last quarter of the nineteenth-century operetta, a form of light opera, became immensely popular in Great Britain. It was a predecessor to the American musical, which came to full maturity in the twentieth century and is the one theatrical genre originated solely by American talent. Shown here is a scene from Gilbert and Sullivan's operetta *The Pirates of Penzance* by W. S. Gilbert and Arthur Sullivan, featuring performers Victoria Joyce and Mark Wilde in a production at the London Coliseum. (Nigel Norrington/Camera Press/Redux)

than earlier musicals. Cohan's shows moved a step closer to today's "book" musicals—musicals that tell a story. (The dialogue and action of a musical are sometimes called the ***book***, though the term libretto is also used.) Around the time of World War I and in the period following, a truly Native American musical began to emerge. It featured a story that was typically frivolous combined with enduring popular songs.

The Book Musical Is Born

Musicals with Black themes were presented on Broadway in the 1920s, some of them written by African Americans, including *Shuffle Along* (1921), with lyrics and music by Noble Sissle (1889–1975) and Eubie Blake (1883–1983). This groundbreaking musical was adapted by Black director-playwright George C. Wolfe (b. 1954) into *Shuffle Along, or the Making of the Musical Sensation of 1921,* which premiered on Broadway in 2016. Wolfe is also the author of the musical *Jelly's Last Jam* (1991).

In 1927, Oscar Hammerstein II (1895–1960), who wrote the lyrics and libretto, and Jerome Kern (1885–1945), who composed the music, combined some of the best aspects of operetta and musical comedy to create *Show Boat.* The story was thoroughly American, rather than an exotic romantic fable, and it dealt with serious material—including the then-controversial love story of a Black woman and a white man. It was also innovative in that the songs were integrated into the plot. (It should be noted, however, that like many early musicals, for later generations, there are offensive racial stereotypes in the text.)

Chapter 11 *Theatrical Genres*

SHOW BOAT: A LANDMARK MUSICAL
When *Show Boat* opened in 1927, it began a new chapter in the history of the American musical. The chorus line was eliminated, miscegenation (a romance between a white man and a Black woman) was treated for the first time, and other problems facing African Americans were touched on. Also, it had a glorious score by Jerome Kern and Oscar Hammerstein. Shown here is a revival staged by Harold Prince. (Anacleto Rapping/Los Angeles Times/Getty Images)

Another milestone of musical theatre was Gershwin's *Porgy and Bess* (1935), based on a book by DuBose Heyward (1885–1940). Set in the African American community of Charleston, South Carolina, was said to be more realistic than *Show Boat*, and its score is so powerful that many people consider it an opera rather than a musical. (For *Porgy* too, in later years the portrayal of the Black characters evoked racial stereotypes and a recent production used a book adapted by African American playwright Suzan-Lori Parks to correct these shortcomings.) With the emergence of these two musical masterpieces, *Show Boat* and *Porgy & Bess*, the *book musical,* an entirely new form— a completely American form—was born.

A High Point of Musicals

In the wake of these two American productions, *Oklahoma!*—which was produced in 1943 and brought the team of Richard Rodgers (1902–1979) and Hammerstein together for the first time—heralded a new form. *Oklahoma!* has been praised for seamlessly fitting together story, music, lyrics, and dances so that tone, mood, and intention became a unified whole. Its choreography, by Agnes deMille (1905-1993), included a ballet sequence that influenced many later choreographers, including Jerome Robbins (1918-1998) and Bob Fosse (1927-1987). Rodgers and Hammerstein went on to create other significant musicals such as *Carousel* (1945), *South Pacific* (1949), *The King and I* (1951), and *The Sound of Music* (1959).

Among other notable musicals during the 1940s and 1950s were Irving Berlin's (1888-1989), *Annie Get Your Gun* (1946), based on the life of Annie Oakley; Cole Porter's (1891-1964), musical version of *The Taming of the Shrew,* called *Kiss Me, Kate* (1948); *Guys and Dolls* (1950) by Frank Loesser (1910-1969); *My Fair Lady* (1956), by the librettist and lyricist Alan Jay Lerner (1918-1986) and the composer Frederick Loewe (1904-1988), based on George Bernard Shaw's *Pygmalion* (1913); and *West Side Story,* a modernization of *Romeo and Juliet,* which was created by the composer Leonard Bernstein (1918-1990), the lyricist Stephen Sondheim (b. 1930), and the librettist Arthur Laurents (1918-2011).

THE POPULAR AMERICAN MUSICAL
Hello, Dolly!, with music and lyrics by Jerry Herman and book by Michael Stewart, is the quintessential popular American musical. Opening in 1964, it was not as serious as many midcentury musicals but nevertheless won ten Tony Awards and has been revived many times, most recently in 2017 starring Bette Midler as Dolly. Lighthearted and tuneful, it tells the story of a matchmaker who supposedly is looking for a wife for a wealthy widower but ends up with the man herself. (Sara Krulwich/The New York Times/Redux)

Chapter 11 *Theatrical Genres*

Some commentators believe that *Fiddler on the Roof* (1964)—with music by Jerry Bock (1928-2010), lyrics by Sheldon Harnick (b. 1924), and book by Joseph Stein (1912-2010)—marks the end of this era of outstanding book musicals. *Fiddler on the Roof*, about a Jewish family whose father attempts to uphold tradition in a Russian village where the Jewish community faces persecution, was directed and choreographed by Jerome Robbins. One example of changes in the musical following *Fiddler on the Roof* was the rock musical *Hair* (1967), by Galt McDermot (1928-2018), James Rado (b. 1932), and Gerome Ragni (1935-1991), which had no actual storyline and was a celebration of the anti-establishment lifestyle of the 1960s.

Musicals after 1975

After *Hair*, the musical scene became increasingly fragmented, with fewer traditional book musicals being written along with other significant changes. Instead there were other approaches, one being the concept musical, in which a production is built around an idea rather than a story. Two examples, both composed by Stephen Sondheim (b. 1930) and directed by Harold Prince (1928-2019), are *Company* (1970) and *Follies* (1971). Two of Sondheim's other works, *Sunday in the Park with George* (1985) and *Into the Woods* (1988), can also be considered concept musicals.

Another significant development in musicals of the 1970s and 1980s was the ascendancy of the choreographer as the director of musicals. Jerome Robbins, director of *West Side Story* and *Fiddler on the Roof*, was generally recognized as the leading director-choreographer in the United States. Following him, *A Chorus Line* was developed by the director-choreographer Michael Bennett (1943-1987). Other significant director-choreographers were Gower Champion (1920-1980), responsible for *Hello Dolly!* (1964) and *42nd Street* (1980); Bob Fosse, who directed *Sweet Charity* (1966) and *Pippin* (1972); and Tommy Tune (b. 1939), who directed *Nine* (1982) and *Grand Hotel* (1989). Other contemporary director-choreographers are Susan Stroman (b. 1954), responsible for *Contact* (1999), *The Producers* (2001), and *Big Fish* (2013), and Kathleen Marshall (b. 1962), director of the Broadway revival of *Anything Goes* (2010).

Still another major development since 1965 has been the emergence of British composers and lyricists. The leading figure in this movement is the composer Andrew Lloyd Webber (b. 1948), who, with the lyricist Tim Rice (b. 1944), wrote *Jesus Christ Superstar* (1971) and *Evita* (1979). Webber has also written *Cats* (1982), *The Phantom of the Opera* (1987), and *The School of Rock* (2015). Two other large-scale British musicals of the period were *Les Misérables* (1987), originally conceived in France, and *Miss Saigon* (1989), both of which have had successful recent revivals. In 2008 *Billy Elliott* and in 2013 *Matilda* arrived on Broadway from London. In 2014, the rock musician Sting's musical *The Last Ship* opened in New York.

Four additional trends are discernible in the contemporary musical theatre from 1990 to the present. One is the unprecedented number of major revivals of past musical successes. One reason for the increase in revivals has been the rising cost of producing musicals, which has led producers to present tried-and-true musical classics that are considered safe investments. At the same time, this is a clear indication that there has not been the same output of new work as in earlier years. On the positive side, the trend confirms that these outstanding musicals from the past form part of an important heritage and have lasting value.

MUSICALS IN TRANSITION
After the impressive outpouring of original musicals in the years during and just after World War II, the musical entered a period of transition. Important new musicals continued to appear but often employing new forms: concept musicals, rock musicals, and "jukebox" musicals. An example of a musical that combines elements of a traditional musical and a concept musical was *A Little Night Music* with lyrics and music by Stephen Sondheim. Seen here is a scene from a Broadway revival starring Angela Lansbury (center). (Sara Krulwich/The New York Times/Redux)

In addition, some revivals have attempted to address the inherent racism, sexism, homophobia, and ableism in many of the historic musicals. We have already mentioned the reworking of Gershwin's *Porgy and Bess*. In 2009 Lin-Manuel Miranda, the creator of *in the Heights* and *Hamilton,* assisted with the Broadway revival of *West Side Story* translating some of the scenes with the Sharks into Spanish. In 2020, a revival of the musical by auteur director Ivo van Hove used multimedia and new choreography to speak to a new audience. The 2019 revival of *Oklahoma!* confronted issues of race, homophobia, and ableism. Ali Stroker, who played Ado Annie, was the first actor in a wheelchair to win a Tony. The 2018 London revival of Sondheim's *Company,* which opened in New York n 2022, reversed the gender of the lead role to confront the sexism inherent in the original version.

A second trend has been musicals based on films. This list would include *The Producers, Monty Python's Spamalot* (2005), *Hairspray* (2003), *Young Frankenstein, Billy Elliott* (2005), *Once* (2011), *Kinky Boots* (2012), *Honeymoon in Vegas* (2015), *Waitress* (2015), *The Devil Wears Prada* (2020), and musicals presented by the Disney organization, such as *The Lion King* (1997), *Mary Poppins* (2004), *The Little Mermaid* (2007), *Aladdin* (2011), and *Frozen* (2018).

The third trend is the creation of productions out of the music of former popular music stars and groups, sometimes referred to as "jukebox musicals." The most successful of these has been *Mamma Mia!* (1999)—a story taking place in the Greek islands and based on the music of the group ABBA. The music of Billy Joel formed the basis of Twyla Tharp's dance musical *Moving Out*. In the years that followed, show after show was created by stringing together hits from one music group or another, good examples being *Jersey Boys* (2005), *Rock of Ages* (2008), and *Motown* (2013). *American Idiot* (2009) created a musical around the rock group Green Day's recordings, *Beautiful* (2014) used the music of Carole King to tell her life story, *Ain't Too Proud to Beg* (2017) details the career of the soul group the Temptations, and *Tina: The Tina Turner Musical* (2019) dramatizes the iconic star's career.

A fourth trend—a refreshing counterpoint to the rush of revivals—has been the appearance of fresh, off-beat musicals, indicating that the genre remains full of vitality. For example, *Rent* (1996), about a group of anti-establishment young people, won numerous awards, including the Pulitzer Prize and the Tony Award for best musical of the year. Another example is *Avenue Q* (2003), a lively, iconoclastic musical featuring puppets operated by onstage characters.

Next to Normal, which was awarded the 2009 Tony Award, concerns a mother who is struggling with bipolar disorder and the effects her disease has on her family. As her condition worsens, other concerns surface—suicide, drug abuse, psychiatric ethics—none of which are typical subjects for a musical. Another example is *Dear Evan Hansen* (2016), with music and lyrics by Benj Pasek (b. 1985) and Justin Paul (b. 1985) and book by playwright Steven Levenson (b. 1984), which deals with a teenager suffering from social anxiety and learning self-acceptance.

Some other original musicals during this time period mix elaborate spectacle with newly composed music; examples include *Wicked* (2003) and *Spiderman: Turn*

AMERICAN MUSICALS IN THE TWENTY-FIRST CENTURY
In the first two decades of the twenty-first century the American musical scene was a cross section of musicals: old and new, classic and experimental, serious and comic, aimed at the mature audience as well as the very young. An important musical of the period was *Hamilton* which opened in 2015. The production, created by Lin-Manuel Miranda, successfully combined a number of elements, including history (the story of Alexander Hamilton, a Founding Father, but with anachronistic elements); rap music; eighteenth-century costumes; modern choreography; and nontraditional casting. Seen here is Miranda in the Broadway production, playing the lead role in front of the ensemble. (Sara Krulwich/The New York Times/Redux)

Part Four   The Playwright and the Play

> ## IN FOCUS: THE APPEAL OF MUSICAL THEATRE
>
> We have pointed out that the book musical is a unique American invention and accomplishment. What is it about this type of dramatic offering that has proved so enduring and appealing?
>
> First of all, it is a combination of various elements. Musicals tend to be based on appealing, timeless stories, which have a fascination of their own. One reason for this is that often the book of a musical is based on a novel or a traditional play that has proved to have an exciting, suspenseful narrative. Often there is a protagonist who faces severe obstacles that must be overcome. Whether it is the cockney flower girl in *My Fair Lady,* the suffering Jewish father in *Fiddler on the Roof,* the put-upon heroine of *Kiss Me, Kate,* the mother fighting desperately for her children in *Gypsy,* or one of the beleaguered founders of the United States fighting political and personal issues, the chief character faces formidable challenges over which to prevail.
>
> Notice, too, that the backgrounds of these stories vary quite widely, ranging from the founding of our nation, a pogrom in a small Jewish village over a century ago, to a western state like Oklahoma, to the South Pacific. Also, as part of the narrative there are usually exceptional roles for star performers: the irresistible con man in *The Music Man,* the appealing rake in *Guys and Dolls,* the lonely, elderly bachelor in *Most Happy Fella,* the indestructible matchmaker in *Hello, Dolly!,* or the founders of our nations presented as contemporary figures in *Hamilton*. Each of these is a role that attracts star performers.
>
> Along with the story and the appealing characters, the book musical features outstanding musical scores. The melodies are appealing, original, and often irresistible and the lyrics are inventive, clever, and poetic. Add to this dance. From ballet to vigorous tap to everything in between, dance early on became an indispensable component of musicals. Finally, it is the blend, the cohesion of these elements when a strong, inventive director pulls all these elements together into a unified whole, that results in the finished, satisfying musical.

Off the Dark (2011). There have also been successful new musicals with original music scores, often using pop and rock music, such as *Spring Awakening* (2006), *Memphis* (2009), *The Book of Mormon* (2011), and *Hadestown* (2016).

A number of contemporary musical theatre composers combine the traditions of the golden era of the musical with the recent trends of the American musical, including Adam Guettel (b. 1964), Michael John LaChiusa (b. 1961), Andrew Lippa (b. 1964), and Jeanine Tesori (b. 1961), whose *Fun Home* (2013) deals with the coming out of its lesbian protagonist and was the first musical to win Tonys for a woman composer and woman author of the book, playwright Lisa Kron (b. 1961).

The contemporary composer who has made a major impact on the American musical is Lin-Manuel Miranda (b. 1980). His first major work *In the Heights,* winner of the 2008 Tony Award for Best Musical, covers three days in the lives of characters in the Dominican American section of Washington Heights in Manhattan and features hip-hop, meringue, salsa, and soul music. Miranda's *Hamilton* (2015), which tells the story of the Founding Fathers by using multicultural, nontraditional casting and hip-hop music, is a theatrical phenomenon, with unprecedented demand for tickets in New York and in other cities.

It is clear that the musical theatre scene at the present time is a patchwork quilt, featuring old and new, revues and book musicals, imports and original material. All in all, the musical remains a mainstay of Broadway and of those large theatres across the United States that feature shows with music, dance, spectacular scenery, and well-known performers.

SUMMARY

1. Tragedy attempts to ask very basic questions about human existence: Why do people suffer? Is there justice in the world? What are the limits of human endurance and achievement? Tragedy presupposes an indifferent and sometimes malevolent universe in which the innocent suffer and there is inexplicable cruelty. It also assumes that certain individuals will confront and defy fate, even if they are overcome in the process.

2. Tragedy can be classified as traditional or modern. In traditional tragedy the chief characters are persons of stature—kings, queens, and the nobility. The central figure is caught in a series of tragic circumstances, which are irretrievable. The hero or heroine is willing to fight and die for a cause. The language of the play is verse.

3. Modern tragedy involves ordinary people rather than the nobility, and it is generally written in prose rather than verse. In this modern form, the deeper meanings of tragedy are explored by nonverbal elements and by the cumulative or overall effect of events, as well as by verbal means.

4. There are several kinds of nontragic serious plays, the most notable being heroic drama, bourgeois or domestic drama, and melodrama.

5. Heroic drama has many of the same elements as traditional tragedy—it frequently deals with highborn characters and is often in verse. In contrast to tragedy, however, it has a happy ending or an ending in which the death of the main character is considered a triumph, not a defeat.

6. Bourgeois or domestic drama deals with ordinary people, always seriously but not always tragically. It stresses the problems of the middle and lower classes and became a particularly prominent form in the twentieth century.

7. Melodrama features exaggerated characters and events arranged to create horror or suspense or to present a didactic argument for some political, moral, or social point of view.

8. Comedy takes a different approach from serious forms of drama. It sees the humor and incongruity in people and situations. Comic dramatists accept a social and moral order and suspend natural laws (a man falls flat on his face but does not really hurt himself).

9. Comedy is developed by means of several techniques. *Verbal humor* turns words upside down and creates puns, malapropisms, and inversions of meaning. *Comedy of character* creates men and women who take extreme positions, make fools of themselves, or contradict themselves. *Plot complications* create mistaken identity, coincidences, and people who turn up unexpectedly in the wrong house or the wrong bedroom. There are also physical aspects to comedy: slapstick and horseplay.

10. From these techniques, the dramatist fashions various kinds of comedy. For instance, depending on the degree of exaggeration, a comedy can be *farce* or *comedy of manners;* farce features strong physical humor, whereas comedy of manners relies more on verbal wit.

11. Another type of comedy is *domestic comedy,* which deals with ordinary people in familiar situations.

12. Depending on its intent, comedy can be designed to entertain, as with *farce* or *burlesque,* or to correct vices, in which case it becomes *satire.* Many of Shaw's plays represent *comedy of ideas.*

13. Serious and comic elements can be mixed in theatre. Many tragedies have comic relief—humorous scenes and characters interspersed in serious material.

14. Authentic tragicomedy fuses, or synthesizes, two elements—one serious, the other comic. We laugh and cry at the same time. Chekhov, Beckett, Dürrenmatt, and writers of theatre of the absurd use tragicomedy in their plays. Some commentators feel that this is the form most truly characteristic of our time.

15. Musical theatre is a popular form that traditionally integrates book (storyline), music, lyrics and dance seamlessly. There are many types of musical theatre: traditional book musical, concept musical, and jukebox musical are just a few of the subcategories.

Design Elements: Audience Sitting in Theatre (theatre): Ron Chapple/Photodisc/Getty Images; Studio Light (spotlights): Exactostock/SuperStock

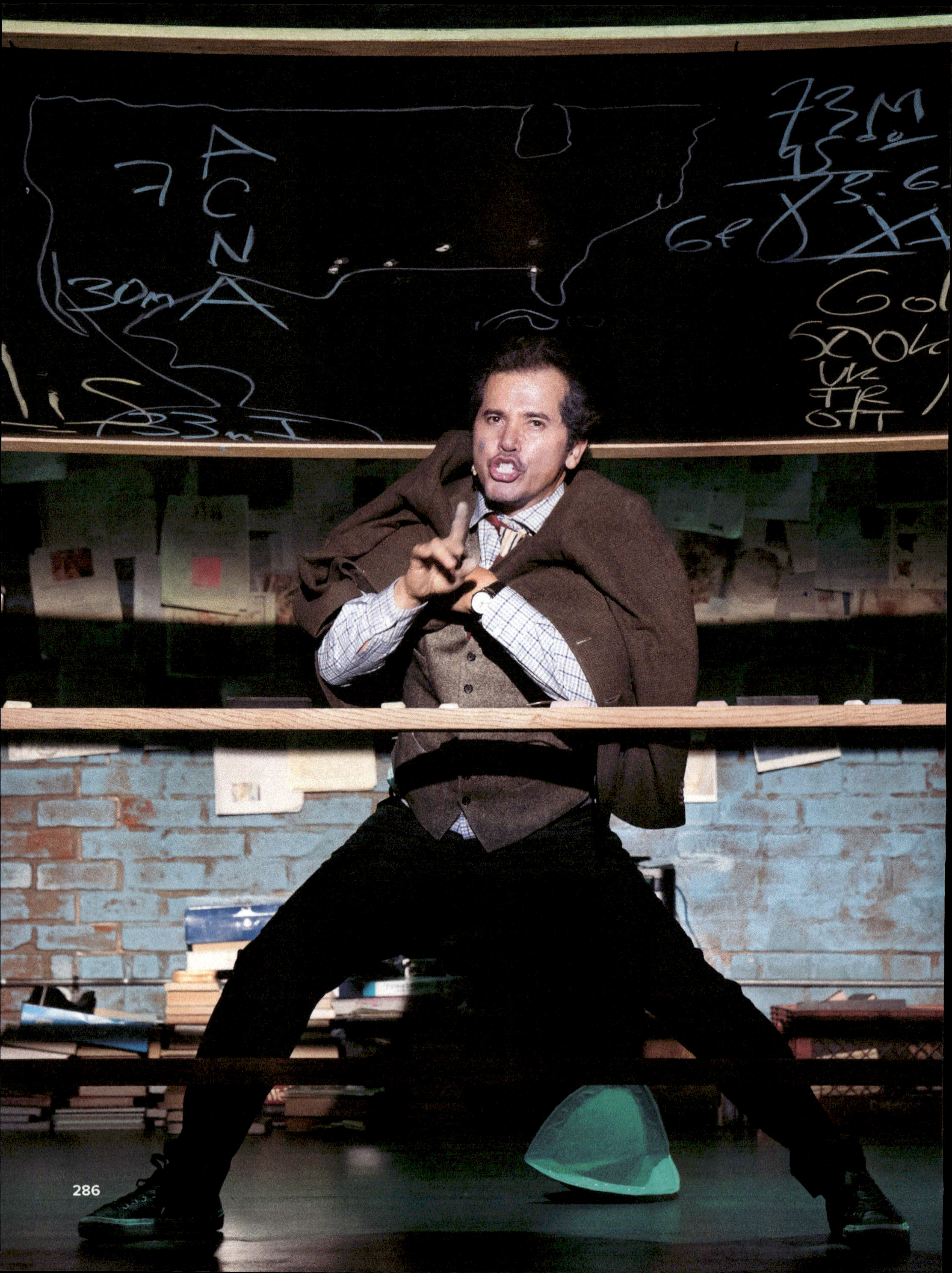

Alternative and Experimental Dramatic and Theatrical Forms

As can be seen in our discussions of tragicomedy and theatre of the absurd in the previous chapter, dramas often defy categorization. Plays frequently mix genres and styles. We have noted how Shakespeare wrote plays that did not clearly fit into either tragedy or comedy and some earlier critics referred to them as "problem" plays.

In the late twentieth century, theorists who are referred to as *postmodernists,* and whose concepts we will discuss more fully later in this chapter, questioned the validity of categorizing dramas by genre. They argued that such categorization led to a hierarchy that was built on sociopolitical and aesthetic biases. Why should tragedy or comedy be privileged over melodrama or domestic drama? Does privileging traditional tragedy over modern tragedy have sociopolitical (and in many cases, gender and racial) implications? Can we really distinguish between any of these genres and do such broad categories even make sense? Do audiences or authors differentiate in this fashion or does each playwright create a unique work and does each audience member have his or her own unique reaction to that work? Is there really a distinction between more popular theatrical forms and entertainments, such as musical theatre, and so-called high art?

We can clearly see the problem of trying to categorize drama since the end of the nineteenth century. Throughout this time period there have been many avant-garde theatrical forms that do not neatly fit into any of the categories. We will discuss some of these in this chapter.

◀ **ALTERNATIVE AND EXPERIMENTAL FORMS**

For almost 150 years, many theatre artists have experimented with forms that departed from realism or expanded on that type of drama. In recent years, one of those forms is performance art, where a single actor either presents autobiographical material or portrays a series of characters. Seen here is John Leguizamo in his one-person show Latin History for Morons. *Leguizamo uses his own experiences to reflect on the sociopolitical issues the Latinx communities confront in the United States. (Sara Krulwich/The New York Times/Redux)*

Expressionism, Surrealism, Epic Theatre, and Theatre of Cruelty

Expressionism and surrealism, forms that developed early in the twentieth century, tried to capture the inner workings of the human mind: expressionism presenting drama from the point of view of the protagonist and surrealism trying to mimic the dream and other subconscious states. Many playwrights have integrated these forms into works that deal with realistic concerns. For example, Arthur Miller in *A Death of a Salesman,* which he said was "a tragedy of the common man," uses expressionistic techniques to get into the mind of the protagonist. Tony Kushner's *Angels in America* uses dream scenes that are surrealistic to underscore the tragedy of the AIDs crisis in the United States in the 1980s.

The German playwright Bertolt Brecht, between the two World Wars and shortly after World War II, created what he called "epic" theatre, in which audience members were constantly reminded they were in the theatre. Songs broke up the action of his plays and underscored his political messages, and narrators were used to comment on the sociopolitical meaning of the dramatic action. The plays, like Shakespeare's dramas, were episodic in form and, therefore, the term "epic." Many contemporary playwrights, such as Caryl Churchill and Suzan Lori-Parks, use Brechtian techniques to create unique sociopolitical dramas.

In the 1930s, a French dramatist and theatre critic Antonin Artaud boldly proclaimed that there should be "no more masterpieces," meaning that texts like the plays of Shakespeare should no longer be revered but rather treated as works that could be updated, restructured, or transformed in any way that make them more relevant to contemporary audiences. Artaud also argued that theatre should be a sensory experience, bombarding the audience visually and aurally, hence the title "theatre of cruelty." He argued that plays should be texts for performance.

Following World War II this movement became more widespread. In the spirit of Artaud, a central element share by many of the new experimental and avant-garde approaches to theatre was a rejection of what was called "text-based" theatre, meaning theatre based on the script as written by a playwright being sacred.

Surrealism, expressionism, epic theatre, and the theatre of cruelty all influenced the absurdist playwrights that we discussed in the previous chapter and influenced many of the other nontraditional and experimental forms we will now discuss.

EPIC THEATRE
Playwright and director Brecht was known for his epic theatre theories and his political plays that reflected those theories. His best known work is *Mother Courage and Her Children.* Shown here is Fiona Shaw as Anna Fierling, Mother Courage, in a production of the play directed by Deborah Warner and translated by U.S. playwright Tony Kushner at the National Theatre in London in 2009. (Robbie Jack/Getty Images)

OTHER NONTRADITIONAL AND EXPERIMENTAL FORMS

In the twenty-first century, as we have seen, traditional genres remain prevalent. At the same time, during the sixty years nontraditional or alternative forms took root and flourished. These forms sometimes downplayed the importance of the playwright and the director and/or an ensemble of actors became the key creators.

There have been many examples of nontraditional or experimental forms that build on earlier avant-garde experiments. Next we will survey some of the key examples of these experimental forms during the past sixty years.

Happenings *Happenings* were raw, thoughtfully crafted theatrical events first created by painters and sculptors in the late 1950s and early 1960s. With little or no theatre training, these visual artists were part of the postmodern movement when artists explored other art forms beyond their own specific practices. Unlike the misleading title, happenings were not spontaneous or happenstance. They were intentional, organized acts that explored time and space. Performances consisted of prepared activities and tasks that were choreographed and blocked. Groups of performers engaged in pedestrian (everyday) movement or stylistic gestures with *found* objects or props and performed in a sculptural set. Nonsensical sounds and spoken text were used without feeling or emotion.

Given circumstances that might identify time and place were removed and the senses of sight, sound, and often scent were evoked. There was no applause or curtain call and audiences usually consisted of forty to fifty spectators invited to the space through mailed invitations, advertising, or word of mouth. Productions were often limited to a few performances. The first happenings were performed in parks, art galleries, studio lofts, museums, storefronts, parking lots, and other unique spaces. Happenings were supposed to be an extension of everyday life, eliminating the boundary of the fourth wall between performers and audience. When a performance ended, the audience often waited in the space until a performer signaled or a brave audience member initiated an exit.

happenings Nonliterary theatrical events, developed in the 1960s, in which the script is replaced with a scenario that provides for chance occurrences, and are performed (often only once) in such places as parks and street corners.

Environmental Theatre The term *environmental theatre* was coined in the 1960s by the American director and teacher Richard Schechner (b. 1934) many characteristics of environmental theatre, however, had developed out of the work and theories of earlier avant-garde artists such as Meyerhold and Artaud. Proponents of environmental theatre treat the entire theatre space as a performance area, suggesting that any division between performers and viewers is artificial. For every production, spatial arrangements are transformed.

The major influence on Schechner's theories was the Polish director Jerzy Grotowski. Works staged by Grotowski with the Polish Laboratory Theatre, originated in Wroclaw, Poland, from its founding in 1959 until 1970, had many characteristics of environmental theatre. For each production, the theatre space and the performer-audience relationship were arranged to conform to the play being presented. Grotowski called his theatre *poor theatre,* meaning poor in scenery and special effects. It relied on the performers for its impact.

environmental theatre A type of theatre, made popular in the 1960s, that attempts to eliminate the distinction between audience and acting space and that emphasizes a multiple focus for the audience rather than a single focus.

Two experimental directors are Robert Wilson (b. 1944) and Richard Foreman (b. 1937). Their work is typically unified by a theme or point of view determined by the director, and their material is often organized into units analogous to frames in television or film. Stunning theatrical images containing the essence of the ideas that interest these directors are often the key to their work.

Important off-off-Broadway theatres in which avant-garde works found a home included Café LaMama, the Living Theater, the Open Theater, the Performance Group, Mabou Mines, and the Wooster Group. These theatres in New York City had counterparts all across the United States. All have experimented with physical performance techniques, improvisation, texts created by performers and directors, and environmental presentations.

Whatever the process, the result was not traditional theatre. Like their counterparts in painting, nonrepresentational theatre artists deal in images, impressions, fragments, and segments. There may be strong elements of improvisation, free association, and audience participation. Each presentation is an event, a time-based event, and it is up to the spectator to integrate its elements in some way, to determine its meaning and its impact. Another way of saying this is that viewing such theatre becomes a different kind of experience from the experience audiences are accustomed to in traditional theatre.

Postmodernism One term used to describe the nontraditional theatre we have been discussing, and much that followed, is ***postmodernism.*** According to the film critic A. O. Scott, postmodernism has several attributes: "a cool, ironic effect; the overt pastiche of work from the past; the insouciant mixture of high and low styles." Although postmodernism is difficult to define specifically, it has certain distinctive characteristics.

postmodernism A contemporary concept suggesting that artists and audiences have gone beyond the modernist movements of realism and departures from realism and such categories as "high art" and "popular art."

For one thing, postmodernism reflects issues of power in art. Postmodernists question the idea of an accepted "canon" of classics; they also ask why certain artists (such as playwrights) and certain groups (such as white males) should have held positions of power or "privilege" throughout theatre history. Accordingly, postmodernists rebel against traditional readings of texts, arguing that theatre productions may have a variety of "authors," including directors and even individual audience members: they argue that each audience member creates his or her own unique reading. Postmodernist directors are noted for "deconstructing" classic dramas and trying to represent onstage the issues of power embedded in the text. When a classic is deconstructed in this way, it may serve simply as the scenario for a production.

One of the most famous groups known for deconstruction of texts is the Wooster Group, under the artistic direction of Elizabeth LeCompte (b. 1944). In 1997, the Wooster Group presented a highly theatricalized and physical version of Eugene O'Neill's *The Emperor Jones* in a run-down theatre in the Times Square area in New York City. In 2007, it presented a version of *Hamlet* that featured various filmed scenes of *Hamlet* interspersed with live action. Postmodernists mix abstraction and realism, so that their works cannot be easily classified. Furthermore, the distinction between "high" art and popular art can no longer be clearly defined: postmodernists mix popular concerns and techniques with those of high art.

An intriguing example is the musical *The Lion King* (1997), based on a popular Disney animated film with music by the rock composer Elton John. The director of *The Lion King,* as well as the designer of the masks and puppets, is Julie Taymor who is a designer, director, and adapter of literature for the stage and is known for her avant-garde use of puppet techniques borrowed from Asian theatres. Many elements of *The Lion King* are based on her previous work. For example, she used puppets in

AVANT-GARDE AND EXPERIMENTAL THEATRE

Aside from large professional theatres, there are many smaller theatres, in cities across the United States, such as off-off-Broadway in New York. Some of these are theatres that reflect our diverse populations. Alternative theatre also includes avant-garde and experimental theatre groups and productions. One of the foremost avant-garde directors of the past quarter century, often cited as a postmodernist, is Richard Foreman. A notable production of his—a sort of retrospective of previous work—is *Old-Fashioned Prostitutes* (*A True Romance*) shown here with Rocco Sisto (right) and Alenka Kraigher (left) at the Public Theater in New York City. (Karli Cadel/The New York Times/Redux)

staging Shakespeare's *The Tempest* (1986) at New York's Theatre for a New Audience; in her frequently revived adaptation of a short story, *Juan Darien* (1988); in a production of Igor Stravinsky's opera *Oedipus Rex* in Tokyo (1992); and in a production of *The Green Bird* (1996), an eighteenth-century comedy by Carlo Gozzi. Taymor also directed a Broadway revival of David Henry Hwang's *M. Butterfly* in 2017 in which she employed some of her visual postmodern techniques.

PLAYING YOUR PART: THINKING ABOUT THEATRE

1. Do you think it is possible to present the workings of the subconscious on stage? Why? Why not?
2. Have you ever seen a film, television show, or theatre production in which you are always made aware that you are watching actors play characters? That the scenery and lighting are not real?
3. How might rock concerts reflect Artaud's theory of the Theatre of Cruelty? What did Artaud mean by "no more masterpieces?" Do you think he was right? Why? Why not?
4. Do you think a theatre production must have a text written by a playwright? Why? Why not?

A POSTMODERN PRODUCTION
As a mark of postmodernism, theatre today is eclectic and widely diversified. Periods, styles, and theatrical intentions are often mixed or coexist side by side. One such mixture of styles and material was a staging of *Hamlet* by the Wooster Group, known for its experimental work. This Shakespearean tragedy was deconstructed by using the film of the 1964 stage production starring Richard Burton as its basis. Elizabeth LeCompte directed. (Robbie Jack/Corbis/Getty Images)

performance art
Experimental theatre that initially incorporated elements of dance and visual arts into performance. Since performance art often is based on the vision of an individual performer or director rather than playwright, the autobiographical monologue and solo performance have become popular performance art forms.

Performance Art In the past three decades, several artists have experimented with forms that force audiences to confront certain issues: What is performance? What is theatre? What is the subject of theatrical representation? Some of these artists are also political-minded; some are not. *Performance art* is often the name given to recent forms that pose these questions and as well as others.

Performance art has important antecedents: earlier avant-garde experiments of the twentieth century, such as dada, surrealism, and happenings, which stressed the irrational and attacked traditional artistic values and forms; the theories of Antonin Artaud and Jerzy Grotowski; and popular forms, such as clowning, vaudeville, and stand-up comedy.

During the past three decades, the term "performance art" has referred to differing types of theatrical presentations. In its earliest manifestations, performance art was related on one hand to painting and on the other hand to dance. In the 1970s, one branch of performance art emphasized the body as an art object: Some artists suffered self-inflicted pain, and some went through daily routines (such as preparing a meal) in a museum or in a theatre setting. Another branch focused on site-specific or environmental pieces in which the setting or context was crucial: Performances were created for specific locations such as a subway station, a city park, or a waterfront pier.

In some of the earliest forms of performance art, story, character, and text were minimized or even eliminated. The emphasis was not on narrating a story or exploring recognizable characters but rather on the visual and ritualistic aspects of performing. This type of theatre was often the work of an individual artist who incorporated highly personal messages, and sometimes political and social messages, in the event. The overall effect was often like a continually transforming collage. As might be expected, there was, as mentioned earlier, an affinity between this kind of theatre—with its emphasis of the visual picture formed onstage—and painting. Often, stage movement in performance art was also closely related to dance, as in the work of Martha Clarke (b. 1944).

In more recent years the term "performance art" changed yet again. It is now also associated with individual artists who present autobiographical extended monologues or present one-person shows in which they portray various characters through interconnected monologues. There are also some performance artists who stage presentations that feature clowning and other popular slapstick techniques borrowed from the circus and other popular arts.

Several such artists—Karen Finley (b. 1956) is one of the most visible—became a center of controversy. These artists often support such causes as feminism and equality for the LGBTQ communities. Often nudity and other controversial representations of sexuality or sexual orientation are used to ask audiences to reflect on their biases. Such was the case in *Alice's Rape* (1989), in which Robbie McCauley performed nude as her great-great-grandmother, a slave on the auction block. These performance artists are continuing a trend begun by early realistic and antirealistic dramatists, whose works challenged the social status quo and were often banned.

Two artists who began performing solo pieces in alternative spaces but later received commercial productions are Spalding Gray (1941–2004) and Bill Irwin (b. 1956). Gray, a monologist who discussed issues that ranged from his own personal concerns to politics, was reminiscent of ancient storytellers who created a theatrical environment single-handedly. Irwin's performances are mimelike, and he uses popular slapstick techniques to reflect on the contemporary human condition.

Anna Deavere Smith (b. 1952), an African American performance artist, won considerable acclaim in the early 1990s for pieces dealing with racial unrest. In her works, she portrays numerous real people she has met and interviewed. For example, her *Twilight: Los Angeles 1992* presented people affected by the uprising that followed the acquittals in the first trial of police officers charged with brutalizing Rodney King.

ANNA DEAVERE SMITH: PERFORMANCE ARTIST
Shown here is Anna Deavere Smith in her piece *Let Me Down Easy,* at the Second Stage Theater in New York in September 2009. Smith creates her works, which deal with sociopolitical issues, by interviewing people connected to those issues and then playing all of them in her one-person shows. In *Let Me Down Easy,* Smith deals with health care issues in the United States. Her best known works, *Fires in the Mirror* and *Twilight: Los Angeles 1992* deal with racial unrest. (Sara Krulwich/The New York Times/Redux)

IN FOCUS: ANNA DEAVERE SMITH AND PERFORMANCE ART

Anna Deavere Smith (b. 1950) over the past four decades has been the most prominent African American performance artist in the United States. She was born and raised in Baltimore, where her family members were the first African Americans in her neighborhood. Smith attended Beaver College, a woman's college in Pennsylvania. In 2021, she wrote an article for *The Atlantic* about the racism she confronted there in the 1960s. She completed an M.F.A. in Acting at the American Conservatory Theatre in San Francisco.

After finishing her graduate work, Smith pursued a career as a performer and acting professor, teaching at Carnegie Mellon University, Yale University, the University of Southern California, Stanford University, and New York University. She has had an active stage, movie, and television career, including roles in *The West Wing, Nurse Jackie, Black-ish,* and *For the People.*

Smith is best known for works in which she portrays real people whom she has met and interviewed; as a performer, she crosses gender and racial lines to represent all of the people with whom she has spoken, asking pointed questions about racial and gender identity. She usually records her conversations with interviewees and creates a mosaic of diverse characters, attitudes, and voices. She has been highly praised for the astonishing way in which she captures both the essence and the idiosyncrasies of the people she portrays and how she uses those individuals to address issues of race in America. Her work is a fusion of performance art, political theatre, and documentary drama.

Among Smith's best-known works are: *Fires in the Mirror* (1992), *Twilight Los Angeles 1992* (1994), *Let Me Down Easy* (2008–2010), and *Notes from the Field: Doing Time in Education* (2016).

Other well-known monologists are Eric Bogosian (b. 1953); Danny Hoch (b. 1970); John Leguizamo (b. 1965), who focuses on Latino American issues; Mike Daisey (b. 1973); Lisa Kron (b. 1961); and Sarah Jones (b. 1973). Ping Chong (b. 1946) is an Asian American performance artist who mixes multimedia into his works.

A number of spaces have become recognized for their presentation of performance artists. These include two in New York City: PS 122, a converted public school in the East Village in Manhattan and after a major renovation now known as Performance Space New York; and the Kitchen, also located downtown. In addition, many museums throughout the United States are known for presenting series of performance artists, including the Walker Museum in Minneapolis and the Museum of Contemporary Art in Chicago. The fact that performance art is most often presented in converted, found spaces or museums again reflects the eclectic nature of the form and its relationship to earlier avant-garde movements and the visual arts.

Along with those in the United States, there are also significant performance artists in most major cities around the world, such as Issei Ogata (b. 1952) in Japan.

TWO FORMS THAT BRIDGE THE TRADITONAL AND NONTRADITIONAL

There are many forms of theatre that are unique because of their subject matter or the material they use to create a drama. They are not easily categorized into the traditional genres. Two such forms are political theatre and documentary drama.

Political Theatre Another type of theatre that could be considered nontraditional, in terms of subject matter, is political theatre, which concerns itself not with primarily exploring the aesthetics or artistic side of theatre but with political ideas, causes, and individuals. Even those political playwrights who explore differing aesthetic approaches do so in order to reinforce their political points of view.

Political theatre can run the gamut from dramas that take a strongly partisan point of view to those with a more even-handed probing of ideas and causes. It can attack a target, espouse a cause, or engage in satire to expose what the dramatist considers a wrongheaded regime or a wrongheaded approach to a problem. Many dramatists of the past, such as George Bernard Shaw and Bertolt Brecht, have incorporated a clear political agenda into their work. Many of the performance artists we discussed focus on political issues.

In the United States, there was a marked increase in political drama during the period of the Vietnam War, with such plays as Megan Terry's *Viet Rock,* Barbara Garson's *MacBird,* and the musical *Hair.* In the 1970s, the Black power movement also created a number of plays that had a strong political purpose. In recent years, there have been theatre artists who have created works dealing with the issues of the Iraq and Afghanistan wars, Middle East tensions, and mass incarceration. There are examples of political theatre across the globe.

In a reaction against the administration of George W. Bush and many of its policies, there was an outpouring of essentially political plays. One of these was *Baghdad Burning: Girl Blog from Iraq* (2005), about everyday life in Iraq during the war; it was based on the blog of a girl living there, with actors reading entries telling of both routine and horrific incidents. Another was *The Treatment* (2006), Eve Ensler's dramatization of post-traumatic stress disorder as revealed in scenes between a male American war veteran and a woman military psychologist. A third play was *My Trip to Al Qaeda* (2007), written by Lawrence Wright (b. 1947) based on a book by Wright, *The Looming Tower: Al Qaeda and the Road to 9/11.*

There have also been recent dramas and theatre productions critical of the administration of President Donald Trump, including a controversial staging of Shakespeare's *Julius Caesar* at New York's Public Theater. *Shipwreck: A History Play About 2017,* a play by Anne Washburn, which premiered in London in 2019, that has Donald Trump as a character at a dinner party attended by liberal friends discussing contemporary politics.

POLITICAL DRAMA
Shown here are Mikéah Ernest Jennings as President George W. Bush and Jeff Biehl as Donald Trump in *Shipwreck: A History Play About 2017*. The play by U.S. dramatist Anne Washburn premiered in London in 2019 and focuses on U.S. politics and social issues during the Trump administration. (Teresa Castracane Photography)

Other political plays do not deal directly with a particular party or administration, but nevertheless have a strong political component. *Nine Parts of Desire* by Heather Raffo is a powerful portrait of a cross section of Iraqi women: their problems, their plight, and their distant hopes. Another political play is *Exonerated* by Jessica Blank and Erik Jensen, which includes actual transcripts of trials and other testimony of people who had been sentenced to death but were later proved to be innocent. This is also an example of a documentary drama, a form we will discuss next, and another example of how plays cannot be easily categorized.

Many of the plays we have discussed in the previous sections of this chapter qualify as political plays. In addition, many of the plays we will discuss when we review our diverse and global theatres later in this textbook also have a political point of view no matter what aesthetic approach the artists take. These plays speak up for the rights and for the recognition of a particular underrepresented or oppressed group. As we shall see in the chapter, "Diverse and Inclusive Plays and Playwrights," this is true of African American, Latinx American, Asian American, indigenous, feminist, and LGBTQ theatres and artists. It is also true of theatre created for and by underrepresented groups in nations across the world.

Documentary drama (or theatre of fact) Term encompassing different types of drama that presented material in the fashion of journalism or reporting. Drama that is supposedly based on factual occurrences and materials.

Documentary Drama

A contemporary dramatic form, ***documentary drama*** (sometimes referred to as *theatre of fact*), has roots in the classical Greek and Elizabethan theatres and in other theatres through the early twentieth century. Often this type of drama is also political.

Documentary dramas are based on historical documents, which give an air of authenticity and historical reality. The goal of documentary drama is to convince audiences that they are watching history unfold, even when the dramatists have modified the documents for dramatic or political effect. One of the most famous documentary dramas is *The Investigation* (1965) by Peter Weiss (1916–1982), which dramatizes the war crimes trials of people who were guards at a Nazi extermination camp.

Documentary drama continues to be prevalent in the twenty-first

DOCUMENTARY DRAMA

A continuing trend in global theatre is documentary drama. This type of theatre is based on historical documents—papers, e-mails, recordings, television images—in order to give it the air of authenticity and historical reality. Some documentary presentations intersperse invented segments or dialogue, but others stick strictly to the public record. There are many documentary dramas dealing with the Iraq War. None has been more successful or more moving than *Black Watch,* the story of a 300-year-old Scottish regiment that saw combat in Iraq. A mixture of dramatic scenes, monologues, musical numbers, and horrific television footage of combat, it evoked the horror and sorrow of war. The production shown here, with Paul James Corrigan as Kenzie, Paul Rattray as Cammy, and Emun Elliott as Fraz, was created by the National Theatre of Scotland and first presented at the Edinburgh Festival. (Geraint Lewis/Alamy Stock Photo)

century. Today, docudramas—as they are sometimes referred to—are also popular as made-for-television movies. Still, docudramas for the stage continue to be written.

A good example is *Exonerated* (2002), which we mentioned earlier, a documentary about former Death Row inmates who were innocent. There have also been numerous docudramas dealing with the war in Iraq, including *Black Watch* (2006), staged throughout the world by the National Theatre of Scotland. *The Jungle,* a docudrama created by Good Chance, a theatre established close to a migrant camp near Calais in France, tells the stories of Afghan and Syrian migrants in that makeshift migrant city called the Jungle. The docudrama also performed at the Young Vic in London in 2017 and off-Broadway in New York in 2019. During the shutdown of theatre in 2020 due to the COVID-19 pandemic, off-Broadway's Public Theatre presented on Zoom *The Line,* a docudrama based on interviews with New York first responders by the authors of *Exonerated*.

There are also examples of documentary drama from the across the globe, including Africa, Latin America, Asia, and the Middle East.

TRADITIONAL GENRES AND FORMS CONTINUE AND TRANSFORM

As we noted, plays and theatrical forms often mix genres and styles and cannot be easily categorized. Many playwrights in the contemporary theatre mix realistic and nontraditional forms and structures.

The traditional patterns set and the forms established from the Greeks to the present day continue to influence contemporary playwrights. Beginning with the Greeks in 2500 BCE and continuing through the Renaissance in Western Europe, Elizabethan theatre in England, Renaissance theatre in France and Spain, late-nineteenth-century theatre in Europe and the twentieth century in the United States, the form and shape of our theatrical creations have been established and entered the Western mainstream. To this day, William Shakespeare remains the most frequently produced playwright in the United States. Shakespeare's episodic structure was copied by the Romantics in the early nineteenth century. The comic forms of the Greeks and Romans continue to impact our theatre today. The crisis structure devised by the classical Greeks influenced many of the early realistic playwrights. As a further testament to the continuing impact of that realistic, domestic drama tradition in drama, in 2017 a new play by Lucas Hnath, *A Doll's House, Part 2,* a sequel to Henrik Ibsen's drama of 1879, opened on Broadway, and in 2019 British Indian playwright Tanika Gupta adapted the play, setting it in colonial India.

MERGING THE TRADITIONAL AND AVANT-GARDE
In the second half of the twentieth century there were playwrights who merged traditional realistic domestic drama with avant-garde dramatic techniques. One such dramatist was Sam Shepard. Shown here is a scene from his play *Buried Child* starring actor Ed Harris.
(Sara Krulwich/The New York Times/Redux)

Chapter 12 *Alternative and Experimental Dramatic and Theatrical Forms*

> ## PLAYING YOUR PART: EXPERIENCING THEATRE
>
> 1. How might you turn your classroom into a space for an environmental theatre production? What type of play might be best suited for that environment?
> 2. What political issues today might be turned into an interesting play? What would your point of view be about that political issue? Who would be the leading characters?
> 3. What documents from the past 10 years might be turned into documentary dramas?
> 4. How might you structure the events of your own life into a solo performance art piece?

However, many playwrights in the late twentieth and early twenty-first centuries, mix forms, structures, and genres in unique ways.

Three late twentieth-century U.S. playwrights who merged traditional realism with alternative forms were Sam Shepard (1943–2017), David Mamet (b. 1947), and August Wilson. Shepard's plays, such as *Buried Child* (1979), dealt with American mythology, emphasizing the violence and degeneration of the American family. His plays have surreal and absurdist techniques merged into the traditional domestics drama. Mamet dealt with sharp-edged characters in confrontation in such plays as *Glengarry Glen Ross* (1983), with his language influenced by the work of the absurdists.

A playwright of great importance later in the century was the African American dramatist August Wilson, who wrote a series of ten plays about the African American experience, one play for each decade of the twentieth century. Wilson's plays are filled with poetic symbols that echo the African American experience.

Across the globe, the plays and playwrights of our twenty-first century theatre continue to merge traditional forms and genres in unique ways. As we will see in the chapter, "Diverse and Inclusive Plays and Playwrights," there are also plays and playwrights that reflect our diverse world and work to make today's theatre more inclusive and equitable.

SUMMARY

1. Expressionism and surrealism attempt to show the workings of the subconscious. Expressionism presents a play from the point of view of the protagonist while surrealism stages the workings of the subconscious often structured like a dream.
2. Epic theatre was a form developed by the German playwright Bertolt Brecht. Brecht always wanted his audiences to know they were in the theatre and wanted his plays to teach a lesson.
3. Theatre of Cruelty was a theatrical concept by the French theorist Antonin Artaud. Artaud wanted theatre to bombard the audiences senses.
4. There have been many experimental forms that developed in the second half of the twentieth century including happenings, environmental theatre, and performance art.

All of these move away from the idea that theatre is text based. Postmodernism questions traditional dramatic forms and structures.

5. Political theatre and documentary drama are often traditional in form but nontraditional in subject matter. Political theatre focuses on a specific political issue and point of view. Documentary drama, which is often political in nature, uses actual texts, transcripts, and interviews and presents them on stage.

6. Many contemporary playwrights merge traditional genres and forms with alternative and experimental ones.

Design Elements: Audience Sitting in Theatre (theatre): Ron Chapple/Photodisc/Getty Images; Studio Light (spotlights): Exactostock/SuperStock

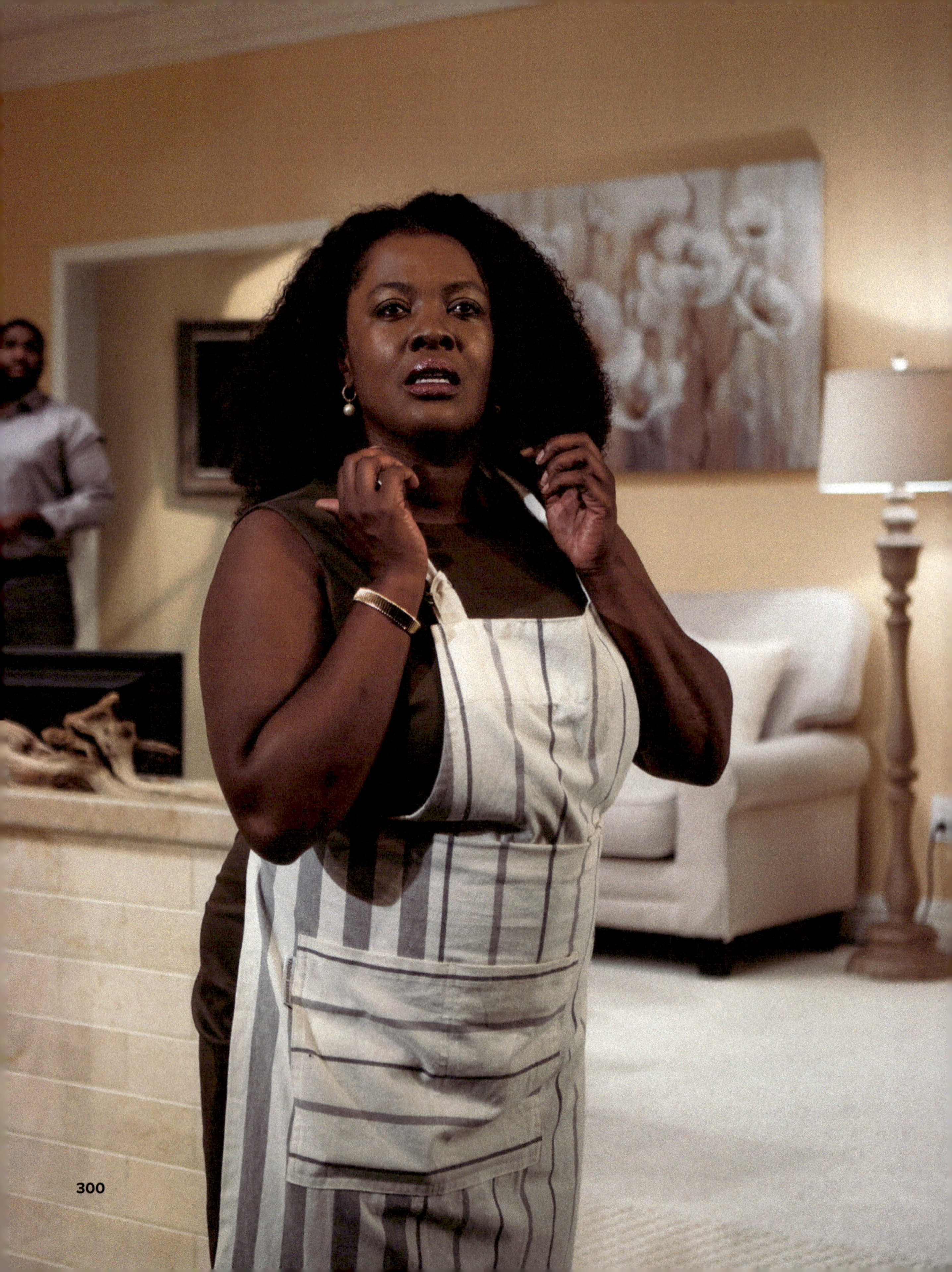

13

Diverse and Inclusive Plays, Playwrights, and Theatrical Forms

In this chapter, we review diverse forms of theatre, playwrights, and other theatre artists that have come from historically underrepresented and marginalized groups in the theatre in the United States. (We should note that underrepresentation of specific populations has also been true in theatre communities across the Western world.) We will review theatre created by African Americans, Latinx Americans, Asian Americans, indigenous peoples, women, and those in the LGBTQ communities. (Of course, there are many other theatres created by diverse groups in the United States and other Western societies.)

As we noted earlier, inspired by the Black Lives Matter movement and the widespread protests following the horrific murder of George Floyd by police officers, a group of BIPOC (Black, indigenous, and People of Color) theatre artists authored a document entitled "We See You, White American Theater" in which they called for changes in representation in the U.S. theatre. These artists called for rejecting the traditional repertoires of commercial and regional theatres by producing the current and past works by marginalized playwrights and theatre artists and truly committing to inclusivity and equity.

We will, therefore, first turn our attention to the past and current theatre works created by Black, Latinx, Asian American, and indigenous artists, and then review works created by women and LGBTQ theatre artists.

DIVERSE MULTICULTURAL THEATRE AND PLAYWRIGHTS

Before we discuss specific diverse theatres and playwrights, it should be noted that while many theatre artists wish to write from a specific ethnic or gender viewpoint, others who are members of an underrepresented group or the LGBTQ community, or

◀ **TODAY'S DIVERSE THEATRE**

Jackie Sibblies Drury's Fairview, *which won the 2019 Pulitzer Prize in Drama, turns the traditional family drama into a theatrical examination of systemic racism in the United States. Drury is one of many contemporary playwrights writing in today's diverse and multicultural theatre. Shown here are Heather Alicia Simms, in the foreground, and Charles Browning during a 2018 dress rehearsal of* Fairview *at the Soho Rep Theater in New York. (Emon Hassan/The New York Times/Redux)*

who espouse feminism or a political outlook, do not want to be identified primarily on that basis. For instance, there are Latinx or African American playwrights who want to be known as playwrights without any ethnic or racial identification. Also, there are people who are gay or lesbian or strong feminists, but they want to be regarded chiefly as dramatists, not gay dramatists, lesbian dramatists, or feminist dramatists.

African American Theatre and Playwrights: Introduction

African American theatre—also referred to as *Black theatre*—is a prime example of theatre reflecting the diversity of American culture and the contributions of a particular group to that culture. African American theatre is theatre written by and for Black Americans or performed by Black Americans. It partakes of two important traditions. One is the Western traditional theatre, in which actors like Paul Robeson (1898–1976) and writers like Lorraine Hansberry (1930–1965) have been significant. The other is a tradition that traces its origin to theatre in Africa and the Caribbean. Let us first look at some of the African traditions and current theatres that have influenced many Black playwrights and theatre artists.

African Theatres and Drama

Early African societies had many traditional performances connected to ceremonies and rituals that employed music, song, and dance. Colorful, symbolic costumes were also a key element of many rituals and ceremonies. African theatre artists in the twentieth century used these traditional forms and subverted forms of popular Western theatre in order to create work that reflects anticolonial struggles as well as attacks against totalitarian regimes in the newly independent African nations.

Contemporary African theatre and society are divided into English-speaking Africa; French-speaking Africa; Portuguese-speaking Africa; and Arabic-speaking Africa, which includes the northern African countries Egypt, Tunisia, Algeria, and Morocco. In the nations that were originally defined by nineteenth-century racist colonial powers, there are also attempts to experiment with the indigenous languages of the peoples of the regions of Africa.

In Portuguese-speaking Africa, which includes Angola, Cape Verde, Guinea-Bissau, Mozambique, and São Tomé and Principe, missionaries introduced religious drama in order to spread Catholicism. Before independence in 1975, much of the theatre in these regions was like vaudeville, although some anticolonial dramas were written as well. After independence, there was a greater focus on theatre that would arouse social consciousness, and plays followed the model of agitprop dramas; theatrical companies created collaborative works that focused on political and social issues.

French-speaking (francophone) Africa includes areas south of the Sahara as well as some nations in northern Africa. There is a vital theatre in the sub-Saharan nations, influenced by traditional forms of storytelling and music as well as by French theatre traditions. Many of the plays written in this part of French-speaking Africa have been produced in festivals organized in Paris.

English-speaking (anglophone) Africa, which includes Nigeria, South Africa, Uganda, and Zambia, has had a significant international impact. Anglophone theatre became highly developed in the 1950s because of the influence of universities in this region that encouraged the work of dramatists and also organized traveling theatre troupes. Among the influences on the theatre of English-speaking Africa are traditional forms, popular theatre, and the indigenous languages of the peoples; in fact, there has been considerable debate over whether theatre should be created in the language of the African peoples or in English. South Africa produced many significant playwrights and theatre companies in the 1970s; these companies frequently produced works that questioned South Africa's apartheid, in which races were defined and separated by law.

Concern for political and social equality is at the heart of the works of the South African playwright Athol Fugard (b. 1932) and the Nigerian playwright Wole Soyinka (b. 1934), and these two authors have become the most internationally renowned of all contemporary African playwrights. Fugard, who is white, attacked apartheid in such plays as *Sizwe Banzi Is Dead* (1973) and *Master Harold ... and the Boys* (1982). Some of Fugard's early works were written in collaboration with Black actors. His works represent the racial turmoil of South Africa during apartheid and post-apartheid.

Nigerian dramatist Wole Soyinka, who is also a poet, essayist, and novelist, began his career with the Royal Court Theatre in London in the late 1950s. His politically charged works led to his arrest in Nigeria in 1967, and two years in prison. Soyinka received the Nobel Prize in Literature in 1986. Among his best-known dramas are *Death and the King's Horsemen* (1975) and *Play of Giants* (1985).

In recent years an important group of dramatists, writing in Arabic, emerged in northern Africa, many dealing with sociopolitical issues.

WOLE SOYINKA: A NOBEL PLAYWRIGHT
Wole Soyinka, a remarkable playwright from Nigeria, is outspoken and has faced many hardships, including being jailed for his beliefs. Undeterred, he has continued to write plays, and in 1986 he was awarded the Nobel Prize in Literature. The scene shown here is from his play *Death and the King's Horseman* in a recent London production. (Donald Cooper/Shutterstock)

IN FOCUS: MARGINALIZED PLAYWRIGHTS AND PLAYS: EARLY AFRICAN AMERICAN THEATRE

While some Black theatre artists were able to work in the mainstream theatre, for the most part African American theatre artists were marginalized well into the twentieth century. However, there were many playwrights and other theatre artists whose work was extremely significant to the development of the U.S. theatre.

During the eighteenth and nineteenth centuries it was rare to see Black performers on the American stage. An exception to this were the actors appearing with the African Grove Theatre—a Black company founded in New York during the 1820-1821 season by William Brown (an African American) and the West Indian actor James Hewlett. The company was particularly noted for Shakespearean plays. Hewlett was the first Black to play Othello, and the renowned actor Ira Aldridge (c. 1806-1867) made his stage debut with the company. Here, too, the drama *King Shotaway* (1823)—believed to be the first play written and performed by African Americans—was presented. The African Grove closed in 1827, however, after attacks by white audience. Instead, throughout much of the nineteenth-century, horrific stereotypes of African Americans were performed by white actors in blackface in the popular minstrel shows.

As we noted in the discussion of musical theatre, African American composers and writers exerted a strong influence on the emerging musical theatre early in the twentieth century. During that same time, a number of African American stock companies were organized. The most significant was the Lafayette Players, founded in 1914 by Anita Bush (1883-1974). By the time it closed in 1932, this company had presented more than 250 productions and employed a number of Black stars. Black performers and writers were also making inroads into commercial theatre in the 1920s. Twenty plays and musicals with Black themes were presented on Broadway in this decade, five of them written by African Americans. The decade also saw some Black performers achieve recognition in serious drama, among them Charles Gilpin (1878-1930), Paul Robeson (1898-1976), and Ethel Waters (1896-1977). In the 1930s there were a few Broadway productions of plays by Black authors, such as the folk musical *Run Little Chillun* (1933) and *Mulatto* (1935) by Langston Hughes (1902-1967).

Even though there were few commercial productions of plays by African American playwrights during this time period, there were a number of women Black playwrights whose works were published or produced by community theatre groups, including: Mariette Bonner (1899-1971) and Angelina Weld Grimke (1880-1958), whose play *Rachel* deals with lynching.

Possibly the most significant development for Black theatre during the 1930s was the Federal Theatre Project, which was meant to help theatre artists through the Depression. This project formed separate Black units in twenty-two cities that mounted plays by Black and white authors and employed thousands of African American writers, performers, and technicians.

In 1932, *The Great Day* by Zora Neale Hurston (1891-1960) was produced on Broadway. In 1941, Orson Welles directed, for his Mercury Theater, a dramatization of the controversial novel *Native Son* by Richard Wright (1908-1960). Other important Broadway ventures included Paul Robeson's record run of 296 performances in *Othello* in 1943, and *Anna Lucasta* (1944), adapted by Abram Hill (1911-1986).

The 1950s saw an explosion of Black theatre that would continue over the next six decades. *Take a Giant Step* by Louis Patterson (b. 1922), a play about growing up in an integrated neighborhood, premiered in 1953. In 1954, the playwright-director Owen Dodson (1914-1983) staged *Amen Corner* by James Baldwin (1924-1987) at Howard University. Off-Broadway, the Greenwich Mews Theater began casting plays without regard to race and produced *Trouble in Mind* (1956) by Alice Childress (1920-1994), which she also directed. All of these plays would influence later Black dramatists, including Lorraine Hansberry and August Wilson.

African American Theatres and Playwrights

While there were many earlier Black playwrights, most of the works we will see in the theatre today by African American dramatists come from the late 1950s to the present day.

Possibly the most important production of the postwar era was *A Raisin in the Sun* (1959) by Lorraine Hansberry. The play is about a Black family in Chicago, held together by a God-fearing mother, at the time when the family is planning to move into a predominantly white neighborhood where they will be unwelcome. During the play, the son loses money in a get-rich-quick scheme and dashes their hopes, but later assumes responsibility for the family. Hansberry's play was directed by Lloyd Richards (1922–2006), the first Black director to work on Broadway.

IN FOCUS: *A RAISIN IN THE SUN* ON STAGE TODAY

Lorraine Hansberry's *A Raisin in the Sun* opened on Broadway in 1959. The play deals with a South Side Chicago Black family that struggles to improve its circumstances after receiving an insurance settlement following the death of the family's father. The family's matriarch wants to move the family into a home in a segregated white neighborhood, which meets with resistance from white residents, while her son wants to use the money to start a business and gain his independence. Hansberry's play depicts how racism is the major obstacle faced by African Americans as they try to access the American dream.

Hansberry's work is now a classic of the American theatre (even being adapted into a musical entitled *Raisin* in 1973) and has received many significant revivals in New York, regionally, and internationally in the twenty-first century. In 2004, a Broadway revival directed by Kenny Leon had a star-studded cast that included Sean (Puff Daddy) Combs (b. 1969), television star Phylicia Rashad (b. 1948), and Audra McDonald (b. 1970), who has won more Tony Awards than any actor in the history of the award. A television version of this production was filmed in 2008. A critically acclaimed production of *A Raisin in the Sun* was staged in Manchester, England, in 2010. (A West End production of the play was staged in London almost immediately after the original 1959 Broadway staging.) In 2014, Kenny Leon again directed a Broadway revival of the Hansberry play. Starring in the lead role was Denzel Washington as the son Walter (some critics argued he was too old to play the part). In 2016, the British Broadcasting Company (BBC) presented a radio play version of *A Raisin in the Sun*.

Many U.S. regional theatres have staged revivals of Hansberry's plays. In 2008, Penumbra Theatre, an African American company in Minneapolis, staged the play to such critical acclaim that it then moved to the renowned Guthrie Theatre in a co-production with the Arizona Theatre Company and the Cleveland Play House, two other significant regional theatres. One of the most recent regional revivals was presented at Washington, D.C.'s Arena Stage in 2017.

The influence of Hansberry's work on contemporary theatre is also reflected in new works that use the plot line, themes, and characters of *A Raisin in the Sun*. Bruce Norris's *Clybourne Park*, which won the Pulitzer Prize in 2011, has as its first act the story of the white family who is selling their home to the Youngers, the Black family in Hansberry's play. The second act is set fifty years later with the Youngers' home now in a Black neighborhood that is gentrifying.

Benethea's Place (2013), by British born Kwame Kwei-Armah (b. 1967), who was artistic director of Center Stage in Baltimore and is now artistic director of the Young Vic in London, deals with the Younger daughter who, in the first act, leaves in 1959 to go to Nigeria with her new husband Joseph Asagai (who also appears in *A Raisin in the Sun*). The second act is set fifty years later as Benethea, who is now a dean of social sciences at a California university, visits the dilapidated family home she still owns. In this way, Kwei-Armah's play deals with the continuing impact of racist colonialism and the oppressiveness of white privilege in the United States.

Revivals of *A Raisin in the Sun*, along with these new works influenced by Hansberry's play, clearly underscore the significant place the play has in the history of the theatre.

JOE TURNER'S COME AND GONE IN REHEARSAL
One of the most profound of playwright August Wilson's ten-part play cycle is *Joe Turner's Come and Gone*. Set in Pittsburgh in 1910, the scene is a boarding house in which African Americans from the South find refuge on their trip from the South to a hoped-for better life in the North. Parts of the play are mystical, especially the character Bynum Walker who says everyone should find his or her "song." The scene here, from a rehearsal at the Mark Taper Forum in Los Angeles, features cast member Gabriel Brown (center) dancing in front of the other boarders, who are portrayed (left to right) by January LaVoy, Glynn Tuman, Vivian Nixon, and Keith David. (Gary Friedman/Los Angeles Times/Getty Images)

Richards later became head of the Yale School of Drama, where in the 1980s he nurtured the talents of the renowned African American playwright August Wilson (1945–2005), author of *Ma Rainey's Black Bottom* (1984), *Fences* (1985), *Joe Turner's Come and Gone* (1986), *The Piano Lesson* (1990), *Seven Guitars* (1995), *King Hedley II* (2000), *Gem of the Ocean* (2003), and *Radio Golf* (2005). These plays are part of an impressive ten-part series in which each individual play focuses on one decade of the twentieth century. The magnitude of Wilson's achievement has led a number of commentators to call him the most important American playwright of the late twentieth century.

From 1960 to the 1990s, there was an outpouring of African American theatre, much of it reflecting the struggle for civil rights. Amiri Baraka (b. 1934) came to theatregoers' attention in 1964 with *Dutchman,* a verbal and sexual showdown between an assimilated Black male and a seductive white woman, set in a New York subway. Among other significant plays of these two decades were Adrienne Kennedy's *Funnyhouse of a Negro* (1964) and *The Owl Answers* (1969); Lonne Elder's *Ceremonies in Dark Old Men* (1969); Charles Gordone's *No Place to Be Somebody* (1969); Douglas Turner Ward's *Day of Absence* (1970); and

Charles Fuller's *A Soldier's Play* (1981), which won a Pulitzer Prize for Drama.

In 1970 the Black Theater Alliance listed more than 125 producing groups in the United States. Although only a few of these survived the decade, many had a significant impact. The Negro Ensemble Company, founded in 1967, holds the contemporary record for continuous production by a professional Black theatre company. The New Lafayette Theatre, which operated from 1966 until 1972, introduced the playwright Ed Bullins (b. 1935), experimented with Black ritual, and published the journal *Black Theater*. Other theatres of this period were the New Federal Theatre (founded by Woodie King) and the National Black Theatre (founded by Barbara Ann Teer).

In addition to the emergence of these producing organizations, another major change in the 1970s was the presence of a larger Black audience at Broadway theatres, which accounted for a significant number of commercial African American productions, such as *Don't Bother Me, I Can't Cope* (1972) and *Bubbling Brown Sugar* (1976). This trend continued in the 1980s and 1990s with such hits as *Jelly's Last Jam* (1992) and *Bring in 'da Noise, Bring in 'da Funk* (1996).

African American artists continued to make an impact on commercial and noncommercial theatre. For example, George C. Wolfe (b. 1955), author-director of *The Colored Museum* (1986), *Spunk* (1990), and *Jelly's Last Jam,* also directed both parts of the award-winning *Angels in America*. From 1993 to 2004, Wolfe was artistic director of a renowned off-Broadway facility, the Public Theater. In 2016, Wolfe directed and adapted *Shuffle Along*, the historic 1921 Broadway musical created and produced by African Americans, which he subtitled, *The Making of the Musical, Sensation of 1921 and All That Followed.*

TODAY'S THEATRE: GLOBAL AND DIVERSE
The work of the playwright Lynn Nottage is an excellent example of contemporary theatrical diversity. *Ruined*, directed by Kate Whoriskey, was jointly produced by the Goodman Theatre in Chicago and the Manhattan Theatre Club in New York. It is set in the Democratic Republic of the Congo in the year 2000 and tells the story of Sophie (Condola Phyleia Rashad) and her horrific experiences at the hands of men. (Liz Lauren/Richard Hein)

Another African American director, Kenny Leon (b. 1955), in 2002 founded the True Colors Theatre in Atlanta; and in 2004 and 2010 he directed revivals of *A Raisin in the Sun* and *Fences* on Broadway. In 2011 Leon staged two Broadway productions of plays by women African American authors: *The Mountaintop,* by Katori Hall (b. 1981), and *Stick Fly,* by Lydia R. Diamond (b. 1969).

Suzan-Lori Parks (b. 1964), Pearl Cleage (b. 1948), and Cheryl West (b. 1956) are contemporary African American women playwrights whose works deal with issues of racism and feminism and have been produced in regional and alternative

CURRENT AFRICAN AMERICAN PLAYWRIGHTS
Shown here are Joaquina Kalukango, left, and Paul Alexander Nolan in a scene from *Slave Play* by Jeremy O. Harris at the Golden Theater in New York on September 9, 2019. Harris's controversial play about interracial relationships, and how they mirror systemic racism, transferred from off-Broadway to Broadway in 2019. (Sara Krulwich/The New York Times/Redux)

theatres. Two additional African American women dramatists whose works are politically charged are Kia Corthron (b. 1961) and Lynn Nottage (b. 1964). Nottage won the Pulitzer Prize for *Ruined* (2008) and *Sweat* in 2016. Other emerging African American women playwrights are Jackie Sibblies Drury, whose *Fairview* won the 2019 Pulitzer Prize for Drama; Antoinette Nwandu, author of *Pass Over;* Dominique Morisseau; and Aleshea Harris.

Also among the current generation of African American dramatists are Thomas Bradshaw (b. 1980) and Branden Jacobs-Jenkins (b. 1985), both of whose works have been staged in off-off-Broadway, off-Broadway, and regional theatres, as well as Jeremy O. Harris (b. 1989), whose controversial *Slave Play* about interracial relationships transferred from off-Broadway to Broadway in 2019. Ike Holter (b. 1985) is an African American playwright who has written a seven-play series dealing with the contemporary Black experience in Chicago, and whose work has been produced at Chicago's storefront and larger regional theatres. His play *Hit the Wall* (2012), which deals in a uniquely theatrical fashion with the Stonewall riots, premiered in Chicago and has been produced around the United States.

Asian American Playwrights and Theatres

Asian American theatre should be seen against its background: the long, important heritage of the theatres of Asia. The Asian continent is immense and includes roughly forty countries and hundreds of ethnicities, languages, and theatre traditions. In the limited space of this book, it would be impossible to do justice to such diversity. Therefore, we will confine our discussion to three Asian countries and their theatre traditions—the Indian, Chinese, and Japanese—all of which reached a high point of artistic excellence many centuries ago at a time when religion and philosophy were central in each culture. This has kept the focus of traditional theatre allied to these realms, even though the societies themselves have modernized and changed. In addition, these three cultures created and sustained forms of theatre in which many facets of theatrical art—acting, mime, dancing, music, and text—were combined.

In all three countries, therefore, classical traditional theatre continues today: Kathakali in India; Beijing (Peking) opera in China; and nō, kabuki, and bunraku in

Japan. At the same time, Asian countries were influenced in the early twentieth century by Western dramatic forms, particularly the modernist traditions of realism and departures from realism.

It is against the backdrop of these ancient traditions that contemporary Asian American theatre developed. As early as the 1850s, puppet shows, acrobatic acts, and traditional operas were imported from China to California. For most of the nineteenth century and the first half of the twentieth century, however, Asians appeared in dramatic offerings strictly as stereotypes. In films, for instance, Asian Americans played such menial parts as cooks, spies, and vamps. Leading parts—even Asian characters—were played by whites in makeup.

With the coming of more cultural and ethnic awareness in the 1960s and 1970s, this situation began to change. In 1965 several Asian American performers and directors founded the East West Players in Los Angeles. In 1973, two more groups were formed—the Asian Exclusion Act in Seattle and the Asian-American Theatre Workshop in San Francisco—and in 1977 the director-actor Tisa Chang (b. 1945) founded the Pan Asian Repertory Theatre in New York. These groups employed Asian American performers, produced dramas from the Asian cultural heritage, and emphasized new plays written by and for Asian Americans. The plays often focused on issues and concerns specific to Asian Americans, such as racism and violence directed against those populations.

A number of plays by Asian American writers were produced in the 1970s and 1980s, including a memory play by Philip Kan Gotanda (b. 1950) called *Song for a Nisei Fisherman* (1982). In 2003 the American Conservatory Theatre (ACT) premiered his play *Yoheen,* and in 2007 ACT presented Gotanda's *After the War,* an epic drama about a group of people of different nationalities living in a boardinghouse run by a former jazzman.

A playwright who came to prominence in the 1980s was David Henry Hwang (b. 1957) who wrote several plays that won wide recognition, beginning with *FOB,* produced in 1980, *The Dance and the Railroad,* produced in 1981, and *M. Butterfly* in 1988, which opened successfully on Broadway. Based on a true story, the play deals with a French diplomat who meets and falls in love with a Chinese opera singer who he thinks is a woman but turns out to be a man and a spy.

The newer generation of Asian American playwrights includes Diana Son (b. 1965); Chay Yew (b. 1965), who between 2011 and 2019 was the artistic director of Chicago's Victory Gardens Theatre; Han Ong (b. 1968); and Young Jean Lee (b. 1974), who is also a director. Her *Straight White Men* in 2018 became the first play written by an Asian American woman produced on Broadway. Other emerging Asian American playwrights are Yilong Liu, Jiehae Park, Lauren Yee (b. 1986), Qui Nguyen, whose *She Kills Monsters* (2011) and *Vietgone* (2015) have been produced at many regional theatres, and Christopher Chen, whose *Caught* won the 2017 off-Broadway award for best play.

There has also been a movement to have more Asian Americans employed as performers in appropriate roles. Hwang and the actor B. D. Wong, who played the Chinese opera singer in the original production of *M. Butterfly,* led a vigorous protest against the hiring of an English actor to play the leading role in the musical *Miss Saigon.* That battle was lost; but by 1996, when a revival of *The King and I* opened on Broadway, it had a large proportion of Asian American performers. The same was true for the Lincoln Center revival in 2015.

ASIAN AMERICAN THEATRE

The Vietnamese American playwright Qui Nguyen has had plays produced regionally and off-Broadway. Shown here is a scene from the New York City Center Stage's production of his best-known work *Vietgone,* which depicts the relationship between two young, in love refugees from the Vietnam War (played by Paco Tolson and Jennifer Ikeda). (Emon Hassan/The New York Times/Redux)

However, there continues to be concerns regarding theatres not casting Asian American actors or employing other Asian American theatre artists. In 2012, the La Jolla Playhouse in San Diego cast a white actor as a Chinese emperor (and had only three Asian performers) in the workshop of the musical *The Nightingale*. The Royal Shakespeare Company in London also created controversy in 2013 when Asian actors were cast only in minor roles in the classic Chinese play, *The Orphan of Zhao*. A study of New York City's 2018–2019 theatre season, done by the Asian American Performers Action Coalition, reported that only 6.9 percent of all roles were played by Asian Americans, only 4.9 percent of all writers were Asian Americans, and only 4.5 percent of the directors were Asian Americans.

Latinx Theatre

Contemporary Latinx (a gender neutral term that replaced Latino/a) or Hispanic theatre in the United States can be divided into at least three groups: Chicano theatre, Cuban American theatre, and Puerto Rican or Nuyorican theatre. All three address the experiences of Latinx Americans living in the United States, and the plays may sometimes written in Spanish or a combination of Spanish and English, but are usually performed in English.

As is the case with all diverse theatres, many Latinx playwrights and theatre artists have been influenced by traditional and popular forms to reflect on specific Latinx American sociopolitical topics.

Chicano theatre, which originated primarily in the West and Southwest, came to prominence during the civil rights movements of the 1960s. The theatre troupe known as El Teatro Campesino ("farmworkers' theatre") grew out of the work of Luis Valdéz (b. 1940), who joined César Chavez in organizing farmworkers in California. Valdéz wrote *actos,* short agitprop pieces dramatizing the lives of workers. (The term *agitprop* means "agitation propaganda"; it was applied in the 1930s to plays with a strong political or social agenda.)

El Teatro Campesino became the prototype for other groups such as Teatro de la Gente ("people's theatre"), founded in 1967; and Teatro de la Esperanza ("theatre of hope"), begun in 1971 in Santa Barbara, California. Valdéz's play *Zoot Suit* (1978), about racial violence in Los Angeles in 1943, opened in Los Angeles to considerable acclaim and later moved to Broadway. Other plays about the Chicano experience followed, one of the most notable being *Roosters* (1987) by Milcha Sanchez-Scott (b. 1955), in which cockfighting is a metaphor used to explore Chicano concerns and family conflicts. Luis Alfaro (b. 1963) is a Chicano performance artist, director, and playwright whose best-known works are adaptations of *Oedipus the King, Oedipus el Rey* (2010) and of *Medea, Mojada* (2013). Two Mexican American women playwrights whose works are currently being produced at regional theatres across the United States are Karen Zacarias (b. 1969) and Marisela Treviño Orta.

Cuban American theatre developed chiefly in Florida. The Federal Theatre Project of the 1930s resulted in fourteen Cuban American productions in 1936 and 1937. A highly regarded Cuban American dramatist who began to be produced in the 1970s was Maria Irene Fornés (1930–2018). Other Cuban American playwrights include Eduardo Machado (b. 1953) and Nilo Cruz (b. 1960), who won a Pulitzer Prize in 2003 for *Anna in the Tropics.*

Nuyorican is a term that refers to Puerto Rican culture, mostly in New York but elsewhere as well. Works by Puerto Rican playwrights began to be produced in the 1960s and 1970s by groups such as the Teatro Repertorio Español; the Puerto Rican Traveling Theatre, founded by Miriam Colon; and the New York Public Theater, founded by Joseph Papp. The Nuyorican Poets' Café presented plays by a number of Hispanic writers, including an ex-convict, Miguel Piñero (1947–1988), whose *Short Eyes,* a harshly realistic portrait of prison life, proved to be very successful and won a number of awards in the 1973–1974 season.

Today many Puerto Rican playwrights have come to prominence. Quiara Alegreia Hudes (b. 1978) won the Pulitzer Prize in 2012 for *Water by the Spoonful,*

A MILESTONE IN LATINO/A THEATRE
A significant event in the emergence of Latino/a theatre was the 1978 production of *Zoot Suit* by Luis Valdez. It was a Brechtian-like musical based on a real event, but it was given a highly theatrical treatment. *Zoot Suit* originated in Los Angeles and moved to Broadway. Seen here is a 2017 revival at the Mark Taper Forum in Los Angeles directed by the author. (Craig Schwartz)

LATINX THEATRE
Lin-Manuel Miranda, center, as Uanavi in his musical *In the Heights* in 2008. *In the Heights* is a rap, hip-hop, and salsa flavored musical about Latinx families in Washington Heights in New York City. The film version premiered in 2021. (Sara Krulwich/The New York Times/Redux)

which is part of a trilogy of plays, and also authored the book for the musical *In the Heights* (2007). Lin-Manuel Miranda (b. 1980), whose heritage is Puerto Rican, is the composer of *In the Heights* as well as *Hamilton* (2015), for which he wrote the book.

The vitality of Latinx theatre is also reflected in the many companies that are dedicated to the presentation of works by Latinx playwrights of various backgrounds. In 1971, a network of Latinx theatres across the country was established. Current examples including Teatro Vista, established by two Cuban-born theatre artists, and Teatro Luna, organized by ten Latina women, including Mexican-born playwright Tanya Saracho (b. 1980), perform works by Latinx artists in Chicago.

Indigenous Theatres and Playwrights

Indigenous peoples are those peoples who lived in areas long before modern states were founded by colonizers. In the United States, for example, we refer to the indigenous peoples who were here prior to the Europeans as Native Americans or American Indians. They belonged to various individual cultures with unique languages and traditions; their lands stolen and they were brutally massacred and relocated by European colonizers. This happened throughout the newly established nations in North and South America. In addition, those who survived were often forced to live in segregate communities and forced to give up traditional ways of life.

Strictly speaking, there was no Native American theatre tradition; rather, there were spiritual and social traditions that had theatrical and performative elements. These were found primarily in ancient rituals and communal celebrations, which were often infused with cosmic significance. Also, unlike traditional Western theatre, these events had no audience as such: those observing were considered participants just as much as the principal performers. Many of these ceremonies and the like were outlawed by the American government in the nineteenth century. Thus the legacy of rituals and ceremonies, which had strong theatrical components—not to mention significant spiritual and cultural value—was lost or forced to go "underground."

The American Indian Religious Freedom Act of 1972 made it legal once again for certain ceremonies, such as the sun dance, to resume. The increased awareness of these rituals and celebrations contributed to the emergence of a Native American theatre. Two groups that led the way in the past three decades were the Native American Theatre Ensemble and Spiderwoman.

The Native American Theatre Ensemble, which was originally called the American Indian Theatre Ensemble, was founded by Hanay Geiogamah. (It is important to note that those familiar with Native American theatre invariably identify theatre companies and theatre artists not with the generic term *Native American theatre,* but in terms of their tribes. Thus, Geiogamah is identified as Kiowa-Delaware.) Geiogamah's organization gave its premiere performance at La Mama in New York City in 1972, and later toured widely, not only in North America but also in Europe and elsewhere.

Spiderwoman Theatre comes under the headings of both Native American theatre and feminist theatre. Founded in 1975, it is the longest continually running women's theatre in North America, as well as the longest-running Native American theatre. Three of its founding members—Lisa Mayo, Gloria Miguel, and Muriel Miguel—draw on storytelling and other theatrical traditions to celebrate their identity as American Indian women and to comment on stereotypes of women in general.

Another important Native American producing organization is Native Voices at the Autry Museum in Los Angeles. Randy Reinholz, a Native American, and his wife, Jean Bruce Scott, had developed a program presenting Native American drama at Illinois State University where they were on the faculty. In 2000, they were invited to bring their project, Native Voices, to the Autry to become a full-time, professional producing organization in Los Angeles. Since that beginning they have presented a series of readings, workshops, and full productions of a wide range of Native American dramatic writing.

Native Voices productions include *Kino and Teresa* (2005), a retelling by James Lujan (Taos Pueblo) of the story of *Romeo and Juliet*. The play pits people from the Taos Pueblo against their Spanish conquerors. Other productions include *Super Indian* (2007), *Stand-off at Highway #37* (2014) by Vickie Ramirez (Tuscarora), and *Lying with Badgers* (2020) by Jason Grasl (Blackfeet), which tells the story of two estranged brothers of the Blackfeet nation using puppets interacting with actors, as well as an annual theatre festival of new plays.

Several Native American playwrights have published single-author anthologies of their works including William F. Yellow Robe Jr. (Assiniboine); Diane Glancy (Cherokee); and E. Donald Two-Rivers (Anishinabe). Another important contemporary playwright is Bruce King (Turtle Clan, Haudenosaunee-Oneida). King and Yellow Robe are also directors who have founded their own companies in the recent past and have taught playwriting and performance at the Institute of American Indian Arts in Santa Fe, New Mexico.

Recognition of the neglect of Native American drama took an interesting turn in the spring of 2018 when three major theatres in Oregon, that had rarely, if ever, scheduled a play by a Native American, presented plays by three such authors, all women playwrights, simultaneously. The Oregon Shakespeare Festival premiered

THE JOURNEY OF A NATIVE AMERICAN THROUGH TODAY'S CHALLENGING WORLD

In this drama, *Ghostlands,* Robert Owens-Greygrass (Lakota, shown here) deals with the conflicting worlds of his native heritage. Greygrass, who also wrote the piece, portrays sixteen characters through the sometimes comic but always challenging journey of Native Americans in today's world. Presented at the Autry Museum in Los Angeles, directed by Kevin Sifuentes (Hopi) in 2012. ((left) Craig Schwartz; (right) Bert Vanderveen)

A NATIVE AMERICAN WALKS THE "TRAIL OF TEARS"

Native American performer and playwright DeLanna Studi (Cherokee) and her father walked the 900-mile journey from the native American Indian territory in the southeastern United States to the Oklahoma territory—a journey known as the "Trail of Tears"—the path American Indians were forced to take on foot after an edict expelling them from their homeland in 1830. From this journey, she fashioned her play *And So We Walked* which she is seen here performing at the Portland Center Stage.

Manahatta, a play by Mary Kathryn Nagle that takes the events of the 1600s when the Dutch inhabitants of Manhattan expelled and walled out the Native Americans of the Lenape tribe, forcing them to leave their native habitat; she relates that to another crisis several centuries later, namely, the financial collapse in the United States of 2008–2012. The Portland Center Stage presented *And So We Walked* by DeLanna Studi, a play that traces the journey of the playwright and her father on the "Trail of Tears," the forced immigration route of Indians from their native home in the southeastern United States to the Oklahoma territory west of the Mississippi River in the late 1830s, an event described in the accompanying photograph. The Artist's Repertory Theatre of Portland premiered *The Thanksgiving Play* by Larissa FastHorse, a satire that challenges theatre companies who claim that they cannot find actors who are able to play the roles of Native Americans. (It is hoped that this

314   Part Four   The Playwright and the Play

coincidence of presentations of Native American theatre does not turn out to be a one-off event.)

There are also many Native American theatre organizations throughout the United States, including Thunderbird Theatre at Haskell Indian Nations University, founded in 1974; Red Earth Performing Arts, founded in Seattle in 1974; and the Tulsa Indian Actor's Workshop, founded in 1993. The American Indian Community House (ACH) in New York City uses its theatre space for Native American performing artists, hosting the Indian Summer Series, a month-long festival; ACH also keeps a database of native performers.

What is important to note about Native American drama and theatre today is that it is not primarily historical or ceremonial. Though elements of tribal traditions may be incorporated, the emphasis among playwrights and producers is really on fusing the problems and aspirations of today's Native Americans with their heritage.

This is also true of indigenous playwrights and theatre artists from many other countries. As examples, we can look at indigenous theatre from Canada and Australia. The popular Australian musical *Bran Nue Dae* (1990) dealt with Aboriginal life. It is also estimated that over the past fifty years, there have been hundreds of productions of plays by indigenous dramatists. Among some of the best known are: Jane Harrison's *Stolen* (1997), Andrea James' *Yanagai! Yanagai!* (2003), and Tammy Anderson's *I Don't Wanna Play House* (2000). The indigenous theatre at Canada's National Arts Centre in Ottawa produces work by and dealing with the indigenous peoples of Canada.

Additional Diverse Theatres, Playwrights, and Theatre Artists While we have discussed many diverse theatres in the United States, there are many other companies (and playwrights) that reflect the ever-expanding diversity of U.S. society.

For example, Noor Theatre in New York City, founded by three women of Middle Eastern descent, strives to present work from the growing Middle Eastern communities in the United States. Silk Road Rising is a Chicago theatre company that presents plays relevant to the Asian American and Middle Eastern American experiences and says in its mission statement that it hopes to "advance a polycultural worldview."

Among the playwrights who reflect this diversity is Pakistani American Ayad Akhtar (b. 1970), whose play *Disgraced* won the 2013 Pulitzer Prize; Stephen Karam (b. 1980), whose dramas include *Sons of the Prophet* (2011) and *The Humans* (2014); and Rajiv Joseph (b. 1974), whose father immigrated from India and who authored *Bengal Tiger at the Baghdad Zoo* (2009) and *Guards at the Taj* (2015).

The impact of multicultural artists on U.S. theatre is also evident in the career of Palestinian American director Joseph Haj (b. 1965), directing at such theatres as the Oregon Shakespeare Festival, the Actors Theatre of Louisville, and the Folger Theatre in Washington, D.C.; serving as producing artistic director at the Playmakers Repertory Company in North Carolina; and then becoming the eighth artistic director of the Guthrie Theater in 2015, following the retirement of the Irish-born director Joe Dowling (b. 1949).

FEMINIST THEATRE AND WOMEN PLAYWRIGHTS

Feminist theatre, as we know it, is a significant movement that began in the socially active atmosphere of the late 1960s and early 1970s. It developed alongside the more general feminist movement, which stressed consciousness-raising to make people aware of the subordinate position women had often been forced to occupy in social, corporate, and political structures. Activists in this period attempted to revise cultural value systems and interpersonal relations in terms of an egalitarian ideology. In theatre, this took the form of theatre groups like the It's Alright to Be a Woman Theatre in New York, one of the first groups to translate consciousness-raising into stage performances.

Feminist theatre developed in multiple directions. For one thing, there was an attempt to make women writers of the past more widely acknowledged and recognized. The other direction for feminist theatre was the very active writing and production that emerged in the late 1960s when many women playwrights questioned traditional gender roles and the place of women in American society.

In the 1970s and 1980s, in response to the women's movement, which spurred women's playwriting and women's theatre companies, there were a number of critically

IN FOCUS: MARGINALIZED THEATRE ARTISTS: WOMEN PLAYWRIGHTS AND THEIR PLAYS

As with the other diverse groups we have discussed in this chapter, early women playwrights' works were often overlooked by theatre historians and those who produced classical works. These women were excluded from what many refer to as the "traditional canon," which was made up of plays almost exclusively by white, male, European authors. However, as noted, the rediscovery of these works by feminist critics and scholars has exerted a significant influence on contemporary women playwrights.

Thus, historical figures like Hrosvitha, a nun who wrote plays in her convent at Gandersheim in Germany in the tenth century, and the English playwrights Aphra Behn (1640–1689) and Susanna Centlivre (c. 1670–1723) were brought to the forefront. Works by Behn and Centlivre provide insights into the Restoration and eighteenth-century worlds through the eyes of women.

In addition, attention is now paid to several women playwrights who had made their mark in the early and middle twentieth century. One significant forerunner, for example, was the American playwright Rachel Crothers (1878–1958), who wrote and directed many successful plays from 1906 to 1937. All of Crothers's plays dealt with women's moral and social concerns, and most of them were set in urban high society. Crothers's plays are skillful, entertaining comedies, but she always focused on the issue of sexual equality.

Other notable women playwrights earlier in the twentieth century were Susan Glaspell (1876–1948), Sophie Treadwell (1890–1970), and Lillian Hellman (1905–1984). Glaspell's one-act play *Trifles,* Treadwell's *Machinal,* and Lillian Hellman's *The Children's Hour* and *Little Foxes* are now considered classics of the American theatre. We also noted earlier a number of women Black playwrights of the early twentieth century, including Angelina Weld Grimké (1880-1958), whose 1916 play *Rachel* dealt with lynching.

A signal event—some would say a transformative event that we noted earlier in our discussion of African American theatre—occurred in 1959 when Lorraine Hansberry's play *A Raisin in the Sun* opened on Broadway, the first play written by a Black woman dramatist to achieve such wide acclaim. Its success became a milestone.

As we shall see all of these early women playwrights set the stage for the many women whose works are now central to the contemporary U.S. and global theatres.

CONTEMPORARY WOMEN PLAYWRIGHTS
An important development in recent years has been the emergence of women playwrights after many years of male domination among American dramatists. Today women playwrights are coming to the forefront in impressive numbers, and among them is Amy Herzog. In her play *Belleville* a young couple have abandoned the stability of their life in the United States for a life in bohemian Paris where their marriage unravels, at the same time that many lessons are learned. Playing the couple in this scene at the New York Theatre Workshop are Maria Dizzia and Greg Keller. (Sara Krulwich/The New York Times/Redux)

and commercially successful women American playwrights. Representative works include *Fefu and Her Friends* (1977) by Maria Irene Fornés, which offered insight into female friendship and the struggles women experience in a patriarchal culture; *Still Life* (1981) by Emily Mann (b. 1952); *Painting Churches* (1983) by Tina Howe (b. 1937); and three plays that won the Susan Smith Blackburn Prize, and later the Pulitzer Prize for Drama: *'Night, Mother* (1983) by Marsha Norman, *Crimes of the Heart* (1977) by Beth Henley (b. 1952), and *The Heidi Chronicles* (1988) by Wendy Wasserstein.

Although the women's movement transformed during the 1980s, women continued to write plays in increasing numbers. The playwrights who had broken new ground in the 1970s continued to write dramas, and now they were joined by other women's voices. *How I Learned to Drive* (1998) by Paula Vogel (b. 1951) is about a girl's coming-of-age. Vogel's most recent play, *Indecent* (2015), deals with the production of a play on Broadway in 1923 that focused on a lesbian love affair. The Pulitzer Prize winning play *Wit* (1998), by Margaret Edson (b. 1962) deals with a college professor dealing with terminal illness. These plays are examples of women's ongoing exploration of new subjects and new forms.

There are many contemporary U.S. women playwrights. Earlier in this chapter, we mentioned significant African American women playwrights: Suzan-Lori Parks (b. 1964), Pearl Cleage (b. 1948), Kia Corthron (b. 1961), Lynn Nottage (b. 1964), Dominique Morisseau (b. 1978), Katori Hall (b. 1981), Alesha Harris sand Jackie

POLITICAL THEATRE: A FEMINIST PERSPECTIVE
A well-known contemporary playwright is Sarah Ruhl. In her play *In the Next Room (*or *The Vibrator Play)*, she presents a feminist point of view about the circumstances of women in the late nineteenth century when society was dominated by men, and women's feelings of sexuality were often suppressed. In such a society, sexual fulfillment for some women could be found only indirectly and infrequently. Shown here are Maria Dizzia and Michael Cerveris as patient and doctor in a scene from the play. (Sara Krulwich/The New York Times/Redux)

Sibblies Drury. We also noted that there are feminist Latina American, Asian American, and indigenous playwrights.

Among other current women playwrights whose works deal with feminist and broader social issues are Sarah Ruhl (b. 1974), Theresa Rebeck (b. 1958), Rebecca Gilman (b. 1965), Carson Kreitzer, and Amy Herzog (b. 1979). Sarah Ruhl was awarded the Susan Smith Blackburn Prize in 2004, an award given annually to a woman who writes for the English-language theatre, and was the recipient of a MacArthur "genius" grant. Ruhl's play *The Clean House,* a Pulitzer Prize finalist, concerns a Brazilian maid who turns out to be a comedian and who refuses to clean the messy house of her disorganized employers. A play by Ruhl on Broadway in 2009 was *The Next Room*. Among recent works by Herzog are *After the Revolution, 4000 Miles,* and *Belleville*.

Theresa Rebeck, a successful writer for television, in her play *The Scene* wrote a sharp, pointed satire about today's television industry. Her play *The Water's Edge* transplanted the Greek story of Agamemnon, the returning warrior, to modern times and developed a seriocomic drama that mixes a tragic situation with amusing observations. Rebeck is also the author of *Seminar*. Claire Barron (b. 1986) is a current playwright whose works, such as *You Got Older* (2015) and *Dance Nation* (2018), deal with how women's roles are shaped in contemporary society.

As noted, there are many feminist theatre organizations. Some scholars estimate that more than 100 such companies have been founded in the United States; these companies include At the Foot of the Mountain, Women's Experimental Theatre, and Omaha Magic Theatre, founded by the playwright Megan Terry. One company, Split Britches, was started in 1981 by Lois Weaver, Peggy Shaw, and Deborah Margolin as an offshoot of Spiderwoman Theatre. Split Britches became well known for its production of *Belle Reprieve* (1991), which made satiric references to Tennessee Williams's *A Streetcar Named Desire* and was created collaboratively with an English gay company, Bloolips.

GENDER DIVERSITY: FEMINIST THEATRE

For some years now, a number of playwrights and theatre companies have treated contemporary issues and concerns confronting women. Shown here is a scene from the 2019 Steppenwolf Theatre production of *Dance Nation* by Clare Barron, which was a Pulitzer Prize finalist in 2019 and the winner of the 2017 Susan Smith Blackburn Prize, which recognizes outstanding playwriting by women. Barron's satrical drama uses adults to play teenagers in the world of dance competitions. (Michael Brosilow)

A PROVOCATIVE PLAY: *UNEXPLODED ORDNANCES (UXO)*

Split Britches is a well-known, well-established Lesbian theatre company founded some years ago by Peggy Shaw and Lois Weaver. One of their recent productions, *Unexploded Ordnances*, shown here, deals with below-the-radar, unknown lethal military explosives that exist in secret places. The group in the play wants to find them and expose where they might be found. In the scene shown here the General (Shaw), far left, has gathered a panel in an attempt to discover the whereabouts of these missiles and munitions. Not shown is the President (Weaver) assisting in the search. (Sara Krulwich/The New York Times/Redux)

IN FOCUS: LAUREN GUNDERSON

During the 2019 to 2020 theatre season, eleven of the top twenty playwrights produced in the United States were women. The most produced playwright was Lauren Gunderson (b. 1982). The year prior to that Gunderson was second on the list and in 2017–2018 she was also the most produced dramatist in the United States. Gunderson is an extremely prolific playwright who has authored over twenty scripts.

Yet, Gunderson, who completed an M.F.A. in Dramatic Writing at New York University in 2009 and now lives and writes in San Francisco, has never had one of her plays produced on Broadway and has had only a small number of New York productions. Instead, her works are a mainstay of all of the country's major regional theatres. In 2019–2020, there were thirty-three productions of her plays at such theatres.

Many of Gunderson's plays focus on strong women characters. She has written about historic figures (these include *Silent Sky*, a 2011 play about the nineteenth century astronomer Henrietta Leavitt and *The Half-Life of Marie Curie*, first staged in 2019); characters adapted from popular novels (such as *Miss Bennet: Christmas at Pemberley*, which premiered in 2018 featuring the popular character from Jane Austen's *Pride and Prejudice*); and a musical *Jeannette*, about America's first congresswoman, which was workshopped in 2019 and early 2020 with a cast comprised of performers who were Black, Brown, Asian, white, indigenous, gay, straight, and transgender. In 2020 during the COVID-19 pandemic, her play *The Catastrophist,* about her husband who is a world renowned virologist, was streamed as "cinematic digital theatre."

The question remains: why hasn't Gunderson had greater recognition and commercial productions. Whatever the reasons, Gunderson has proven that she can be one of the most successful playwrights, if not the most successful, in the United States without commercial theatre recognition.

Lauren Gunderson is one of the most produced playwrights in the United States. Seen here are Kayla Ferguson and Reggie D. White in her play *I and You,* directed by Sean Daniels and produced by Merrimack Repertory Theatre in association with Richard Winkler at the off Broadway 59E59 Theaters. (Sara Krulwich/The New York Times/Redux)

Many of the feminist companies that were started in the 1970s and 1980s, at the height of the women's movement, have closed. But several still remain, including Women's Project and Productions, which was founded in 1978 by Julia Miles. Also, new feminist companies have developed in recent years. Rivendell Theatre, founded in Chicago in 1995, is, according to its mission statement, committed to presenting audiences with "artistically challenging, thought provoking plays that explore the female experience." Feminist theatre companies continue to urge audiences to re-examine their own gender biases and those of their society.

It is important to be aware, as well, that there are feminist companies and women playwrights across the globe. In England, for example, there are a number of significant

A RECENT PLAY BY CARYL CHURCHILL: *LOVE AND INFORMATION*
Caryl Churchill has been the leading woman dramatist in Great Britain for the past half century, having written dozens of provocative, original dramas for the stage as well as scripts for film and television. Her recent play, *Love and Information,* consists of seven brief segments or vignettes which Churchill instructs the director to present in any sequence she or he chooses. The performers shown here are John Procaccino and Kellie Overbey in a 2014 production at the Minetta Lane Theatre in New York. (Sara Krulwich/The New York Times/Redux)

women playwrights, including Caryl Churchill (b. 1938), Timberlake Wertenbaker (b. 1946), Pam Gems (1925–2011), Nina Raine, Rebecca Lenkiewicz (1968), the first living woman dramatist to have her original work staged at London's National Theatre, and Lucy Prebble (b. 1981). In Austria, Nobel Prize-winner Elfried Jelinek (b. 1946) writes plays about current political issues, such as *On the Royal Road: The Burgher King* (2017), which satirizes President Donald Trump.

LGBTQ THEATRE AND PLAYWRIGHTS

Lesbian theatre groups can be part of feminist theatre, but gay, lesbian, and transgender theatre is also a distinct movement. A number of plays and performers introduced gay, lesbian, and transgender themes into theatre before the 1960s. For example, in the nineteenth century and the early twentieth century there was a considerable amount of cross-dressing in performances: Men often appeared in "drag" and women in men's clothing, raising questions about sexual and gender roles. Also, plays included material on this subject; one example is Lillian Hellman's *The Children's Hour* (1934), in which a presumed lesbian relationship between two schoolteachers was presented.

However, the play that first brought gay life to the forefront was *The Boys in the Band* (1968), by Mart Crowley (1935–2020). Crowley depicted a group of men living an openly gay life. In 1969, the year after it opened, gay patrons of the Stonewall Inn in New York's Greenwich Village fought against police officers attempting to close the bar. This uprising, considered an early milestone of the modern gay rights movement, changed attitudes of gay activists, who now rejected what they considered a stereotype

GAY AND LESBIAN THEATRE
Among the many diverse theatres that emerged in the last part of the twentieth century was theatre centering on the gay and lesbian experience. An important drama in this category was *The Normal Heart,* a largely autobiographical drama by Larry Kramer. The play, about the beginning of the AIDS crisis in the early 1980s, pits two characters against each other, one urging a full-throated confrontation with the public calling attention to the epidemic and the other taking a more measured approach. A 2011 revival of the play featured the performers shown here: Ellen Barkin, John Benjamin Hickoy, and Joe Mantello. (Sara Krulwich/The New York Times/Redux)

of homosexuals depicted in *The Boys in the Band.* However, successful New York revivals in 1998, 2010, and on Broadway in 2018 to celebrate the play's fiftieth anniversary, as well as in Chicago in 2020, led to a reevaluation of the play's significance in the history of gay, lesbian, and transgender theatre in the United States.

In the years that followed, complex gay characters were presented unapologetically. Plays in the 1970s and 1980s included *The Ritz* (1975) by Terrence McNally (1938–2020) and *Torch Song Trilogy* (1983) by Harvey Fierstein (b. 1954), which was revived off-Broadway in 2017. Since then, more and more plays have dealt expressly with gay issues. In these dramas, not only are the daily lives of gays and lesbians presented forthrightly but frequently gay or lesbian sociopolitical concerns are also put forward. In addition to a general concern for gay, lesbian, and transgender themes, there was a sense of urgency engendered by the AIDS crisis. This has led to a number of significant dramas, including *The Normal Heart* (1985) by Larry Kramer (1935–2020), which was revived in a Tony award–winning production in 2011; *As Is* (1985) by William M. Hoffman (1939–2017); Tony Kushner's two-part play *Angels in America: A Gay Fantasia on National Themes* (1993–1994); and Terrence McNally's *Love! Valour! Compassion!* (1995). *The Inheritance* (2018) by Matthew Lopez (b. 1977) is a play presented in two parts, each over three hours, that dramatizes the lives of New York gay men a generation after the AIDS crisis and their indebtedness to earlier gay men.

THE FIVE LESBIAN BROTHERS' *THE SECRETARIES*
The Secretaries is a wild, knockabout farce written almost two decades ago by the Five Lesbian Brothers, a long-time women's cooperative in New York. It is concerned with mayhem and comical intrigue among a group of secretaries and deals with lesbian subject matter. It was successfully revived in 2016 in this production at the About Face Theatre in Chicago. Directed by Bonnie Metzgar, the actors shown here are, left to right, Kelli Simpkins, Meghan Reardon, Lauren Sivak, Erin Barlow, and Sadieh Rifai. (Michael Brosilow)

Among the lesbian playwrights who paved the way for the current generation were many who also dealt with feminist and multicultural issues. They include Megan Terry, Maria Irene Fornes, and Paula Vogel, all of whom were mentioned earlier.

Groups that used cross-dressing to break stereotypes of gender and sexual orientation were also extremely important in the past five decades. Among the early "gender-bender" groups were the Cockettes and the Angels of Light in San Francisco and Centola and Hot Peaches in New York. An important company in New York was the Theatre of the Ridiculous, founded by John Vaccaro, which developed an extraordinary writer and performer—Charles Ludlam (1943–1987). Ludlam rewrote the classics to include a good deal of wild parody and frequent cross-dressing; he also created the long-lived Ridiculous Theatrical Company

Another important group was the Five Lesbian Brothers, a collective of five women, including the solo performance artist Lisa Kron, who were based in New York City (1876–1948) and staged plays parodying mainstream attitudes toward gender and sexuality. Chicago's About Face Theatre, founded in 1995, has as a mission "to be Chicago's celebrated center for lesbian, gay, bisexual, transgender, queer and ally (LGBTQA) arts." Though a number of these groups have not survived, individual performers and playwrights in gay, lesbian, and transgender theatre remain very much a focus of attention.

Chapter 13 *Diverse and Inclusive Plays, Playwrights, and Theatrical Forms*

The twenty-first century continues to see plays tackling issues of gay, lesbian, and transgender identity and relationships. Commercially successful plays focusing on gay characters include *Take Me Out* (2003) by Richard Greenberg (b. 1958), *Next Fall* (2009) by Geoffrey Nauffts (b. 1961), and *Significant Other* (2015) by Joshua Harmon (b. 1983). The current generation of lesbian playwrights includes K. S. Stevens, author of *Butch Mamas!* (2009); solo artist Carolyn Gage (b. 1952); Elizabeth Whitney, creator of *Wonder Woman! A Cabaret of Heroic Proportions!* (2009); Meryl Cohen, author of *Reasons to Live* (2012); and Lisa Kron (b. 1961).

There are a number of transgender and non-binary theatre artists working in the contemporary U.S. theatre. Taylor Mac (b. 1973), who in *Hir* (2015) dramatizes a family that includes a transgender sibling; Basil Kreimendehl, Jess Barbagallo, and MJ Kaufman, whose *Sagittarius Ponderosa* (2016) explores the transgender experience, are among the emerging twenty-first-century transgender playwrights. Will Davis (b. 1983) is a transgender director who has staged works off-Broadway and was the artistic director of Chicago's American Theatre Company until it closed in 2018. In 2017, he directed a production of William Inge's 1953 play *Picnic* with transgender performers playing the leads as well as other roles. In 2018, three transgender actors starred in shows on Broadway. In 2019, Danny Younes, a trans actor, played Jack in the musical *Into the Woods* at Ford's Theatre in Washington, D.C., and in 2020 transgender actor Alexandra Billings joined the cast of the long-running Broadway musical *Wicked*. These are just a few examples of trans theatre artists who are affecting and diversifying the U.S. theatre.

A series of Broadway musicals have reflected the growing awareness of gay, lesbian, and transgender concerns. In 1983, a Broadway musical version of *La Cage aux Folles* told the story of a gay couple who run a nightclub located in St. Tropez in the south of France and in which the male performers cross-dress. Based on a play by Jean Poiret, it chronicles the comedic events of a dinner party in which two gay men pretend to be heterosexual in order to impress their son's ultra-conservative future in-laws. The book was written by Harvey Fierstein. *La Cage aux Folles* has had successful revivals, including on Broadway in 2010 and a tour of the United Kingdom in 2017.

In the following decade, *Hedwig and the Angry Inch* (1998), book by John Cameron Mitchell (b. 1963) and music and lyrics by Stephen Trask (b. 1966), opened off-Broadway. It tells the story of a transgender punk rock performer who emigrated from East Berlin and is following her former lover on his more successful tour.

PLAYING YOUR PART: THINKING ABOUT THEATRE

1. Attend or read a play by a diverse dramatist. In what way does the work deal with unique and specific issues? In what ways is the work similar to traditional dramas and forms?
2. How might we make our own theatres more diverse, inclusive, and equitable? How does the goal in theatre relate to the need for diversity, inclusion, and equity in your university and/or workplace? Are there differences and similarities?
3. What can we learn about marginalized peoples by seeing their theatrical presentations? How does theatre compare with news accounts for providing insight into the racism, sexism, and/or homophobia they confront?

HIR AND TRANSGENDER DRAMA

Hir, by Taylor Mac, is a black comedy that tells the story of Isaac, a young man returning from military duty only to find chaos in the family home. The father is ailing and the mother takes this opportunity to declare war on the whole notion of patriarchy. His sister Maxine is in the process of changing gender. Shown here from a 2016 production at Playwrights Horizons are actor Tom Phelan at the left and, playing the crusading mother, Kristine Nielsen on the right. (Sara Krulwich/The New York Times/Redux)

The 2014 musical *Kinky Boots,* which also deals with transgender issues and has a book by Fierstein and music by Cyndi Lauper (b. 1953), tells the story of an encounter between a drag queen and a shoe factory.

As we noted in the our discussion of musical theatre, the 2013 musical *Fun Home,* which moved to Broadway in 2015, was the first mainstream musical about a lesbian protagonist. Based on the graphic memoir of Alison Bechdel, the musical examines her childhood, her recognition of her sexual orientation, her coming out, and her relationship with her gay father. Lisa Kron, a successful lesbian playwright, performance artist, and founder of the theatre group Five Lesbian Brothers, whom we mentioned earlier, wrote the book and lyrics. Jeanine Tesori (b. 1961) was the composer.

GLOBAL THEATRE

We can no longer very easily categorize theatre productions and artists by strictly delineated national boundaries, just as we can no longer always make differentiations between the playwright and other theatre artists who create texts for performance. The fact that communication and travel are so easy makes it difficult to define national theatres and artists. The ability to stream productions also means that audiences from

IN FOCUS: TADASHI SUZUKI, GLOBAL THEATRE ARTIST

Among important global theatre artists who cross national borders, a key figure is Tadashi Suzuki (b. 1938), a director, writer, and teacher who calls Japan his home but has worked with and influenced artists around the world. Suzuki first attracted attention as a part of Japan's *shōgekijō undō,* or "little theatre movement" in the 1960s and 1970s. *Shōgekijō* was a response to what was seen as the restrictive realism and limited point of view of *shingeki*. Like proponents of "little theatre" and avant-garde movements in the West, *shōgekijō* artists largely rejected mainstream success, preferring smaller, more adventurous audiences who were willing to engage with provocative, experimental material. Other directors who were a part of this movement included Shūji Terayama (1935–1983), Shogo Ohta (1939–2007), and Yukio Ninagawa (1935–2016).

A scene from Tadashi Suzuki's adaptation of Euripides's *Electra* at the King's Theatre at the Edinburgh Festival. (Robbie Jack/Corbis/Getty Images)

Today, Tadashi Suzuki is among the world's most famous theatre directors. His Suzuki Company of Toga, in the mountains of Japan is well-known for combining stories and traditions from various cultures; this includes creating theatre pieces that remain distinctively Japanese while also entering into conversation with theatre across the globe. His work also frequently comments on international political situations. In addition to his own company in Japan, Suzuki co-founded the SITI company in 1992 with the prominent American director Anne Bogart.

An example of Suzuki's international work is his production of Euripides's *The Bacchae*. In 1981, Suzuki worked with students at the University of Wisconsin to develop a dual-language version of the play, which he had been working on in Japan for a number of years. In this production, the American actors spoke English and the Japanese actors spoke Japanese, the characters responding as if they understood each other. The production also emphasized the cyclical nature of violence and power, suggesting that one tyrant dies only to be replaced by another. Suzuki has also staged a unique version of *Oedipus Rex*.

Beginning in 1991, Suzuki introduced *Dionysus,* a new adaptation of the play that focused on the clash between religion and government. This production was widely interpreted as a comment on the escalating violence in the Middle East in general and the wars between the United States and Iraq more specifically. At the 2019 Theatre Olympics, an international theatre festival which was held in Japan and Russia, Suzuki was co-artistic director and staged his production of *King Lear*.

Suzuki's actors are praised for their onstage presence and incredible athleticism. His actor-training system, the Suzuki method, combines elements of traditional Japanese theatre techniques with the experimental work that emerged from international theatre in the 1960s and 1970s. Actors spend a great deal of time focusing on their feet and the ground beneath them, building strength, flexibility, and balance through a physical connection to the earth. Many observers feel that Suzuki's most lasting impact on world theatre will be his work on actor training.

(Prepared by Frank Episale.)

IN FOCUS: IVO VAN HOVE, GLOBAL DIRECTOR

A European director who has received global recognition and whose work is truly multinational is the Belgian-born postmodernist Ivo van Hove (b. 1958). Van Hove, who is gay, collaborates with his partner, the designer Jan Versweyveld (b. 1958), whom he credits as helping conceptualize his productions. Van Hove has worked across the world. He is the artistic director of Toneelgroep in Amsterdam and his productions have been staged in England, the United States, Russia, Austria, and other countries.

Van Hove has made a specialty of reinterpreting traditional texts in unique ways, often using minimalist, stripped sets that symbolically represent issues in the action. In his production of *A Streetcar Named Desire* (1996), for example, the character Blanche DuBois spends a good part of the play naked in a bathtub.

In his production of *The Misanthrope* (2007) by Molière, van Hove not only drastically reworked the text but employed such contemporary devices as cell phones and computer notebooks. In his *Angels in America* (2007), the stage is bare and the final appearance of the angel is not a theatrical revelation but a nurse.

As with many global directors, van Hove has toured his productions and directed in other countries. In the United States, he has directed productions at the off-Broadway New York Theatre Workshop, including the earlier-mentioned *Misanthrope*, *The Little Foxes* (2010), *Scenes from a Marriage* (2013), and Enda Walsh (b. 1967), and David Bowie's *Lazarus* (2015). He directed an acclaimed, minimalist production of Arthur Miller's *A View from the Bridge* at the Young Vic in London in 2014 that moved to Broadway in 2015, as well as Arthur Miller's *The Crucible* on Broadway in 2016. In 2020, just prior to the closing of Broadway theatres due to the pandemic, van Hove's unique staging of the classic musical *West Side Story* opened. The director cut the musical so it ran 2 hours without intermission, used large filmed scenes, and had new choreography designed to replace the iconic dance numbers that had traditionally been employed in revivals.

---

across the globe can see examples of plays and theatre works from across the globe. This became quite apparent during the COVID-19 pandemic when we could watch productions of new plays and revivals streamed across continents.

The artists highlighted in boxes in this section clearly reflect the globalization of our contemporary theatre. All of them are significant figures in their home countries, have been influenced by their cultures' traditional theatres, and have impacted theatre artists and audiences across the world. In addition, they have often created and adapted stage works with actors rather than traditional playwrights, illustrating the blurring of how texts for theatre are devised.

While we have looked at diverse and inclusive theatres and playwrights primarily in the United States, as we have frequently noted, the global theatre is also being pushed to become equitable and inclusive. In European countries, there are movements to end the marginalization of BIPOC, women, gay, and transgender theatre artists and dramatists. There is the call to open up the stories presented on stage to better reflect the diverse nature of our global society. In addition, there is greater recognition of traditional global theatres and their histories, unique traditions and conventions, as well as influences on Eurocentric theatre.

So in approaching global theatre (which as we have noted, would be impossible for us to cover in its entirety), we should keep in mind that in most global cultures, theatre has a long, illustrious history. Unlike American theatre, which has a relatively short history, world theatre goes back more than 2,000 years in Europe and over 2,000 years in Asia. In Europe, preceding contemporary theatre, the theatre tradition of the past begins with Greek theatre and moves through Roman, medieval,

IN FOCUS: AUGUSTO BOAL AND THE THEATRE OF THE OPPRESSED

If ever there was a global theatre figure in recent times, it was Augusto Boal (1931–2009). Born in Brazil, Boal (pronounced Bo-AHL) attended Columbia University in the United States. Returning to Brazil, he began working in the Arena Theatre in São Paulo. At first he directed conventional dramatic works, but Boal was a man with a powerful social conscience. During his early years he began to develop his philosophy of theatre. He determined, for example, that mainstream theatre was used by the ruling class as a soporific, a means of sedating the audience and inoculating it from any impulse to act or revolt. In other words, conventional theatre was oppressive to ordinary citizens, especially the underprivileged.

Boal also became fascinated with the relationship of actors to audience members. He wished to establish a partnership between the two, and he felt strongly that spectators should participate in any theatre event, that a way must be found for them to become performers and a part of the action. In putting these theories into practice, he began to present agit-prop plays, that is, plays with a strong political and social message. He experimented with several versions of such plays. One was the Invisible Theatre in which actors, seemingly spontaneously, presented a prepared scene in a public space such as a town square or a restaurant. Another was his Forum Theatre in which a play about a social problem became the basis of a discussion with audience members about solutions to the problem.

Considered an enemy of the authoritarian government in Brazil for his work in the 1960s, he was jailed in 1971 and tortured. Released after a few months, he was exiled from his native land. Following that he lived in various countries: Argentina, Portugal, and France. He decided along the way that his approach should be less didactic than it had been, that he would be more effective if he engaged the audience in the theatrical process rather than confronting them. This was the basis of his Theatre of the Oppressed, which became the cornerstone of his life's work from then on. He authored a book by that title, which appeared in 1974.

Augusto Boal (Sucheta Das/AP Images)

In 1985 Boal returned to Brazil. From that point until his death, for the next quarter-century, he traveled all over the world, directing, lecturing, and establishing centers, furthering the Theatre of the Oppressed. He also authored other books that were widely read. Altogether, his approach to theatre found adherents in more than forty countries. Wherever the Theatre of the Oppressed was established, its productions challenged injustice, especially in poor and disenfranchised communities where citizens are often without a voice or an advocate. In his later years he was looked upon by many as the most inspirational person of his time in propagating socially oriented theatre.

Renaissance, eighteenth-century, and nineteenth-century theatre into modern theatre. In Asia, theatre in India began perhaps 2,000 years ago and Chinese theatre a few centuries after that; Japanese classic theatre tradition was established by 800 CE.

In other parts of the world—for instance, in Africa, in Latin America, and in the indigenous cultures of North America and Australia—there are rich traditions of rituals and ceremonies imbued with theatrical elements: costumes, song and dance, and the impersonation of people, animals, and divinities. There are also popular theatres, experimental theatres, and practice unique to these cultures.

When we look at European, Asian, and other theatres, therefore, we are looking at traditions that precede the theatre that exists in those parts of the world today. At various points in *The Theatre Experience,* we have referred to some of these theatres and to their playwrights, stage spaces, production practices, and acting companies.

We should, however, always keep in mind that we are most familiar with our Western, Eurocentric theatre traditions, practices, forms, and playwrights. For us to have a more representative, diverse and inclusive theatre, we must embrace the traditions, practices, and writings from across the globe and from those peoples who have been and continue to be marginalized because of racism, sexism, and homophobia. Our hope is to have an equitable theatre that represents all of the peoples in our diverse and global world. Theatre has always been referred to as a reflection of its society. In the diverse and global twenty-first century, for theatre to be an honest reflection, we must see all of us represented on our stages.

IN FOCUS: ARIANE MNOUCHKINE, GLOBAL THEATRE ARTIST

Since her founding of the avant-garde Théâtre du Soleil in Paris in 1964, Ariane Mnouchkine (b. 1940) has become one of the most globally respected directors. She is especially known for her effective use of Asian theatre techniques. Born in France, she was the eldest daughter of Russian émigré and film producer Alexandre Mnouchkine. While studying psychology at Oxford University, she became involved with the Oxford University Drama Society. When she returned to Paris in 1950, she helped form a student theatre association at the Sorbonne. In the early 1960s, Mnouchkine travelled to Asia and became interested in the theatrical forms and rituals there, that later highly influenced her works.

When she returned to Paris in 1963, she and several friends came together to establish the Théâtre du Soleil, a company that has produced everything from loose collections of improvised materials to acclaimed versions of Shakespeare's works to a powerful ten-hour staging of the *Oresteia,* the cycle of Greek tragedies about the house of Atreus.

Among the best-known collectively created productions of the Théâtre du Soleil are *The Clowns* (1969), *1789* (1970), a dramatized history of the French Revolution, the 1991 adaptation of the *Oresteia,* and *Les Ephemeres* (2009).

Mnouchkine gained significant attention in the United States through presentations by the Théâtre du Soleil at the Olympic Arts Festival in Los Angeles in 1984, at the Brooklyn Academy of Music in 1992, and Lincoln Center in 2009.

Among her other well-known company created productions are: *And Suddenly Sleepless Nights* (1997), which treats the plight of illegal immigrants, and the two-part, six-hour *The Last Caravan Stop Odysseys* (2003), which deals with the horrors faced by refugees. Mnouchkine received an honorary doctorate from Oxford in 2008, the Ibsen Award in 2009, the first woman to receive this honor, and the Goethe Medal in 2011.

PLAYING YOUR PART: EXPERIENCING THEATRE

1. Have you ever found yourself in a circumstance in which you were interacting with individuals who spoke only another language? How did you negotiate that circumstance? How might that be similar to experiencing a theatre production that uses the unique traditions of a different nation?
2. Are there issues in contemporary American society that might be dramatized by playwrights of other nations in a fashion that would be different than the way in which a U.S. dramatist would represent the same situation? What might those differences be?
3. Read a play by a contemporary playwright from Latin America, Africa, or Asia. How is the play similar to U.S. dramas you have read? How is it different?

SUMMARY

1. Diverse theatres include theatre by and for African Americans, Asian Americans, Latinx Americans, and indigenous peoples. Even though marginalized in the United States, these artists have produced historically significant plays and theatre productions.
2. Feminist theatre and women playwrights came to the forefront in the 1960s and 1970s and have continued to accelerate ever since.
3. LGBTQ theatre in all its aspects became well established by the close of the twentieth century and beginning of the twenty-first century.
4. The modern era is marked by increasing globalization in theatre, with more and more communication and cross-pollination—a feature of much of modern society, including the arts.
5. A number of countries in Asia and the West have theatre traditions that stretch back hundreds, and in some cases thousands, of years
6. Asian theatre has both traditional and modern branches. In places like Japan, China, and India, both types of theatre remain particularly active.
7. Theatre in Africa builds on traditional forms and influences from the various colonizers.

Design Elements: Audience Sitting in Theatre (theatre): Ron Chapple/Photodisc/Getty Images; Studio Light (spotlights): Exactostock/SuperStock

Plays That May Be Read Online

The following is a list of plays that are used as examples to highlight key concepts in *Theatre Experience*, 14th edition, and that can be read online. Any play in this edition that can be found on the Internet is highlighted in blue typeface. Should you want to read any of these plays, or if your teacher has assigned one, you can refer to this list and find an online version.

Abraham and Isaac www.wwnorton.com/college/english/nael/noa/pdf/13BromePlay_1_12.pdf
Adding Machine, The (Rice, Elmer) www.scribd.com/doc/25952449/Elmer-Rice-The-Adding-Machine
Alchemist, The (Jonson, Ben) www.gutenberg.org/ebooks/4081
All for Love (Dryden, John) www.gutenberg.org/ebooks/2062
All's Well That Ends Well (Shakespeare, William) www.gutenberg.org/ebooks/1125
Antigone (Sophocles) http://classics.mit.edu/Sophocles/antigone.html
Antony and Cleopatra (Shakespeare, William) www.gutenberg.org/ebooks/2268
Arms and the Man (Shaw, George Bernard) www.gutenberg.org/ebooks/3618
Bacchae, The (Euripides) www.gutenberg.org/ebooks/35173
Birds, The (Aristophanes) www.gutenberg.org/ebooks/3013
Blood Wedding (Lorca, Federico Garcia) www.poetryintranslation.com/klineasbloodwedding.htm
Brand (Ibsen, Henrik) http://archive.org/details/cu31924026309199
Busie Body, The (Centlivre, Susanna) www.gutenberg.org/ebooks/16740
Caesar and Cleopatra (Shaw, George Bernard) www.gutenberg.org/ebooks/3329
Candida (Shaw, George Bernard) www.gutenberg.org/ebooks/4023
Chantecler (Rostand, Edmond) www.gutenberg.org/ebooks/10747
Cherry Orchard, The (Chekhov, Anton) www.gutenberg.org/ebooks/7986
Cid, The (Corneille, Pierre) www.gutenberg.org/ebooks/14954
Clouds, The (Aristophanes) www.gutenberg.org/ebooks/2562
Comedy of Errors, The (Shakespeare, William) www.gutenberg.org/ebooks/23046
Country Wife, The (Wycherley, William) http://archive.org/details/countrywifecomed00wych
Cymbeline (Shakespeare, William) www.gutenberg.org/ebooks/1133
Cyrano de Bergerac (Rostand, Edmond) www.gutenberg.org/ebooks/1254
Doctor in Spite of Himself, The (Molière) http://archive.org/details/dramaticworksofm01moliiala
Doll's House, A (Ibsen, Henrik) www.gutenberg.org/ebooks/2542
Dream Play, The (Strindberg, August) www.archive.org/details/playsbyaugustst00bjgoog
Electra (Euripides) www.gutenberg.org/ebooks/14322
Electra (Sophocles) http://classics.mit.edu/Sophocles/electra.html

Emperor Jones, The (O'Neill, Eugene) http://archive.org/details/emperorjones00onegoog
Enemy of the People, An (Ibsen, Henrik) www.gutenberg.org/ebooks/2446
Eumenides, The (The Furies) (Aeschylus) www.gutenberg.org/ebooks/8604
Everyman http://archive.org/details/everyman00newy
Every Man in His Humour (Jonson, Ben) www.gutenberg.org/ebooks/3694
Every Man Out of His Humour (Jonson, Ben) www.gutenberg.org/ebooks/3695
Faust (Goethe, Johann Wolfgang von) www.gutenberg.org/ebooks/14460
Frogs, The (Aristophanes) www.gutenberg.org/ebooks/7998
Ghosts (Ibsen, Henrik) www.gutenberg.org/ebooks/8121
Government Inspector (The Inspector General) (Gogol, Nikolai) www.gutenberg.org/ebooks/3735
Great God Brown, The (O'Neill, Eugene) http://gutenberg.net.au/ebooks04/0400091h.html
Hairy Ape, The (O'Neill, Eugene) www.gutenberg.org/ebooks/4015
Hamlet (Shakespeare, William) www.gutenberg.org/ebooks/1524
Heartbreak House (Shaw, George Bernard) www.gutenberg.org/ebooks/3543
Hedda Gabler (Ibsen, Henrik) www.gutenberg.org/ebooks/4093
Henry IV, Pt. 1 (Shakespeare, William) www.gutenberg.org/ebooks/2251
Henry IV, Pt. 2 (Shakespeare, William) www.gutenberg.org/ebooks/1117
Henry V (Shakespeare, William) www.gutenberg.org/ebooks/1119
House of Bernarda Alba, The (Lorca, Federico Garcia) www.poetryintranslation.com/PITBR/Spanish/AlbaActI.htm
Importance of Being Earnest, The (Wilde, Oscar) www.gutenberg.org/ebooks/844
Julius Caesar (Shakespeare, William) www.gutenberg.org/ebooks/2263
King Lear (Shakespeare, William) www.gutenberg.org/ebooks/2266
King Stag, The (Gozzi, Carlo) www.epc-library.com/freeview/F_1814.pdf
Libation Bearers (Aeschylus) https://www.theoi.com/Text/AeschylusLibation.html
Life Is a Dream (Calderon de la Barca, Pedro) www.gutenberg.org/ebooks/2587
Little Clay Cart, The (Sudraka) www.gutenberg.org/ebooks/21020
London Merchant, The (Lillo, George) http://archive.org/details/londonmerchanto00lillgoog
Love's Labour's Lost (Shakespeare, William) www.gutenberg.org/ebooks/1109
Lysistrata (Aristophanes) www.gutenberg.org/ebooks/7700
Macbeth (Shakespeare, William) www.gutenberg.org/ebooks/1129
Major Barbara (Shaw, George Bernard) www.gutenberg.org/ebooks/3790
Marriage of Figaro, The (Beumarchais, Pierre) https://oll.libertyfund.org/title/holcroft-the-marriage-of-figaro-or-the-follies-of-a-day
Master Builder, The (Ibsen, Henrik) www.gutenberg.org/ebooks/4070
Measure for Measure (Shakespeare, William) www.gutenberg.org/ebooks/1126
Medea (Euripides) www.gutenberg.org/ebooks/35451
Menaechmi, The (Plautus) www.perseus.tufts.edu/hopper/text?doc=Perseus:text:1999.02.0101
Merchant of Venice, The (Shakespeare, William) www.gutenberg.org/ebooks/2243
Merry Wives of Windsor, The (Shakespeare, William) http://shakespeare.mit.edu/merry_wives/full.html
Midsummer Night's Dream, A (Shakespeare, William) www.gutenberg.org/ebooks/1514

Misanthrope, The (Molière) http://archive.org/details/comedies00molirich
Miser, The (Molière) www.gutenberg.org/ebooks/6923
Miss Julie (Strindberg, August) www.gutenberg.org/ebooks/14347
Mrs. Warren's Profession (Shaw, George Bernard) www.gutenberg.org/ebooks/1097
Much Ado About Nothing (Shakespeare, William) www.gutenberg.org/ebooks/2240
No Exit (Sartre, Jean Paul) http://archive.org/stream/NoExit/NoExit_djvu.txt
Oedipus the King (King Oedipus) (Sophocles) http://classics.mit.edu/Sophocles/oedipus.html
Othello (Shakespeare, William) www.gutenberg.org/ebooks/1531
Peer Gynt (Ibsen, Henrik) http://archive.org/details/peergyntadramat01ibsegoog
Phaedra (Phedre) (Racine, Jean) www.gutenberg.org/ebooks/1977
Pirates of Penzance, The (Gilbert, W. S., and Sullivan, Arthur) www.gutenberg.org/ebooks/808
Prometheus Bound (Aeschylus) www.gutenberg.org/ebooks/8714
Pygmalion (Shaw, George Bernard) www.gutenberg.org/ebooks/3825
Richard II (Shakespeare, William) www.gutenberg.org/ebooks/1111
Richard III (Shakespeare, William) www.gutenberg.org/ebooks/2257
Rivals, The (Sheridan, Richard Brinsley) www.gutenberg.org/ebooks/24761
Romeo and Juliet (Shakespeare, William) www.gutenberg.org/ebooks/1513
R.U.R. (Capek, Karel) https://www.gutenberg.org/ebooks/59112
Saint Joan (Shaw, George Bernard) http://archive.org/details/SaintJoan
School for Scandal, The (Sheridan, Richard Brinsley) www.gutenberg.org/ebooks/1929
School for Wives, The (Molière) http://archive.org/details/comedies00molirich
Sea-Gull, The (Chekhov, Anton) www.gutenberg.org/ebooks/1754
Second Shepherds' Play, The www.gutenberg.org/files/19481/19481-h/19481-h.htm
Servant of Two Masters, The (Goldoni, Carlo) http://gutenberg.ca/ebooks/goldonident-twomasters/goldonident-twomasters-00-h.html
Shakuntala (Kalidasa) www.sacred-texts.com/hin/sha/index.htm
Six Characters in Search of an Author (Pirandello, Luigi) www.ibiblio.org/eldritch/lp/six.htm
Sotoba Komachi (Zeami) http://etext.virginia.edu/toc/modeng/public/WalSoto.html
Tamburlaine the Great (Marlowe, Christopher) www.gutenberg.org/ebooks/1094
Taming of the Shrew, The (Shakespeare, William) http://shakespeare.mit.edu/taming_shrew/full.html
Tartuffe (Molière) www.gutenberg.org/ebooks/2027
Tempest, The (Shakespeare, William) www.gutenberg.org/ebooks/23042
Three Sisters, The (Chekhov, Anton) www.gutenberg.org/ebooks/7986
Tragical History of Dr. Faustus, The (Marlowe, Christopher) www.gutenberg.org/ebooks/779
Troilus and Cressida (Shakespeare, William) www.gutenberg.org/ebooks/1790
Twelfth Night (Shakespeare, William) www.gutenberg.org/ebooks/1526
Two Gentlemen of Verona, The (Shakespeare, William) www.gutenberg.org/ebooks/1108
Uncle Vanya (Chekhov, Anton) www.gutenberg.org/ebooks/1756
Volpone (Jonson, Ben) www.gutenberg.org/ebooks/4039
Way of the World, The (Congreve, William) www.gutenberg.org/ebooks/1292
Would-Be Gentleman, The (Molière) http://archive.org/details/comedies00molirich

Glossary

Aesthetic distance Physical or psychological separation or detachment of audience from dramatic action, usually considered necessary for artistic illusion.

Allegory Symbolic representation of abstract themes through characters, action, and other concrete elements of a play.

Alley or traverse space In this type of space the audiences its on opposite sides of the stage facing each other.

Antagonist Opponent of the protagonist in a drama.

Arena Stage entirely surrounded by the audience; also known as *circle theatre* or *theatre-in-the-round*.

Auteur French term for "author." When used to describe a director it suggests one who makes drastic alterations and transformations to a traditional script.

Black box A theatre space that is open, flexible, and adaptable, usually without fixed seating. The stage–audience configuration can be rearranged to suit the individual requirements of a given production, making it both economical and particularly well suited to experimental work.

Blocking Pattern and arrangement of performers' movements onstage with respect to each other and to the stage space, usually set by the director.

Bourgeois or domestic drama Drama dealing with problems—particularly family problems—of middle- and lower-class characters. There are serious and comic domestic dramas.

Box Small private compartment for a group of spectators built into the walls of traditional proscenium-arch and other theatres.

Build To create a costume from scratch in a costume shop.

Burlesque A ludicrous, comic imitation of a dramatic form, play, piece of literature, or other popular entertainment.

Casting Fitting performers into roles.

Climax The highpoint in the development of a dramatic plot.

Comedy of ideas A comedy in which the humor is based on intellectual and verbal aspects of comedy rather than physical comedy or comedy of character. A drama whose emphasis is on the clash of ideas, as exemplified in the plays of George Bernard Shaw.

Comedy of manners Form of comic drama that became popular in the English Restoration, that is set within sophisticated society, while poking fun at its characters' social pretensions, usually through verbal wit.

Comedy In general, a play that is light in tone, is concerned with issues that point out the excesses and folly of human behavior, has a happy ending, and is designed to amuse.

Comic premise Idea or concept in a comedy that turns the accepted notion of things upside down.

Commedia dell'arte Form of comic theatre, originating in Italy in the sixteenth century, in which dialogue was improvised around a scenario involving a set of stock characters, each with a traditional costume, name, and often mask.

Complication Introduction, in a play, of a new force, which creates a new balance of power and entails a delay in reaching the climax.

Computer-assisted design (CAD) Designs created by computer. All features of a set design, including ground plans, elevations, and walls, can be indicated by computer, and variations and alternations can be easily created and displayed.

Concept musical A musical that is built around an idea or a theme rather than a story.

Corral Theatre building of the Spanish golden age, usually located in the courtyard of a series of adjoining buildings.

Crisis A point in a play when events and opposing forces are at a crucial moment, and when the course of further action will be determined. There may be a series of crises leading to the definitive climax.

Cues Any prearranged signal—such as the last words in a speech, a piece of business, or any action or lighting change—that indicates to a performer or stage manager that it is time to proceed to the next line or action.

Deus ex machina ("DEH-oos eks MAH-kih-nah") Literally, "god from a machine," a resolution device in classic Greek drama; hence, intervention of supernatural forces—usually at the last moment—to save the action from its logical conclusion. In modern drama, an arbitrary and coincidental solution.

Director In American usage, the person responsible for the overall unity of a production and for coordinating the work of contributing artists. The American director is the equivalent of the British producer and the French *metteur-en-scène* ("meh-TURR ahn SENN").

Directorial concept The controlling idea, vision, or point of view that the director feels is appropriate for the play; it should create a unified theatrical experience for the audience.

Distressing Making a costume look weathered or worn.

Downstage Front of the stage, toward the audience.

dramaturg The individual who works on literary and historical issues with members of the artistic team mounting a theatre production.

Dramaturg (or literary manager) On the staff of a theatre, a person who consults with and advises authors and directors, writes program notes, and edits scripts.

Drapers Technicians who pattern, pin, and drape the fabric to fit the actors in a production perfectly.

Dress rehearsal The first full performances of a production before performances for the public.

Emotional recall Stanislavski's exercise that helps the performer present realistic emotions. The performer feels a character's emotion by thinking of the conditions surrounding an event in his or her own life that led to a similar emotion.

Ensemble playing Acting that stresses the total artistic unity of a group performance rather than individual performances.

Environmental sounds Noises of everyday life that help create a sense of reality in a production.

Environmental theatre A type of theatre, made popular in the 1960s, that attempts to eliminate the distinction between audience and acting space and that emphasizes a multiple focus for the audience rather than a single focus.

Exposition Information necessary for an understanding of the story but not covered by the action onstage; events or knowledge from the past, or occurring outside the play, that must be introduced so that the audience can understand the characters or plot.

Expressionism The attempt in drama to depict the subjective state of a character or group of characters through such nonrealistic techniques as distortion, striking images, and poetic language.

Farce A subclass of comedy with emphasis on exaggerated plot complications and with few or no intellectual pretensions.

Flashback In a narrative or story, movement back to a time in the past to show a scene or an event before the narrative resumes at the point at which it was interrupted.

Flat A scenic unit consisting of canvas stretched on a wooden frame often used with similar units to create a set.

Fly loft Space above the stage where scenery may be lifted out of sight by ropes and pulleys.

Fourth wall Convention, in a proscenium-arch theatre, that the audience is looking into a room through an invisible fourth wall.

Front of the house Portion of a theatre reserved for the audience; sometimes called simply the *house.*

Genre A French word meaning category. In theatre, genre denotes the category into which a play falls: for example, tragedy, comedy, or tragicomedy.

Ground plan A blueprint or floor plan of the stage indicating the placement of scenery, furniture, doors and windows, and the various levels of the stage, as well as the walls of rooms, platforms, and the like.

Hamartia ("hah-MARH-tee-ah") Ancient Greek term usually translated as "tragic flaw." The literal translation is "missing the mark," which may suggest that hamartia is not so much a character flaw as an error in judgment.

Happenings Nonliterary theatrical events, developed in the 1960s, in which the script is replaced with a scenario that provides for chance occurrences, and are performed (often only once) in such places as parks and street corners.

Heightened realism Also known as *selective realism,* refers to plays in which characters and their actions resemble real life but a certain license is allowed for other elements in the play.

Heroic drama Serious but basically optimistic drama written in verse or elevated prose, with noble or heroic characters in extreme situations or unusual adventures.

Hubris ("HEW-brihs") Ancient Greek term usually defined as "excessive pride" and cited as a common tragic character flaw.

Glossary **335**

Imitation To simulate or copy behavior observed in real life.

Immersive theatre In immersive theatre, audience members play an active role in some way, often moving through a performance space, sometimes even choosing where they should go within that space and what they should see and do. Many such productions use transformed, redesigned spaces as well as requiring audience members to engage in a complete sensory experience (touch, smell, even taste of foods and drink).

Incongruity In comedy, incongruity usually refers to a character's inappropriate behavior or actions for a specific circumstance resulting in our laughter.

Magic if Stanislavski's acting exercise that requires the performer to ask, "How would I react *if* I were in this character's position?"

Managing director In nonprofit theatre organizations, the individual who controls resources and expenditures.

Mediated arts The mediated arts, which include radio, film, television, digital streaming, and the like, are performances captured or recorded through the use of other types of media.

Melodrama Dramatic form made popular in the nineteenth century that emphasized action and spectacular effects and also used music to underscore the action; it had stock characters, usually with clearly defined villains and heroes.

Motivated sounds Sounds called for by the script.

Multifocus theatre An environment in which there is more than one playing area.

Multimedia theatre Use of electronic media, such as slides, film, and videotape, in live theatrical presentations.

Naturalism Attempts to put onstage exact copies of everyday life; sometimes also called slice-of-life drama.

Nonrealism (or departures from realism) All types of theatre that depart from observable reality.

Obstacle That which delays or prevents the achieving of a goal by a character. An obstacle creates complication and conflict.

Orchestra A circular playing space in ancient Greek theatres; in modern times, the ground-floor seating in a theatre auditorium.

Pantomime A form of theatrical presentation that relies on dance, gesture, and physical movement without speech.

Performance art Experimental theatre that initially incorporated elements of dance and visual arts into performance. Since performance art often is based on the vision of an individual performer or director rather than playwright, the autobiographical monologue and solo performance have become popular performance art forms.

Platform stage Elevated stage with no proscenium.

Plot As distinct from story, patterned arrangements of events and characters in a drama, with incidents selected and arranged for maximum dramatic impact.

Postmodernism A contemporary concept suggesting that artists and audiences have gone beyond the modernist movements of realism and departures from realism and such categories as "high art" and "popular art."

Previews Tryout performances of a production before an audience, preceding the official "opening" performance.

Producer In American usage, the person responsible for the business side of a production, including raising the necessary money. (In British usage, a producer for many years was the equivalent of an American director.)

Prop Properties; objects that are used by performers onstage or are necessary to complete a set.

Proscenium ("pro-SEEN-ee-um") Arch or frame surrounding the stage opening in a box or picture stage.

Protagonist Principal character in a play, the one whom the drama is about.

Pull To choose a costume from an inventory owned by a theatre company or costume warehouse.

Rake (1) To position scenery on a slant or at an angle other than parallel or perpendicular to the curtain line. (2) An upward slope of the stage floor away from the audience.

Realism Broadly, an attempt to present onstage people, places, and events corresponding to those in everyday life.

Reinforcement The amplification of sounds produced by a performer or a musical instrument.

Rendering A complete drawing of a set, usually in color.

Ritual Ceremonial event, often religious, that takes place in a prescribed sequence.

Role playing In everyday life, the acting out of a particular role by copying the expected social behavior of that position.

Romanticism Nineteenth-century dramatic movement that imitated the episodic structure of Shakespeare, and thematically focused on the gulf between human beings' spiritual aspirations and physical limitations.

Satire Comic form, using irony and exaggeration, to attack and expose folly and vice.

Scrim Thin, open-weave fabric that is nearly transparent when lit from behind and opaque when lit from the front.

Site-specific companies Theatre groups that create productions for specific nontheatre locations.

Slapstick Type of comedy, or comic business, that relies on ridiculous physical activity—often violent in nature—for its humor.

Soliloquy Speech in which a character who is alone onstage speaks inner thoughts aloud.

Spine Also known as *main action,* the spine is determined by the goal or primary objective of all the characters in a play, both collectively and individually.

Stage house Stage floor and the space around it to the side walls, as well as the space above it up to the grid.

Stage left Left side of the stage from the point of view of a performer facing the audience.

Stage right Right side of the stage from the point of view of a performer facing the audience.

Stitchers Technicians who sew all of the costumes for a production.

Stock characters Two-dimensional, stereotypical characters.

Subplot Sometimes referred to as parallel plot, a secondary plot that reinforces or runs parallel to the major plot in an episodic play.

Superobjective What the character wants above all else during the course of the play.

Symbol A sign, a visual image, an object, or an action that signifies something else; a visual embodiment of something invisible. A single image or sign stands for an entire idea or larger concept—a flag is a symbol for a nation; a logo is a symbol for a corporation.

Technical director Staff member responsible for scheduling, construction, and installation of all equipment; he or she is responsible for guaranteeing that designs are executed according to the designer's specifications.

Technical rehearsal A rehearsal that focuses on running through the production with scenery, props, lighting, costumes, and sound for the first time.

Thrust stage Stage space that thrusts into the audience space; a stage surrounded on three sides by audience seating.

Tragedy A serious drama in which there is a downfall of the primary character.

Tragicomedy During the Renaissance, a play having tragic themes and noble characters but a happy ending; today, a play in which serious and comic elements are integrated. Many plays of this type present a comic or ironic treatment of a serious theme.

Turntable A circle set into the floor of a stage that is rotated mechanically or electronically to bring one set into view as another disappears.

Upstage At or toward the back of the stage, away from the front edge of the stage.

Wagon stage (or, Wagon) Low platform mounted on wheels or casters by means of which scenery is moved on- and offstage.

Well-made plays Type of play popular in the nineteenth century and early twentieth century that combines apparent plausibility of incident and surface realism with a tightly constructed, highly causal, and contrived plot.

Notes

Chapter 1
1 Walter Kerr, "We Call It 'Live Theatre,' but Is It?" *New York Times*, January 2, 1972.
2 Jean-Claude van Itallie, *The Serpent: A Ceremony,* written in collaboration with the Open Theater, Atheneum, New York, 1969, p. ix.
3 www.theguardian.com/culture/2003/may/02/artsfeatures
4 Bernard Beckerman, *Dynamics of Drama: Theory and Method of Analysis,* Knopf, New York, 1970, p. 129.

Chapter 3
1 Michael Gioia, "How the Great Comet Transformed the Imperial Theatre into an Immersive Russian Supper Club," *Playbill*, December 1, 2016.
2 "Mimi Lien on the Set Design of 'The Great Comet of 1812'," interview conducted and edited by Victoria Myers, *The Interval*, January 4, 2017.
3 Material on the proscenium, arena, and thrust stages was suggested by a booklet prepared by Dr. Mary Henderson for the educational division of Lincoln Center for the Performing Arts.
4 Antonin Artaud, "The Theater and Its Double," Grove, New York, 1958, pp. 96–97.

Chapter 4
1 Konstantin Stanislavsky, *An Actor Prepares,* Theatre Arts, New York, 1948, p. 73.
2 Konstantin Stanislavsky, *An Actor Prepares*, Theatre Arts, New York, 1948.
3 Christopher Marlowe, *Doctor Faustus* (1592).
4 Jean Benedetti, *Stanislavski*, Routledge, New York, 1988, p. 217.
5 www.backstage.com/advice-for-actors/professional-tips/how-has-technology-changed-your-acting-career/
6 David Bridel, "In the Beginning Was the Body," *American Theatre*, January 2011.

Chapter 5
1 Robert Viagas, "Playwright Katori Hall Expresses Rage over 'Revisionist Casting' of *Mountaintop* with White Dr. Martin Luther King," *Playbill*, November 9, 2015.

Chapter 6
1 Robert Edmond Jones, *The Dramatic Imagination*, Theatre Arts, New York, 1941, p. 25.

Chapter 11
1 Horace Walpole, letter to Anne, Countess of Ossory, August 16, 1776.
2 William Shakespeare, *King Lear* (1606), act V, scene 2.
3 William Shakespeare, *Antony and Cleopatra* (1606), act IV, scene 5.
4 Oscar Wilde, *Lady Windemere's Fan* (1893).
5 Terry Pinkard, *German Philosophy 1760–1860: The Legacy of Idealism*, Cambridge University Press, Cambridge, UK, 2002, p. 354.
6 Albert Camus, *Le Mythe de Sisyphe*, Gallimard, Paris, 1942, p. 18.
7 From *Waiting for Godot* by Samuel Beckett. Copyright 1954 by Grove Press; renewed copyright 1982 by Samuel Beckett.

Index

About Face Theatre, 323
Abraham and Isaac, 17
Absurdist plots, 272
Abyssinia, 276
Accessories and costumes, 175
Acting. *See also* Actors
   believable characters, 77, 87-94
   challenges of, 77-78, 80
   classical, 80-81
   in daily life, 72-73, 75-76
   performances, evaluating, 97-99
   personal roles and, 76
   physical, 86, 87-89
   profession of, 87
   realistic, 20, 75-77, 87
   role playing and, 75
   stage, 75-99
   Stanislavski system, 78-83
   synthesis and integration of, 94-97
   training for special forms of, 94
Acting One (Cohen), 86
Action onstage, Stanislavski technique of, 82
The Actor at Work (Benedetti), 86
Actors. *See also* Acting
   audience, relationship with, 7-8, 9-10
   audience and, 2, 3, 13-15, 75, 85
   body mikes on, 196
   and costumes, 162-163
   and directors, working with, 111-121
   fascination of, to audiences, 98
   range of, 84-85
   social status of, 80-81
   technology and, 88

Actors' Equity Association (AEA), 119
Actors Studio, 83
Actos, 311
Adapted spaces, 64
The Adding Machine (Rice), 105
Adler, Stella, 83
Aeschylus, 31-32, 80, 208, 256
   as director, 106
Aesthetic distance, 14
African American stock companies, 304
African American theatre, 302-308
   audience background for, 28
   regional theatres of, 34
   traditions of, 302
African Grove Theatre, 304
African theatre, 161, 302-304
After the Revolution (Herzog), 318
After the War (Gotanda), 309
Age of enlightenment, 221
Agitprop plays, 13
Aladdin, 51, 53
Albee, Edward, 20, 211, 242, 246, 261
Alchemist (Jonson), 244
Aldridge, Ira, 304
Alice's Rape (McCauley), 293
Allegory, 104-105
All My Sons (Miller), 259
All's Well That Ends Well (Shakespeare), 270
Alternative theatre, 35, 291, 307. *See also* Avant-garde and experimental theatre
Amateur theatre, 37
Amen Corner (Baldwin), 304

American contemporary theatre. *See* Contemporary theatre
An American in Paris, 144
American Indian Religious Freedom Act, 313
American Repertory Theater, 34
American Theatre magazine, 92
Amphitheatre, Greek, 56
Amplification of sound, 193-194
Anachronism, 17
Ancient Greek theatre. *See* Greek theatre
And So We Walked (Studi), 314
Angels in America (Kushner), 17, 230, 288, 307, 322
   departure from realism of, 20
Anna in the Tropics (Cruz), 311
Annie Get Your Gun, 279
Antagonists, 211, 247
Antigone (Sophocles), 213, 247
Antony and Cleopatra (Shakespeare), 227, 240
Appia, Adolphe, 181, 192
Arena stage, 48, 53-55
Argand, Aimé, 180
Argand lamp, 180
Aristophanes, 31, 263
   comic premises of, 264
   nonhuman characters of, 246
Aristotle, 217, 256
Arms and the Man (Shaw), 269
Arsenic and Old Lace (Kesselring), 254, 264
Artaud, Antonin, 61, 288, 292
   theatre space and, 61-65
Asaro "mud men," 172
Asian American theatre, 308-310

339

Asian theatre, 308–310
 actor training for, 87, 92
 Chinese theatre, 60, 170, 214, 329
 demands of, 80–81
 heroic drama of, 260
 Indian theatre, 214, 313
 influence of, on the West, 214
 Japanese theatre, 60, 81, 96, 253, 326
 make up in, 171
 masks in, 172
 movement and gestures in, 80, 91
 puppetry in, 96
Assistive listening devices (ALDs), 191
Athalie (Racine), 81
Atmosphere. *See* Scenery; Sound; Stage lighting; Theatre spaces
Audience, 1–25
 actors, relationship with, 2, 88
 background of, 27–33
 character types and, 247
 composition of, 12
 criticism, relation to, 43–44
 direct action of, 14–15
 directors as eye of, 113–115
 dramaturg for, role of, 42
 expectations of, 27, 33–38
 group experience of, 10–11
 imagination of, 16–19
 judgment of, 43
 participatory and immersive theatre, 15–16
 and physical arrangement of theatres, 47
 role of, 5–25
 scenery, view of, 133
 sound, view of, 133
 stage lighting, view of, 133
 transitory and immediate theatre, 8–9
Auditions, 112
Aural designers, 131, 195
Australian theatre, 16
Auteur directors, 109–111, 205
Automated light fixtures, 190–191
Avant-garde and experimental theatre, 41, 94, 291. *See also* Nontraditional theatre

European, 312
Japanese, 308
special techniques for, 94, 97
staging of, 61–62, 136
structure in, 234–235
Avenue Q, 17, 96, 282
Awake and Sing, 113

Bacchae (Euripides), 246
Backstage magazine, 88
Baghdad Burning: Girl Blog from Iraq, 295
Baker, Annie, 15
Balance of forces in plays, 212
Balconies in theatres, 48
The Bald Soprano (Ionesco), 275
Baldwin, James, 304
Baraka, Amiri, 306
Barbagallo, Jess, 324
Barn doors, 190
Battlefield, 108
Beale, Simon Russell, 22
Bean, Richard, 268
Beats, Stanislavski technique of, 82
Beauty and the Beast, 20, 168–169
Bechdel, Alison, 325
Beckerman, Bernard, 8
Beckett, Samuel, 94, 234, 272, 275
Bedroom farce, 267
Behn, Aphra, 316
Beijing opera, 214
Bel Geddes, Norman, 181
Believable characters, 77, 83–94
Belle Reprieve, 318
Belleville (Herzog), 317, 318
Benedetti, Robert, 86, 86
Bennett, Michael, 280
Berlin, Irving, 279
Bernstein, Leonard, 279
Bibiena, Giuseppe di, 51
Bibiena family, 49–51
The Big Bang Theory, 19
Binkley, Howell, 179
Biomechanics, 90
The Birds (Aristophanes), 246, 264
The Birthday Party (Pinter), 271
Black boxes, 48–49, 66, 194
Blackout, 191

The Blacks (Genet), 169
Black theatre. *See* African American theatre
Black Watch, 296, 297
Blank, Jessica, 296
Blocking, 114
Blogs, 39
Boal, Augusto, 13, 14, 328
Bock, Jerry, 280
Body mikes, 196–197
Body movement, 87–90
Body movement exercises, 90
Bogart, Anne, 92, 111
Bolton Theatre, 50
Book musicals, 277
The Book of Mormon, 48, 283
Border lights, 190
Bourgeois drama, 260–261
The Bourgeois Gentleman, 218
Boxes in a theatre, 49
The Boys from Syracuse, 266
The Boys in the Band (Crowley), 321–322
Bradshaw, Thomas, 308
Brand (Ibsen), 208, 232
Bran NueDae, 315
Brantley, Ben, 35
Bread and Puppet Theatre of San Francisco, 96
Breathing exercises, 89
Brecht, Bertolt, 214, 225, 240, 288
 Asian theatre influence on, 214
 and narrators, use of, 245–246
 theory of storytelling of, 28–29
Breuer, Lee, 111
Bridel, David, 92
Bring It On: The Musical, 77
British theatre, 263, 305
Broadway theatres, 34, 47
Brook, Peter, 139
 profile of, 108
Brooklyn Academy of Music, 21
Brown, William, 304
Built costumes, 164
Bullins, Ed, 307
Bunraku puppets, 81, 96
Buried Child (Shepard), 297–298
Burlesque, 263, 267
Burton, Kate, 115

Bush, Anita, 304
Bush, George W., 295
Bus Stop (Inge), 138

Cabarets, 35
Caesar and Cleopatra (Shaw), 159
Calhoun, Jeff, 93
Camera point of view, 217
Camus, Albert, 272
Čapek, Karel, 246
Carousel, 204
Carroll, Tim, 89
Case, Sue-Ellen, 217
Casting, 112
   color blind and nontraditional, 113
   against type, 112
Casting director, 112
Cat on a Hot Tin Roof (Williams), 113, 227
Cats, 280
The Caucasian Chalk Circle (Brecht), 214, 245-246
Centering, 93
Centlivre, Susanna, 316
Central image
   directorial concept and, 106-109
   lighting and, 186
   stage design and, 140
Century of progress, 221
Ceremonies, as theatre, 72
Chang, Tisa, 309
Chantecler (Rostand), 246
Characters, 238-249
   audience and, 247
   believability of, 77, 94
   and climactic drama, 227
   comedy of, 265-266
   contrasting, 247
   costumes indicating relationships among, 159-162
   with dominant traits, 244, 247
   extraordinary, 238-239
   juxtaposition of, 247
   minor, 245
   narrators or chorus as, 245-246
   nonhuman, 162, 246
   orchestration of, 248-249
   realistic *vs.* departure from realism, 20
   representative or quintessential, 239-243
   stock, 238, 243-244
   superobjective of, 82, 95
   symbolic, 162
   in theatre of the absurd, 275-276
Charlie and the Chocolate Factory, 51
Chavkin, Rachel, 48
Chekhov, Anton, 82, 133, 271
   balance of forces in, 212
   dramatic structure of, 232-233
   orchestration of characters of, 248-249
   and realism, 77
   scene design of, 129
   sound design of, 194
   tragedy and comedy of, 270, 275
The Cherry Orchard (Chekhov), 82, 115, 212, 233
   scene design of, 129
Chicano theatre, 310
The Children's Hour (Hellman), 321
Children's theatre, 35
Chinese theatre, 60, 171, 308, 329
Chong, Ping, 294
Choreography, in musical theatre, 279-282
Chorus, 245-246
A Chorus Line, 280
Christie, Bunny, 129, 136
Churchill, Caryl, 288, 321
The Cid (Corneille), 260
Cinderella, 174
Circle Mirror Transformation (Baker), 15
Circle of attention, 79
Circle theatre, 48
CiVil WarS: A Tree Is Best Measured When It Is Down, 236
Cixous, Hélène, 217
Clarke, Martha, 293
Classical acting, 80-81
Cleage, Pearl, 307
The Clean House (Ruhl), 318
Cleopatra, 227
Climactic structure, 215-216, 225-232
   acts in, 227
   construction of, 227
   and episodic structure, combining with, 232-233
   episodic structure *vs.,* 231
   plot in, 226-227
   segments or acts in, 227
Climax of play, 215-216, 226
Close-up point of view, 217
The Clouds (Aristophanes), 264
Clurman, Harold, 19
Cohen, Robert, 86, 86
Cole, Bob, 276
Coleridge, Samuel Taylor, 24
Collaboration in theatre, 204
   in costume design, 168-169
   in lighting design, 192-193
   of scene design, 150-151
Collective mind, 10
College and university theatre, 36-37
Collins, Pat, 188
Color
   in costume design, 166-167
   of light, 186, 188
   in scene design, 142
Color-blind casting, 113
Color changers/scrollers, 190
The Colored Museum (Wolfe), 307
The Color Purple, 140-141
Comedy, 244, 263-269
   of character, 265-266
   characteristics of, 263-265
   forms of, 266-266
   photo essay of forms of, 268
   plot complications in, 266
   techniques of, 265-266
A Comedy of Errors (Shakespeare), 266
Comedy of ideas, 269
Comedy of manners, 267-269
Comedy of menace, 269
Comic opera, 275, 297
Comic premise, 264
Commedia dell'arte, 175, 243-244, 266
Commercial producers, 123-124
   responsibilities of, chart of, 124
Community theatre, 37
Complications, 215

Composition, in scene design, 142
Computer-assisted design (CAD)
   in costume design, 164
   in scenery design, 148, 150-151
Computers, for scene changes, 146
Concentration, Stanislavski
     technique of, 79, 82
Concept, directorial, 105-109
   and central image, 106-109
   period, 105
   and purpose, 109
Concept musical, 280-281
Congreve, William, 106, 232, 269
Consciousness raising, 76
The Constant Prince, 64
Contemporary theatre, 62, 297,
     305, 316-318. *See also* Diverse
     multicultural theatre; Global
     theatre; Musical theatre
   Asian American, 308-310
   feminist, 217, 296, 316-319
   gay and lesbian, 322
   Latino/a, 310-312
   LGBTQ theatre, 296, 301,
     321-325
   Native American, 312-315
   nontraditional, 294-297
   performance art, 294-295
   political, 295-296
   special techniques used in, 28-29
Contentless Scene of Robert
     Cohen, 86
Contrast in episodic drama, 230
Contrasting characters, 247
Copeau, Jacques, 90-91
Corneille, Pierre, 86, 260
Corrales (Spanish stages), 57-58
Corthron, Kia, 308
Costume design, 134-135
   collaboration in, 161-162
   color in, 166-167
   elements related to, 168-175
   evaluating, 177
   fabric in, 164
   line, shape, and silhouette,
     166-167
   objectives of, 157-158
   process of, 158-164
   technology and, 168

   work of, 167
Costumes, 157-177
   actors' requirement for, 163-164
   consistency in, 164
   coordination of, 176-177
   line of, 164-166
   realistic *vs.* departure from
     realism, 20
   relationships among characters,
     indicating, 158-159
   role of, 141
   status and personality of, 159
   for symbolic and nonhuman
     characters, 162
   time and place of, 158
   tone and style, establishing, 158
Counterpoint, 245
COVID-19 pandemic, 11
Coward, Noël, 269
Crafts and costumes, 175
Craig, Edward Gordon, 181
Created and found spaces, stage
     design in, 61-65
Crimes of the Heart (Henley), 317
Crisis, characters involved in,
     215-216
Crisis structure, 226. *See also*
     Climactic structure
Critics/criticism, 38-39
   audience's relationship to, 42
   criteria for, 41-42
   fact and opinion in, 40-41
   reviewers as, 39
Cross-fade, 191
Crothers, Rachel, 316
Crowley, Mart, 321
The Crucible (Miller), 105, 209, 261
Cruz, Nilo, 311
Cuban American theatre, 311
Cuban theatre, 310
Cues, lighting, 191
Culture, modern theatre and, 31-33
Cunningham, Merce, 92
*The Curious Incident of the Dog in
     the Night-Time,* 136, 146

Dance, 6, 172, 204, 276
   demand of, 86
   in musical theatre, 276-77

   performance art and, 292-294
Dance Nation, 319
The Dance and the Railroad
     (Hwang), 309
Darwin, Charles, 31
Davies, Howard, 129
Davis, Will, 324
Day of Absence (Ward), 169
Death and the King's Horseman
     (Soyinka), 303
Death of a Salesman (Miller), 242,
     257, 261, 288
Deconstruction of the text, 111
deHartog, Jan, 169
DeLoutherbourg, Philippe Jacques,
     180
Dennehy, Brian, 242
Departures from realism. *See*
     Nonrealism
Design, role of, 130
Design concept, scenery, 139-140
Designer/front elevations, 151
Designers, 130-131. *See also*
     Costume design; Lighting
     designers; Scene designers
Desire Under the Elms (O'Neill),
     184
Deus ex machina, 227
Dialectic, 245
Diamond, Lydia R., 307
Diapolyekran, 143
Dimmers, 187
Dinner theatres, 35
Dionysus in 69, 61
Direct action, 14-15
Directorial concept, 105-109
Directors, 101-128
   as audience's eye, 114-116
   auteur directors, 109-111, 205
   casting and, 112
   dramaturg and, 120
   dress rehearsals and, 117
   duties of, chart of, 121
   evaluating, 127
   evolution of, 106
   movement, pace, rhythm
     and, 116
   in noncommercial theatres,
     124-125

Directors (*Cont.*)
   and performers, 71-99
   physical production and, 111-112
   postmodern, 111
   power and responsibility of, 121
   previews and, 117-118
   production managers and, 125-127
   rehearsals and, 114
   scripts and, 102-107
   stage managers and, 118-119
   technical rehearsals and, 116-118
   traditional, 102-107
Distressing costumes, 167
Diverse multicultural theatre, 301-315
   African American theatre, 27, 34, 305-308
   Asian American theatre, 308-310
   Latino/a theatre, 310-312
   Middle Eastern theatre, 315
   Native American theatre, 312-315
The Doctor in Spite of Himself (Molière), 265
Docudramas, 23, 297
Documentary dramas, 296, 297
Dodson, Owen, 304
A Doll's House (Ibsen), 211, 226, 232-233
A Doll's House, Part 2 (Hnath), 297
Domestic comedy, 268
Domestic drama, 254, 260-261
Dominant trait characters, 244
Donahue, Mike, 208
Doran, Gregory, 22, 171
Doubt (Shanley), 20
Dowling, Joe, 133
Downstage, 52
Doyle, John, 140-141
Drama
   bourgeois, 254, 260-261
   comedy, 244, 263-265
   domestic, 260-261
   heroic, 257-260
   melodrama, 262-263
   nature of, 208-209
   theatre of the absurd, 272-276, 298
   tragedy, 219-221, 254-255
   tragicomedy, 269-272, 275
Drama therapy, 15
Dramatic characters. *See* Characters
Dramatic structure, 225-249
   climactic, 225-226
   patterns as, 234
   rituals as, 225, 233-234
Dramatists, 205. *See* Playwrights
Dramaturg, 42-43, 120
Drapers, 163
The Dream Play (Strindberg), 20, 192
Dress rehearsal, 117
Dromgoole, Dominic, 230-231
Duchess of Malfi (Webster), 255
Dürrenmatt, Friedrich, 275
Dutchman (Baraka), 306

East West Players, 309
Edison, Thomas, 180
Editing sound, 198
Edson, Margaret, 20, 317
Einstein, Albert, 31
Einstein on the Beach, 21, 236
Electra (Aeschylus), 208
Electra (Euripides), 208
Electra (Sophocles), 20, 208, 247, 260
Elizabethan theatre. *See also* Shakespeare, William
   costumes in, 159
   culture and, 31
   demands of, 81
   music of, 277
   stage design of, 134
   tragic drama in, 220
   women in, 32
Elizabethan thrust stage, 46-47, 58-60
Elizabeth I (queen of England), 31, 238. *See also* Elizabethan theatre
Elliott, Geoff, 183
Ellipsoidal reflector spotlights (ERSs), 190
El TeatroCampesino, 311
Emotional Creature (Ensler), 30

Emotional recall, 86
Empathy, 14
The Emperor Jones (O'Neill), 84, 111, 290
The Encounter (McBurney), 111
En Route (One Step at a Time Like This), 16
Ensemble playing, Stanislavski technique of, 82
Ensler, Eve, 30, 295
Environmental sounds, 195
Environmental theatre, 289
Environment of a theatre, 47-48
Epic theatre, 275, 288
Epigrams, 265
Episodic dramatic structure, 225, 227-232
   and climatic structure, combining with, 232-233
   climatic structure *vs.,* 231
   juxtaposition and contrast in, 230-231
   overall effect of, 232
Esslin, Martin, 272
The Eumenides (Aeschylus), 32
Euripides, 31, 80, 208, 246
Eurydice (Ruhl), 183
Everyman, 104-105, 246
Evita, 280
Executive directors, 124
Exercises
   body and voice, 90
   breathing, 89
Existential characters, 273, 275
Exonerated (Blank and Jensen), 296-297
Expectations of the audience, 27, 33-38
Experimental theatre. *See* Avant-garde and experimental theatre
Exposition, 226
Expressionism, 105, 272, 288
Extraordinary characters, 238-239
   photo essay of, 240-241

Fabric in costume design, 167
Facebook, 39, 88
Fact-based theatre, 23-24
Facts, in criticism, 40-41

Fade, 191
Farber, Yael, 23
Farce, 266-267, 136
FastHorse, Larissa, 314
Faust (Goethe), 238, 260
Federal Theatre Project, 304
Fefu and Her Friends (Fornés), 40-41, 238, 317
Feminism and Theatre (Case), 217
Feminist theatre, 217, 237, 275, 313, 316-321
Fences (Wilson), 242, 306
Fichandler Stage, 55
Fiddler on the Roof, 280, 283
Films
   in India, 308-310
   musicals based on, 281
   point of view in, 216-217
   and television, 6-7
   theatre *vs.*, 7-8
Finley, Karen, 293
First hand to the costume designer, 167
Five Lesbian Brothers, 323
Flashbacks, 17
Flat, 145
Floodlights, 190
Flower Drum Song, 113
Fly loft, 145
FOB (Hwang), 309
Focus and composition of stage lighting, 182
Follies, 280
Followspot, 190, 193
Footlights, 187-188
Forbidden Broadway, 267
Foreman, Richard, 235-236, 289, 291
   as auteur director, 109
Fornés, Maria Irene, 41, 217, 238, 311
Forum Theatre, 13
Fosse, Bob, 279
The Fourposter (de Hartog), 169
4000 Miles (Herzog), 318
Fourth wall, 48-49
Frayn, Michael, 266
French theatre, 302
Fresnel, Auguste, 190

Fresnel soft-edged spotlight, 190
Freud, Sigmund, 31
Friedman, Thomas, 38
Fringe theatre, 194
The Frogs (Aristophanes), 32, 246
Front of the house, 49, 125
   lighting of, 188
Frozen, 164
Fry, Stephen, 84
Fugard, Athol, 303
Fun Home, 283

Gaines, Barbara, 161
Galati, Frank, 185
Garcia Lorca, Federico, 33, 257, 283
Garrick, David, 180
Garson, Barbara, 295
Gattelli, Christopher, 93
Gay and lesbian theatre, 322
Gehry, Frank, 205
Geiogamah, Hanay, 313
Gels and stage lighting, 187
Gender-bender groups, 323
General mike, 197
Genet, Jean, 169
Genres, theatrical
   additional forms, 280
   bourgeois drama, 260-261
   comedy, 244, 263-265
   domestic drama, 260-261
   heroic drama, 257-260
   melodrama, 262
   theatre of the absurd, 272-276
   tragedy, 219-221, 254-255
   tragicomedy, 269-272, 274
   types of, 244-245
George II, duke of Saxe-Meiningen, 106
Gershwin, George, 278
Gershwin, Ira, 278
A Gentleman's Guide to Love and Murder, 171
Ghostlands (Owens-Greygrass), 314
Ghosts (Ibsen), 20, 226, 232
Gibson, William, 169
Gilbert, W. S., 276-277
Given circumstances of Stanislavski, 79

Glaspell, Susan, 316
The Glass Menagerie (Williams), 23, 79, 245, 261
Glengarry Glen Ross (Mamet), 298
Global theatre, 37-38, 325-329
   in Africa, 172, 329
   in Canada and Australia since World War II, 315
   documentary dramas, 296
   in India, China, and Japan, 92, 260
   in Latin America, 297, 329
   in Middle East, 295, 315
   overview of, 325
   in Russia and eastern Europe, 326-327
   in western Europe, Britain and Ireland, 326-327
God of Vengeance, 83
Goebbels, Heiner, 88
Goethe, Johann Wolfgang von, 238, 260, 260
Gold, Sam, 15
Golda's Balcony (Gibson), 169
Golden Boy (Odets), 260
Goldsmith, Oliver, 295, 269
Goldstein, Jess, 159
Good Woman of Setzuan (Brecht), 214
Gotanda, Philip Kan, 309
Gozzi, Carlo, 291
The Grapes of Wrath (Steinbeck), 185
Gray, Meghan, 183
Gray, Spaulding, 293
The Great Day (Hurston), 304
The Great God Brown (O'Neill), 174
Greek theatre, 211, 247
   amphitheatre of, 56
   chorus in, 245-246
   climactic structure of, 225-226
   culture and, 31
   demands of, 80-81
   heroic drama of, 260
   masks in, 80, 172, 244
   music of, 280
   stage design for, 49, 53, 134
   tragic drama in, 220-221, 255
   women in, 32

The Green Bird (Gozzi), 291
Greenidge, Kirsten, 184
Grimm, David, 173
Grotowski, Jerzy, 61, 92, 292
   dramatic structure and, 234
   theatre space and, 61-65
Ground plan, 142
Groups, psychology of, 10
Guerrilla theatre, 64
Guthrie Theater, 68
Guys and Dolls, 279
Gwynn, Nell, 81
Gypsy, 283

Hadestown, 140
Hagen, Uta, 86
Hair, 280, 295
Hairspray, 165, 171
Hairstyles in costume design, 171
Hall, Katori, 113, 317
Hall, Michael C., 97
Hall, Peter, 246
Hallinan, Frank, 118
Hamilton, 34, 113, 166, 281-283, 312
Hamlet (Shakespeare), 106, 189, 213, 220, 290, 292
   conflict in, 212, 215
   departure from realism of, 20
   juxtaposition of scenes in, 230
   spine of, 103
   staging of, 106-109
   theatrical genres and, 253, 269
Hammerstein, Oscar II, 277-278
Hand puppets, 96
Hansberry, Lorraine, 21, 261, 302
   A Raisin in the Sun, 20, 261, 305
Happenings, 289
Happy Days (Beckett), 94-95
Hard flat, 145
Harnick, Sheldon, 280
Harper, Elizabeth, 185
Hart, Lorenz, 266
HeddaGabler (Ibsen), 128, 226, 248
The Heidi Chronicles (Wasserstein), 317
Heightened realism, 104
Hellman, Lillian, 316, 321
*Hello, Dolly!,*279, 283

Hemesath, Matthew, 160
Henley, Beth, 317
Henry IV, Part I (Shakespeare), 270
Herman, Jerry, 279
Heroes, tragic, 255-256
Heroic drama, 254, 257-261
Heroines, tragic, 255-256
Herzog, Amy, 318
Hewlett, James, 304
Hilferty, Susan, 162
Hir (Mac), 324-325
Hispanic theatre, 310-311
Hitchcock, Alfred, 145
Hnath, Lucas, 297
Hoffman, Constance, 246
Hoffman, Miranda, 138
Hollywood flat, 145
Honeyman, Janice, 161, 225
Hope, Roxanna, 203, 226
House, in a theatre, 49
The House of Bernarda Alba (Garcia Lorca), 257, 283
Howe, Tina, 317
How I Learned to Drive (Vogel), 317
Hrosvitha, 316
Hudes, QuiaraAlegreia, 311
Hughes, Ted, 108
Human beings, theatre's focus, 9
Hunt, Helen, 245
Huntley, Paul, 171, 174
Hurston, Zora Neale, 304
Hwang, David Henry, 291, 309

Ibsen, Henrik, 111, 203, 297
   character traits in plays of, 208, 248
   climactic drama of, 226
   A Doll's House, 211, 238
   episodic drama of, 232
   Ghosts, 20
   HeddaGabler, 226
   and realism, 77
The Iceman Cometh (O'Neill), 85, 261
*I Do! I Do!,*169
Illusion, creation of, 16
The Illusion (Corneille), 86
The Imaginary Invalid (Molière), 244

Imaginary worlds of theatre, 21-25
   realistic *vs.* nonrealistic elements, 21-22
   stage reality, 23-24
Imagination of the audience, 16-19
   metaphors, 18-19
   symbols, 18
Imitation, acting as, 72-73, 75
Immersive theatre, 15-16
I'm Not Your Perfect Mexican Daughter, 61
The Importance of Being Earnest (Wilde), 265
The Impromptu of Versailles (Molière), 106
Improvisation, 235
Incentive in plays, 212
Incongruity, 265
In Dahomey, 276
Indecent (Vogel), 83, 233, 317
Indian theatre, 312-315
Indonesian rod puppets, 96
Inge, William, 138, 324
Inner truth, 82
Integration, 94-95
Intensity of stage lighting, 187
International Centre for Theatre Research, 108
In the Heights, 113, 149, 312
In the Next Room (or the Vibrator Play) (Ruhl), 318
The Investigation (Weiss), 296
Invisible Theatre, 13
Ionesco, Eugene, 246, 275
Irving, Henry, 81
Irwin, Bill, 293

Jacobs, Sally, 139
Jacobs-Jenkins, Branden, 308
Japanese theatre, 60, 253, 308
   kabuki in, 81, 170, 308
   puppetry of, 81, 96
Jekyll and Hyde the Musical, 171
Jelinek, Elfried, 321
Jelly's Last Jam (Wolfe), 307
Jensen, Erik, 296
Jesus Christ Superstar, 179, 280

Joe Turner's Come and Gone (Wilson), 71, 306
John, Elton, 290
Johnson, Philip, 50
Johnson, William, 276
Jones, Robert Edmond, 135
Jones, Tom, 169
Jonson, Ben, 31, 238, 244
Journey to the West, 91
Juan Darien, 291
Jukebox musicals, 281
Julius Caesar (Shakespeare), 185, 159, 295
Juxtaposition
　of characters, 246–247
　in episodic drama, 230
　in musical theatre, 236

Kabuki, 81, 171, 308
Kall, Thomas, 34
Kang, Suhyun, 169
Kani, Atandwa, 224–225
Kathakali, 91, 170, 308
Kaufman, MJ, 324
Kaur, Lynn Japjit, 23
Keen, Julie, 184
Kern, Jerome, 277–278
Kerr, Walter, 7
Kesselring, Joseph, 254, 264
Khon dancers, 172
Kierkegaard, Søren, 271
Kinetic stage, 143
King, Bruce, 313
King, Rodney, 293
The King and I, 113, 166, 279
King Lear (Shakespeare), 28, 111
　episodic structure in, 227–232
　subplot of, 230
　tragedy of, 219, 221, 255
King Shotaway, 304
Kinky Boots, 281, 325
Kinney, Terry, 211
Kiss Me, Kate, 279, 283
Kitchen (performance space), 35
Kopit, Arthur, 217
Kraigher, Alenka, 111
Kramer, Larry, 322
Kreimendehl, Basil, 324
Kreitzer, Carson, 318

Kron, Lisa, 324
Kurt, Stefan, 235
Kushner, Tony, 17, 20, 86, 288

La Cage aux Folles, 324
The Ladies of the Camellias, 159
Lafayette Players, 304
Language
　realistic *vs.* nonrealistic, 20
　in theatre of the absurd, 275
Lansbury, Angela, 281
Laternamagika, 143
Latin American theatre, 297, 329
Latino/a theatre in the United States, 310–311
Lauan, 145
"The Laugh of the Medusa" (Cixous), 217
Laurents, Arthur, 279
Layout, physical, 142
Lazarus, 97
Lebow, Will, 210
LeCompte, Elizabeth, 111, 290
Lecoq, Jacques, 91
Lee, Young Jean, 309
Lenkiewicz, Rebecca, 321
Lennox, Amy, 97
Leon, Kenny, 27, 307
Lerner, Alan Jay, 237
A Letter to Queen Victoria, 94, 236
LGBTQ theatre, 296, 321–323
　musicals of, 324
Lien, Mimi, 48
Lies Like Truth (Clurman), 19
Light boards, 191–192
Lighting. *See* Stage lighting
Lighting controls, 191–192
Lighting design, 131. *See also* Stage lighting
　objectives and functions of, 181–186
　process of, 186–187
　special effects in, 191–201
Lighting designers, 186–193
　collaborators for, 192–193
　resources for, 189–192
Light plot, 186

Lillo, George, 260
Lin, Maya, 19
Lincoln, Abraham, 213
Line
　of costumes, 165–166
　in stage design, 143
The Lion King, 51, 162, 281, 290
　departure from realism of, 20
Literary manager, 42–43, 120
Little Foxes (Hellman), 316, 327
A Little Night Music, 281
Live theatre, defined, 5
Living Theater, 234
Lloyd Webber, Andrew, 173, 280
Locales
　and climactic drama, 226
　establishing, 139
Loewe, Frederick, 237, 279
The London Merchant (Lillo), 260
Long, William Ivey, 165
Long Day's Journey into Night (O'Neill), 212, 257–258, 261
Lope de Vega, 227
The Lost Colony, 165
Loudspeakers, 197
Louizos, Anna, 149, 188
Louw, Illka, 161
Love and Information (Churchill), 321
Love! Valour! Compassion! (McNally), 20
Luck of the Irish (Greenidge), 184
Ludlam, Charles, 323
Lyricists, 279–280
Lysistrata (Aristophanes), 264

Mabou Mines, 234
Mac, Taylor, 324
Macbeth (Shakespeare), 63, 137, 162, 212
　acting in, 79
　comedy in, 270
　direction of, 120
　episodic drama of, 230
　fantasy in, 16, 20
　tragedy of, 221
MacBird (Garson), 295
MacDonald, Karen, 210
Macy, William H., 86

Madison Square Garden, 67
Magic *if,* 82
Magrath, Monette, 184
The Mahabharata, 108
Main action, 103
Makeup, 168–171
   for fantastic or other nonrealistic characters, 86, 169–170
   realistic *vs.* departure from realism, 20
Malaprops, 265
Mamet, David, 86, 86, 298
Mamma Mia!, 281
Managing directors, 123–127, 124–125
Manahatta (Nagle), 314
Mann, Emily, 317
Marat/Sade, 108
Marionettes, 96
Mark Taper Forum, 58, 60, 311
Marlowe, Christopher, 31, 80, 238–239
Martin, Nicholas, 115, 138
Martin, Steve, 188
Marx, Karl, 31
Mary, Queen of Scots, 238
Masks, 171–175
   in Asian theatre, 172
   in Greek theatre, 80, 172, 253
   photo essay of, 172–173
Mass, in scene design, 142
The Matchmaker (Wilder), 113
Matilda, 147
Maxwell, Richard, 35
Mayo, Lisa, 313
M. Butterfly (Hwang), 291, 309
McBurney, Simon, 111
McCauley, Robbie, 293
McGuire, Joshua, 231
McKintosh, Peter, 145
McNally, Terrence, 20
McPherson, Conor, 8
Measure for Measure (Shakespeare), 230, 270
Mediated arts, 6–7
Medieval drama
   morality plays, 104–105
   mystery and morality, 17
   stage design for, 56, 134
   women in, 32

Medium point of view, 217
Mei Lanfang, 214
Meir, Golda, 169
Meisner, Sanford, 86
Melodrama, 254, 262
The Menaechmi (Plautus), 266
The Merchant of Venice (Shakespeare), 173, 180
Metaphors
   functions of, 18–19
   stage design and, 141
   for theatrical productions, 106–109
Metteur-en-scène, 101
Meyerhold, Vsevolod, 109, 289
   body movement exercises of, 90
Michetti, Michael, 185
Mickey, Susan E., 161
Microphones, 197
Middle Eastern theatre, 315
A Midsummer's Night's Dream, 1, 47, 108, 139, 175, 253
Miguel, Gloria, 313
Miguel, Muriel, 313
Miller, Arthur, 88, 110, 258, 288, 327
   The Crucible, 105, 209
   Death of a Salesman, 242, 288
   domestic drama of, 261
   The Price, 212
Miller-Stephany, John, 71, 118
Millinery and costumes, 175
Mime, in Roman theatre, 81
Mimicry, as acting, 72
Minor characters, 244
The Miracle at Naples (Grimm), 173
Miranda, Lin-Manuel, 34, 166, 283, 312
The Misanthrope (Molière), 161, 327
The Miser (Molière), 36
Miss Julie (Strindberg), 211
Miss Saigon, 113, 309
Mixing sound, 197–198
Mnouchkine, Ariane, 329
Modern drama, 111
Modern theatre, 31–33. *See also* Contemporary theatre

   culture and, 31–33
   emergence of, 307
   European, 312
   musical theatre, 280–283
   nontraditional theatre, 294–297
   tragedy and, 254–255
   tragicomedy and, 269–272
   variety of experiences in, 33–38
Modern tragedy, 254–256
Modern tragicomedy, 270–272
Molière, 161, 218, 263, 267
   burial of, 81
   college and university theatre, 36
   comedy of, 265, 267
   as director, 106
   and dominant trait characters, 244, 247
Monologists, 293–294
Monzaemon, Chikamatsu, 96
Mood
   lighting and, 181, 183
   stage design and, 139
Morality plays, 104–105
Most Happy Fella, 283
Mother Courage and Her Children, 288
Motivated sounds, 195
Motivation in plays, 212
Mouawad, Jerry, 210
The Mountaintop (Hall), 113, 307
Mourning Becomes Electra (O'Neill), 166–167
Movement
   in Asian theatre, 91–92
   director's role in, 116
   lighting and, 189
Movie flat, 145
Moving light, 189–191
Mozart, Wolfgang Amadeus, 260
Mrs. Warren's Profession (Shaw), 269
Multicultural theatre, 283, 301. *See also* Diverse multicultural theatre
Multifocus theatre, 65
Multimedia theatre, 65, 281
Muppets, 96
Musical revues, 234

Musical theatre, 236, 276-283
　appeal of, 283
　coordination in, 94
　films, based on, 281
　jukebox, 281
　juxtaposition in, 236
　LGBTQ characters and issues in, 293
　opera and operettas, 6, 276-277
　from 1920s and 1930s, 277-280
　from 1940s and 1950s, 279-280
　from 1960s through 1980s, 280
　from 1990s to present, 280
　revivals in, 280
　scene design of, 146
　sound amplification in, 193-197
　structure in, 236-237
　training for, 94-95
The Music Man, 283
My Fair Lady, 237, 283
The Myth of Sisyphus (Camus), 272
My Trip to Al Qaeda (Wright), 295

Nagle, Mary Kathryn, 314
Narrative, abandonment of, 111
Narrators, 245-246
Natasha, Pierre & the Great Comet of 1812, 47-48, 153, 192
National Theatre, 321
Native American theatre, 313-314
Native American Theatre Ensemble, 312
Native Son (Wright), 304
Native Voices, 313
Naturalism, 103-104
Natural laws, suspension of in comedy, 263-264
Negro Ensemble Company, 307
Neighborhood theatre, 64
Neutral Hero (Maxwell), 35
New Lafayette Theatre, 307
Newsies, 93
The Next Room (Ruhl), 318
Nguyen, Qui, 309
Nicolao, Stefano, 163
'Night, Mother (Norman), 210, 317
The Nightingale, 310
Nine Parts of Desire (Raffo), 296
Nirbhaya, 185

No Exit (Sartre), 210
Noises Off (Frayn), 266
Noncommercial theatres, producers in, 124-125
Nonhuman characters, 162, 246
Nonrealism, 21-22, 105
　realism and, 20-22
　scene design for, 137-139
Nonsense, 275
Non sequitur, 235, 275
Nontheatre buildings, staging in, 64
Nontraditional casting, 113
Nontraditional theatre, 294-297. *See also* Avant-garde and experimental theatre
　environmental theatre, 289
　happenings, 289-290
　multimedia theatre, 294
　performance art, 292-294
　postmodernism, 290-291
Nonverbal theatre, 234-235
Noone, James, 138
The Normal Heart (Kramer), 322
Norman, Marsha, 210, 317
Nottage, Lynn, 31, 209, 317
A Number (Churchill), 321
Nuyorican, 311

O'Brien, Barret, 208
Observation, Stanislavski technique of, 79
Observed theatre, 14
Obstacles, 215
Oedipus Rex (Sophocles), 241
Oedipus Rex (Stravinski), 326
Off book rehearsals, 114
Off-Broadway theatre, 324, 327
Off-off-Broadway theatre, 290, 308
Offstage, 52
Ogata, Issei, 294
Oh Dad, Poor Dad, Mama's Hung You in the Closet, and I'm Feelin' So Sad (Kopit), 217-218
Oklahoma!, 278
Old-Fashioned Prostitutes (A True Romance) (Foreman), 110, 236, 291
Old Hats, 268

O'Neill, Eugene, 111, 257, 261, 290
　costumes in, 166-167, 175
　domestic drama of, 261
　family conflict in, 212, 257
　staging of, 184
One Man, Two Guvnors (Bean), 268
One Step at a Time Like This, 16
On the Royal Road: The Burgher King, 321
Opening scenes, structure in, 213, 215
Open Theater, 234
Operas, 6, 280
Operettas, 276-277
Opinions, in criticism, 40-41
Opposition in plays, 211-212
Orchestra, 49, 56
Orchestration, of characters, 248-249
Orghast (Hughes), 108
The Orphan of Zhao, 310
Oskar, Pall, 5
Othello, 24, 217, 247
Our Town (Wilder), 23, 214, 245
Owens-Greygrass, Robert, 314

Pace, 116
Paint charge, 150
Paint elevations, 152
Painting Churches (Howe), 317
Palestinian theatre, 315
Paltrow, Gwyneth, 17
Pan Asian Repertory Theatre, 309
Panorama point of view, 217
Pantomime, 22, 94
Parabolic aluminized reflector (PAR), 190
Parallel plots, 230
Parks, Suzan-Lori, 20, 307
Participatory theatre, 14, 15-16
Patterns, as dramatic structure, 234
Patterson, Louis, 304
Peer Gynt (Ibsen), 208, 232
Performance art, 293-294
Performance Group, 61, 64, 234
Performers. *See* Actors
Period, of a production, 105, 140
Period background of an audience, 29-30

348　　　　Index

Personality, costumes indicating, 159
Personal roles and role playing, 76
The Phantom of the Opera, 51, 147, 280
Phèdre (Racine), 218
Photo essay
　actor's range, 84-85
　comedy, forms of, 268
　extraordinary characters, 238-239
　masks, 172-173
　modern domestic drama, 258
　stage costumes, 160-161
　stage lighting, 184-185
Photo opportunities, 24
Physical acting, 86-89
Physical layout of the stage, 142
　proscenium stages, 49-53
Physical production of a play, 111. *See also* Scenery; Sound; Stage lighting; Theatre spaces
The Piano Lesson (Wilson), 20
Picnic (Inge), 324
Picture-frame stage, 49. *See also* Proscenium stages
Piñero, Miguel, 311
Pinter, Harold, 272
Pippin, 280
The Pirates of Penzance, 276-277
Place
　costumes indicating, 158-159
　lighting for, 181
Platform stage, 56
Plautus, Titus Maccius, 266
Playhouse of the Ridiculous, 272
Playing area, 142
Play of Giants (Soyinka), 303
Plays, background information on, 28-29
The Play That Goes Wrong, 263
Playwrights, 127, 204-221
　background information on, 28-29
　and directors, 102-103
　dramatic structure set by, 213-216
　educational tools and, 15
　point of view of, 216-221
　role of, 127, 208-209
　society's point of view and, 219-221
　structural conventions used by, 209-212
　women, 316-321
Plot
　in climactic drama, 226-227
　comedic complications of, 265-266
　in episodic drama, 227, 230
　vs. story, 213
　structure from, 213
　in theatre of the absurd, 275
Plum, Paula, 210
Poetics (Aristotle), 217, 256
Point of view, 216-221
　in film, 217
　and genre, theatrical, 254
　individual, 218
　of playwright, 216-221
　of society, 219-221
Polish Laboratory Theatre, 234
Polish theatre, 289
Political theatre, 295-296
Politics and theatre, 24
Polyekran, 143
Poor theatre, 111, 289
Porgy and Bess, 278-281
Porter, Cole, 279
Postmodern directors, 111
Postmodernism, 290-291
Postmodernists, 287
Practical aesthetics, 86
Previews, 117-118
The Price (Miller), 212
Pride and Prejudice, 12
Prince, Harold, 278, 280
Private Lives (Coward), 269
Problem plays, 270
Producers, 123-127
　British, 101
　in commercial productions, 25, 123
　in noncommercial productions, 124-125
　role of, 124
Production managers, 125-127
Projection, in scenic design, 146-147, 151
Prometheus Bound (Aeschylus), 256
Property designers, 150-151
Props, 146, 150
Proscenium arch, 49, 52-53
Proscenium stages, 49-53
　explanation of, 48
　physical layout of, 50, 52-53
Protagonists, 212, 247
Protagoras, 221
Psychodrama, 15
Psychophysical actions and Stanislavski, 82-83
Publicity, 125
Puerto Rican theatre, 312
Pulcinella Goes to Hell, 173
Pulling costumes, 164
Punchdrunk, 16, 64
Puns, 265
Puppetry, 81, 96
　in Asian theatre, 91-92
Pygmalion (Shaw), 237

Quartley, Mark, 22
Quintessential characters, 239-243

Racine, Jean, 81, 218
Radio Golf (Wilson), 162
Raffo, Heather, 296
Ragni, Gerome, 280
A Raisin in the Sun (Hansberry), 20-21, 27-28, 261, 305
Rake, 49
Ramakian, 172
Realism, 21-22
　explanation of, 77
　heightened, 104-105
　naturalism, 103-104
　and nonrealism, 20-22
　scene design and, 139-140
　Stanislavski system and, 77-83
Realistic acting, 20, 77
　modern approaches to, 86
　Stanislavski system, 77-83
Reality television, 23
Real-life roles onstage, 77
Rebeck, Theresa, 318

Regents Park Open Air Theatre, 12
Regional theatre, 34, 320
Rehearsals
   director's role in, 114-115
   dress, 117
   technical, 116-118
Reinforcement of sound, 196
Reinholz, Randy, 313
Relaxation, Stanislavski technique of, 79
Religious celebrations, 72
Rendering, 150
Rent, 282
Representative characters, 239-243
Reproduction of sound, 195-196
Resident professional theatre, 34-35
Respect for Aging (Hagen), 86
Restoration period in England, 158, 233
Reviewers, 38-42. *See also* Critics/criticism
Revues, 234, 283
Rhinoceros (Ionesco), 246
Rhythm, 116, 183-186
Rice, Elmer, 105
Rice, Tim, 280
Richards, Lloyd, 305
Ridiculous situations, 266
Rituals
   as dramatic structure, 225, 233, 234
   Native American, 312-314
   as theatre, 72
The Rivals (Sheridan), 265
Rivendell Theatre, 320
Robbins, Jerome, 279-280
Robeson, Paul, 302
Rock concert lighting, 192
Rodgers, Richard, 266, 278
Rod puppets, 96
Rodriguez, Dámaso, 184
Role model, 72
Role playing, 72-73, 75
Role reversal, 15
Roman theatre, 81
   stage design for, 57
   women in, 81
Romantic drama, 260

Romanticism, 260
Romeo and Juliet (Shakespeare), 162, 213, 215
Roosters (Sanchez-Scott), 311
Rosenberg, Philip, 138
Rostand, Edmond, 246
Royal Shakespeare Company, 22, 145, 310
Ruhl, Sarah, 33, 183, 318
Ruined (Nottage), 307, 308
Run-through of play, 116
R.U.R. (Karel), 246
Russian theatre, 329
Rylance, Mark, 89

Sagittarius Ponderosa (Kreimendehl, Barbagallo, and Kaufman), 324
Saint Joan (Shaw), 159, 237, 241, 260
St. Patrick's Day Parade, 73
Sanchez-Scott, Milcha, 311
Sartre, Jean-Paul, 210
Satire, 137, 267
Saxe-Meiningen, George II, duke of, 106
The Scene (Rebeck), 318
Scene design, 134, 134. *See also* Scenery
   collaboration and production process of, 150-154
   contemporary, 139-140
   elements of, 141-147
   evaluating, 154
   history of, 134-135
   materials and machinery of, 144-146
   objectives of, 135-141
   physical layout and, 142
   practical design problems of, 135
   process for, 148-150
   special effects and, 146-147
   for total environment, 154
Scene designers, 134, 134-150
   central image or metaphor of, 140
   coordinating with the whole, 141
   design concept of, 140
   design problems, solving, 141

   locale and period, establishing, 139
   tone and style, establishing, 135-139
Scenery, 133-154. *See also* Scene design
   audience's view of, 133
   coordination of, 141
   environment for a play, 137
   realistic and departure from realism, 20, 138
Scenes and climactic drama, 227
Scenic charge artists, 150
Scenography, 143
Schechner, Richard, 289
Schmidt, Harvey, 169
The School for Lies, 161
The School for Scandal (Sheridan), 266
School of Rock, 280
Schuman, Peter, 96
Schwartz, Stephen, 170
Scott, A. O., 290
Scott, Jean Bruce, 290
Screen projection, 145-146
Scrim, 144-146
Scripts, choice of, 102-103
Scrollers and stage lighting, 187, 190
The Sea-Gull (Chekhov), 82
Seascape (Albee), 246
The Second Shepherds' Play, 270
The Secretaries, 323
Segments as structure, 234-235
Selective realism, 104
Seminar (Rebeck), 318
Serial structure, 234
The Servant of Two Masters (Goldoni), 268
Shadow puppets, 96
Shakespeare, William, 31, 287, 297. *See also* specific plays
   actors, demands on, 87
   casting the plays of, 113
   conflict in plays of, 212
   costumes in, 159, 162-163, 173, 175
   episodic dramatic structure in, 227-232

Shakespeare, William (*Cont.*)
  lighting for, 180
  music of, 262
  nonrealism of plays of, 20, 22
  scene design for, 139
  staging plays by, 59–60
  structure of plays of, 225
  theatrical genres and, 253
  tragicomedy of, 267–272, 275
Shakespeare festivals, 35
Shakespeare in Love (film), 17
Shakespeare's Globe Theatre, 1, 3, 215
Shanley, John Patrick, 20
Shape and form of stage lighting, 181–182
Shape of costumes, 164–167
Shaw, Fiona, 95, 288
Shaw, George Bernard, 237, 241, 263, 279
  comedy of ideas of, 269
  costumes in, 159
  heroic drama of, 260
Shaw, Peggy, 318
The Sheep Well (Lope de Vega), 227
Shepard, Sam, 297–298
Sher, Antony, 224–225
Sheridan, Richard Brinsley, 265–266
Shingeki, 326
Short Eyes (Piñero), 311
Shotgun mike, 197
Show Boat, 277–278
Silhouette of costumes, 166
Simon, Neil, 267
Sisto, Rocco, 111
Sitcoms, 267
Site-specific companies, 62–64
Slapstick, 136, 263
Slave Play, 308
Surrealism, 288
Sleep No More (Punchdrunk), 16, 64
Slice-of-life drama, 104
Smith, Anna Deavere, 293–294
Social issues in theatre, 31
Social media, theatre reviews on, 39
Social roles and role playing, 75–76

Social status of actors, 80–81
Society, point of view of, 219–221
Society, theatre and, 31, 32–34
Sociodrama, 15
Socrates, 264
Soft-edged spotlights, 190
Soliloquy, 22
Son, Diana, 309
Sondheim, Stephen, 279–280
Song for a Nisei Fisherman (Gotanda), 309
Soo, Phillipa, 166
Sophocles, 31, 80, 208, 241, 260
  contrasting characters of, 247
  Electra, 20, 208
  glorifying humans of, 220
Sound, 193–199
  amplification of, 193–199
  audience view of, 133
  evaluating, 200
  reinforcement of, 196
  reproduction of, 195–196
  technology and, 193–199, 197–198
Sound designers, 131, 195
Sound effects, 194–195
Sound recordings, 197–198
Soyinka, Wole, 303
Space. *See also* Theatre spaces
  director's use of, 116
  limited, 210
Spamilton, 267
Spanish thrust stage, 57
Special effects
  lighting and sound, 199–201
  scenic, 144–147
Specifics, importance of, in Stanislavski technique, 79
Spectators. *See* Audience
Spiderman: Turn Off the Dark, 43
Spiderwoman Theatre, 313
Spill of light, 182
Spine of a play, 103
Spine of a role, 82, 95
Split Britches, 318–319
Spunk (Wolfe), 307
Stage costumes. *See* Costumes
Stage house, 55, 57
Stage left, 52

Stage lighting, 179–201. *See also* Lighting design
  audience view of, 133
  and central image in, 186
  color of, 187–188
  controls for, 191–192
  departure from realism of, 20
  distribution of, 187–189
  evaluating, 200
  focus and composition of, 182
  history of, 179–181
  intensity of, 187
  mood and style of, 182–183
  movement in, 189
  photo essay on, 184–185
  properties of, 187–189
  realistic *vs.* departure from realism, 20
  rhythm in, 183, 186
  role of, 131
  shape and form of, 181–182
  special effects in, 199–201
  technology and, 180, 192
  time and place of, 182
  types of, 189–191
  visibility and, 181
Stage managers, 101–102, 118–119
Stage pictures, 115
Stage right, 52
Stage spaces. *See* Theatre spaces
Stanislavski, Constantin, 77–79, 86, 103, 271
Stanislavski system, 77–83
Star Wars, 22
Status, costumes indicating, 158
Stein, Joseph, 306
Steinbeck, John, 185
Steppenwolf Theatre Company of Chicago, 86
Sternheim, Carl, 188
Stewart, Michael, 279
Stick Fly (Diamond), 307
Stifter's Things, 88
Still Life (Mann), 317
Stitchers, 163
Stock characters, 237, 243–244

Story
  plot *vs.*, 213
  realistic *vs.* departure from realism, 20
The Story of the Chalk Circle, 213
Strasberg, Lee, 86
A Streetcar Named Desire (Williams), 212, 258, 261, 318, 327
  realism of, 20
Streetcar Named Desire (van Hove's version), 110
Street theatre, 64
Strindberg, August, 110, 192, 211
  The Dream Play, 20
  Miss Julie, 211
  and realism, 77
Strip lights, 190
Structure. *See also* Climactic structure; Episodic dramatic structure
  creation of, 213–216
  in experimental and avant-garde theatre, 234–236
  in musical theatre, 236–237
  plot as, 213
  realistic *vs.* departure from realism, 20
  segments and tableaux as, 234–235
  serial, 234
Studi, DeLanna, 314
Style
  of costumes, 158
  lighting and, 181, 183
  of a production, 103–104
  of scene design, 134–139
Subplots, in episodic drama, 231
Sullivan, Arthur, 276
Sullivan, Daniel, 219
Superobjective of a character, 82, 95
Superrealism, 101
Surrealism, 314, 318
Suzuki, Tadashi, 92, 326
Svoboda, Josef, 143
Sweat (Nottage), 31, 209, 308
Sweeney Todd: The Demon Barber of Fleet Street, 262

Sweet Charity, 280
Sword fights on stage, 86, 87
Symbolic characters, 162
Symbols, function of, 18–19
  in scene design, 134
Synthesis and integration, 94–97
Syrian theatre, 297

Tableaux as structure, 235–236
Tai chi, 92
Taichman, Rebecca, 233, 184
Take a Giant Step (Patterson), 304
Tamburlaine, 239
Tartuffe (Molière), 267
Tarver, Jennifer, 203, 226
Taylor, James P., 184
Taymor, Julie, 162, 290
Tazewell, Paul, 157, 166
Technical directors, 150–151
Technical rehearsal, 116–118
Technology
  actors and, 88
  costume design and, 171
  lighting and, 180, 191
  sound and, 193–199
Technology and acting, 88
Teichman, Rebecca, 86
Television, films and, 6–7
The Tempest (Shakespeare), 20, 22, 145, 224–225, 291
  costumes in, 162
  staging of, 110
Tent theatres, 55
Terry, Megan, 295
Tesori, Jeanine, 325
Text-based directing, 102
Texture, in scene design, 142
The Thanksgiving Play (FastHorse), 314
Theatre directors. *See* Directors
The Theatre Experience, 329
Theatre genres, 253–283. *See also* specific genres
  additional forms, 280
  bourgeois, 260–261
  comedy as, 253, 263–265
  domestic, 260–261
  heroic drama as, 257–260
  melodrama as, 262

  theatre of the absurd as, 272–276
  tragedy as, 254–257
  tragicomedy as, 269–272, 275
  types of, 253–254
Theatre-in-the-round, 48. *See also* Arena stage
Theatremania.com, 39
Theatre of fact, 23, 296
Theatre of the absurd, 272–276
  characters in, 275–276
  language in, 275
  plot in, 266
Theatre of the Oppressed (Boal), 13, 14, 328
Theatre spaces, 48–66, 234
  adapted, 64
  arena stage, 48, 53–55
  black box, 48, 66, 194
  created and found, 61–65
  environment, creating, 47–48
  evaluating, 68
  limits of, 210
  multifocus environments, 65
  in nontheatre buildings, 62
  popular, 66
  proscenium stages, 48, 49–53
  site specific, 62–64
  special requirements of, 67
  street theatre as, 64
  thrust stage, 48, 55–60
Thirty Nine Steps, 146
Thomas, Brandon, 71
Thompson, John Douglas, 84–85
Threepenny Opera (Brecht-Weill), 235
Three Sisters (Chekhov), 133, 212, 249
Through line of a role, Stanislavski technique of, 82
Thrust stage, 55–60
  Elizabethan, 46–47, 58–60
  explanation of, 48
  Spanish, 57
Thumbnail sketches, 148
Time
  costumes and, 158–159

Time (*Cont.*)
   director's use of, 116
   lighting and, 181
   limited, 210-211
   stage design and, 139
Tolstoy, Leo, 47
Tone
   in costumes, 158
   in scene design, 135-150
Tony Administration Committee, 193
Topdog/Underdog (Park), 20
Torelli, Giacomo, 49
Touring theatre, 34
Townsend, Justin, 184
Traditional directors, 102-107
Traditional theatre, 294-297
Traditional tragedy, 254-257
Tragedy, 254-257
   effect of, 256
   modern, 256-257
   and society's point of view, 219-221
   traditional, 254-257
The Tragical History of Doctor Faustus (Marlowe), 80, 238-239
Tragic circumstances, 255
Tragic irretrievability, 255
Tragicomedy, 269-272, 275
   modern, 270-271
Tragic verse, 255-256
Transitory and immediate theatre, 8-9
Trapdoors, 144
Treadmills, 144
Treadwell, Sophie, 316
The Treatment (Ensler), 295
Trestle stage, 57
A Trip to Coontown, 276
Trump, Donald, 295, 321
Tryouts of plays, 117-118
Tune, Tommy, 280
Turntables, 144
Twelfth Night (Shakespeare), 89
Twilight: Los Angeles 1992 (Smith), 293
Twitter, 39
The Two Gentlemen of Verona, 3
Typecasting, 112

Uncle Vanya (Chekhov), 194, 248, 271, 274
Undergarments, 166
The Underpants, 188
Underscoring of sound, 196
Unexploded Ordnances, 319
University theatre, 36-37
Unto These Hills, 12
Upstage, 52

Vaccaro, John, 323
Valdéz, Luis, 311
Valk, Kate, 111
van Hove, Ivo, 97, 110, 327
van Itallie, Jean-Claude, 8
Van Teighem, David, 194
Vaudeville, 302
Vecsey, George, 73
Verbal humor, 265
Versweyveld, Jan, 327
Video design, 147
Vietgone (Nguyen), 310
Vietnam War memorial, 19
Viet Rock (Terry), 295
A View from the Bridge (Miller), 88, 107, 110
Viewpoint. *See* Point of view
Viewpoints theory, 92
Visibility in stage lighting, 181
The Visit (Dürrenmatt), 275-276
Visual composition, 115
Vocal exercises, 90
Vogel, Paula, 233, 317
Voice, 87-89
   warm-up exercises for, 90
Voice training, 93
Volpone (Jonson), 237

Wagon, 144
Wagon stage, 57, 144
Waiting for Godot (Beckett), 65, 234, 272-273, 275
Walker, Alice, 141
Walker, George, 276
Walpole, Horace, 217, 254
Wannamaker, Zoe, 129
War and Peace (Tolstoy), 47
Ward, Douglas Turner, 169

War Horse, 96, 146
Warm-up exercises for voice, 90
Warner, Deborah, 95, 288
Wasserstein, Wendy, 317
Water by the Spoonful (Hudes), 311
The Water's Edge (Rebeck), 318
The Way of the World (Congreve), 232
Weaver, Lois, 318
Webster, John, 255
Weiss, Peter, 108, 296
Welles, Orson, 304
Well-made plays, 227
West, Cheryl, 307
Western European theatre, 297
Western theatre, demands of, 80
West Side Story, 162, 211, 279
   departure from realism of, 20
Wheeldon, Christopher, 204
When We Are Married, 118
Whoriskey, Kate, 31, 307
Who's Afraid of Virginia Woolf? (Albee), 20, 242
Wicked, 51, 170, 180
Wigs in costume design, 171-172
Wilde, Oscar, 265, 269
Wilder, Thornton, 23, 113, 245
   Asian theatre influence on, 214
Williams, Bert, 276
Williams, Tennessee, 258, 261, 318
   Cat on a Hot Tin Roof, 226
   domestic drama of, 261
   The Glass Menagerie, 23, 79, 245, 261
   A Streetcar Named Desire, 20, 258, 261
Wilson, August, 113, 162, 298, 304, 306
   Fences, 242, 306
   The Piano Lesson, 20
Wilson, Robert, 21, 94, 110-111, 138, 306
   dramatic structure of, 234-236
Winged Victory statue, 5-6
The Winter's Tale, 86
Wit (Edson), 20, 317
Wolfe, George C., 307

Women in theatre, 32, 81
  feminist theatre and, 217, 316–321
Wong, B. D., 309
Woods, Jeannie M., 36
Woolard, David C., 188
Wooster Group, 111, 234, 292
The World Is Flat (Friedman), 38
The Would-Be Gentleman (Molière), 265
Wright, Lawrence, 295
Wright, Richard, 304
Wycherley, William, 106, 269

Yavich, Anita, 173
Yellow Robe, William F., Jr., 313

Yew, Chay, 309
Yoheen (Gotanda), 309
Young people's theatre, 36
Youth theatre, 36
YouTube, 39

Zoot Suit (Valdéz), 311